MW01039804

Catapult: The Biography of Robert A. Monroe

Bayard Stockton

Catapult: The Biography of Robert A. Monroe

Bayard Stockton

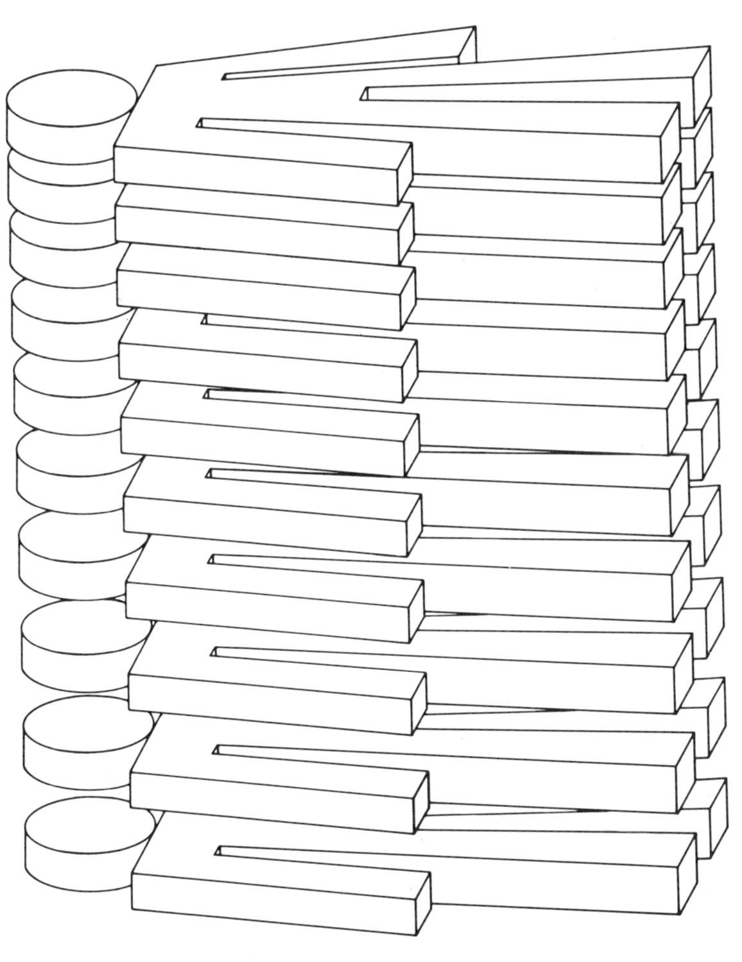

For

Tara, Philip and Vanessa

For information, write:

The Donning Company/Publishers
5659 Virginia Beach Boulevard
Norfolk, Virginia 23502

Library of Congress Cataloging-in-Publication Data
Stockton, Bayard
Catapult: the biography of Robert A. Monroe
by Bayard Stockton
p. cm.
Bibliography: p.
Includes index.
1. Monroe, Robert A. 2. Consciousness 3. Physics—United States—Biography. I. Title.
BF1027.M65576 1989 133.9′092′4—dc 19 [B]
ISBN 0-89865-756-3 : $19.95

Printed in the United States of America

CONTENTS

BOOK ONE: THE MAN

BOOK TWO: HIS WORK

BOOK THREE: WHO IS BOB MONROE?

APPENDIXES

Perhaps we are part of some global nervous system, currently passing through a very rapid phase of development, capable of being to the planet everything that our own brains are to us. Yet this nervous system has, at a very critical stage, appeared to have gone out of control, threatening to destroy the very body which supports its existence.

If then we are to fulfill our role as a part of the planetary brain, our malignant behavior must be stemmed and the negative trends reversed. If we are to achieve this, it is imperative that we change, in the most radical way, our attitudes towards ourselves, others and the planet as a whole. As we shall be seeing, such changes are going to require a major transformation in human consciousness.

—Peter Russell, The Global Brain, *Pp. 20-21*

THE GATEWAY AFFIRMATION

I AM MORE THAN MY PHYSICAL BODY.
BECAUSE I AM MORE THAN PHYSICAL MATTER,
I CAN PERCEIVE THAT
WHICH IS GREAT THAN THE PHYSICAL WORLD.
THEREFORE I DEEPLY DESIRE TO EXPAND, TO EXPERIENCE;
TO KNOW, TO UNDERSTAND; TO CONTROL, TO USE SUCH GREATER
ENERGIES AND ENERGY SYSTEMS AS MAY BE BENEFICIAL AND
CONSTRUCTIVE TO ME AND TO THOSE WHO FOLLOW ME.
ALSO, I DEEPLY DESIRE THE HELP AND COOPERATION,
THE ASSISTANCE, THE UNDERSTANDING OF THOSE INDIVIDUALS
WHOSE WISDOM, DEVELOPMENT AND EXPERIENCE
ARE EQUAL OR GREATER THAN MY OWN.
I ASK THEIR GUIDANCE AND PROTECTION
FROM ANY INFLUENCE OR ANY SOURCE
THAT MIGHT PROVIDE ME WITH LESS THAN
MY STATED DESIRES.

—Robert A. Monroe and the Explorers, 1973

Authors Note: The responsibility for interpretation in the book is entirely mine and, unless otherwise labelled, the conclusions are mine alone.

Many of the times contained in the following text are approximate. Some physical life entities and all non-physical friends have difficulty in dealing with physical, worldly time. Many of those who are in close contact with their superior consciousness likewise find it difficult as well as irrelevant to keep precise track of time. So it is with Bob Monroe. That he often cannot recall precise dates, although he does remember places and names clearly, is a significant sign of his indifference to one of the guideposts we more mundane humans use.

Prologue: Into The All

Many people know of Bob Monroe from his books, which have sold in the hundreds of thousands of copies. A certain proportion of those readers, and some who have learned of Bob's work elsewhere, feel drawn to the Monroe Institute in Virginia* to sample the techniques he has pioneered. The basic course the Institute offers is called the Gateway Voyage. The Gateway Experience is the subject of a companion volume to this one, due to be published in 1990.

There is no generic Gateway Voyage. Gateway is an experience hard to define in words because so much of it is impressionistic, or visionistic. No one's experience of the intense week of self-revelation can be exactly the same as anyone else's, because all of what happens is rooted in the individual's consciousness, more unique than his or her fingerprint yet, it could be philosophically argued, the same as anyone else's.

I include here an account of my own initial week at the Institute, because—short of fictionalizing—I can think of no other way to convey the flavor of Monroe's techniques and some of what they achieved in one human being. In so doing, I know fully that my subjective reality may be your alphabet soup.

My life till then had been that of the journeyman journalist, almost all of it spent abroad. My world had been that of the professional, skeptical bystander at greater and lesser events which often made headlines. I had too often seen the folly of man to have much faith in anything I could not prove to my own satisfaction.

I am a recovering alcoholic and have, over a few years, become fairly well anchored in a spiritual program. I got there at last, after decades of drinking, only through a spiritual intervention which took clearly-tangible form. Both during my boozing days and since, I have often wondered why I survived the rigors of dedicated alcoholism. From time to time, I have ventured out from the secure base of the program to search for further esoteric knowledge and sustenance. On the first such excursion, I was the subject of what I later came to regard as a diabolical recruitment attempt.

I met a man, by one of those non-coincidences, who asked me if I knew why I was a survivor, and then offered me "The Keys to The Kingdom," if I would but allow myself to be instructed by him. He gave me some meditational rote, on which I concentrated mightily for a period of weeks. My fluent, near-hypnotic guru urged me to jump out of "the lifeboat" of my recovery program, so I could swim freely in his vast new ocean of revelation.

* The Monroe Institute, Route 1, Box 175, Faber VA 22938

But I felt myself inexorably held back by an unseen force—or by my deep intuition—from the final plunge into union with The All he offered. I later concluded it had been an undefined fear which restrained me: Not so much fear of the unknown, as subconscious fright at the prospect of losing the security that very lifeboat afforded me. And yet there had, on several occasions, been that near-physical feeling I was being gently restrained, tugged back from the brink by unseen forces.

I became gunshy of spiritual salvation. I took a while to return wholespiritedly to the precepts of my program, but in a few months, I was fully back on board, and once again feeling at one with myself.

In late 1986, I again became deeply interested in broadening my spiritual horizons, for reasons I cannot clarify. It was simply an irresistible urge. I had reached another plateau in the program, and again felt I had learned all it had to offer. Apparently involuntarily, I started to quest again. Another man with whom I talked sporadically introduced me to the rudiments of meditation, and answered some of my spiritual questions. He suggested a writing project involving paranormal research.

One day I was in a secondhand bookshop gathering material for the new task. A dusky dust jacket caught my eye. It was Bob Monroe's *Journeys Out Of The Body.* I put it in my stack of purchases, went home, started reading and hardly put it down. I knew I had to get in touch with Monroe. My copy was a first edition, published in 1971, which gave no clue to his whereabouts. I wondered whether, indeed, he was still alive.

Within two weeks, I happened on a mention of Monroe's second book, *Far Journeys (FJ),* and also came upon the Monroe Institute's address in Prof. Charles Tart's parapsychology newsletter of the time. I grabbed a copy of *FJ* and devoured it. I was so near levitation, I wrote Bob ever-more-enthusiastic letters after reading each chapter, but, slightly more coolly, had the sense to hold them till I had finished the entire book. Then I let fly, with an impassioned blast of adulation. I later learned that as many as one hundred such letters arrive each week at the Faber, Virginia, rural delivery box. The most interesting are sent to Bob for attention. Those which fall into the customary pattern are dealt with by the office staff.

Mine was one of the latter. Mere enthusiasm. The reply I got was an application form for a Gateway Voyage. I filled it out, then impatiently telephoned. Helen Warring, the soft-spoken, ever-considerate Institute registrar, gave me the stock answer: there was a long wait for admission.

Several days later, Helen phoned to say a berth had opened; could I come? Within a week, I was in Virginia. One woman in my group made air reservations from the Canary Islands, in mid-Atlantic, to Charlottesville, without a confirmed booking for the course, so sure was she that she was supposed to participate.

My Voyage took place during Easter week 1987, a timing I regarded as no coincidence.

I drove down from Washington with a fellow-student, a shy woman health program-administrator, who was as excitedly expectant of the week ahead as I. We stopped along Route 29 for a fastfood biscuits-and-gravy snack, then headed in gentle rain up to the fifteen hundred-foot elevation of the Institute. It is in Nelson County, one of Virginia's best-kept secrets. Neighboring Albemarle is home to the horsey gentry. Nelson is less status-hooked.

Bob and Nancy Monroe relate they knew they had to buy the property after they first saw it, in its wild state. Part of the lure of Roberts Mountain Farm may have been the fact that it is situated on a strong and deep cap of granite which makes the site practically unshakable. It is also located in one of the areas metaphysicists adore, stretching from the headquarters of the Edgar Cayce Center at Virginia Beach into the interior: One of the "safe" areas if the violent geological earth changes predicted by Cayce ever hit the North American continent.

A writer from *Omni* fancifully called the Monroe Institute Center an "exotic complex."[1] My first impression of it that drizzly Sunday afternoon was definitely not exotic: an unkempt parking lot, surrounded by meadow spiced with wild spring onions. The Institute's three unpretentious, cream, red-roofed buildings did not promise much.

When observed from a distance, there is jarring inconsistency in the rooflines of their architecture. The Center building itself looks stunted in comparison with the other two structures, which are the lab building and an auditorium-and-seminar hall. Much later, the explanation for this very un-Monroelike lapse in design consistency comes out: The Center was originally financed by a partner who suddenly withdrew; Bob's grandiose plans had to be scrapped.

No one objects to the sylvan surroundings, stretching up beyond hills to the ancient Blue Ridge, nor to the Center as constituted. To the contrary, most students who attend develop an emotional bond to the place, and would probably vehemently oppose any lavish improvements—except, perhaps, for the addition of more bathrooms, which are called for in a planned expansion.

We are first greeted in the hallway that April afternoon by soft-spoken Dave Mulvey, a former radio and television reporter from Tennessee via Lynchburg, whose darkly sandy hair is beginning to grey at the temples. He dashes out unbidden, in the wet, to hoist our bags, show us our rooms. He asks me to join him for an Intake Interview, of which all I now remember are the soft, friendly questions, "Why did you come? What do you hope to get out of Gateway?"

"I don't have any expectations. Some hopes, yes. My main purpose is. . . ." The answer catches in my throat. I am not used to discussing my inner life with strangers. "Well. . . I came for spiritual advancement." Dave nods encouragingly, and makes a brief note on his clipboard.

We eat an amazingly appetizing vegetarian supper, then troop the few steps across to Francis Hall—named for David Francis, a West Virginia mining executive who was one of Monroe's closest confidants.

Some administrative details are explained by Mulvey and the other trainer, Darlene Miller, a white-haired, young-faced psychologist, who, before she came to the calm of the Institute, ran a 160-bed home for mentally-handicapped adolescents in Denver.

With grins, Darlene and Dave collect our watches. We begin to enter a state of timelessness.

There is a mild touch of theatricality to the first view the newcomer has of Bob Monroe. The seminarians sit in comfortable leatherette armchairs at tables artfully angled to funnel down towards another chair, strategically placed at the apex of the design.

Mulvey kills time tossing off a string of jokes from his inexhaustible supply. Despite the laughter, the twenty-two novitiates sit restlessly, waiting for the moment when The Man will arrive.

There's a crackling thunder of static, transmitted through the room's loudspeakers. Mulvey smiles broadly.

Some of the students turn. Others, not knowing what to expect, sit rigid in their chairs, staring straight ahead.

Bob Monroe progresses down the room slowly, not ponderously, but with the gait of a man who has time. I am surprised at how pale he is. He grins, mutters, "How are you?...Good to see you...Glad you're here." He makes sure the lapel microphone is clipped to his shirt, clenches his hands in that trademark gesture.

"Well, now! Tell me why you're all here! Looking for some excitement?" He chuckles and eases himself into his seat. Darlene brings a mug of coffee.

Monroe thanks her with inborn courtesy. "I try to hold with two of these a day," which may be his intent, but it's breached more often than observed.

"So, why *are* we here?" Ever so gently, Bob Monroe launches into a soft, rambling, soliloquy—a yarning I know he has given more times than he can remember, but one that is always fresh, intriguing, exhilarating. There is professionalism in his performance—the use by a master of voice modulation and emphasis, the seemingly effortless movements. I recall Bob Monroe was once a radio director who, in the words of his sister Dorothy, used to wave his arms and conduct a radio program just like someone leading a full orchestra. He is also a master of timing, another hangover from radio drama days. And he is a teacher, perhaps with many of the traits of his professorial father.

Now, he's telling us he'll provide the technology to let us experience in some small measure new patterns of Consciousness—new to this era, that is.

People have scribbled down reasons they have come distances and paid considerable sums for the Gateway Experience: To diminish ego; achieve personal growth; simply let themselves be, accept. Someone says, simply, "We're all searching."

A flip chart at the front of the room lists the official objectives of the Gateway: To develop and explore human consciousness; To learn and experience profound areas and expand awareness; To know and understand the Higher Self.

I fix on Monroe's face. The image of Socrates immediately springs to mind. Deep-fold streams cross his forehead to join at a canyon, which runs deep down to the bridge of Bob's nose. The branches intersect the crow's feet of laugh lines crinkling outwards from his deepset eyes, across high cheekbones. These horizontals are, in turn, bisected by verticals which slash diagonally down across the cheekbones, making a checkerboard pattern, in turn furrowed by curves which end at the root of the nose. It is a face which has known agony and joy, ecstasy and sorrow, and it reflects the eroding of physical time and of a fully-lived life.

The eyes are remarkable, deep-socketed in puffy flesh, watery, rapidly-blinking, penetrating, calm, wise. His ears are huge, jug-shaped. Under Bob's chin hang turkey-like wattles.

His hair is white now, and spare on top. There's a scraggly fringe of beard, maybe half an inch long, sprouting weedlike from his chin and meandering up his cheeks. "It's taken me two months, and it's no great success." He later says he can't for the life of him grow decent whiskers, because he has had skin transplants on his cheeks.

On this occasion, in April 1987, my impression is of a man who has served his term, and is now slumping on the brink of irreversible fatigue. I get the feeling he's saying inside, "I've done my job here. I'm tired. I want to go Home." There's an air of wistfulness to him, even despite the smile which, make no mistake, is still genuine and fresh. Yet something dictates that he stay on and complete a task as yet unspecified.

What manner of man is it who, in his seventy-second year, sits in the Chair, addressing his newest squadron? In the first year the Center operated, some sixty people came to listen to him in Gateway courses there. In 1987, it was three hundred fifty, and the waiting list now often stretches out six months.

* * * *

Monroe eases into a different pose just on the rim of the spotlights' pool.

"We got a lot of business to attend to, so I'm sure you won't mind if we get going." I glance at the rear of the room. Two women I later came to know as Nancy Penn Monroe and their daughter Scooter McMoneagle, sit, their arms propped on a table, listening as if they had never heard Bob before."

"Who are we? We're an energy form...Like a vortex or tornado. Always in action, not lying idle...We're talking about those highly complex wave forms that are You."

Then, a throwaway line to break the awe that permeates the room: "There's one First Timer in this group, the rest of us are Repeaters; I'm referring to our human physical lives. All you Gateway people are familiar faces. We have met before." There is a rustle as the Voyagers pridefully adjust their postures.

For the rest of the week, the One-Timer remark bothers me with increasing intensity: Am I that individual, on a fast track through this physical life, compiling as much experience as I can, to be applied There as soon as I make my exit? For a while, I am convinced he means me.

But now, Monroe is serious again: "I challenge you to find out: What is your Ultimate Illusion?"

A volley of answers bounces back at Bob. Throughout the week, Our Man from Dallas—bustling ex-Navy combat flyer, glider pilot, marketing executive—sticks up his hand at every opportunity. "Bob, about your own Ultimate Illusion? Will you tell us?" And the same grin, "Nope. Maybe at the end of the week. Ask me then."

That Sunday evening, he continues, "You wouldn't be here unless you were pretty well accelerating towards escape velocity.

"It's not accidental that some of you are Here, to remember There." Now, there is no joking in the honeyed voice.

"Gateway brings intense knowledge of self, gets the ego under good control.

"The program asks: 'What would I *really* like to do?...It's a crib sheet, that's all. It's sort of sneaky. Gives you control of your options.

On another occasion, Monroe describes Gateway thus: "It's a multipurpose guidance system designed to get past unconscious fear of the Unknown...Get over the barrier we all have –fear of the Law of Change...and to make change exciting."

Now, in David Francis Hall, Bob uses an analogy which extends into his business affairs: Interstate Industries is the corporate name for the company that markets his Metamusic and other tapes:

> "It goes something like this:
>
> "The Path—To reach for Adulthood.
>
> "The Road—Maturity: A number of illusions are let go. You release your unconnected responsibilities.
>
> "The Highway—Wisdom. How do you measure it? It creates a vacuum. How do you fill it, to make you gladder and wiser? With what you insert by thought, action, being!
>
> "The Interstate—Freedom."

It's the Interstate that Monroe seeks to have Gateway graduates travel thenceforth. "The only requirement is that you bring curiosity. And have fun!"

Monroe hitches his chair farther out of the glare of the overhead spot. He is almost visibly now talking from There.

"Let's take and say an entity gets a whiff of the Here action. He tastes it, smells it. It's discordant, but it's attractive. He thinks, 'Looks pretty good. Let's take a shot, see what it's like.' So he goes to the entry station and applies to be Human.

"The Entry Director—that's Ed—says there's a long waiting list for the choice locations. But Africa, or India, you can get there right away.

"He tells you, 'Of course, there are some conditions. One is to be disconnected from your true identity. Second, you've got to accept Time-Space as real: that this earthly planet you're entering does exist in the Twentieth Century.' "

"You take what you can get, and suddenly a 14-year-old girl in a Harlem tenement gives birth. The baby feels, hears, smells." Bob Monroe's voice drops to a barely-audible whisper:

"Now, you're on stage. You come back for periodic check-ins and to get proper alignment." But, he continues, your entity's commuting between Consciousness Here and There is not necessarily chronological.

"You can go back in time to pick up special knowledge; for instance, maybe you need to look at the Crusades. Or at the Creation."

Then, "Why do we become human?"

"No one forces you to return to Earth. It's your own decision. Maybe it's simple curiosity.

"Or, there's the Remittance Man approach: You're being 'paid' to flee from another energy system, and dive into Here, use the Earth as a refuge." I scribble "Nightmares?" in my notes.

There are those who become addicted to the Human Experience. "They're the Human Junkies. They get locked in to what they have Here: The worldly lures of material acquisition and power." They find it impossible to yield their attachment to earthly totems. They choose to recycle, to come back again and again, to get more, ever more.

At some point, however, even the predators begin to see that property and the pursuit of power don't provide the answers they need. They start to adjust their styles, to drop their addictions to the "appurtenances" of physical life. Eventually, they become more selective in their recycles: Then they may even choose to wait a thousand of our years for another entry.

Bob muses on, in full, allegorical spate. "There are the missionaries who come to change it all, but get hooked on the physical. Rescuers who get trapped helping their buddies.

"Best of all, there's the Graduate.

"What makes one? Massive growth. Divining the purpose of the physical world.

"This Earth is an experience system, a compressed learning machine.

"It's *the* Learning School. It creates stress, crisis, conflicts which teach us cause and effect, polarities, comparatives.

"You would be bored by physical serenity.

"If you have a short interval between lives, you are addicted heavily. If you take a long interval, you're getting selective, and maybe you go into service There."

"Service to humankind is a fine goal, but there are others. For instance, there might be other intelligent life Here. We might know, if we knew how to communicate better non-verbally."

I can't resist the image of a pod of dolphins, smiling compassionately at the writhings of human species. Much later, other images of more immediate, pressing import occur to me.

"And, of course, there are other schools. The closest one we've discovered is sixty light years away. It's an alligator culture, only they have bigger bumps."

In a later exercise, I ask to view this life system: I come to a liquid planet and see friendly creatures who look like a cross between alligators and frogs. But perhaps that's merely the differing perceptions of two reporters.

The Sunday evening session winds down. Bob Monroe has taken us on a verbal voyage to the seldom reaches of Beyond, of There. Now, slowly, gently, he readjusts to the Here and Now.

He looks a bit startled to find himself back, land-bound. "Well, this is the beginning of my third work cycle. Time to go have supper.

"Don't forget: Have fun!"

And, with the broad grin of a man sharing a huge, joyous secret with old friends, he places his coffee cup on a side table and strolls back up the aisle.

A woman scrambles to her feet. "Mr. Monroe, I have to hug you." Bob looks momentarily taken aback, then quickly adjusts to the unexpected intrusion on his person, and wraps his arms around the neophyte with genuine pleasure.

We shuffle back over the redbrick pathway to the Center, excited yet privately puzzled by Bob's talk, perhaps slightly apprehensive.

* * * *

Monroe has a friendly but firm word of advice for all who start out on his taped exercises. "Empty your bladder first." Facilities at the Center are limited. Before each exercise, one of the trainers clangs a brass bell. By the end of the week, students react to the peal galvanically, troop en masse to the restrooms, but all too often find the red light of occupancy lit by someone quicker off the mark. As the group coalesces, the embarrassment of hanging over a banister gazing with absorption at nothing at all disappears and all—men and women—wait their turn with grins of patience.

All Monroe exercises are conducted in what are cumbrously called "Chec Units" (for Controlled Holistic Environmental Chamber). Bob's books talk of waterbeds, three of which were used in the lab at his previous headquarters. Today's Chec units are bunks with normal mattresses, faintly reminiscent of the old Pullman sleeping-car berths. One perpetual student calls them "Jefferson Beds" after the syle of sleeping niche Thomas Jefferson built into his nearby Monticello homestead.

This cavern, which is home for the week, is equipped with a headset, a microphone on a gooseneck arm, a cassette recorder, volume control for the overhead speakers, controls to mix a light display projected at the foot of the bunk, and a switch to indicate to the trainers in the control room the occupant is ready for the exercises to begin.

It lacks the convenient net sling in which the Pullman passenger could stow his loose oddments. By the final day, my cubbyhole had become a comfortable, if crumb-strewn nest. I burrow crannies around the mattress to store fruit and snacks, a water glass, wallet, spare glasses, extra pens and the other flotsam of daily physical life.

When the student is settled, usually prone, he draws a black curtain across the Chec Unit's entry gap, and is alone with himself—and the taped voice of Bob Monroe. It's not sensory deprivation, but fairly close to it.

After Bob's talk that first night, I notice my heart is throbbing faster than usual. As the initial cassette starts to pulse through the earphones, all of us in the building hum in keeping with the swooping harmonics of the tape's resonant tuning. I feel heat accumulating in my body, but, oddly, my skin remains cool. A faint waveform of sibilant noise coaxes a tingling in my brain: A sense of confluent crests of Energy lapping back and forth through my thought processes. Every filament of my being seems alive, alert, although, as Bob urges, my physical body relaxes into sleep.

What I hear are not the patented signals which unify the action of my brain's hemispheres, and take me into the theta state, between awake and asleep: Hemi-Sync is barely audible. What I hear and at first think of as Hemi-Sync is an artfully-conceived sound pattern which impresses the physical sense as being Hemi-Sync, but is, in fact, a mask.

Then, suddenly, unexpectedly...a sense of weightlessness, of soaring and plummeting. I actually feel the energy of our twenty-two disparate selves combining, grouping. I want to shout in glee. I no longer feel apart, as I have for so much of my life. I have the uncanny sensation that the sum of our energies is so great, the Center will burst its pinnings and its roof will fly off at any second. I note a rushing sensation I later think of as love for the group of which I am now an integral part, though I yet hardly know their names.

We come down after an indeterminate time, reluctantly; throughout the week, I and others are often annoyed that Bob always, unrelentingly, calls us back from our reverie-explorations. It is blissful Out There.

After each session, we gather in a conference room unlike most others: no tables, just a large open space. Originally, it had a white carpet, now somewhere off-beige because nearly a decade of bare feet have ground fine, red Virginian dust into it.

We lie around the floor on cushions, a few choose to sit in armchairs. At one of the early sessions, someone starts talking of "good" and "evil." Gently, the trainers interpose, "We don't usually talk of good or evil, bad or good. They're value judgements. We do talk of constructive and destructive. Positive and negative. Beneficial and harmful." It's a simple system which avoids semantic or doctrinal pitfalls.

The exercises follow throughout the week. I begin slowly to appreciate I am working towards freedom, learning to discard traces of fear which indeed still lurk unsuspected, deep inside me.

At the outset of each lesson, I dutifully stuff my worldly concerns into the Energy Conversion Box. It's a handy mental repository to hold the static of everyday concerns which can interrupt progress to the Interstate. Since we design our own boxes, I image mine to be an ancient Spanish chest of burnished leather, bound by stout iron straps. Its lid is heavy enough to slam down authoritatively whenever I wanted to leave behind the jumble of my physical life.

We master a basic step to protect ourselves on trips, the awkwardly-named Resonant Energy Balloon. The technique allows the voyager to surround his body with a swirling cocoon of shimmering light as he prepares to embark on altered-consciousness travel

Early in the program, we go to Focus 10, Monroe's term for the first level of higher Consciousness; the condition of "Mind Awake, Body Asleep." Having yielded easily to the tape's instructions, I find myself entering something which looks much like Van Gogh's "Room at Arles." I see the scene and amd part of it; I believe I smell the freshness of the air, and the slight perfume of Midi spring flowers; I know I feel the texture of unsanded wood and stuccoed walls and rough cotton bedding. (When I later checked a print, I discovered my vantage point was the reverse of the artist's: I saw the scene from the window, not from Van Gogh's doorway.)

During one Monday morning exercise, I hear a sound like that of an old-fashioned tin roof rattle crackling in a wild thunderstorm. I laugh like a little boy. Eagerly, I think I am about to separate from my physical body. My mind says, "Here we go!" I feel an intense tugging, an undeniable physical sensation, but after an incalculable period of seething turmoil, I relapse, knowing I will not then separate, nor be able to shove my ethereal hand through the cedar paneling of the Chec Unit, as Bob Monroe learned he could do in 1958. My disappointment, and that slight, nagging feeling of rejection is shortlived, however.

Something better happens. I behold an adored and respected uncle who died in the mid 1950s, one of the most gentle and wise men I have ever known. He had appeared to me, before I came to Gateway, on a number of occasions, taking identifiable shape as he gradually replaced an earlier, roguish being who was my first distinguishable guide.

Now, my uncle's red beard reflects the sun iridescently as he sits on the top rail of the ranch corral, a robust, vibrant figure, chewing a straw, smiling broadly. It is a vignette I could have dredged from a childhood vacation in Wyoming, but it's a vivid image, and I have no physical memory of my uncle in that pose. "Come on over, it's great," he calls. I yearn to join him. I later conclude the setting was intended as verification, an identifier, or a bona fide.

Monday afternoon I conjure up a wand. In Monroe terms, it's called the Energy Bar Tool, an all-purpose gadget to take on voyages, more useful than a Swiss Army knife and far less dangerous. Mine at first looks like a multi-colored neon tube. I use it as a baton to direct a Mahler symphony, then plunge my unseen orchestra into the booming cadences of the theme from Star Wars. I telescope it, lengthen it into infinity. I puzzle over its practical use, but shrug and merely keep it with me henceforth.

That afternoon, Bob's taped voice tells us we are on our own to go out and reconnoiter. It is our first "Free Flow" exercise in Focus 10—Mind Awake, Body Asleep. I ask for the blessing of God on my adventures—and take off, without fear.

I meet my uncle again. My mother—his sister—who died after lengthy illnesses, in 1957, is a radiant presence in the background. She is dressed in a Mother Hubbard, her face averted under its cowl. She, a happy gardener in physical life, seems to be hoeing.

My uncle and I join energies. For the first time I experience what I can only describe as a tumultuous, exhilarating surge of Wholeness: An energy of Knowing which takes over and stimulates my entire being. Although I feel as if my body is embraced by an infinite, beneficial energy, I know it is happening to far more than my mere physical self. I begin, slowly, to understand that I am more than body and brain.

I am entering my mind, the altered state of consciousness. My uncle flashes me an understanding that what lies ahead will be difficult for me, and that we have a considerable path to go together.

That evening in David Francis Hall, we watch a beauteous movie of twin gliders slipping, spinning, wafting over craggy landscapes. The film is The Sonnet of a Soaring Pilot, trying to evade his alter ego. No spoken message. Just images close to the heart of a man who soared the Andes, for us now to digest.

Monday night, from the cozy protection of my Chec Unit, I myself loft. First, I waft over the Center. I notice I cast no shadow on its roof, even though the moon is full. I swoop over the Institute's nearby lake, then—on my command—I circle over the wonders of America's dazzling night-time cities. But they are sights I have seen from planes. I whimsically change course, and look at Moscow as it starts to gather strength for another day, at London and Paris, still slumbering. And I get a nonverbal message that millions and millions of people, in sleep, crave for themselves the release and joy of my effortless prospecting.

* * * *

On the Tuesday morning, we are ready to advance to Monroe's second level. Focus 12, the state of Advanced Conscious Awareness. My Energy Bar Tool accompanies me as I climb a short stepladder to board the fuzzy-wispy pink cloud-carriage that awaits me there. I become a newborn babe, trampolining in space. My Energy Bar Tool spontaneously turns into Ilios, a rod of pure light. From somewhere, a hymn from childhood chapel services choruses, "These things shall be a loftier race. . . .

Next, fun and games abate. I am firmly shown shortcomings that still linger in me. They are an uncomfortable revelation; I smugly thought I had dealt with them in my recovery program. I must tackle ego, pride, fear, material attachment; I must learn to love and be loved—to open up for the first time in my physical life, truly and innocently.

By now we neophytes have melded into a group and are, in many cases, sharing our experiences in the debriefing sessions after each exercise. Some are highly personal, many uproarious. One of the two British artists with us reports he has been looking out of a spaceship's cockpit at—a field of strawberries. A young man in our group says he saw me flying over the Institute's lake in a red plane, and yelled, "Hey, wait for me!"

In the Chec Unit, I try again to separate from my body. I feel a hollowness inside my chest. My frame is weightless. I have by now been joined by other guides, who augment my uncle. One is a Crusader knight named Tristan, in white tunic, with the familiar red cross on his chest. Another is a more mystical figure, whose purpose I know is to act as my spiritual guide; I later identify him as the physical William Temple, Archbishop of Canterbury in the 1940s. To me, he is Synchron.

Four unseen pairs of hands tug and push at me. I know they belong to my Non-Physical Friends and family. I feel my blood-energy vibrating at the boil, but my skin still remains dry. I cannot get out! I despair. Why am I not qualified to emulate Monroe? Am I not worthy? What am I doing wrong? How am I blocking myself? I decide my spiritual evolution has not proceeded far enough, and am morose.

Next an exercise poses some basic questions. For a start, "Who am I?" Some of the answers are serious: "You are one of Us," flashes at me from a group of energies I vaguely perceive.

In another scene, I behold one of my companions in the course, the woman from the Canary Islands, coming towards me through a cloud, singing huskily, "Come to Me, My Melancholy Baby." It's sort of campy "Here Comes Mr. Jordan" stuff. The German lady, when I later confide my experience, immediately asks, "Well? Did we?" I had to regretfully tell her we didn't.

The events of the exercises begin to blur as we progress along Bob Monroe's carefully-guided path. By Wednesday, we are practicing Non-Verbal Communication (NVC)—the transmission, receipt and retention of fleeting visualizations or images. Some of our group complain they fall asleep during the lessons. The trainers assure them it doesn't deprive them of the experience. What comes to them through the headphones is imprinted in their consciousnesses and will stay part of their beings.

The Energy Bar Tool takes another, sudden turn. While trying to absorb NVC, I make

Ilios into an antenna for my non-physical friends to home in on. Suddenly, in Focus 12, it changes from being a sort of mast into an unmistakable, but puzzling, symbol. Afterwards, I sketch the simple device into my notebook, but I cannot, today, recall showing the sketch to anyone in the course.

Several weeks later, a small box tumbled out of my post office box: A dear Gateway lady, a librarian who lives near Detroit, included a brief note: "When I got home, I showed the sketch to a sculptor friend of mine. This is the result." I wear the pendant around my neck, and treasure it still today. Although I have asked several people, knowledgeable in such matters, no one has been able to tell me anything about the design: It "looks familiar" but it seems to have no historical precedent.

We go on to Monroe's third level, Focus 15, the state of No Time. I look first at my own entry into Earth—a clinical examination of the acts of conception and birth. Then, for the fun of it, I examine the Manhattan of the mid-nineteenth century, a brawling melting pot a-bubble, of which I may have been a part. I go back in time and look at the stoa under the Acropolis in Athens, and watch Plato discoursing in a Periclean Age cafe.

Back in the conference room, I remain skeptical. The act of making a baby is no big deal. A New Yorker by upbringing, I have read books describing Manhattan in its uncouth early days. I wandered the Athenian stoa with an archeologist who described life in the Golden Age in vivid detail. I suspect what I am doing is merely visualizing knowledge already lodged in my brain.

But am I requesting those specific visions, or are they coming unbidden, to show me something of value? I can't decide where the dividing line between voluntary self-guidance, or "aspecting," and passive acceptance of unfathomable events, lies.

That night, perhaps suffering from overload, I blank out, and have no recall of anything. Next day, we take a trip without tapes, to prove to ourselves we can travel without external boosting. I, who knows next to nothing about pro football, make a Super Bowl prediction (which turned out totally wrong). Then I watch sympathetically as laborers haul massive blocks of stone up wooden inclines in the desert. Again, the construction of the pyramids is something I know about, as does any schoolboy; but here the picture is presented unbidden, complete with sound effects and sweat. At the time, I had next to no conscious interest in pyramids, except as pieces of mysterious architecture, and knew nothing of their energy properties.

Wednesday afternoon, I go through an intensely personal experience: I begin to open those channels of self-limitation which block my progress towards Self. Simple recognition of the controls still imposed on my being by my ego, self-will, materialism seem almost to be enough to remove some of the barriers.

Then, I meet my mother, guided by her ever-present, ever-so-gentle brother. She is a joyous, lustrous young woman with flowing red hair, gowned in simple white linen, not the sorely pain-ravaged being I had last seen in physical life. We surge together in a rapturous absorption of energies and, non-verbally, exchange assurances of deep, abiding love. The omissions and commissions of our intertwined lives, which had haunted me since her death, instantly resolve themselves. I take another step towards Freedom, and dissolve, not for the first time that week, in a catharsis of shuddering sobs.

Soon, I am involved in several other highly-charged spiritual and emotional encounters, including one with my dead father, which I feel are too wrenchingly personal to discuss in the group debriefings. Yet I feel I have to share them with someone, or explode. I think I may be flitting on the borderline of sanity.

I choose Darlene Miller, and unload my exhilaration, my ecstasy, my doubts, my disbelief, my feelings of unworthiness, my tears on her. Darlene serenely and tenderly encourages me to continue, not to falter. It's an assurance I badly need, and I renew it with her later, as experience piles on experience.

The trainers firmly urge us to use the long mid-day break to get out-of-doors, to ground ourselves. A combination of the taped exercises, swimming in the lake and walking over the rolling ridges of the farm run us the gamut of mind-body activity. I am burning energy at an exorbitant rate. I am amazed at my appetite.

There comes next an "emotional cleansing" exercise. I catalogue the recognized anxieties still lurking in my being. They bubble away into the metaphysical never-never, to the soothing tones of Bob on tape: Fear of lonesomeness; of intimacy, abandonment and rejection; apprehension of unworthiness; above all, Fear of the Unknown. A message comes through: "Perfect Love casts out Fear." I accept it willingly, and with tears of gratitude.

I begin to wrestle consciously with the concept of love; to wonder why I have blocked it all my life; to overcome my ingrained, defensive skepticism. More than a year later, I am aware I still have a long way to go to accept and give of true, limitless love, in both the individual and the universal senses. But Gateway brings me to conversance with the feeling, where nothing else had.

Centered after the Thursday lunchtime break, I look at the future again, to see what it holds for me and those close to me. Something like 90 percent of the visualizations come true within the year. They include the writing of this book. A woman in the course comes up to me and says she has been told I have an important message for her; we cannot determine what the message is, but she has intuited other information about me she had no way of otherwise knowing.

Thursday night. The week has been exhausting, draining, euphoric. I feel fully cleansed, but more lies ahead: We are taken to Focus 21, the borderline between Here and There. First I pass through the tunnel familiar to those who have had a Near-Death Experience, and meet my welcoming committee, composed of my immediate family. Thereafter, I part from my uncle, who indicates he has chosen to stay in a level close to Earth, to help others who have their transitions yet to make—including his wife, who dies within the year. He yields to a new guide, whose identity comes only with difficulty. After a period of ambiguity, I discover his name is Menton, which then elides to Mon.

Mon brings me to an open forum, its simplicity of line and columns broken by the green of plants. I later learn it is called the Hall of Love. I intuitively prostrate myself on low, shelving steps during an encounter with the God presence. During the first stage of the encounter, I register a rending-healing-pulsing through my entire being. I identify God as Love-Sharing-Service. God has no human physical features or attributes.

I am told I must return to physical life, that I have now "qualified" but that my task is not complete. I am drenched in tears. I register a three-pulse beat below my left ear. My body throbs rhythmically.

Rising from the steps, I am moved to a side alcove or chapel, and am seated on a simple bench. There, I have a bolstering, warming conversation with the energy I identify as Jesus Christ. When Bob's voice calls us back, I am still soaked in tears. Later, as I let my overwhelming sense of unworthiness flow, I am told "Tears are liquid Love." It seems a barely adequate phrase to get me out of my sense of abject lowliness.

I come awake the morning of Good Friday and, in the first exercise of the day, return to the Hall of Love to receive some more messages. It is bare; I ask Mon where the foliage has gone. He replies cheerily, "Oh, we only had the plants here to help you feel at home." Again, I sit on the bench with Jesus. Thereafter my day is euphoric.

We learn to pattern our requests to the Non-Physical Friends, starting with smaller desires, working up to the big ones. Darlene comments that it is perfectly acceptable to ask for a fair share of the abundance of material things the Earth offers. Her comment is reassuringly worldly in our near-gossamer state.

Friday morning, we stroll around the campus in silence. I watch business executives and housewives kneel down to talk to blades of grass, or hug trees. I wonder briefly what a television crew would make of the scenes.

The silence paves the way for yet another series of spiritual encounters. Although I can now accept that I am a participant in these scenes, they still shake me to the core. If they are but figments of my over-heated imagination, they seem, at the least, presumptuous and perhaps even irreverent.

Am I projecting or "aspecting?" Is it all wish-think? Do I *know* the experiences have happened? I cannot hope to gain proof, but the weight of repetition works for acceptance of a reality I have no way of checking. I yield to faith that what I envision is true, yet I cling to some skeptical defenses, in case the whole structure of witnessing should collapse.

I glory yet again in a bath—an infusion—of "the light." Not surprisingly, I blank again completely during the following exercise. I am close to overload.

And then Dave and Darlene start gradually to bring us back into the physical world of roads and airlines and bank accounts. We list changes we anticipate in our daily lives and in our Inner Selves. We also consider how we can sabotage the benefit of the week, by inattention to what we have learned or total reimmersion in daily concerns.

We form a circle, arms-around, and speak our final thoughts of thanks and love, to each other, to the trainers, to our Friends, and to ourselves. There aren't many totally dry eyes in the conference room.

At his windup appearance Friday night, Bob Monroe instills his enthusiasm in us. "Well, now you know what it's all about. You've experienced the birth of a new kind of energy in yourselves. You're now a small part of the vibration of the earth changing. Accept it."

The familiar hand from Dallas shoots up one last time. Would Bob now, finally, please answer that recurrent question. The Progenitor pauses. "Sure. You should know it by now. It's simple."

"The Ultimate Illusion is that Man has limitations."

Our Gateway had one failure. I had brought a bagful of avocados with me from California, plucked from a tree the day I left. They were hard. About the second day of the week, I asked the group to concentrate energy on the bag, placed in the middle of the conference room floor, to ripen the fruit. Unfortunately, by the end of the week, the avocados had not softened.

There comes the graduation sock hop, at which big beat music thumps through the Center, as the group dances off the intensity of the week. I feel unable to indulge in the exuberance. Instead, I drag one of my fellow-students away from the rock-n-roll, to fill his ear with all the details of my week's highly personal events, some of which I have withheld from Darlene. He listens gravely and reassuringly. Maybe I am not crazy.

At 5:30 Saturday morning, I go on the week's final voyage. I ask some particular questions in The Library at Focus 15, and get highly useful answers. At Level 21, I am told that Tristan, the Crusader figure, is my militant protector. I express open skepticism about the reality of Mon and am told I will have confirmation, which did soon come, to my satisfaction.

Bob comes by for Saturday morning breakfast, one of his traditions, and autographs copies of his books. He glances at the recipient, goes in on himself, and then scrawls, in his angular, left-handed script, some legend, like "See you in. . . ." (and the number of a Consciousness Level he has been directed to give for that individual).

Our watches are returned. We dawdle over packing, sensing the loosening of a bond rarely forged. The group which knit together in the shared adventures of a week's mystical experience starts to unravel. We stand at the Center's entrance, hugging one another, as participants head for Germany, Britain, Venezuela, California, Michigan, Texas. We promise to stay in touch and send our experiences to a newsletter. It was actually published only once, with only eight contributions from our class of twenty-two.

The hospital administrator and I climbed into her battered car. At the Institute's exit, I briskly told Margaret, "Turn right." She shyly demurred: "I think we go left here."

"Margaret, I have traveled all my life. I have an infallable sense of direction. Go right."

Meekly, Margaret did as I bade her. Somewhere in the interior, where whiskered Virginians were out looking for possum, I admitted, "Something's wrong. Turn back." Margaret finally navigated us onto the highway back to the District of Columbia, without further help from me.

* * * *

It took me nearly ten days to come down from the week, and even longer to assimilate what had happened. No one realizes immediately after a Gateway how much it has affected him or her.

The Voyage was the beginning of a lengthy process of change within me, which continued during later Monroe courses. It started an accommodation with another reality which has become ever-present in my life. It also loosened the shackles of my conformity to social expectations. I shuffled my priorities. Some things no longer seemed particularly important.

Oh, I continue to stroll the streets of the city, and to behave in acceptable patterns. But, increasingly, I question whether that conformity is necessary to my inner wellbeing.

Gateway also, ever-so-gently, gave me acceptance of my Inner Self. Previously, I had often paused in one headlong plunge or another, to hear a chiding but gentle voice ask, "Why are you doing this?" or, "Oh no! Not again!" Now, I can identify that voice, and it has become my constant consultant, if I choose to heed it.

I walk freer. I know I can never rid myself totally of my earth-binding bonds of ego, pride, fears, and material attachments. My behavior will never be all that it might be. But I have gained more sense of the needs of others, and reduced the sense of my own importance. I have to try continually not to exploit the powers that reside in me to the detriment of others, but to employ them beneficially. The renunciations came easily, and have been greatly comforting.

I also learned another lesson I had only dimly realized—and distanced myself from—before: That men could love men unabashedly. That men can hurt inside, and comfort each other, even hug, without shame. That men and women are truly equal. I begin now to know what love for man as well as woman is, and I have started to accept as well as to give it, for the first time. I also learned that there is an unimaginable amount I do not know.

Over the months that followed, I yearned for the reinforcement of being able to talk to other Monroe graduates, to compare experiences, and to assure myself that what I had undergone had truly happened—to tell me, in short, that I was not a freak. It is an unfortunate shortcoming of the Institute that no arrangements for regional meeting points have been made that have lasted. Once away from Virginia, Monroe people are on their own, unless they are able to maintain contact with their own course-mates. Perhaps it is meant to be so.

Within months, my life, my beliefs, my code had changed 180 degrees, to an extent that surprised not only me, but many around me. I became used to the bewildered question, "You've changed somehow! Lost weight? Shaved your beard?" I knew the change was there, although I was hard put to explain it in words. What surprised me was that friends thought they detected an actual physical difference in my face, in my being.

They are changes wrought by Bob Monroe's Gateway, and for them I shall always be grateful.

Introduction

If Bob Monroe had asked for a philosphical guidebook to chart his lifetime course, it would probably have been fairly close to Peter Russell's stunning book, *The Global Brain* which appeared in Britain and the United States in the early 1980s. Russell intricately yet dramatically, and above all optimistically, outlines the malaise of this planet and emphasizes a remedy is available to us and within us all; a remedy which could jump-start the earth and its life-forms into a new level of evolution. The remedy is the much-talked-about, so little acted-upon development of Consciousness.

On first reading, Mr. Russell's huge and comprehensive canvas may seem to be too vast to concern one of the infinitesimal dots on it, yet that canvas has to do with each of us, and with The All. In fact, Peter Russell was unaware of Bob Monroe and his work when he wrote.

But Robert A. Monroe is one of a small number of people who hold keys to the Russell equation. What makes Bob Monroe different from most of the others is that he is a purely American product, at a time when the United States, though in decline, can still provide the moral, spiritual, and technological leadership which may permit mankind and other lifeforms to survive. Bob Monroe by virtue of his background and his mainstream Americanism may be just the person to make Conscious Awareness a factor in some important levels of America's creative society, because he is credible in our materialistic, skeptical age. If America can lead in the evolution of consciousness, it is more than probable that other nations and societies will follow—enough, according to Russell and others, to make a difference.

There are many blocks to achieving Conscious Awareness, most of them of our own, ultra-human fashioning. Society's expectations and demands present the main obstacles to people's covert yearning to be more than they are; the daunted school of thought that says, privately, 'Sure, I'd like to experiment, to see what it's all about, but I don't want to be caught doing anything kooky.' More than a bit of courage is needed to ignore the frown of our culture on things which are not solidly anchored in or condoned by the preachings of our various establishments.

The second major barrier to sucessful contact and accommodation with Supra-Consciousness is fear. It is with us all, until identified, confronted, and, eventually, accomodated or overcome. We, as a society, are riddled with fears so pernicious they go beyond cataloguing. But once the seeker has acknowledged his fears, half his way to higher Conscious Awareness is clear. The rest can be dealt with by techniques such as Bob Monroe's. Fears, especially fear of the unknown, fall away in the exhilaration of Knowledge.

It is no coincidence that Monroe has perfected techniques of Supra-Conscious awareness at a time when the new science of Chaos is emerging; when a prominent astronomer-computer scientist speculates on close contact between Earth and other dimensions; when Time-Life issues a small shelf of books on the paranormal, and the Public Broadcasting System (PBS) runs a series of programs on the role of myth and consciousness in our society.

* * * *

This is the story of Bob Monroe, a remarkable, unique American, whose influence on our society cannot yet be defined or measured. He interacts in a field which defies our "normal" standards of quantity or quality control. Most of his present success cannot easily be traced directly to him, because it has gone through too many filtrations after leaving his workbench. But his influence has already been profound, and will continue to build.

Bob Monroe does not recognize the scope of his success. He is more comfortable acknowledging the achievements which are obvious, although even then, he is hesitant about claiming any particular credit. It's all part of the Monroe Paradox.

Monroe has done much to ease a certain terror of doubt and confusion that haunted many people, who are sure singular events happened in their lives about which they could talk to no one until well after Monroe went modestly public with his own *Journeys Out of the Body (JOOB)* in 1971. Beyond that, he has at least indirectly offered reassurance and comfort to some of the estimated 60 percent of the American population who have had some kind of paranormal episode.

Of more importance, he has developed a late-Twentieth Century, American, hi-tech method which offers all who care to use it an easy, painless, drug-free method to access the Altered State of Consciousness. This method provides quick familiarity with, and some understanding of both the physical and non-physical realms. He also has developed techniques of mental relaxation, resourcefulness, agility, and development which will stand us in good stead in the years to come if, as many are convinced, those years are tough in the extreme.

The application of his techniques in medicine and education, especially, have yet to be fully explored. Monroe's pioneering has helped push staid science to question its laws; he has sparked a sub-industry in the mind-expansion business, issued tapes to help bring sleep, control pain and dramatically ease surgery. Monroe can even help improve your golf and tennis games.

Edgar Cayce was an All-American phenomenon, who introduced trance-channeling to a broad public, and whose work, more than forty years after his death, is still the basis of research; Cayce books are still widely read. Bob Monroe is also American through-and-through. He has gone a step farther than Cayce. Cayce was passive, a channel. Monroe is an explorer in the realm of Altered Consciousness. They were followed, in the 1960s, by the serious drug-experimenters, who saw visions and raised questions novel to society; and, nearly simultaneously, by the hesitant rise in medium-like channeling. Cayce and Monroe have been imitated since by charlatans and hucksters; but, far more important, they have been joined by other sincere professional and amateur researchers, in a quiet quest for ultimate sources—and truths.

Monroe's true achievement has been his contribution to opening up, making acceptable and accessible to the ordinary person the field of Conscious Awareness.

He summed up his objectives best in an undated paper, probably written in the early 1980s.

"The Monroe Institute is devoted to the concept that the future of man lies in changes and/or improvement in his function of consciousness. . . .

"The Institute maintains a unique position of credibility in a controversial field, among educators, professionals, academicians and socio-political structures (including local), by strictly adhering to the following:

> 1. It does not foster any philosphy, religion, religious belief system or life style. . . .
>
> 2. It expresses itself as an authority *only* in areas where it has gathered information, knowledge and experience. . . .
>
> 3. As its origins are within a Western culture, Institute activities are geared totally by and for the Western mind. . . . It does not denigrate the vast accumulation of human knowledge and experience engendered by "Eastern" philosophy. . . .

"The Institute holds these precepts:

> 1. Late Twentieth Century man finally is approaching a level where he might begin to perceive. . . facets of reality ever before elusive and/or rejected.
>
> 2. Such perceptions may lead to forms of freedom inconceivable to the present consciousness of man, therefore it is his consciousness that first must begin to change.
>
> 3. The first freedom is from release (not loss) of illusions promulgated and instilled by others. He can do this only by discovering validity by and for his own self.
>
> 4. The second freedom is total self-determination.
>
> 5. The Institute attempts to provide tools now acceptable in a cultural context to begin this process. These are offered with full realization that no cult of personality is needed for their proper and expanded use. Conversely, any such dependency appears to violate the process itself.

"To this extent, the Institute has been and will remain unique, offering and teaching only that with which it is familiar. In the broad view, apparently it is only one part of a growing undercurrent in Western culture, spontaneous and unorganized.

"The end result is yet in the possibility stage. Perhaps 100, 500, 1,000 years from Here-Now. It will have come into full-bloom."

* * * *

Bob Monroe, in his contemplative years, is an extraordinarily complex being: down-home yet intellectual; loving yet hard to grasp; public yet secluded—an influence which future years may come to be recognized as having been enormously positive, beneficial and constructive for other humans.

Much of what follows deals in the shadowland which straddles the frontier of the reality we encounter daily, and in a series of non-physical realities we are now, as a culture, beginning slowly to recognize. This side of the border is familiar, much-trampled territory. The other side is mystical, to some extent imponderable, and certainly immeasurable. It is broadly derided, scorned, ignored; yet serious academics, albeit a handful, are doing their utmost to make the world of Consciousness an acceptable part of our daily regimens, for reasons that seem to them and to many others vital.

The story of Bob Monroe ranges afield—from business peaks to financial canyons, from enthusiastic subject of scientific research to go-it-alone laboratory investigator. The way stations in between have been in the fields of music, radio, TV, gliding, flying, scuba-diving, surfing, marriage, property-ownership, housing-construction, philosophy, cattle-raising, poker-playing. . . you name it. Chances are Bob Monroe has done it.

It is not my purpose to rank Monroe with advanced, evolved Tibetans or Yoga Masters, although as his story emerges, certain similarities will become evident. Bob is a totally American phenomenon. He has arrived at the same truths they have achieved by a far different, homegrown, but no less valid path.

* * * *

Who is Robert A. Monroe? Galactic explorer? Radio Nut? Writer? Super-Channeler? *Nostalgiste*? Inventor? Recluse? Egocentric businessman? P.T. Barnum of the Aquarian Age? Just a guy who loves to beat the System?

One Virginia autumn day, Monroe and I came schussing down a Blue Ridge mountain road in his well-used four-wheel drive Blazer, talking about an earlier enthusiasm for racing cars at Watkins Glen.

As we negotiated a hairpin curve, Bob, suddenly reflective, said, "I've made some mistakes. . . but I have nothing to be ashamed of." A simple statement of a man who has lived life, and then some.

He's a determined, self-protective loner yet a man who still remembers and acknowledges the worldly friends who helped mold him, even way back to his childhood. He's not unduly modest, and has no reason to be, yet at times he exudes the remarkable, humility of true innocence.

He is a man who has made and lost large sums of money. In the late 1970s, he and his wife, Nancy, sold a luxurious Virginia estate to buy and build the Monroe Institute on an out-of-the-way farm in one of the state's most rural counties, and in so doing took a drastic cut in lifestyle. The capital investment in land and buildings and expensive equipment to build the Monroe Institute came out of his own pocket. For years he paid for much of the Institute's operations in research and training as well. His explanation? Disarmingly, "I had a lot to learn."

The Monroes' physical comfort took second priority for more than seven years. Now that he has made the major outlays, Bob is content to follow an intuition which says, "Enjoy!" The couple's new house is well-stocked, beautifully-furnished, air-conditioned, and warm in winter. Monroe wears no hair-shirt to prove anything to anyone.

Bob has difficulty talking of himself, and often takes refuge in the passive to cover an emotion: "It was felt." He tends to glide artfully over revelation which would give the listener a key to his inner self.

Monroe adamantly rejects the role of guru. He refuses flatly to impose his own beliefs on others. He rarely uses the word "metaphysical" because he feels it sounds too pompous, yet has been too cheapened. He talks instead of philosophy or, in very recent times, occasionally, almost hesitantly, of spirituality.

His physical-life exploits in the days when individuality was cherished would have been flamboyant, if played to an audience, but they were solos, just for the hell of it. The exhilaration was what counted—that and the bite of a thin edge of danger.

He is, too, a man's man who knows how to meet a payroll, work to a deadline, run a company, and by the way, he goes Out of Body (OOB) most every night.

He's a guy whose non-physical experiences blast the mind: Someone who weaves back and forth across the last frontier, is friends with death, returns with knowledge vouchsafed heretofore to lamas, hermit monks, saints, deep-meditators.

Bob Monroe has demystified the occult. The innovation he has made public in his books is that practically anyone can take similar voyages. He provides a method, using technology instead of long years of focussed concentration.

Along the way to perfecting his techniques, he has become well acquainted with terror and agony, has suffered depression, has endured massive physical ailments. His face is carved by the frequent knife of pain, but its folds are softened by a serenity of Knowing beyond the limits most of us can grasp.

There are many streaks of inconsistency to the Man, part of the purposeful configuration of his inboard defense system. Bob is intensely loyal to those who helped him in the past, and refuses to cut ties to some who don't match up to the standards he sets for himself. He has difficulty in finding words of thanks, but expresses gratitude in other, more subtle ways.

Conversely, he leans over backwards to stay free of commitment to any other person, and he is almost ferociously adamant about maintaining iron control of his own activities.

Bob Monroe is a man who finds himself terribly alone. A major part of his story is the wrenching gap between his pragmatic, executive Left Brain function and the soft, joyous, naive, but at-times melancholy yearning of his Right Brain. The mistakes he has made in his life are those of an ordinary mortal. He followed his heart too often in the past. He trusted too many people whose motives turned out to be questionable. Now, he finds difficulty in trusting anyone.

Bob's brilliance and shifting enthusiasms make him loath to keep his attention centered on a project for long. He still has a lot to do, and not much time left Here, this time around. Monroe warns people against expecting anything of him—but perhaps not emphatically enough; many feel themselves under his spell and throw caution to the winds in acts of impulsive fealty.

Some have hoped to use Monroe as a springboard into the lucrative New Age Movement. What they forget is that Bob Monroe has a long track record in the business world.

Part of Monroe's sense of beleaguered aloneness has come through experiences with do-gooders who have offered to donate large sums of money to his Institute, yet at critical moments reneged. Bob looks at offers of philanthropy these days with skepticism. He will simply not allow himself to be taken over. This reserve has undoubtedly also hindered exploitation of the mass of information held in thousands of hours of recorded tape which are Institute property.

They are the records of Monroe's own non-physical journeys and of the discoveries of his Explorers—OOB volunteers who probe the world of the super conscious and report their other-worldly experiences. It would take a large sum of money to transcribe, catalogue and index the tapes. If the job were done, the Monroe Archive would at least complement the Edgar Cayce material.

* * * *

Bob Monroe had to know what was happening to him in the early days of his OOBs or, he felt sure, go insane. He offered himself for scientific study, but was not generally welcomed. Feeling excluded, he resolved to use his business acumen and his own scientific technology to "prove" what was unprovable. He has done so, by the sheer credible weight of "experiential data" accumulated by himself and others; but he is still largely unrecognized by the establishments. He takes no solace from the fact that the worlds of psi, parapsychology and the study of the paranormal are barely accorded the status of establishment stepchildren.

Solid proof does not and cannot exist, except in the authentic ring of Monroe's accounts, and in the experiences of countless of his students. What consitutes evidence of the metaphysical world? Could anyone have such a wild imagination? Is he merely a latter-day Jules Verne? The search for credibility has long plagued Monroe.

Monroe's trainers say, "Reality is what you perceive it to be." Brainwashing? Subliminal manipulation? It's a charge often levelled by Bob's detractors. What Bob Monroe has developed is a hi-tech, binaural method of "entrainment," or of bypassing the indoctrination of society, to get at the real identity, the true consciousness of the trainee. Any mind-shift which temporarily comes during a Monroe taped exercise is the result of the student's own desires; and, again, Monroe pushes no ideology at all.

The courtly Virginian pioneered the intensive use of tape cassettes to expand Conscious Awareness. The system feeds different frequencies into the student's ears, thus linking the hemispheres of the brain. Monroe patented his Frequency-Following Response process as "Hemi-Sync" in 1975. Since then, others have recognized the effectiveness of his discovery and have published similar techniques.

Monroe seeks to introduce the student to a system which allows him to operate in constant touch with his or her inner guidance, if he so chooses. But there is no coercion, at any step along the way. A participant who begins to feel uneasy has a childishly simple method to break out of the supranormal state and center himself in the physical. Nothing in any of the Monroe courses goes against the grain of social behavior. To the contrary, the exercises are specifically designed to be integrated with daily life.

Monroe's conviction is that all that is necessary for an individual to know will be forthcoming, if he makes the right paranormal connection. The ponderous harness of everyday life becomes less important as the student learns to free himself from fear, deal with his ego, access his consciousness and, thenceforward, operate in concert with his Guidance.

Another explanation of Monroe's isolation is that it reflects his passionate distrust of anything that smacks of guru-ism. Although he works to achieve an effect when he appears in front of a class, he is puzzled and at times uncomfortable that his words—some them jesting throw-aways—excite adulation among those who come to listen and learn. Not entirely self-deprecatingly, he may complain about the number of amateur enthusiasts who take astral trips to call on him: "You wouldn't believe Monday nights around my house! Everyone seems to want to prove they can make contact with me!"

Monroe is disturbed by the excesses of cult leaders, yet knows he could easily have been one. He constantly dismantles the pedestals his admirers construct for him. He does not even dream of competing with any of the public soothsayers of our time.

Bob recalls with amusement an evening in Tampa, where he had been invited to "say hello" to J. Z. Knight's Ramtha. "J. Z. came over to me and gave me a big, warm, feminine hug. Then, later in the session, along came Ramtha and gave me a great big, man's hug. That little girl couldn't have done that!

"Afterwards, I went up in the receiving line. I communicated with him on another level.

"He said, 'What are you doing here?' I told him I just came to see the show. Everyone thought we were discussing deep philosophical questions."

Still going strong in his seventies, Monroe lets those around him wonder just how long he will stay on the earthly plane—a question which he adroitly parries, or to which he gives conflicting answers. Yet the listener feels sure Bob knows when his time will come.

Monroe—The Ultimate Adventurer. The Ultimate Player. A skilled and experienced showman. A Scorpio who's a man's man, and a woman's man as well. He protests he's unaware of the flirtation issuing from his liquid, appealing eyes. But he sternly rejects the label of "womanizer," and he is irretrievably, deeply in love with his wife, Nancy.

Monroe—the technologist and iconoclast who thoughtfully provides a tape to increase or decrease sexual potency, and of whom one participant in a training course jokingly said, "He gives good headphones." Master of a taped voice which has been known to bring female participants in the basic Gateway Voyage course repeatedly to orgasm. He's a leading Consciousness-Movement figure who smokes cigarettes, watches "Jeopardy" on TV, cheers the Washington Redskins ardently, and marvels over the orchestration of the Super Bowl halftime show.

Yet he's a philosopher for his world-scattered audience, far more than king only in his small part of rural Virginia.

Monroe is the mud-on-the-boots idealistic planner behind the New Land community on the 840-acre farm he bought. He has resigned in dismay from active participation in the utopia which, at times acerbically, struggles to govern itself but has dissolved into a sharply-curtailed version of his self-sufficiency dream.

Bob Monroe keeps his own schedule of three working shifts a day, broken by brief naps. Sometimes, in search of companionship, he suddenly pops up at someone's house to yarn, or make serious business decisions.

Flow-charts mirror Monroe's engineering attitude, yet paradoxically his non-physical friends don't worry about "The Time-Space Illusion" which dictates deadlines, or even demands paper and filing systems. Bob Monroe reflects a rapid-blinking skepticism about the value of man's cultural appurtenances, yet he is grounded in them. It befits someone who lives in the Now, yet has access to the Library—which other metaphysicists call the Akashic Records—or the sum of knowledge.

There are moments of rare, treasured Monroe. He listens intently, one foot tucked under his expansive frame, as a student tells of the miraculous disappearance of a brain tumor; then he clenches his hands in a familiar, baseball-seaming gesture and says, with a glow of satisfaction, "You've done it once. Do it again. It can be learned. Then pass it on."

He sits in shadow while his old friend Dr. Elisabeth Kubler-Ross speaks of her life's work. At the end of her talk, Bob Monroe saunters into the light to embrace the sparrowlike pioneer of thanatology in a hug of love which seems nearly to smother her.

He leans back with a glow of amusement and pure joy to sketch the outlines of several novels he plans after his main work is done. Of course, he'll write them nested in the overflowing stuffing of an office chair he has clung to, despite female attempts to provide him with a new one.

Bob Monroe is a man in balance with his surroundings—all of them. Although, or perhaps because, he opens doorways and paths to new understanding of self and cosmos, he can sit on the deck of a house in the Virginia outback, and literally commune with nature's creatures in his determinedly 1930-ish manner of speech.

Monroe has chosen, or been directed, to soar glidepaths which elude—or frighten—conformist Man. He offers a roadmap of such highways-of-the-soul to others, if they are willing to accept the challenge.

There are a number of parallels, and the analogy is easy to carry too far, between the persons and the experiences of Bob Monroe and Bill Wilson, the co-founder of Alcoholics Anonymous (AA). The physical lives of Monroe and Wilson bear some striking resemblances. Wilson and Dr. Bob Smith, the other AA prime-mover, were guided in much that they did. AA, of course, has spread to become the greatest spiritual movement of the twentieth century. Monroe has not had that effect among the broad populace, perhaps because his efforts lack the precise focus of AA and its offshoots. But the two men may have been working towards the same end, in response to a far calling they both acknowledge.

Monroe provides a transition from the drug-shadowed, giddy, spiritual voyeurism of the misfired 1960s. His appeal potentially is to all, not only to those who have suffered from one or another readily-identifiable addiction. Yet relatively few yet heed the call.

He offers the restless individual a comfortable, private accommodation with the era of the media-washed corporate state: A bold, personal escape from The Age of Fear. He recognizes the need of chained man, trying to define and free himself from the tangible, material leash of a society dancing wildly to establishment cymbals.

Monroe's approach is completely pragmatic. The Gateway Affirmation is directed at no power or force in particular: It's thrown "out there," for whomever or whatever to act on, to the benefit of the person invoking it.

Bob Monroe has pioneered his often-painful, solitary way so others may follow, but not in cloying, spotlighted groupiness. In the Monroe technique, you're soloing from your first hour of instruction.

A new audience of those who may benefit from Monroe's technology seems almost to designate itself in the late 1980s. As scattered individuals, seemingly at random, advance new, revolutionist ideas in the sciences and in the adjoining realm of metaphysics, there is increasing reason to believe that, at last, all Bob Monroe has developed as a result of his Out-Of-Body experiences has subtle meaning for mankind, if it is acted upon by the right persons, in time.

Does anyone in this world really know what the sum of Bob Monroe is? A man of many facets, difficult to fathom: Is he still far ahead of his time? Or is he a man whose time may now, at last, have come?

Book One

The Man

It is for experience, for growth of the individual being that the soul enters rebirth; joy and grief, pain and suffering, fortune and misfortune are parts of that experience, means of that growth; even the soul itself may of itself accept or choose poverty, misfortune and suffering as helpful to its growth, stimulants of a rapid development ....
"The principle is. . .the development of the nature through cosmic experience so that eventually it may grow out of ignorance ....

—Elmer and Alyce Green quoting Aurobindo Ghose,
"The Synthesis of Yoga"; in 'Beyond Biofeedback,' p 309

1920s

Robert Allen Monroe had a Mark Twain-Norman Rockwell sort of boyhood in Lexington, Kentucky. During Bob's early years his father, Robert Emmett Monroe, was a junior professor and entrepreneur at Transylvania College in Lexington. He exploited the knowledge of Europe he gained in World War I by organizing vacation tours to the Continent. Bob's mother, Georgia Helen Jordan Monroe, had been one of six University of Michigan medical doctor graduates in 1906, long before women were usual in medical ranks, but she did not practice for long after she married. She was a talented musician, too, who never found full outlet for her gifts.

"We were different. We didn't entertain the neighbors or socialize. Oh, my parents said, 'Hello,' and were friendly, all right," Bob recalls. But the Monroes kept mostly to themselves.

When Bob Monroe reminisces about his early years, one of his first statements is, "We probably had a family Bible lying around somewhere, but I don't remember it ever being used. We weren't religious. We were unconventional in that sense.

"Maybe it was because we were an academic, and therefore, for those days, an 'intellectual' family. My parents read a lot, my father, especially had a library of books, most of them in French.

"I guess you might call it an intellectual resistance to religion.

"Oh, I knew about religions. There was a family in the block in Lexington, and their boy wouldn't play with us. He was 'different.' Only later did I learn it was because he was Catholic." Bob's younger brother, Emmett, observes, "Church was simply not a factor in our upbringing, although our parents abided by the proper code. Smoking, drinking and divorce were bad."

Bob's was the molding of a prototypical American lad in the early 1900s, until a surging curiosity about all manner of things started to interrupt the pattern. It was a curiosity which went, perhaps, just that shade further than Mark Twain's.

Father expected young Bob to learn life on his own, with perhaps a paternal nudge here and there. He tossed his son in a pond at the age of one, and Bob started to flounder till pulled out by the Monroe females. It was Bob's first realization that he was mortal.

"My first meeting with a dead body was when I was a Boy Scout in Lexington. I had to do a tour of duty in a guard of honor at the casket of our dead scoutmaster. I chose the time between two and four in the morning because I thought, 'Now's my chance. I've never been awake at that time.'

"I touched the body. I was disappointed. Hard. . .cold . . .It felt like a human body, but not like flesh. It was stiff, but certainly not scary."

There was another escapade, clearly remembered. "When I was six or seven years old, we were visiting at my grandmother's house on North Cass Street in Wabash, Indiana. We kids were sitting in the front yard one evening, telling ghost stories. Someone suggested. . ." the listener can't help but know who the someone was ". . . maybe we ought to go to the graveyard to get better results.

"Well, we got just inside the gates of the cemetery, right among the tombstones. It did improve the stories, tremendously. But suddenly behind us, there was a tremendous scream, and a ghostly form emerged. We were paralyzed. We broke and ran, panting. The question was, then, whether to tell our parents or not.

"Months later, my father told me he heard us talking, had gotten a sheet and was waiting for us. . . It disillusioned me about ghosts."

* * * *

Today Bob recalls feeling he grew up "surrounded by sisters," where in fact, there were just two, both older than he. Finding the mobile home in which Dorothy Monroe Kahler now lives in an unfamiliar corner of Ohio at night is a tall order.

But the search is worth it. When Dorothy, the Monroe family historian, opens the door of her home, she embraces the visitor at once in the familiar Monroe smile—a grin which lights her face from ear to ear. She eases her walker along the narrow corridor, plumps into an easychair, and can hardly wait to start talking about that younger brother of hers, "Who doesn't pay any attention to the family stuff, of course. But I keep telling him he can't avoid it." She's talking of that stubborn Bob who still really hasn't grown up.

Dorothy is convinced that some of their ancestors have helped position the Monroe of today. She pulls out an unknown genealogist's quotation, copied in a scrawl reminiscent of Bob's left-handed scratchings:

We are your ancestors.
We may be forgotten,
But we are ever-present.
We are the men and women
Who long ago shaped the civilization of our time,
Not even aware that we were also shaping yours.
By a multitude of invisible but potent hands
We reach out and change you.

Dorothy repeats, "By a multitude of invisible but potent hands," softly. She is six years older than Bob, who was born on October 30, 1915.

Her view is different from that of brother Emmett, who is eight years Bob's junior. His is that of the hero-worshipping youngster who watched his senior cut a wide swathe in various meadows and halls. In his adult years, Emmett has carved out his own distinguished niche in the medical world.

Dorothy's is the firm, no-nonsense stance of the oldest child who, regrettably, wasn't able to keep up with all the shenanigans the lad got up to, both in adolescence and thereafter.

A binder full of history traces the family from the time in 1651 when the original immigrant—who spelled his name with a 'u'—was banished from England to the Massachusetts Bay Colony, a prisoner of Oliver Cromwell in England's Civil War. William Munroe was apprenticed and freed by 1657, whereupon he began to sire the first in a long line of revolutionaries. An early ancestor was a special dispatch-carrier for General Washington. Others were wanderers, frontiersmen, story-tellers, inventors, and even one healer. The Munroe's became Monroe's about Revolutionary times.

Mother's family were hardy pioneers as well. Among her forebears were four brothers who surveyed what is now Ohio for Washington in 1782. All four were killed by the Indians, two burned at the stake.

Dorothy starts the family tale, and as she swings into speech, her mental agility is reminiscent of a hummingbird in flight. Enthusiasm tumbles over into passion. Bob's own warmth lances out of her deep-set eyes. She is easily identifiable as a member of what a minister once called, "This fantastic family." Her own disappointment at not having made it to the top—she came close to being lead singer for Phil Spitalny's All Girl Orchestra before World War II—is masked in her talk of Bob's career.

There's another surprise, immediately. "Bob weighed twelve pounds at his birth in Wabash, which was Mother's home. She always went back there to have her babies. Bob looked like he was already two or three years old." Young Monroe was christened "Bob Allen" in accordance with the double-name custom of the South. Bob could already read and write at the age of four, so he skipped kindergarten, and went directly to the first grade, two months before his fifth birthday. He became Robert Allen not by choice, but because school authorities automatically penned the more formal monicker on official forms.

The family spent summers in Wabash with Mother's relatives. In the early days, they made the trip on a series of connecting "Interurbans," from Lexington. Once a friendly driver let young Bob hold the controls, which was a major thrill for the youngster.

Dorothy says, "See if Bob remembers the bunch of bananas that always hung in the basement of the house in Lexington. He would eat half a dozen a day." She recalls Bob, scooping peanut butter out of a bucket which materialized from a shelf in the Transylvania College pantry. Bob planned and executed the operation: His smeared face reflected his combination of pleasures, "In the days when peanut butter stuck to the roof of your mouth."

Another time, "Uncle Charlie sent a shipment of beans and popcorn from Michigan. The sack burst, and we kids had to spend hours at the kitchen table, sorting it all out, kernel by kernel." Uncle Charlie was the kids' folk hero. A crusty Michigan man who refused to be tamed by society, drifted and wandered as the whim took him, and lived to be ninety-seven. "And he only died then because he was thrown from a horse!" says Bob, his voice full of admiration.

"Most of the sparks around our house flew between Bob and Father," recalls Emmett.

Bob continues, "We had an unusual childhood. While at Transylvania, at first we lived in a dorm, and we ate in the dining room. We were spoiled brats.

"It was a very fine childhood. As long as I did the chores—carried out the ashes, things like that—then I was free to do whatever I wanted."

From a position six decades of physical life later, Bob says with a twinkle, "Except for occasionally on something he thought was important, my Father generally left me alone.

"It left me free to explore areas that were not of interest to him. I learned not to talk about the dangerous things I got up to; I knew he would make a misinformed judgment call.

"As long as I was home for dinner, he didn't ask where I'd been. I didn't give him any problems.

"I could have killed myself any number of times, but I didn't tell my parents."

Bob gives an instance, "There was the time when another guy and I—we were probably eight or ten—climbed up through the scaffolding around a new tower they were building on the high school, maybe ten stories up. The watchman suddenly looked up, when we kicked something loose, and it dropped. He just about had a fit, and hollered at us to come down."

On another occasion, Father did flare at Bob after he slithered down a very narrow tunnel into a limestone cave which opened up into a hall of stalactites and stalagmites. "It was very dangerous. But even though he was angry, my Father was calm. He merely said, 'Now why would you want to do something like that?' Firm, definite. You can't argue with that kind of authority. "Father also took a switch to the back of Dorothy's legs for misdemeanors, and Mother would remonstrate with him, 'You're stronger than you think.' But discipline was a household rule."

Emmett Monroe comments, "Bob wasn't slowed down by Father's lack of interest. He was always pushing, pushing ahead. He doesn't look back, even today.

"He was always exploring the boundaries, looking at the limits. 'Gotta find out what's out there,' that was his motto. He never accepted the rules just because someone said they're so. He had to see for himself. But he was always careful not to be destructive of anyone else."

Emmett Monroe adds, "Dorothy and Bob tested things out for me, so our parents treated me differently. I guess I didn't push them quite as much."

Bob: "Why did I pull some of those stunts? Maybe it was curiosity. I had the freedom to explore my curiosity." Simultaneously, he was sampling that sharp bite of fear that puts that edge into real life adventure.

"There were certain things I seem to have been born with. Music. The desire to fly. And an innate mechanical ability."

* * * *

There still exist some early evidences of Bob Monroe, the successful writer. On February 13, 1923, the seven-year-old pecked away at his father's typewriter, on the back of a carbon copy of one of Prof. Monroe's business letters.

Bob Allen Monroe

The Story of Abraham

part 1

Abraham was born in Kentucky. He lived in a log cabin. He was very poor. By the time he grue up to be a man they made him presedent. Every body was happey when he was presedent. But long after that he got .shot. every body was sad when he was dead. along time after that. his wife died. Every body was more sad. They berryed her about 10 miles from Winchester. And put a stone wall around it.

part 2

Stoory of George Washington

Once to boys were playing with a ax. George was one of their names. The other boy said. Ibet you cant cut as well as ican. Well lets see. so the boys tried. George cut down his fathers cherry thee. That night his father said Never mind. After a few years he grew to be a man. And they made him presedent.

Several days later, Bob wrote his Uncle Paul, with considerably improved typing:

My dog got lost but we found him agin. And one night we had to go and get a blanket for we were afriad the reater of the auto would frease. And we looked in the wood shed and guess what we saw. It looked like a mouse. It was sitting up. In the morning I went in thed and guess what i saw: Isaw a cat lying down. I was so surprised that I nearly fell back. But we found out that its legs were broken. I felt sorry for her. A few days later she died. I hope you have A fine dinner on George Washingtons Birthday.

the end.

Bob's love of music may have been intuitive, too. Dorothy has a suggestion: "You know, there's a theory that children learn when they're still in the womb. Well, when she was pregnant, my mother used to play cello in an orchestra. Her favorite piece was "Serenade".

An uncle let him strum a mandolin when he was about two; at about the same age, he helped John Phillip Sousa lead the latter's touring band at a concert—from his mother's lap.

Bob's initial exposure to religion came primarily because he enjoyed the music, and wanted to be part of it. He got his sisters to agree that they would all be baptized at the local church. Thereupon he became a member of the boys' choir. In the choir he discovered he could read music, at the age of four. He still doesn't know how he did it. "Did I memorize it? I dunno. I don't think Dad ever came to hear us perform or even mentioned it to me. I suspect Mother had something to do with the permission to get in the choir.

"My mother also played the old upright. I didn't get to take piano lessons. My sisters did. But not me. Wasn't manly.

Dorothy adds, "He could pick out things on the piano. Somewhere, too, he learned to play the marimba. He had it in him. When he was eight or ten, we even had a little neighborhood orchestra.

"When he was only two years old, Bob would always look for the Caruso records in their paper jackets, and he knew which ones they were—at two! And 'Glow Little Glow Worm.' He always found that one. And he loved 'Serenade.' "

Bob continues, "We had one of those old windup Victrolas in a stand-up cabinet. I used to climb up on a chair to place one of the old 78's, so delicately on the turntable, and so gently put the steel needle in the groove!

"Music was a prime divergence of mine from my Father. Dad's position was that music was for sissies. But music was inside me, pleading for recognition, from a young age.

By junior high school, Bob was "singing like Caruso," while Dorothy seemed to be on the verge of making her living using her deep contralto voice.

Bob still recalls the event when music came in his life to stay. "In 1920, we lived on the first floor of the house on North Broadway, and upstairs there was a fraternity house. There was a guy up there who played the sax. He passed me a couple of records. One of them was called, 'Ain't We Got Fun!'

"The first time I heard Louis Armstrong, on the old OK record label, something fell into place."

* * * *

Bob as a kid made scooters with wheels—forerunners of today's skateboards—and cars out of wooden boxes, of the type which later became entrants in soapbox derbies.

The Professor was often absent on his summer tours to Europe, or otherwise preoccupied, "Yet I was not all that wistful I didn't have a father who participated in activities with me." After the Monroes moved to their new quarters in Ashland Avenue, Bob's closest buddy was Harry Bullock, who lived down the block. The Bullocks were wealthy coalmine owners.

"Because I was Harry's friend, Mr. Bullock included me on trips to the Kentucky River to fish, boat, and swim. I learned to ride horses and shoot guns on the Bullock farm, outside of Lexington." There the Monroe passion for speed and solo adventure began to develop. Mr. Bullock bought the two lads a hydroplane—"You wouldn't remember. Sort of a chip with an outboard engine on the rear." Bob still remembers the joy of skid-speeding along a river.

Harry Bullock's father taught him baseball, too, and how to shoot a 30.06, and a "moosegun". "Boy, when I fired that thing from the prone position, it kicked me back about a foot!" Mr. Bullock provided the kind of basic training a young man needed in those days.

"I learned what a rough cob was. And what the Sears and Roebuck catalogue was really for. If you ever been in an outhouse, you'll never forget that unique smell. Those seats were rough at the edges!"

At Christmas, young Bob got out his model train and laid down tracks in the family living room. Father bought up Christmas cards after the holidays, saved them and then commissioned the children sell them for a penny apiece as the next holiday season approached.

Bob has a priceless recollection of his father, which ranks him with the classic, impractical academic: "I realized very early how different we were in certain areas. For example, I was a near-genius in mechanical functions at a very early age, while my father was totally unmechanical. At ten, I intuitively understood and repaired car engines.

"My father always drove his car in high gear. He simply raced the engine and let the clutch out slowly until the car was under way. He shifted only when he needed to head backward. His practice was a tremendous insult to my mechanical integrity. No matter how much I pleaded with him, he wouldn't do otherwise.

"Dad never trusted a car again after it had a flat or a breakdown, or simply ran out of gas. He would then contemplate getting another car again—always a used one.

"When I was thirteen, he recognized my abilities in the automotive field, and would ask me to help him decide which car to buy; then he took my advice implicitly. Years later, that's how he became known on the Ohio State campus as the professor who drove hot cars with big, souped-up engines. At least all that extra power let him drive in high gear much better. But he never knew the difference, or if he did, he didn't mention it."

Young Bob hung around the old Baltimore and Ohio railroad roundhouse at Lexington, and rode out on the switch engines, at the invitation of the engineers. There was something about the boy's reverence for the big machines which appealed to the oldtime railway workers.

Shortly, the appeal of locomotives palled; it was the beginning of his love affair with flight.

Dorothy and Bob made kites together, she remembers, "Not with tails. We knew how to bow the wood. How did we know to do it? I don't know."

Bob says, "I was a leading kite-flyer in Lexington. I built one that was taller than I was, maybe six to eight feet. It was so heavy, I had to get baling cord, couldn't use the standard string. So heavy, when it flew, it almost lifted me off the ground. The other kids, why they were just flying conventional kites."

Then he graduated to aircraft. "I was immensely attracted to planes. When they went overhead, I'd have to rush out and look. That was tremendous stimulation. I never bought a kit. I'd make models of planes I had actually seen."

The Gates Brothers Air Show, featuring ex-World War I pilots, came though Lexington, and to this day, Bob Monroe can remember one of the Lund brothers being killed when the wing of one plane sliced across the tail of another.

"My parents were horrified. I didn't feel the tragedy. I was curious about it."

Bob was a regular visitor to Lexington airfield, especially after a hangar was built. "I pestered one guy, who was eighteen years old, and he was even named Monroe... Monroe Bradley...to take me up. But he wouldn't.

"I had my first plane ride in Knoxville, when we were visiting my aunt. I heard a plane taking off nearby, and I sort of drifted away from the family. And I'm damned if some guy doesn't say, 'Hey, kid, want to take a ride?' It was an old O.X. Robin. The ride was too short.

"I couldn't have been more than ten at the time. I got back to the family, all excited, and then I had to cool it. I just explained, 'Well, I just been out running around.'" Father, who might have suspected the truth, was off conducting one of the his tours.

Young Monroe also coveted a wing from an old Curtiss P-6 fighter which had been totalled by an Army Air Corps pilot and found its way to an alley behind a Lexington garage. But try as he might; he could not get the garageman to part with the wing. "I don't know what I would have done with it, but I just wanted it, bad. It was a symbol to me."

Both Bullocks died in air tragedies: Harry Senior when his private plane crashed; Harry Bullock Jr. in a pilot training accident in Florida during World War II. Bob remembers his childhood friend with deep affection today; Harry was one of three men close to Bob who shared his passion for music and his mechanical interests, and all of whom were killed flying.

In 1928, Bob had a "serious run with scarlet fever, which I was told nearly killed me, and that only an untested new antitoxin saved me. I only remember being out of school for weeks, and going around with dark goggles, to protect my eyes. I'm sure I never thought of dying."

Immediately after he recuperated Bob went to Scout camp. Dorothy says, "He stepped on a nail! He was always in trouble."

Bob submits, "Later, I was stunned by a lightning bolt when it hit a nearby power pole."

Already young Bob knew he was a soloist, yet a leader. "I had followers, but I spent a lot of time on my own."

* * * *

During the First World War, Father Monroe was an American Army middleweight championship boxer and boxing instructor in France, for a while on temporary duty with the French Army. He was decorated by the King of the Belgians for post-World War I athletic work on behalf of the YMCA.

In one of father's rare involvements with his older son, the elder Monroe saw to it that Bob learned the manly art. Dorothy recalls, "Our father got a small pair of gloves for Bob, and put them on him, even on us girls. Bob at first wasn't the least bit inclined to box. I can still remember Father slapping Bob in the face with one gloved hand, saying, 'Come on. Do it,' and Bob refusing. Father was very disappointed."

"Dad did teach me to box," Bob confirms, "starting at about six or seven years old. I was a reluctant, then a willing student. He taught me well. It has been of good value at several points during this lifetime."

Another Lexingtonian says, "The genteel culture of Lexington was a tiny fraction of the whole: the educated middle class felt swamped because it didn't quite fit in the jigsaw of Kentucky in the early twentieth century.

"You had to know how to fight to establish yourself at the beginning of every school year. It was inevitable. The girls just didn't like you if you didn't."

Bob adds, "Really, Dad was no different in the handling of his older son from any of the fathers in our neighborhood. A lot of my contemporaries actually feared their fathers, with good reason. As a matter of fact, he was calmer and far more lenient than most of them. Dad never beat me either in anger or as punishment. I was never actually afraid of him.

"One illustration of a conversation: When I was around four or five, he asked me to come help in his garden, about 500 feet down a lane from the house. I went happily, and was assigned to weed the potato patch. I found two potato bugs, which were glued one on top of the other.

"I took them over to where Dad was hoeing, and asked what was the matter with the bugs.

"He glanced at them. 'There's nothing the matter with them,' and went back to his hoeing. I asked why the bugs were stuck together.

"Dad didn't look up. 'They're reproducing.'

' "What's that?'

' "Making new potato bugs.'

"He continued hoeing, and I took the bugs back to the potato patch and studied them for a while. But I couldn't figure out how they were doing it.

"That proved to be the total sexual education I got from my Father. Not much to go on."

When Bob joined the Boy Scouts, his scoutmaster was a man we may call Roper. It was not unknown for Mr. Roper to play favorites in the Scout troop, and even to ask a particular boy to stay after meetings, to "help clean up." When the Scouts went on an outing, Roper would invite one of his favorites into his sleeping bag, "to help him stay warm." Bob and the others were amused and speculated pruriently.

"I had a paper route then. Not the Lexington paper, that was reserved for college boys who had money to pay for their papers up front. I delivered the Louisville *Journal*, into a part of town where Black people lived.

"On the route was a large house staffed by white girls. One day, I was delivering the papers, and who should come out, but Mr. Roper. He didn't see me.

"Years later, I worked up a pretty good plot about those episodes."

* * * *

Dorothy remembers other wrinkles in Bob's childhood. "He was absolutely left-handed. Our parents put a cuff on his left wrist, so he couldn't get a spoon to his mouth with that hand. But he couldn't feed himself with his right, so I fed him. Nowadays, of course, no one would try something like that."

There were puzzling contradictions in Father's character, still recalled by Dorothy. "Once we were fishing at Lake Patterson in Michigan. Father and some other men were scaring us kids with stories. One, especially, about rattlesnakes and pulling the rattles off. He sent us on a snipe hunt at night.

"He could tell us tall tales, that was OK. But we were punished for lying. Things like that made me not like Dad very much.

"Why even when I was fifty, and living at home, he wouldn't let me go shopping in the mall at night. He'd say, 'And where do you think you're going!' "

Dr. Emmett Monroe says, "Father had a hard time. Dorothy was constantly pushing. She was the rebel. She got very emotional when she was crossed."

Dorothy remembers, "Bob Allen always had a wild imagination. He would tell us he had seen things in his dreams. Father would spank him for telling lies, but Bob would scream, "I did see it! Really, I did!" Dorothy pauses. "You know, I never thought about Bob's childhood dreams till I read *Journeys Out Of The Body.* That must have been what they were!"

Bob himself disagrees, although he doesn't exclude the possibility: "I have absolutely no recollection of those dreams. My first Out-of-Body Experience was in 1958, as far as I know."

Dorothy, Bob, and Emmett have a sister, Peggy, who was institutionalized for schizophrenia at about thirty. In childhood, Dorothy was the family star. She had the big voice. She had pretty curls in her hair, and dimples. Peggy tried to curl her hair, and one night cut off Dorothy's locks. Peggy kept poking her cheeks to try to make indentations. When Dorothy said she feared the worst, Mother Monroe said, shocked, "How can you say such a thing about your own sister!"

Their father paid through the years for private hospitalization for Peggy. When he died and the money ran out, Dr. Emmett assumed the responsibility, and provided medical services for the institution, in return for Peggy's care.

Mother was the skillful negotiator in the middle of the family tugs-of-will. "Mother took the brunt of it all. She always tried to smooth it over. She said, 'I'll make it up to you one day.' " Or, Emmett Monroe continues, "Mother was behind the scenes all the time, encouraging and nurturing us. She was a strong, loving personality, more demonstrative than Father."

There's a touch of sadness in Dr. Emmett's comment, too, that his mother was not able to practice medicine. "It was the day and the age, and she had us kids to care for. But mostly, it was Father's attitude. Working in medicine was just not what a wife and mother was supposed to do." Yet Mother was an incurable optimist. "Anything that was undesirable, she'd sweep it under the carpet," says Emmett. "She'd never let the dark side show."

If she was the picture of a post-Victorian mother, Father was the prototypical Victorian parent. The younger brother continues, "Father always gave us the feeling that he had high expectations of us. But he gave us little positive feedback. He'd say, 'You did well, but we expect better.' Almost never, 'That's great!' Any compliments, we had to earn."

Father rarely showed emotion. "The only time we could read his feelings was when he'd tap his fingers on his knee," remembers Emmett. "Bob's not very effusive with his emotions, either. Maybe he got used to repressing his outward expression of feelings when he was a child. You can't help but wonder how he was feeling inside."

Bob puts it all into perspective. "I had a very interesting relationship with my Father, which never really changed throughout our lives. I'm sure he expected me to be much like him, and more or less to follow in his footsteps.

"However, as early as I can remember, I did not have that desire. It wasn't that I didn't look up to him, because he certainly was the authority figure in my childhood — calm and sure-footed, the one who made important decisions in the family, without even questioning the needs of other members, or at least the children.

"I didn't question that authority openly, probably because I watched Dorothy butt heads with him. Even as a pretty and capable high school girl, she had firepower I lacked.

"I automatically respected and probably admired Dad. He was an intensely active person in his prime as a college teacher, later university professor, a European-tour conductor, and a super linguist.

"He was always deeply involved in what he was doing. I'm sure there was much I didn't know or understand about him.

"My father really didn't know me and didn't particularly make any attempt to find out about me. This neither frustrated nor disappointed me. Other than the boxing lessons, he never participated with me in any sports or recreational activities, except for a rare walk to the lake to fish.

"He was distant, reserved, busy elsewhere virtually all of the time. Any words of encouragement were also rare. He didn't take the trouble to attend my high school senior play, where I had the leading role, nor see my graduation, and I didn't expect him to. I had no sense of deprivation.

"Although the relationship was frustrating at times, I didn't think of this as bad. We had little or no private, confidential conversation; but I didn't miss it because I really didn't expect that kind of communication.

"With one or two exceptions, I'm sure Dad always did what he thought was best for me. Not as it might affect him and his welfare, but for my own growth. He thought he was doing right, and I expected no different.

"I would have been astonished if Dad had ever said he loved me. It wasn't until I was forty and back on a visit in Ohio that he gave me a hug in farewell when I left.

"With my mother, it was different. It was quite obvious that they deeply loved one another, although all we children saw was a tender kiss of hello or goodbye. I know I felt satisfied this was the way it should be.

"I also know that his vigor, appearance, and worldly sophistication—in the true sense of the word—made him particularly attractive to intellectually-mature women. He may have succumbed to such enticements, but I doubt it."

The question of Bob's relationship with his parents is one which arose much later, when psychiatrists probed Monroe to check his mental balance.

Father Monroe may have been a stunted parent, but he was a fine teacher. Some of his students went on to chair university Romance language departments. One wrote a long-enduring textbook.

For Bob Monroe today, Dad remains a paradox: "He was a college professor, all right. But he was a highly successful businessman. He went into a real estate agent's office in Lexington and plunked down $18,000 cash as a deposit on our new house in Ashland Avenue.

"He made an awful lot of money running those European trips of his. In a good year, they netted him $50,000 or $60,000, which was a lot in the late 1920s."

Today, Dr. Emmett Monroe wonders audibly whether what happened next might not have been an indication that Father Monroe was prescient. "Really, he left the academic world to concentrate on his tour business. He was the Lexington agent for Temple Tours out of Boston. Summers, he'd be in Europe, and we'd be in Wabash. Winters, he was away a lot, recruiting customers on campuses for the next season."

Suddenly, in the Spring of 1929, Father saw trouble looming. "I never heard him say, 'There's a crash coming.' But he had that shot at a full professorship at Ohio State, and he took the security it offered, at $5,000 a year." There were other occasions, which Emmett cannot now recall, Father also showed "he had some sort of feeling" about what was going to happen.

* * * *

When the family moved from the small-town bliss of warm Kentucky to the urban chill of Columbus, Bob Monroe started his progress from benchmark, smalltown America to the big league.

Father could not sit still, and he passed that trait onto Bob. "He felt the economic pressure of the Depression. He had us kids to feed. He had to do something to get more money in." So he arranged a property trade through a bank which gave the Monroes a 370-acre farm at Mount Air, now a Columbus suburb. It had all that the Bullocks' farm in Kentucky had—a lake, barns, and woods.

Bob recalls an anecdote of the time: "One time, I won with Dad, only I didn't have the heart to mention it.

"Out at the farm one year, he put in an unusually large garden. Emmett and I would have had to work extra hours on it, so I pushed hard for a used garden tractor I knew could be bought for $25. Dad could see the need, so he went down the road one Saturday. But he came back with a grey mare—an old one to boot.

"One morning a week later, we went out to hitch up the mare, and there she was, dead in her stall.

"Dad looked at her for a long time, told us to drag the carcass over to the chicken yard with the big tractor, then walked away. Mother later told me he had paid $50 for the horse. We never did get the garden tractor."

The farm turned out to be "an economic disaster," perhaps in part because the elder Monroe insisted on embarking on projects wholesale: When he raised turkeys, he didn't get just a few, to get experience before building the flock up; he started big. Same with chickens and sheep. He always grew vegetables for the family and to give to the neighbors. "You could never take the farmer out of our father," comments Dorothy.

In time, he sold the farm, moved to Oakland Park Avenue in Columbus, and acquired four or five rental properties which Emmett cared for. "I'd work with him on the houses, being his peon, as Bob used to say. But it was fun. I learned a lot from him, working together. He was handy."

Father's attitude was, "Work is what you're supposed to do." Mother would say, quietly, "Do your work, then you're free." And Emmett would zoom off on his bicycle to play golf—a passion which remains to this day.

Dorothy's voice is suddenly firm. "My father was a tyrant! He always knew better than we did what we should do. Even when we were grown up!" Professor Monroe allowed his children no choice in their high school and college courses.

Dorothy secretly changed her college courses back to what she wanted to study — engineering and math—too late for Father to do anything about them. "He always blamed my math ability on Mother."

A unique perspective on the Monroe parents and their sons is proffered by Alice, Emmett's wife, who has known the family since the late 1940s.

"Bob was very close to his mother, but not so close to his father. In fact, he had to develop his own strength to get around his father. He had his mother's covert blessing to do so. I never saw any of them disagreeing openly. They were a strong unit.

"Bob probably always felt stifled. My impression was that he had to get out of Columbus. He was always anxious to do things on his own. Not—certainly not—what his father specified.

"In fact, I think Father Monroe was probably secretly very proud of what Bob did accomplish.

"They were remarkably rich and wonderful people. Mother was very Victorian, for all the freedom of spirit she had. A Southern lady. Nothing formally religious, but she had a lot of true spirit.

"Father was a Michigan farm boy. He was about the only one of his generation in the family to get away. And what did he do? He learned French! At first I thought he was a kind of intellectual, but he wasn't.

"He did develop new ways of learning foreign languages which were used by the armed forces during World War II.

"He was a farmer. When our first child was coming along, he rented another acre of riverbottom land in Columbus to farm, just to help feed us. He developed a new cross between a yellow and red tomato, and took it to the agricultural department at the university. He did a lot with the faculty—president of the Faculty Club, chairman of the Athletic Board.

"Yes, he was authoritarian. Bob had his adventures. Emmett found his escape in golf. Dorothy had none."

Bob, says Alice, "got his imagination and his sense of adventure into the Unknown from Mother. From Father, he derived his practical and productive sides."

1930s

Columbus, Ohio, may have been chilly in comparison to Lexington's warmth, but it had its compensations. By now adolescent, Bob stayed up late to listen to the early broadcasts of Duke Ellington's band coming live across the radio networks' scratchy ether. The big, memorable moments were when Ellington came for one-night stands at the Valleydale dance pavilion.

Still too young to get in legally, Monroe sneaked past the ticket-takers. "I'd stand down front, just absorbing the music. Why, the band was so big—forty pieces! He had four bass violas on each side of it! And sousaphones in the middle!"

And—girls. Bob is a Scorpio, a fact which has been noted by many women. Perhaps his sign showed even in those pre-horoscopic times: "In junior high school, I had the option to take a music class. I wanted the music badly, but I was the only boy in a bunch of nearly thirty girls! Being alone with that many girls wasn't a bad thing, either.

"Very early in life, I knew what little girls were. I carried their books, but, well, I had to defend myself. The other boys called me a sissy. The boxing Dad had taught me came in real handy."

His father was reserved and interfered in Bob's life rarely. "Well. . .during my high school period, at about eight one Saturday morning, Dad came in and yanked me out of bed, red-faced and angry.

"He stared at me intently. 'What happened last night?'

"I told him. Three of us had dates, and we drove out to the summer cottage of one girl's family. We built a fire in the fireplace and played records.

"Dad was urgent. 'Did you do anything to that girl?'

"I told him, No, I didn't, and I hadn't. What I didn't tell him was that my date had indeed wanted to have sex, but I backed away.

"She became angry at me for my refusal. Why I declined, I don't remember; probably because of fear I'd get her pregnant.

"Dad didn't question me further, but marched purposefully back downstairs and picked up the phone. I heard him coldly tell the girl's father that his son said he did not have intercourse with the man's daughter, that his son did not lie, and that if he wanted to make more of it, he'd see the man in court.

"Later, I learned my date had told her father we had lured the girls out to the cottage for an orgy, which was not the case. We didn't know what orgies were.

"I was very proud of Dad at that moment. He never mentioned it to me again, and I didn't mind too much the two weekends of staying-home imposed on me simply for causing trouble.

"It was one of the two times in our lives that I saw him actually angry."

In Columbus' North High School, Bob had his first taste of theatre; it became an avocation, then a passion which, in turn, led to his first fortune in radio. Bob was Aladdin in a school play. The genie appeared and rubbed his lamp. Smoke billowed, but a back-projected film of Aladdin's castle failed to materialize. Undaunted, Aladdin Monroe did appear, and the show went on.

Dorothy had argued to be allowed to stay on at the University of Kentucky when the family moved, so she could play in an all-girl band. After graduation, she joined the family in Columbus, and got a good job in a bank.

She enlisted Bob's help in the purchase of a Model A Ford. "It was a brown convertible. Quite something for the day." Bob borrowed the car on Friday nights for dates. Sometimes they went double. His sister kept a cautionary eye on the rearview mirror, surveilling Bob and his girl-of-the-moment in the rumble-seat. "Can you imagine!" asks Bob.

Dorothy wed a teacher-protege of her father's. The Ford was hidden in a garage, ready for the honeymoon getaway. Bob, of course, loaded it with tin cans. "Dorothy was furious. But she would have been mad if I hadn't, too."

Monroe was usually two years younger than his classmates, and, again, his knowledge of boxing was useful. He made desperate efforts in school and later, in college, to overcome his youth. "There were a thousand kids at North High in Columbus. I ran the half mile and the mile—behind a team member who went on to get an Olympic Gold. I wanted to play football, but the coach wouldn't have me: I was six foot, and weighed 137. He pointed at a six-foot-six tackle weighing over 200, and said, 'If that guy falls on you, you're dead.'"

Monroe checked his manhood in another way. As early as his high school years, Bob knew about booze, which he later came to detest, and speakeasies. It was the era of Prohibition. Conveniently close to North High was an unassuming house.

"You could buy a glass of homemade wine in the kitchen there." Bob even today grins in boyishly-embarrassed recall.

"Another thing. I was in high school with the daughter of a man we'll call Tagliatelli, though I didn't know her very well.

"Well, the nearest real honest-to-goodness speak was in the basement of a house a couple of blocks from the Ohio State campus. Nicely decorated, comfortable. Just a lounge, really. No music. Just drink.

"One night, I was there, and who should come down the stairs but this girl. I gaped, and asked what she was doing there. She laughed and said the place belonged to her father.

"When I got to Ohio State, the campus bigshots sort of disdained me: The son of a professor!

"But I knew the right numbers to get into Tagliatelli's, and I took them there. It changed their attitude towards me.

"Tagliatelli had a warehouse in the industrial section of Columbus. Downstairs, you could drive your car in and park. No vehicles on the street, see? He was probably paying the cops off, too.

"Upstairs, he had a really lush joint." The set-up sounded rather like *The Sting*, or the speakeasies of New York.

"Tagliatelli saw me hanging around one night with his daughter's group, and asked, 'You need money, kid?'

"Well, of course I did. But I immediately asked him, 'Not killing anyone, hunh?' "

Tagliatelli assured the college boy there was no contract involved in the assignment. Bob soon found himself behind the wheel of a "huge sedan, with extra springs."

He was dispatched to Toledo to pick up a load of contraband booze. "It was stuff coming in from Canada. I only made one run, and Tagliatelli gave me fifty bucks for the job. Big money in those days.

"I didn't run into any cops, but I was ready if I did. That car could have outrun anything they had on the road. It was quite a feeling, driving that big car." There's a tinge of regret in Monroe's recollection that the run was trouble-free.

Bob and a pal bought a wrecked racing car; they rebuilt it and ran it on local dirt tracks, but never won anything.

"When he was fifteen," Dorothy remembers, "he took a parachute jump, at an airshow in Columbus, trailing flour as he fell. He missed the mark."

Flying was a growing passion. Bob saved enough money to pay for lessons. Dorothy remembers, "One time, he flew down to Lexington from Columbus in a plane belonging to his training school, completely illegally. Another time, he went to Dayton to pick up a plane and fly it to Buffalo at night. At night! Can you imagine it?" Her mock-anguish is tinged with admiration.

Bob Monroe was in a cockpit, fully qualified as a pilot, by the age of seventeen. In time, Bob got his limited commercial pilot's license. Soon, he "talked a racing pilot into letting me fly his special plane around the competition circuit at an airshow—just once. I'm still amazed he let me do it."

In 1934, "a teenager without direction," Monroe applied at Wright-Patterson Field in Dayton to join the Army Air Corps, as it then was. "It was still the Depression. They were taking maybe one in ten thousand people." He was rejected because he had 20/30 vision in one eye, not the required 20/20.

Later, he tried to enlist on the Loyalist side in the Spanish Civil War, but was refused—probably because of his age. He applied to join Gen. Claire Chennault's Flying Tigers, the American volunteer unit that flew for Chiang Kai Shek against the Japanese, prior to America's entry into World War II. "I even had an appointment at the Chinese Embassy. But they turned me down. I don't know why.

"Don't get me wrong. I wasn't volunteering for idealistic reasons. I just wanted to fly the hottest planes available at the time." And if that meant being shot at, well, that was the price.

He continued to fly, until finances forced him to take a break. In the early days, "I never got into any life-or-death situations, no high-risk stuff, you understand.

"Oh, sure, I lost engines, but I always had a landing site in mind. And we did aerobatics. Once, I was in an inverted spin, just testing the plane's capabilities. I had a chute, though. I never got into a 'no option' situation.

"Of course I was afraid. Anyone who does those kinds of things and doesn't know fear is a liar."

Dorothy remembers a near-tragedy of a different sort from the spring of 1934. "Bob was at a girl's house nearby, french-frying potatoes, and the oil caught fire."

Bob thought fast. "He wrapped his arm in a wet towel, grabbed the pan with a pair of pliers, and tossed it out the door. Only, the burning grease flew back into his face.

"I went to see him in the hospital. His face was swathed in bandages."

Bob recalls. "I had third degree burns. I was a walking mummy. My eyes and mouth were free, but the rest was bandaged. I couldn't even laugh."

Dorothy adds, "When they took the bandages off, his face was painted in a red, mask-like, tannin substance. But he scared the little kids at Halloween that year."

The doctors repaired the scars. Since then, Bob Monroe has been unable to grow a full beard. Whether the flaming oil damaged his eyes is moot; Monroe's eyes are ultra-sensitive to bright light.

At least one early romance ended almost literally in disaster. Dorothy remembers, "Father took each of us on one European trip, including Bob. He took a girl out sailing on a boat in the Bay of Naples, and almost got run down by a freighter. They jumped overboard and shoved the boat out of the ship's path at the last minute. He had never sailed before."

Monroe's first brush with marriage came when he was seventeen. He got involved with a girl we'll call Joanne. One thing led to another, and they ended up making furtive love. If you slept with a girl, went the reasoning of the time, you married her. Bob hastened downtown to put ten dollars on an engagement ring, and the young couple drove across the Ohio River into Kentucky one Friday night.

They arrived at a small town about eleven, to discover the Justice of the Peace who could oblige them was "out fishing." Bob glosses over his feelings of thrill and fright as the young couple waited, and waited. About four in the morning, they gave up their vigil, and drove back to Columbus.

Bob and Joanne agreed that marriage between them did not seem to be in the cards. "I don't know what protective coloration prevented it. If I had married her, I would have had to give up college, go out and get a job to support a wife.

"And I was on the hook for that ring. The jewelers started to dun me for it. I had to go to Joanne, and ask for it back. She gave it to me, very gracefully. I have admired her forever for that, and I hope she knows it.

"I took the ring back to the jewelers. They smiled and were very nice about it. They kept the ten bucks. It probably happened all the time."

Throughout the passages with girls and planes, and anything else that came along, music remained part of Bob's life. At high school, he says, "I stubbornly went out to join the school orchestra. The leader asked me what I could play. I bluffed. 'I'm a percussionist.'

"He didn't know I couldn't really read music. But it was simple. I just memorized it. The director got angry when he found out."

As an Ohio State freshman, aged sixteen, Bob wangled himself a seat in a pickup band playing fraternity hops. The gigs paid some useful money. "I was still a drummer, a poor one, I might add. But I was a good scat singer. Remember what scat singing was? I guess the others in the band forgave me my poor drumming."

Bob's remembers the academic side, too. "I started OSU in pre-med, but I got to thinking the medical profession was too confining. You spend your whole life in one place, dealing with the same people."

Monroe switched to mechanical engineering, "where I felt more at home." Also, it was the closest thing available at State in those days to aeronautical engineering.

"Then, I cherry-picked myself out of engineering, too. I can't tell you, now, how I did it.

"While I was still in the hospital, recovering from those burns, it was Father who had the unhappy duty of informing me I had flunked out of college under the sophomore 2.5 rule—you had to have a C+ or better to stay on. I remember still the hesitant compassion in his voice when he told me—even though he was a scholar."

Bob Monroe continues, "There were no jobs in Columbus. It was still the

Depression. So in 1935, I went on the road." At one point, he sold tombstones ("job bad, pay good"); then he sold Real Silk hosiery ("job good, pay bad").

"I started hitch-hiking. Now there's one rule to that game: If you're clean, you'll get rides. If you're dirty, forget it. So as I got dirtier, I drifted to the rails.

"I rode in boxcars and gondola cars. I never actually rode the rods, down below the car bodies. I was never in that much of a hurry." Bob points to a small bluish mark on his forehead."I've kept that there as a reminder. It's a scar from a fight, when someone threw a piece of coal at me. I bled like a pig."

He made a circuit, and every once in a while would check back into Columbus. "Cincinnati, Lexington—although I didn't stop to see any old friends—Louisville, St. Louis, down to Memphis, Knoxville.

"I stopped there to see my aunt. She helped me clean up and fed me, and I was offered a place as cub reporter on the Knoxville *Sentinel*. But my aunt didn't want me in the same town, so she paid my fare home.

"Who knows...If I'd have taken that....?"

When he first entered Ohio State, Bob was in the class of 1936. Following the hobo days on the road, "After much pleading and persuasion at the university, I was conditionally reinstated in the class of 1937. I'm sure my Father had something to do with it, although he never mentioned it.

"Then came the question of tuition, which amounted to about $200 a year."

The entrepreneurial professor and the knockabout son talked it over, man-to-man. Father suggested a deal. "Dad offered to pay my tuition, provided I worked all summer on the farm, six days a week, sunup to sundown. I politely and calmly declined, stating I felt I could do better working in Columbus. He calmly and politely replied I was welcome to do so if I thought I could. I packed a suitcase, hitched a ride into the city, and began life totally on my own. I was eighteen."

He got a job at the Olen Bishop Company grinding and polishing blades for lumbermill rotary saws. It was a complex, delicate series of operations, and Bob had, of course, no industrial experience. The job paid $31.50 a week to start, pretty good money for those days.

He was put on trial for one week, at half-pay. "Willie, the guy who trained me was dirty, unshaven. He spat tobacco juice and he swore at me all the time. I didn't worry. I could handle myself by then, but how that man cussed me!

"By the Wednesday, we had a sort of camaraderie. I was 'The College Kid.' His language toned down. By Friday, he said, 'If that bastard doesn't give you the job....'" Monroe got the spot.

"What they wanted was a substitute, because Willie took off and got drunk three or four days at a time.

"I got to be the hotshot. I could grind thirty blades without ruining one!

"Then the foreman asked me if I'd like to work on the Blanchard, which was a horizontal grinder that required more precision and high tolerances. It always had to be adjusted, just right. I learned it in a day.

"When I went back to college, I had a neat deal. They gave me a quota. I'd come in at five in the afternoon, and I'd do my shot. The rest of the time, I could study.

"Sometimes, I'd do 125 percent of my quota, get finished at midnight, grab a hamburger at the White Castle, and be home in bed by one o'clock in the morning."

Bob and Father occasionally crossed paths on the OSU campus. "We'd stop to say hello, but we had no long conversations about how I was getting along; he didn't ask, and I didn't report. Nor did I particularly ask what he was doing.

"I'm sure he was aware of the brown bag of food my mother secretly stashed every day in the car trunk. Actually, in retrospect, I'm sure my mother handed him the bag every day as he left the house, and he himself put it in the trunk."

There were already signs of the drive to achieve which has persisted through Bob's life. "I signed up for the Advanced ROTC outfit, which paid part of my tuition, and was a member of the close-order drill team, the Pershing Rifles.

"I went into journalism, which put me into the Commercial College of the University. I worked on *The Lantern*, the college daily, and I enjoyed it." He also joined WOSU, the university radio station.

Eventually, Bob was nominated for the salaried editorship of the *Sun Dial*, Ohio State's literary and humor magazine. "It paid good money, enough to put me through the rest of college, and it automatically led to a good career in writing or journalism after graduation.

"I was the top candidate for the job, but to my consternation, I didn't get it. Over a year later, I learned my Father had used his influence to prevent me from getting the post. The reasons he used were 'conflict of interest', as he had put it to the nominating committee; more likely, it was that the magazine was too *avant-garde* for him to want his or his son's name associated with it.

"By the time I found out, I was headed in another direction, and did no more than get his confirmation that he had been involved in the school's decision. He simply said, 'You wouldn't have liked a job like that.' I offered no comment nor recriminations, because there was no point in them. Maybe in one or two ways, I was more mature than I realized."

Monroe fell into the thrall of entertaining an audience. He joined the OSU dramatic and musical society, Strollers, and stage-managed the annual Spanish Play tour to other Ohio colleges.

Another Ohio State dramatic group, The Scarlet Mask Society, was nearly extinct. It had schooled people like Elliot Nugent and James Thurber. "I started to revive it in my junior year, and we eventually put on a couple of musicals," to the embarrassment of Professor Monroe.

One of the major influences on Monroe was Professor Herman Miller, who taught drama. Years later, Monroe told Earl Wilson, the New York gossip columnist, that he got his sense of stagecraft from Miller:

"He was a good friend of mine, just as he was a good friend to Nugent and Thurber. Miller was constantly struggling to get some decent plays done at school."

Here Bob's spell of raw life on road and rails first paid off, as it was to again, in far more substantial terms. He entered a playwright's contest put on by Strollers. "I waited till the last day, then wrote it overnight. It took second prize."

The one-acter was to be staged with the other two prize-winners. The Wilson column continued, "But Monroe was dissatisfied with it and before rehearsals started, he got back his copy and rewrote it. Somehow, Strollers never noticed the switch.

"'When it was produced,' he laughed, '*The Lantern* carried an editorial asking indignantly, 'How could Strollers have chosen any other play for first prize?' The judges stuttered a little and finally said they were sorry they hadn't noticed before what a fine play it was.'"

But it was far more than a light-hearted triumph. Bob stood in the wings, and gradually the rapt attention of the audience transmitted itself to him.

It was a peak moment that still lives with Bob. He was nearly-mesmerized by his accomplishment, "I knew by their silence they were being affected by the play. Eight hundred people! It was the first experience I had of communicating with an audience ....That something like this could happen, such rapport with an audience! It deeply affected my life."

Monroe got a standing ovation, and cries of "Author, Author!" to ring in his ears.

"It was mystical, really." The story was based on a true incident the eighteen year-old Bob had in a St. Louis flophouse, "And in those days, flophouses weren't what they are today, be-lieve me." The old man in the bunk next to Bob's died during the night.

"In the play, I had the young kid hear the old guy coughing, and go over to his bed to ask him to shut up.

"I made the old man a mystical figure. In essence, the old man passed the torch to the wandering, starving kid. The boy was very angry, very cynical, on the verge of violence. Resentful, anti-social.

"But when the kid took the torch, it changed him, totally.

"I dunno what it was...my imagination...or whatever." But Monroe had experienced the power of words over an audience.

Bob made another curriculum change. "I finally majored in English. It was easy. I took three theatre courses, stuff I already knew. And a couple of English lecture courses; all I had to do was attend and listen, and I was in." He also taught freshman English to engineering students, one of the few undergraduates to hold such an appointment. The sum of campus obligations, however, ended Monroe's industrial moonlighting career.

The colorful patchwork of pre-med, engineering, commerce and arts eventually gave Bob enough credits to fulfill the degree requirements. What with one thing and another, "I finally graduated in the Arts College with a 4.0 average during my last quarter."

Around this time, Monroe sold a short adventure story to one of the nationally-circulated pulp magazines, for fifteen dollars. But, "I was never able to repeat the process, despite many attempts.

Dorothy Monroe Kahler sorts through some papers on her table, and triumphantly pulls out the Ohio State graduation photograph of Bob: He poses like a bandleader, or a nascent movie star, a young man with dimples, an impish grin tossed back over a shoulder, hair slicked back, impeccable pin-stripe suit and carefully-knotted tie—the image of a young man in a hurry to go somewhere.

* * * *

It was the spring of 1937. Bob Monroe met a girl named Jeanette, the daughter of a "beanpole smalltown lawyer who knew he was absolutely right in everything he said." She was a graduate student who had local theatre experience. Together, they hatched an idea to open a summer stock company which would offer students acting and technical experience. "Thinking carefully was not the trait of a college senior," says Bob dryly.

"We wanted to borrow $8,500 seed money from Jeanette's father." But only after another matter had been settled. Those were the days of the Mann Act, which prohibited the transportation of females across interstate lines for immoral purposes, and her father was moral.

Jeanette reported to Bob, "Father won't allow me to go across the state line with you unless we're married."

Monroe recalls, "I had a close relationship with her, so I agreed. A big church wedding came off one Sunday. Graduation was the following weekend. I wasn't there. Someone picked up my certificate for me...I have no idea where it ever got to."

By commencement, Jeanette and Bob Monroe were at an amusement park near Pittsburgh. The owner had two empty theatres he didn't know what to do with, and was more than happy to let the attractive, energetic young couple rent them. The Monroes engaged two professionals from New York, and signed up some students.

"One Friday night, we had our grand opening. It was a popular Broadway piece, *Good-Bye Again.* We played to all of three people, in a house which seated four hundred. We never had more than ten. It closed by Wednesday."

The second show was a play Bob wrote. He was determined to get an audience, so he and his troupe gave free tickets to the crowd at a medicine man's truck nearby. "We got our audience, but we had to paper the house to do it."

Two weeks later, the theatre project was dead. The couple made frantic calls back to Columbus, and Jeanette's brother jumped in his car. "We slipped away from the amusement park in the dead of night, our tails between our legs.

"My last significant incident with my father took place in Columbus following that disastrous venture. Two of the men I had contracted to teach at the theatre threatened action against me for 'fraudulently' breaking their agreements.

"Dad attended the meeting at the lawyer's office. I don't remember how he got into it—possibly because those guys somehow thought they could attach his assets, since I didn't have any.

"When someone used the word 'criminal,' Dad rose to his feet in cold fury.

"'Stop right there,' he thundered. 'My son may be a poor businessman and may make some poor decisions, but he is not a criminal.

" 'I know that, and if you attempt to prove otherwise, I will fight you to the last dollar I can find. I trust I have made myself very clear.

" 'Come on, son, let's get out of here.'

"We left, and the matter never came up again, either from Dad or in any legal action. No 'I told you so's'—not one. If I had to assume my father's role now, I would say the same thing about the young me, but with the difference, I'd laugh, heartily."

And with a grin, Bob recalls it took him more than seven years to pay back Jeanette's father. "It was one of the first things I did when I finally hit it big in New York."

A period of frustration and footloose migration followed. The couple stayed with the elder Monroes because Bob couldn't face the prospect of life with father-in-law. He started checking the want ads in the *New York Times,* and chased down any local leads he could find.

In time, he got a slot as a continuity writer at station WHK in Cleveland and had his first taste of radio directing. Jeanette joined him there after two months. Radio seemed to offer a bright future since, in the late 1930s, it was the big new medium, much as TV was the boom of the 1950s.

After about six months, the station's continuity chief, Eleanor Hanson, told him he would have to go. "Why?" asked Bob. Eleanor would give him no reason. Just...the general manager wanted him out. Years later, Monroe encountered Eleanor at a lecture he was giving, and asked her again, "Why?"

She laughed. "The General Manager saw you in your office, typing with your feet on the desk. He thought it was undignified."

Back to Columbus, to the senior Monroes'. "Well, on reflection, maybe they weren't all that happy to have us. But they didn't kick us out." Monroe next landed a job at station WLW in Cincinnati for $75 a week—up from the $31.50 he had gotten at Cleveland. "It was a great jump for me. It totally suited me." Bob wrote continuity and commercials.

Soon Bob was involved in direction and production on various shows at the big, clear-channel station: "The Boone County Jamboree," which had more than a hundred country artists of all types on its roster, and went on tour; "Rainbow Ridge," which was purely "mountain drama"; "Moon River"—a latenight pot-pourri of poetry and music which Monroe describes today as "a pipe-organ deal." Some of the shows Monroe directed were fed to the Mutual Broadcasting System, and to NBC's Blue Network.

During his stay at WLW, Bob also refined his musical abilities. "I'd help score the shows, sitting next to a guy playing an old Hammond electric organ. I'd hum or sing the part I wanted. Make noises like a sax or a violin, or whatever, and the guy at the organ would get it, then write it down. It's the damndest method there is, but it works, and a lot of arrangers do it that way."

The exposure whetted Bob's appetite. "I'd sneak into the studios on weekends and work that old Hammond. It opened up a lot of music in me."

Although Bob was reluctant to have Jeanette in Cincinnati, she insisted on joining him. By now, "I realized I had made somewhat of a mistake."

The job lasted short of a year. Monroe agreed to join the WLW local of the radio artists' union. As soon as the union contract was signed, and while Bob was rehearsing a show, he was called out and fired. Management told him he was being canned not for joining the union, but because he was junior on the staff, and the AFRA (as it then was) agreement called for higher salaries; the money had to be found somewhere. But under the contract, no one was supposed to lose his job. Monroe quickly appealed to the union office to intercede. An AFRA official refused: "We just got the contract; we aren't going to take them on for one guy." Monroe argued. No dice. Then he walked out. "The unions lost me forever."

There were bright sides to the Cincinnati spell, however. Bob met Mike Hinn, a star announcer at WLW, and discoverd both Mike and his brother Bill shared his passion for flying. Mike was "very wealthy. He made good money as an announcer with top ratings."

The Hinns bought a 1930-vintage plane called 'Golden Eagle' and dubbed it 'The Blue Goose.' "We stooged around in it a lot. It was a neat-looking, underpowered, two-cockpit monoplane, but it was fun!" Around the same time, Monroe graduated from building racing cars in the backyard to driving them. He worked the dirt tracks and, even more happily, drove the midget racers of the time. He didn't have the money to maintain his own car, so he found an owner who let Bob drive, just for the experience and thrill of it.

Jobless again, the young Monroe's returned to Columbus. Father wanted him to try banking, but Bob was less than thrilled. Eventually, he signed on as an apprentice toolmaker, and lasted one day. Monroe was unmoved by the job's security. "I can't explain why. I just felt a sense of entrapment.

"I had to go either to New York or Hollywood. That's where the entertainment business was."

With thirty-five dollars from his last unemployment check, he boarded a bus to Manhattan. "It was a long, bumpy, up-and-down-hill ride in those days."

Arriving, disheveled and tired in the metropolis, he booked into a Times Square fleabag. It was 1938. Bob Monroe was in that never-ending stream of young people seeking to shake the dust of provincial America off their shoes, to walk the avenues in glistening brogans. "I don't know how I survived those first few weeks."

Monroe had one contact, Sometime earlier, he had answered a *New York Times* ad. A doctor needed help with scripts for his radio show. The medic replied to Bob in Columbus civilly, saying, 'Look me up if you ever get to New York.' Now, Bob took the doctor at his word.

Dr. Matthew Goudiss took pity on the Ohioan and gave him a chance as a twice-weekly freelance contributor. He also gave Bob an advance on the material, which eased the hunger pangs. "I was good at it. Got fifty dollars a spot, which was almost survivable in New York." On the strength of the job, he rented a basement apartment, inevitably in Greenwich Village. Bob soon found out why it was vacant and the rent cheap: The flat was directly over a subway line; when the trains roared through the tunnel below, the apartment shook wildly. "I felt like a real king," but soon the Goudiss deal ended. Bob started beating on doors. "WLW had qualified me as a radio writer, director and producer. I got a lot of interviews. But no work.

"I sold an occasional magazine or newspaper article. A letter from my Mother with a twenty-dollar bill enclosed came just often enough."

Monroe moved to a brownstone at 32 West 53rd Street. First, to a skylight room, long and narrow, no window, fifth-floor rear; four dollars a week. "A long walk up in a house that had twelve-foot ceilings, and the phone on the ground floor." There were stints of survival dish-washing to pay the rent. "I was probably living on about thirty dollars a week, and was hard-put to find that much."

After a month, he and three actors joined forces to move into a huge room with a kitchenette in the same building, at fourteen dollars a week. One of them was Ben Green, who remained a close friend. Another was Charlie Holmes, who appeared later in Bob's life, too.

Despite mutual poverty, "It was a joyous period. Each night, we reported our failures and shared our ambitions." The quartet had one job between them, soda-jerking in a Bronx drugstore. Whoever was hungriest took the work detail, because the pharmacist-boss was lenient and allowed the counterman to eat on the job.

Sometimes, the starving artists patronized the White Rose Bar on Sixth Avenue, bought a couple of beers, and stuffed its free lunch into their pockets—thoughtfully lined in advance with brown paper. When they got back to the walkup, they concocted a stew of the sandwich makings. "Oh, it was good. Knockwurst and sauerkraut." And whatever else they had managed to liberate from the counter.

The three actors were out, pounding the pavements in search of work. Bob Monroe stayed in the apartment, writing and answering ads; sometimes he ventured forth to make calls on advertising agencies. His parents had sent him the battered, vintage electric typewriter he had bought and put into working order.

"I sent out pilot scripts for my radio shows," and waited. "For nearly two years, I survived by writing: the health lecture scripts; Sunday supplement stuff for the Toronto *Star*, a monthly column in *Argosy Magazine*; some syndicated radio stuff and an occasional pulp magazine piece."

One day, Mother happened to see a wire agency story in the Columbus paper, detailing the exploits of a pilot who flew under the bridges on New York's East River. Mother immediately dispatched a pleading letter to Bob: "You'd better stop doing that, or you'll get in trouble." Monroe recalls, "She never questioned it wasn't I. I wrote back, and said, 'No, Mom, for once it wasn't.'"

But there were constant letters and occasional phone calls from Jeanette—back in the days when long distance was connected (and sometimes listened to) by the operator—all adding up to, "When can I come?"

Bob had been agonizing: "Would I want her to be the mother of my children?" The answer was a firm "No. Probably for snob reasons. She was a capable girl, supportive. A doer. A fine arts graduate. But she didn't fit my mental set at the time. Her English was poor. She made all the familiar grammatical mistakes." Still, he didn't have the heart to tell Jeanette the marriage was washed up.

One night, the phone rang. It was Jeanette, not from Columbus, but just arrived in New York. "Ben Green went over, picked her up at the station and put her in a hotel. Then I went.

"It was a dramatic scene. She had come, under pressure from her family. It took guts to tell her 'No more.' It was sad as hell. If I had stayed with her, I might have softened.

"Dear old Ben went back over to the hotel when I left, and put her on a train back to Columbus."

There was another tragedy at the time. Bob says, "About a month before her psychotic break, Peggy called me from Ohio. It was something she had never done before. She hadn't even written me.

"She pleaded, in her quiet way, to let her come and live with me in New York, where I was just barely surviving. She didn't give me a reason, but I understood her plight. She was a quietly pleasant person, living with two dominant people, and a third nearby. She was always passive, non-intrusive. It took an extreme effort for her just to call me to ask for help.

"Yet I hesitated. She noticed the hesitation, and didn't press the subject again; merely asked how I was getting along, and eventually hung up.

"At the time, there was no way I could see that I could support Peg in New York, and I was sure my parents or Dorothy would not subsidize her in the City. Even if I had the money, she couldn't have lived in that room with the four of us.

"But when she called, I had no idea of the severity of her problem.

"Later, when I discussed the incident with psychiatric friends, they all agreed it was problematical whether coming to New York would have helped her. That helped me a little.

"Still, if I had said, 'C'mon over here. . . .'

"Peggy's illness hit me hard. Can you understand my sense of sadness? I still put it in the 'what if. . . .?' category." The sorrow of the moment was stored away, deep within Bob. It has never truly disappeared.

* * * *

Months went by, and even on a shoestring, life in the bright lights of New York was an appealing adventure. The brownstone was an exciting transition for a young star-to-be, fresh out of the Midwest.

"You should have seen the personalities! We had an attractive blonde with a German accent, who was never there. We speculated she was a German spy. A year later, the Feds picked her up. She was!

"Then there was the prostitute in the first floor flat, a short stubby woman." Monroe steeples his fingers judiciously. "No, none of us patronized her. But we were friendly. . . .

"We had a schizophrenic woman from Philadelphia somewhere upstairs. She always wore a housecoat, and she only ever went out to buy booze and cigarettes. Her family paid to keep her away from home.

"There was Mr. Chisholm, the janitor, and then there was Ria McKee, second floor front. Horsey kind of woman in her sixties. She kept telling us how rich her parents were. Fifty-room house up the Hudson.

"We didn't believe it, of course. Then one day, she asked us out to her place, and it was true! Fifty rooms, can you imagine that!"

* * * *

Monroe had been the lead in the high school's senior play. "After graduation, all the guys said, 'See you in New York or Hollywood.'" Funny thing, none of them ever showed up." He had tasted success with the hobo play, and knew the power of his writing. He had hard evidence from Cincinnati to prove he knew his trade, but doors just didn't open.

Manhattan didn't react to his good provincial credentials. "I was one of the best dialogue writers around, but I couldn't break in. It was frustrating. I didn't know what in hell I was doing wrong."

A possibility dawned on him: "Don't forget I was always young for my age. In school when I was fifteen, the eighteen year old girls would say, 'Come back when you're grown up.' I felt out of cycle all along the line.

"So I grew a mustache, just to make myself look older.

"Then, there was. . . ." there's a brief pause at the admission, ". . . .fear of failure. I didn't want to have to go back to Columbus again."

Bob hastens to add, "Oh, I wasn't trying to show my father anything. Later, when I made it, I didn't even send the clippings back home."

His was an experience of dismay felt by tens of thousands down through the years. Many who fail, even today, go home to comforting anonymity. Monroe persevered. But in the New York City of the late 1930s, even Bob's confidence began to ebb.

1940s

It's another evening in David Francis Hall. Bob Monroe tucks a white loafer, grimed with red dust, under his expansive frame and grins, glad to be diverted by a chance prompt, and to play to an audience, even a small one.

Bob has conducted a lifelong love affair with cats—of any parentage and description. "It's part of my fun stuff.

"Now I'll take and tell you the story of Joe The Cat." Dates are elusive, as ever, but it must have been in the late 1940s.

"I was walking along Sixth Avenue—in those days they still called it Sixth, not Avenue of the Americas—one cold winter day, and I passed a pet shop around 55th Street.

"There was a windowful of Siamese kittens. One of them put his paws on the pane and talked to me. 'I want you,' he said, looking straight at me. He made a few other comments, and, well I had to go in and get him.

"Tucked him in my overcoat pocket. A year later, I had an apartment at 7 Park Avenue, and I used to walk him around Murray Hill, on a leash. Joe had grown into a muscular, self-assured attack cat, but he didn't like being thumped on the nose. Every time he went after a dog, I'd thump him. He learned, but the dogs avoided him, too.

"I wanted to accustom Joe to the water, because summers, I was living on my ketch down at Huntington and Northport harbors, commuting on the Long Island Railroad.

"He'd do just about anything for raw liver. I'd toss some into the empty bathtub in the apartment, and Joe would go for it. Then after a while, I let a couple of inches of water into the tub, and still he'd go in for the meat. Gradually, I filled the bath higher, and there'd go Joe, swimming for the liver, surface diving, even. That's how he learned survival at sea.

"Come summer, I'd get home from the train late in my business suit and row out to the boat in the dark, and I'd call. 'Hey, Joe!' He would answer. He was my directional signal.

"What I'd done was hang a knotted rope over the side, so he could climb back on board, if he went off on a fishing expedition, which he did.

"One night, old Joe wasn't there on deck. I got worried, but I found him all right. There he was, lying on some rope in the locker up forward, all wet. Looked like maybe he'd nearly drowned. He was bloated, too.

"I carried him up on deck. His head hung limp. I figured I'd have to take him to a vet in town to save him.

"Then I noticed an overturned pail on deck. I'd left six fish in it, for my dinner. It clicked. Old Joe had knocked the pail over and gobbled the fish. He was just feeling sorry for himself.

"The end of Joe's story came a few years later. By then, I was living on a farm outside Bethel, Connecticut. I got old Joe a collar with our phone number on it, and let him roam. Now, Joe like to cat around in our barnyard, or anywhere else, for that matter.

"One morning he came home, all ripped open, his intestines hanging out. We sewed him up ourselves.

"When I went to get some gas at the filling station, the owner just happened to say, 'Boy, there was some cat fight out here last night.' I didn't make any comment.

"It took Joe six or eight weeks to recover from his wounds. Then he went out again. He came back the next morning, tired but smug, with his tail up.

"On a hunch, I dropped by the gas station. The owner said, 'Someone got my cat last night. Tore his throat out. Sure would love to know who done it.'

"But, well, Joe's time came. Too many fights behind him. Too many infections. He had five years of glorious life.

"One day, he just flopped over. That's all she wrote."

* * * *

By 1940, when he was an impatient twenty-five, and after several years of frustration, Bob Monroe's life in the brownstone on West 53rd began to edge onto the fast-track. Every once in a while, when Ben Green's brother came into town, the quartet of roommates got a taste of New York's high life. The brother was a merchant marine sailor, on convoy duty in the North Atlantic, for which he got extra hazardous-duty pay.

When he signed off his ship, "He'd have a fat, fat roll, which he wanted to spend. Cabs everywhere. All the clubs. Sometimes, he'd blow a thousand dollars in a night. We'd try to restrain him, but he wasn't interested."

Bob Monroe's first big break came in 1940. One day, NBC called the Monroe house in Columbus to express interest in a radio script Bob had submitted even before he moved to New York. Bob's parents promptly relayed the news.

* * * *

Bob looks back from the late 1980s at those days, and what ensued. "That was the beginning of the next phase of my life. It was a whirlwind of high-drive excitement, a roller-coaster of extreme highs and lows, rags to riches and back again, in an almost continuous cycle, until I finally got it stabilized...From a rooming house west of Fifth Avenue to a home in Westchester County, in a long series of unforgettable lessons.

"I am amazed that the 25-year-old kid I was did as well as I did, with little or no business training, unaware of the sharp operators in big-time broadcasting and advertising, only partially experienced with high-ego personalities, and certainly relatively unsophisticated.

"But I never missed a deadline with scripts or programs; later, I directed big-name stars and got top performances out of them with no problems. I innovated new sound techniques, negotiated multi-million dollar contracts, created and produced musical scores and songs, wrote over a million words in radio drama and other scripts, ran my own organizations, each with its own budget, served as the sacrificial vice president of a radio network amid the cross-currents and manipulations of a large corporation. And I more or less kept my personal life from getting completely out of control."

A bit ruefully, looking back along the corridor of years, Bob remarks, "One price I paid was a duodenal ulcer within two years of my first success. Another was that I missed many opportunities, in all categories, due simply to my lack of experience. It would have been so easy to have done them, if I had known better.

"But I did play! Not so much in the night clubs and around Broadway, but I did have my own airplane, finally. I flew sailplanes, owned and loved sailboats—each one larger than the last. I got up to a forty-four-foot ocean-going ketch in the final days.

"Before we moved to Virginia, we had a five-bedroom house on twenty-seven acres in Westchester County, complete with swimming pool and bath-houses and guest cottage. I was a charter member of the Sports Car Club of America, and built my own sports car from the frame up; its registered and licensed brand name was The Rogue: 450 horsepower; nine-foot hood, three-feet-nine-inches high. Only it never placed better than fourth in a race.

"By the time I was 41, that period had ended, of my own choice.

"I'm still not fully sure of the reason. The only thing I didn't get to do was write and direct my own Broadway show.

"It was a great period in my life, and I remember it fondly, but not wistfully."

* * * *

The show NBC liked, which started Bob's ascent was "Rocky Gordon," based on Monroe's adventures as a hobo, and an outgrowth of his Ohio State dramatic success. "I went from ten dollars a week to one thousand, overnight!" exults Bob, "I stayed on in the brownstone, and we'd celebrate every second week, when the check came in." He kept the treasured electric Remington hard at work. "It made a terrible noise, but no one in the apartment minded. They knew it was making money."

The cast was a freight train crew, the series was humorous as well as full of adventure. It ran five times a week, just before the legendary "Amos 'n' Andy" show and Lowell Thomas's news broadcast.

Monroe started as the writer on the NBC network show, but soon moved on to production. The *New York Times* ran a good-sized photograph of a be-spectacled, gallused Bob Monroe in its edition of Sunday, July 7, 1940. It shows the young producer bending over a couple of portable recording turntables at the New York Central's yard in Weehawken, New Jersey. The turntables, on a railroad pushcart, are set up next to a locomotive's wheels, a microphone stands even closer to the iron horse. It was this show (and perhaps this photograph) that gave Monroe a reputation for being a pioneer in the recording and use of ambient, real-life sound in his radio productions.

"When I first got flush, from 'Rocky,' " one of the first priorities was to buy his first plane. "It was a low wing, 90-horsepower Aeronca, the only classy plane those people ever built. I kept it at Flushing Airport. It was great.

"Oh, I had a couple of forced landings, stuff like that. But nothing really risky. Can't remember why I sold it. Probably financial reasons."

World War II came to America, and "Rocky Gordon" left the airwaves. Earlier, Mike Hinn, the announcer friend with whom Bob had flown in Cincinnati, came through on his way to Ontario to volunteer for the Royal Canadian Air Force. "I would have gone, too, but I was locked in."

People started going to war. After Pearl Harbor, Bob's younger brother, Emmett, volunteered for the Army Air Corps, the branch which had years earlier rejected Bob. Today, Emmett wonders whether he emulated Bob, even though he had earlier worried his older brother would recklessly kill himself in the air.

Emmett became a pilot on B-24's, flying out of England. After the war, he attended California Institute of Technology at Pasadena for two years, majoring in chemistry. Finally he decided to follow in his mother's footsteps, switched to medicine, and got his M.D. from Ohio State. In 1947, he married Alice.

With time, Bob Monroe got his draft notice, but, "I had ulcers by then, and I was made 4F. I went back into engineering, and worked for a manufacturing firm. We designed a flight-simulator prototype which was superior to the Link trainer. It used a five-foot globe and an optical device. The pilot would nose down or nose up, and see all kinds of topographical features." For reasons Bob cannot recall, the simulator was not put into production, although the prototype ended up at Wright-Patterson Air Base.

He did some trouble-shooting travel—once to North Africa to look into a problem involving dust in the filtering systems of aircraft, and again to New Guinea, to investigate the sabotage of a fuel pipeline.

Bob was writing a monthly aviation column for the old *Argosy* men's magazine. That, in turn, led to a position with the National Aeronautic Association(NAA), a private group which had close ties with the government. Monroe commuted weekly to Washington for meetings, but worked out of an office the NAA provided for him in New York.

By 1943, his primary assignment was to produce a weekly radio show for the NAA called "Scramble!", Friday nights on NBC's Blue Network. The show was broadcast in front of a live audience from studios in the RCA Building at Rockefeller Plaza, and its host was Believe-It-Or-Not's Robert Ripley. In the course of the show's run. Monroe met most of the Air Corps brass, including Generals Carl Spaatz, Hap Arnold, and Jimmy Doolittle.

"Scramble's" prime job was to interest youth in aviation and pilot training. The program broke stories on how American pilots flew desparately-needed anti-tank ammunition to British troops in Egypt in June 1942; it featured returned war heroes, such as Marine dive-bomber machine-gunners back from Guadalcanal. Bob Monroe, said *Newsweek* on February 15, 1943 was "a slim 27-year-old 6-footer who writes the shows (on an electric typewriter he bought in a pawn shop), directs the production and serves as cadet recruiting officer."

The *New York Daily Mirror's* feature, "Only Human", by Sidney Fields found another angle. The piece appeared on February 19, 1943 and used some artistic license to explain why Bob wasn't in uniform, as well as to tout his show.

The artist in Fields took flight: "Youth is always the bright Summer of promise, promise that is mostly unfulfilled. All of Bob Monroe's promise always buds and blooms. He's as intense as a white flame, as restless as the wind, isn't happy unless his mind and hands are at work."

The hyperbolic caption under the photograph of a skinny, disheveled Monroe gesticulating at a Blue Network microphone, reads, "A promising novelist, a capable inventor and an established radio producer. He's 28. Most of all, he loves to fly....He writes, directs and produces the radio show, 'Scramble' which dramatizes flying and fliers....At 15, he was an auto racer....(his parents) didn't know about his auto racing until he won two first prizes, and smashed through a fence. Then they ordered, "From now on you fly. There are no fences in the air.' "

The breezy piece concluded, "At his home, Bob writes and plays his fine collection of Ellington records. He built his own huge, two-speaker radio, that does everything but make love to the maid, and invents gadgets like a timer to turn a radio on and off without getting up, an aviation device the Army is using now, and new things in air equipment. . . .

" 'Know what an inventor really is? He's a lazy man trying to get out of doing things.' " The final quote, at least, was pure Monroe.

Monroe made Walter Winchell regularly in those years, too, but the clippings are lost in time. A faded cutting from a 1943 Columbus paper in Dorothy Monroe Kahler's archives shows the hometown editor gave the New York story a different twist, but promoted the legend, a bit late, and using different figures from Bob's: "Idea Jumps Salary from $5 to $150 a Week Overnight." The lead paragraph exults, "Robert Monroe, the radio producer whose salary jumped from $5 to $150 a week has crowded so much adventure into his 28 years that even a soap opera listener would find the true story of his life implausible. . .At 18 he cracked up a plane and was forced to discontinue flying. . . ."

Back in the workaday world, Bob started to do radio programs for the Federal government's Coordinator of Inter-American Affairs, even though he knew little Spanish and no Portugese. He even got an agent.

All of this activity brought Monroe to the attention of Donahue & Coe, a medium-sized advertising agency, with offices in Rockefeller Center. E.J. Churchill, the agency's president, offered him a job. Churchill was a "highly-sarcastic, cynical" man who, Monroe surmised, probably had the boss's job because he was the brother-in law of a top MGM mogul. Donahue was the house agency for MGM as well as for Republic Pictures.

The job introduced Bob to L.B. Mayer, Sam Goldwyn, and other movieland names, and while he held it, he commuted to Hollywood. Bob stayed at Donahue & Coe for two years.

Bob Monroe rapidly became "Radio Production Manager" for the company—a resounding title for a one-man department. He recalls, wryly, overcoming the network "acceptance" people—the radio censors—to be allowed to air a particular commercial. "The product was Lydia Pinkham's, which helped women who were having period pains. Well, in those days, you just didn't mention such things on the air.

"We had a doctor-like voice which would ask, 'Do you suffer when you are tired, lonely, easily depressed, on certain, particular days?' The network censors were usually fifty-year-old women, but we got it through.

"There was another time, in the '50s, when I convinced one of them to allow us to use 'Hell.' I just told the woman it was perfectly normal. If there was a Heaven, there was a Hell. She let it run."

Churchill gave Bob the freedom to explore the boundaries of his potential. "E.J. backed me up. Even if he was crusty, he was also kind." When Monroe's big break came, in 1944, Churchill could have insisted that the show was Donahue property, but he let Bob go off on his own to form Monroe Productions.

It was a daily half-hour prime-time radio show he developed for MGM called "Screen Test," broadcast live out of an eight hundred-seat Broadway theatre. A different male or female hopeful was featured each evening in a dramatic skit, backed up by live orchestra. If an MGM star happened to be in town, the Big Name would drop by to wish the novice actor luck. One of the writers on the show was Charlie Holmes, one of the three actors with whom Monroe had shared digs on West 53rd Street.

"It was big. Lights on the marquee. We never had trouble filling that theatre. There were lines around the corner each evening. We gave them a warm-up, the broadcast, and an after-show."

It was a lot of work. Bob, the perfectionist, paid attention to all aspects of production, even to the lighting, although it was radio. He also spent a lot of time on the music, especially with Lou Davis [1], who became a close collaborator in later enterprises. "The music had to be scored and arranged. I did some stuff I'm particularly proud of. I had a partner who handled the scripts."

Bob Monroe had reached the pinnacle of showbiz by the age of thirty. He moved to the more respectable neighborhood, where young *arrivistes* felt more comfortable than in the roiling tumult of a midtown rooming-house; lower Park Avenue, on the southern slope of dignified old Murray Hill, below Grand Central Station, was good cat-walking country.

"Of course," says Monroe ruefully, "there was another side to that story. I was making maybe $300,000 a year, and that put me in the top tax bracket.

"Do you know what the government's bite was during the War? It was ninety-two percent! We had liberal expenses, of course. But. . .!"

The network publicity department fed Earl Wilson, the Broadway gadabout nighttime columnist, one-liners, to keep the jaunty Monroe image burnished: "When a fan told Radio Producer Bob Monroe, 'Your cast is just like one big family,' he answered, 'It's a lie! We're just very good friends.' "

"Screen Test" ran on the network for about a year, to solid ratings. "Scramble!"; programs for Inter-American Affairs in Spanish and Portugese; music; writing; directing; producing; engineering: All of them made Monroe a reputation as a "broad-based" producer.

MGM closed down the radio show in 1946; peace came on the United States. Bob was between engagements, but he wasn't resting, nor hurting financially. Radio had been good to him.

After he and Jeanette divorced, Bob took up with another woman, named Marianne, who was a concert pianist. Bob and Marianne developed "a profound relationship." They moved out of Manhattan and into a house in suburban Mt. Kisco. Joe The Cat came along.

Around 1943 Monroe met Mary Ashworth. Marianne and Bob separated, by mutual consent.

"Mary was an aspiring actress and singer from Boston, just starting out in show biz. Her mother was supposed to have been an Italian countess. She was pretty, a blonde, and she had a beautiful singing voice. I used her whenever I could in "Screen Test," and we had a wonderful relationship.

"But suddenly, she just didn't call me any more, or she wouldn't answer when I called her. Years later, I found out it was because her agent—who was the wife of our orchestra leader—told her not to stay involved with me, because it tied her down.

"Mary went on to be the Chesterfield Girl on the 'Perry Como Show.' She toured for the USO, entertaining the GI's, and then she went into club dates."

Bob then met and married Frances, a Russian. "Well, she wasn't actually Russian, but she was of Russian descent," and Bob thought she had potential as a writer.

Bob and Frances first lived in the farmhouse outside Bethel, Connecticut, south of Danbury, the hat town. "We lived off what I had earned on 'Screen Test.' They moved on to Stormville, east of Beacon, in New York's Dutchess County. "There was a fellow named Pete O'Brien at the local airport, who had a Navion. It was the nicest piece of equipment I ever saw. Four places, 175 horse, low wing, retractable gear, a G-Meter." Monroe rented the Navion regularly.

He flew it on weekends to Wurtsboro near Monticello in lower mid-state New York, because there he had discovered a gliding club. "The club bought six sailplanes which were surplus after the War. Someone had sold the military on the idea they would be good to train glider pilots, which was ridiculous. A sail-plane is meant to soar on the rising currents. A glider is meant to come down. It was a boondoggle; they were never actually used for training.

"The club got these $50,000 planes for $400 apiece, brand new, still packed, each on a trailer. We used four to fly, and kept two to cannibalize the spares. We called the club The Metropolitan Air-Hopper Soaring Association". Bob kept his membership valid until 1961.

During that period, Bob recalls a memorable flying junket. "I was still a member of the Aviation Writers Association. The Air Force gave us a non-pressurized DC-4 to fly out to our convention in Los Angeles. We were a raucous group. Everyone took turns flying the plane.

"On the way back, they had us stop at Colorado Springs to take a look at the new Air Force Academy. When we got back to the airfield, there was a bad front predicted on the way to Chicago, but we decided to leave anyway. We had about ten hours of fuel in the plane. Of course there was no airborne radar in those days.

"We took off and most were sleeping and eating. We went north and couldn't get through the front. We couldn't climb over it, because the top was too high for our cabin pressure. We went south and couldn't even get through it over Texas. I was flying, and we decided to go through it.

"Well, we made it. But back in the cabin, people were on the roof, they got airsick, there was food and clothing all over the place.

"At one point, I watched the altimeter unwind 8,000 feet at 2,000 per minute. I wondered if it was going to bottom out." Monroe didn't pause to describe the feeling in his stomach as he watched.

"It was wild, fun, exciting. We left Colorado Springs at 4.00 p.m. and we got into Chicago at 1.30 a.m. That C-54 was one sturdy aircraft!"

The money Monroe had made from "Screen Test" began to dwindle. Monroe Productions was standing still. "I figured I had to get something going. So around early 1947, I took the top show I had in my portfolio to Mutual, and talked to the vice president in charge of programming. I had a deal for him."

It's not hard to imagine the lean, hungry-eyed Monroe pitching to the network vice president.

"Look, put the show on the net in Class A prime time for a month, for free. Don't pay us. You provide the studio, the sound effects, the orchestra.

"I'll give you the script, actors, director.

"If you like it, you can pay me for it at the end of the month. If you don't. . . . '

"I could see the VP, calculating, 'What have I got to lose?' " Bob Monroe was a known, reliable figure with a good reputation. The probationary deal was clinched, and the show went on MBS Sunday nights.

"At the end of that first month, the VP called me in, and he played it cool.

"He just sat there, holding me in suspense, deliciously. Then, at just the right moment, he opened a drawer and handed me a check for the month!"

The second big hit in Bob Monroe's career was "High Adventure!", a weekly series that ran on Mutual, later on NBC, for seven years. George Sanders was host for a gamut of dramas, many of them based in World War II, featuring the peak experiences of ordinary people.

Then there were the quiz shows, in the era of the original "64 Dollar Question." The Monroe company ran "Take A Number," "Meet Your Match," and "Name That Tune," two of which went on to TV. After his partner died, Bob gave the copyright to "Tune" to his widow;

it was revived on network TV in the 1980s.

Bob's biggest quiz hit was "Take A Number," which had a huge merchandise jackpot of $50,000 to $60,000. "Number" played live in front of an audience, again in a Broadway theatre. A studio contestant picked a number from the twenty-five displayed on a board, answered a question, and got a prize.

Part of the show's popularity lay in the fact that questions were submitted by listeners. Monroe figured it would do the ratings no harm if someone at home won the pot every once in a while. So another production novelty was that the jackpot question was often nearly impossible to answer; if the studio contestant couldn't respond, a listener automatically got the loot. One high school teacher survived for six weeks, collected more than $200,000 in prizes, and became a short-lived national celebrity.

"We didn't rig the show, as they did in later years. But we controlled it, to make it more interesting."

When a listener won the jackpot in some small town, "We'd beat the drums and really do a publicity number, truck the prizes out in vans, and then dump it on the guy's front lawn. Boats, cars, freezers, refrigerators, you name it. We got the publicity we wanted, and the show boomed."

Dorothy Monroe remembers visiting Monroe in New York during the heady days of his radio career. "There he was in the booth, waving his arms around, yelling out orders to everyone. He really did run those shows, down to the smallest detail."

* * * *

There were, of course, enormous pressures on the young man-in-a-hurry. Many years later, he recalled[2], "Way back in 1940, I began to have pains in my stomach.

"I had an ulcer. A duodenal ulcer. Dr. Richard Gordon put me on a diet of cooked carrots, soft-boiled eggs and milk, with very little deviation. He added some tincture of belladonna, a popular medication at the time to slow up the spastic action in my stomach. I asked him if there was anything else I could do, and he muttered something about it being the price of my work.

"I stayed on this particular diet for nearly a year, as best I could. To this day, I have no particular liking for cooked carrots and soft-boiled eggs.

"Finally, with no improvement over such a long period of time, I asked Dr. Gordon what could be done next. He replied it was up to me. I replied he was the doctor, therefore he should prescribe for me. . . .

"'Well, we can always operate and remove the ulcer.' Dr. Gordon did not bother to look up as he spoke.

"'All right, so I have the operation. Then what? Am I cured?' Dr. Gordon stared at me intently, but said nothing. 'You mean I might grow another one in another part of my stomach?' He nodded ever so slightly.

"'Come on, Dick, what is it?!' I wasn't going to let him get away with this one.

" '*You* are doing it to yourself!' he yelled angrily. 'Don't blame it on anybody else!'

"After an embarrassed silence, I finally got up and told him I would let him know.

"The following week. . . . I went out all alone on my small sailboat and spent many hours on Long Island Sound. I came up with an answer.

"I phoned Dr. Gordon, and told him I would need no operation for the moment, that I was trying something else.

"I began to eat whatever I desired and went off the belladonna. Within three weeks, the pain had almost completely disappeared. Three months later, I returned to Dr. Gordon for a checkup. The fluoroscope showed a healed-over scar, no bleeding.

"After the examination, Dr. Gordon stared at me, waiting for an explanation. I smiled smugly, thanked him, and left. A year later I explained to him what I was doing."

Monroe's formula, later applied to many other problems, was to confront the malady and inaction. "A hole in the stomach is a hole in your mind.

"Write down an "A" list of anxieties and concerns over which you have no power. It is fruitless to dwell on these immutables. Burn the A List.

"Make also a "B" list of those things which you can change. Do something about each problem—not necessarily a total remedy; merely acknowledging the problem may, at first be enough of a change.

"Each night make a new A and B List. The A List will grow smaller and smaller, the B List becomes incorporated in your 'Tomorrow Activity Notes.'

"No more fighting the Law of Change. You can't beat that machine."

But you can self-heal an ulcer. It was a lesson which bore much fruit many years later.

1950s

By the time he was forty, in 1955, Bob Monroe merited twelve lines in *Who's Who in America*: "Pres. Robert Monroe Prodns., radio program producers, 1946-49; pres. RAM Enterprises, 1950-54; sec.-treas., dir. Laury Associates, 1950-54; v.p. charge programming activities, dir., MBS, Inc., 1954-56. Club: Lambs (N.Y.C.). Home: Quaker Bridge Rd., Croton-on-Hudson. Office: 509 Madison Av., N.Y.C. 22."

There are a number of themes that run through Bob Monroe's life, from early childhood. Some are familiar to anyone who has seen today's Monroe Institute brochures, which, in discreet capitals, declare its purpose to be, "Inquiry. Innovation. Information." Bob might have added a sub-category, "Adventure!", but it would have creased the dignified image he sought to achieve.

Monroe innovated in the entertainment world of New York after World War II. He spotted early the potential of magnetic recording tape, which started to come into commercial use shortly after the war, and made it his medium. Then, as now, he combined the artistry of his creative right brain with the engineering savvy of the left brain function to produce a leading edge technology.

One surprise is that Monroe's radio experience did not lead him to shift alignment as TV began to take over American life in the early 1950s. In fact, he did skirmish in the new field.

Bob, then as now ever with his eye on useful new gadgetry, says, "Our company had an option on the number three and four production models of videotape machines produced by Ampex. We sold the options at a good profit when other people realized what tape would do for TV."

His company dabbled, but Bob couldn't get interested in television. "We did some sixteen millimeter shows. Lilli Palmer worked for us for a while. We did a daytime soap called 'Crossroads' which we couldn't sell. We did some live TV, like 'Meet Your Match.'

"It was the same thing I had already been doing for a long time, but simply supplying pictures as well. It was repetitive." Television was Hollywood. Monroe was New York. In Manhattan, the pace was frantic enough.

The decision to stay with audio—'the theatre of the mind'—was highly significant for his future.

Bob today reckons that Monroe Productions put out more than two thousand radio and TV programs in the nine years from 1947; at the peak, he delivered twenty-eight shows weekly.

"High Adventure" played to top radio ratings, even as TV stormed into the popular market. With that series as its star, Monroe Productions became a major team in the network leagues. The company packaged other dramatic series: "Nightmare" with the fabulous European menace, Peter Lorre, for Mutual, which also carried "John Steele, Adventurer"; "Story Time," which featured Madeleine Carroll, one of the luminous stars of the period; and a show which headlined Titus Moody, an acerbic New England character, played by Parker Fennelly, who had been featured in Fred Allen's comedy shows.

Bob achieved the recognition which was the era's equivalent of today's "People" magazine: his hard-working publicist got him more brash puffery in Earl Wilson's Cafe Society column:

". . . . Bob, the younger Monroe, made a Grand Tour of the OSU campus, touching lightly at several schools and hanging around till he got bored.

"He told me at Lindy's, while he chopped away at a dish of ice cream. . . .

"'I had a checkered career at Ohio State.'"

Monroe told The Midnight Earl he had avoided his father's classes: "'He, uh, would not have understood my methods of studying.'

"Monroe is the sort of guy who's known in radio as a 'three-headed man.' That is, he writes, directs, and produces his own shows. In addition, Bob has a couple of other heads: He writes the music for them and for his television shows, he designs the sets.

"His most popular is 'High Adventure,' which has the highest Hooper (radio's then-equivalent of today's TV Neilsen ratings) of any sustaining show. . . . The first film made from a Monroe story will be *The Crooked Way,* with John Payne and Sonny Tufts. Payne's already said he would like the rest of the radio series for future movies."

Four or five of the "High Adventure" radio stories were actually made into movies. Bob is phlegmatic: "They butchered them. I cringed when I saw them."

He introduced a movie technique to the theatre of the air. Previously, entire radio shows had been laboriously rehearsed from start to finish before a recording was made. The cast was engaged for a full day's work. Monroe cut production costs by taping from the moment the players started reading script in the studio, then selecting the right takes, and splicing the whole together. Only then, with the voice track complete, did he lay down sound effects, music, commercials, and the rest of the package. "We paid our people for one or two hours work. That's all we needed.

"We had a stock company of twenty-eight actors, and our writers knew them. Say we'd have a part for a little guy's voice. The writer would come in and say, 'Mort, this is for you,' and Mort knew immediately what he had to do. It was a customized system."

New York also gave Bob a chance to expand his musical side. He began scoring his own productions. "I'd work out melody lines, harmony patterns."

In due course, he expanded the music into a profitable sideline. Monroe started making a "lot of money" underscoring the music for other dramatic shows on the networks. The underscore is the music which leads the listener to emotional response—provokes the tears, triggers the laughter, sets the scene in the old West or the hurly-burly of a city street.

"We took up the idea of looping tapes to produce continuing music sequences. You could build twenty minutes of music out of eight or ten phrases. It was a breakthrough." Today, the Monroe Institute produces and sells Metamusic tape cassettes based on identifiable themes, with a Hemi-Sync underlay; individuals use them for relaxation, meditation, and sleep. They have found application as well in psychotherapeutic work, in education, medicine and, undoubtedly, in other, unreported fields.

Monroe Productions began to build a stock library of musical phrasings to cover any dramatic situation. But one of the notable figures of the show business world was James Caesar Petrillo, then the baron of New York's Local 802, American Federation of

Musicians. Petrillo, a cigar-chomping champion of musician-protectiveness, hated the idea of tape, and even more of canned, repetitive themes which would deprive his live-session-men of work. Monroe was stymied in his attempts to record new library material in the United States.

Bob flew his precious underscores, Ampex audio recorders and a couple of engineers to Cuba, then under the leather heel of Fulgencio Batista, the dictatorial cause for Castro's success. "We went down there and hired local musicians, under the Hungarian director of the Havana Symphony.

"It was a six-day session. On the third day of the session, a new guy showed up in the control room, with a gun in a holster.

"One of the Cuban technicians said, 'Don't throw him out. He's Batista's nephew.'

"So for the rest of the time, we recorded with this guy sitting there." Nerves frayed, especially among the Cubans, but the band played on into the microphones.

"Then, the guy disappeared. We really thought he would confiscate our music. We packed the big tape reels in different suitcases, and held our breath until our plane was airborne.

"Maybe he just liked what we were playing."

Later, Bob sent Lou Davis to Italy to repeat the pattern, but didn't take that trip himself. Today, Bob says, "We were the leaders in the field for a while." The side business gave Monroe a chance to practice on the electric organ, but, "I never had the dexterity to perform and write music. I'd dream up the themes and give them to Lou or a copyist." The same remains true today. Bob is more of a creative innovator at the keyboard than an orthodox composer or performing musician.

There were corporate shuffles. Monroe Productions expanded to become RAM Enterprises, which evolved in later years to Monroe Industries. Then and later, Bob spun off subsidiary companies to handle some of the properties and other of his activities as well.

There was some delightful confusion: A prominent fashion photographer of the time was also named Robert Monroe. "We used to get a lot of beautiful models coming by. I suppose he got a lot of aspiring starlets."

By 1956, the allure of the music trade dimmed. Four or five other firms had built up scoring libraries. Monroe leased his musical properties out, and that aspect of his operations quietly folded.

In 1976 he told a *Penthouse* interviewer, he "quit show business to escape from glamor, which is not only romance but illusion.

"'One of the things that turned me away from production and directing,' he says, 'was my feeling that it was nonreality and that reality was taking place outside that studio somewhere.'"

* * * *

Bob Monroe today comments, "I was a fairly conventional person in those days, caught up in my business."

"Fairly conventional" has never been an apt description of Bob Monroe, no matter how much he may protest—and he knows it. It's that touch of comfortable, self-deprecating modest-immodesty which is part of his 1930s character-set.

In 1950, Monroe went unconventional in another direction. "There was a guy named Edgar Wynn. No relation to the great comic, which is why he called himself Edgar. He had been Eleanor Roosevelt's personal Military Air Transport Command pilot during the war.

"Well, Edgar and I bought a couple of planes from war surplus—a Lockheed Lodestar 14-seater and a Grumman Goose amphibian, and we went into the charter business.

"Called ourselves Trans-American Airways, out of Laguardia Airport. I was chairborne, of course. Ed handled operations.

"Well. . . . I did make some runs, even though I didn't have a full commercial pilot's license.

"The operation did three turn-arounds a week to Florida, and we made money, even deadheading back from Miami to New York. When the Lodestar was on maintenance, we'd use the Grumman to fly people to the New York state lakes. Or we'd take off for a weekend somewhere.

"How much fun that was!"

Taking the Grumman off from water was "interesting." Its prop churned a heavy spume onto the windshield. "For about eight to ten seconds, you'd be blinded, just while you were getting airborne.

"When we weren't out on charter, we were just doing kid stuff. Once, Ed flew right through a powerline when he was landing on a lake. We'd stooge around New York, sightseeing, and see how close we could get our wingtip to the Statue of Liberty. I don't know why we were never cited."

Trans-American ended when Ed was killed flying a converted Navy fighter at the Miami Air Show. "He went in, right in the middle of the field. When we got to him, there he was, looking natural, as if nothing had happened. But the crash had snapped his neck." Bob sold the company and gave the proceeds to Ed's widow, a sweet, beautiful blonde showgirl, who had witnessed it all.

"Ed was a fine guy. A jet-setter. He'd work sixteen hours, play four, sleep four, then call me at five in the morning and say, 'Let's go somewhere.' One of the guys I really miss very much."

There were other, physical-life incidents which could have been preparation for the change in Bob Monroe's life in 1958. Some of those indicators involved Bob's passion for physical-life adventure. They could be regarded as testing or tempering the steel of his courage.

"Over the years, I've been in many marginal situations, but I rarely had time to contemplate the possibility of death. Even when flying, I had the utmost confidence." But adventure wasn't only flying.

The first time Monroe as an adult realized he could drown, he nearly lost his life while he was being body-towed by a drunken friend in Long Island Sound. "I was hanging onto a rope, and my lungs filled with water. I let go and voided the water out of my lungs. My friend noticed I wasn't on the rope when he was a mile away, and came back to pick me up." It was an intimation of mortality, but didn't provoke much after-thought.

Bob survived another challenge at sea. He took his sixteen-foot sloop out off Long Island into the Atlantic. Squalls blew up. Waves crested over ten feet. Bob couldn't get back into harbor; he stayed out all night. "I had no business being there, but I felt I could come through. It was just a super deal, matching myself against the elements, fighting to hold the boat's lee rail out of the water and keep water from entering the cockpit. I never thought I wouldn't get through. I didn't really have any fear of dying . . ." A peak moment.

Then, however, there was another supreme incident. "In 1950, I was commuting every week to Los Angeles from New York, to produce a program using star performers." This was in the days before jet travel, and the gruelling trip was usually through the night, either way. "Often I would stay over and take a side trip just to relax from the hectic pace of New York.

"On an impulse, I decided to spend a weekend at one of those hotels on Waikiki Beach in Hawaii. The series of events is blurred, but it was three weeks before I finally got back to New York. To say that my office was frantic is an understatement." The delay was caused by one of Bob's peak moments—and the lure of life in the tropics.

Bob had never tried surf-boarding. One morning, "I rented a twelve-footer, and went into the water." He practiced getting onto his knees from sitting, then standing, and then he started to enjoy himself.

Finally, he noticed, "I was a hundred and fifty feet farther out from shore than anyone else, and going farther. There was an offshore breeze and a current, too.

"I paddled like mad, but I didn't have the energy to leave the board and swim for land on my own. By now, it was around 11:00 a.m.

"By about one, I was out of sight of the island. I jumped into the water to avoid sunburn. Then I got to wondering if this was shark country, and I hopped back on the board.

"No one knew where I was. I lost track of where land was." The afternoon dragged by very slowly.

"The sun was sinking low. I was sitting on the board thinking, 'I'm going to die out here.' I had given up hope. I was prepared.

"Just at sunset, here came a fishing cruiser, aiming straight for me.

"It was a miracle boat. The guys on board laughed. They said I was fourteen miles offshore.

"They dumped me off at Waikiki, and I paddled into the beach in the dark.

"You know, the rental guy was angry! He said, 'I was damn sure you stole my board.'

"I'm a water person. Up till then, I never thought I could die in the ocean.

"It was an interesting coincidence that the boat was on an exact compass course to where I was."

Bob reflects, "I was raised inland, but I feel this pull to the ocean. I can stick my toe in the Atlantic, and feel I'm part of the world. I know the land is down there, under the sea, stretching from continent to continent.

"Sailing. Flying. It's all part of the same."

* * * *

Something else very important in Bob Monroe's life happened around 1950. Mary Ashworth called to check in after a silence of several years. "By then, she had married and divorced, and she had a two-year-old daughter, Maria."

Bob and Mary married, after he had eased out of his third entanglement, and Mary worked as a member of the Monroe Productions stock company. In 1951, their own child, Laurie was born. And by 1956, they were installed in fashionable suburbia, at Croton-on-Hudson, New York where Mother and Dorothy came to visit.

Mother remonstrated privately with her son for the number of women who had passed through his life. Bob replied calmly, "Well at least I marry my women, don't I!" The discussion ended.

There came another turning point in Bob Monroe's career. The Mutual Broadcasting System, one of the original big four radio networks, was in trouble with its affiliates. RKO General, Mutual's parent company, invited Bob to come on board as vice president for programming. Monroe knew precisely what the score was: "They wanted me to be their sacrificial goat. I had the credits. I took the job, but the bonus in it for me was big: They had to buy four of my shows to give me a capital gain." Monroe stayed at Mutual from 1954 till mid-1956. "I was surprised I lasted that long."

He was also in charge of the network's owned-and-operated stations in key metropolitan areas. The job gave him a taste of the excitement, and the profits to be made, in ownership.

He commuted two hours each way each day, from Croton to 1440 Broadway, and the nineteenth floor executive offices of Mutual-RKO General, and he attended to his other businesses on the side. "I was on dexedrine and barbituates much of the time." He left Mutual with few regrets, and as soon as he did, Bob had no further need for drugs.

* * * *

A year and a half before his first involuntary Out-Of-Body-Experience, a series of events occurred which can be interpreted as a major test, to see whether Monroe bit on an opportunity which was, in every sense, golden. To this day he cannot adequately explain why he did not choose to grasp the burnished ring that was easily within his grasp.

"Not too long after I left the network in 1956, a neighbor came by with an option to an oil concession in Ecuador. He offered a partnership if I would fund a trip there to examine an asphalt lake, oil seeps, that kind of thing."

It was 1956, midway in the Eisenhower boom years. Monroe jumped at the chance. "It was a couple of months after I left Mutual, and I was looking for something to do. Why not? We started to make plans.

"Then I remembered Chicho. His full name was Ernesto Estrada, and all I knew at the time was that he was a native Ecuadorian. He came to the U.S. every summer, and he was always a guest at the Air-Hoppers Club in Wurtsboro. We had a lot of fun, chasing each other all over the sky and hopping thermals.

"He was a strapping six-foot-six, blue-eyed but very dark-skinned, which caused him some trouble in 1950s North America. He was a superb athlete.

"I got his address from the club secretary and cabled him we were coming on business. I got a reply next day, saying simply, 'WONDERFUL CALL ME IN GUAYAQUIL WHEN YOU ARRIVE.' "

The partner, Bob and Mary took off for Quito, planning to spend three weeks, and about $15,000, as a tax write-off.

"We flew over a seemingly-endless ridge of snowy peaks—the spine of the Andes. As it got dark, I was surprised to see flashes of fire far below, maybe fifty or more. I finally asked the stewardess about them; she said they were small, active volcanoes.

"When we checked into the hotel in Quito, I intuitively knew we ought to work through the oil concession business before I got involved with Chicho."

The Monroes took time for a bit of sight-seeing, and marveled at the *burritos*, the men of burden who carried such heavy loads on their backs, the strap-marks were permanently grooved into their foreheads. They saw a three hundred year-old cathedral whose ceiling was gold-plated, and which gave solace to ragged parishioners kneeling in the pews. They looked at Chimborazo—a twenty thousand-foot extinct volcano, snow-covered and glistening in the spring cool—and the Andes behind the peak.

"They didn't like *norte-americanos*. A well-dressed, middle-aged woman spat at my feet and muttered a curse as she passed us by."

Bob was troubled by Quito's eleven thousand foot altitude. "Whenever I dropped off to sleep, I awoke sitting up in bed, gasping for breath. Evidently, when my blood pressure fell as I relaxed, I didn't get enough oxygen, so my mental alarm bells went off. I was grateful when we left for the tropical lowlands a couple of days later.

"We flew down to Esmeraldas, on the Pacific, in an ancient, corrugated-metal Ford Trimotor belonging to the local air service. I hadn't even seen one, much less ridden in one, for twenty-five years. The passenger list included humans, ducks, geese, chickens, and dogs.

"The tricky part came early in the flight. Just after takeoff, we entered the cloud cover that always seems to be on the lee side of the high Andes ridge. The air was smooth enough, but I noticed the young man who passed for steward looking at his watch intently.

"Suddenly, the old Ford banked steeply to the left, then leveled off, still in cloud. The young man nodded, but continued to gaze fixedly at his watch. After some five more minutes, the plane started to descend, and not long after that, we broke through the cloud base. Far below was the tropical jungle.

"When we got down on the grass strip, I asked the pilot what was going on back in the cloud. Luckily, depending on your viewpoint, he spoke some English.

"He chuckled. 'Are you sure you want to know, *senor*?' I nodded.

"'Well, it's all a matter of timing. Exactly three minutes from the time we start rolling down the runway, we have to make a 90-degree turn left. This puts us through a pass in the Andes. Six minutes after that, we're past the mountain ridge, and we can make our letdown out of the cloud.'

"I asked the pilot about radio beacons, radar and such things.

"He smiled. 'Look, this isn't New York. We're doing pretty well. Haven't hit the ridge yet, not once in two hundred runs.'

"Something inside me shivered. Sometimes I'm not as bold as I think I am."

Esmeraldas looked to Bob remarkably like a village in the Old West: A street lined with small, weatherbeaten, one-story wooden stores. Each had a swing-up panel through which the residents made their purchases. About half of the stores seemed to be permanently closed.

The main street itself was a sluggish swamp of mud, channeled occasionally by trucks from the nearby banana plantations, or by mule-drawn wagons. Bob was told the street had been paved by American Point IV money, but the truck traffic had brought in the mud over time, and no one troubled to clean the surface.

The Monroe party stayed in the only "hotel" available—four rooms around a courtyard. The town's mayor invited the gringos to the town council meeting in a relatively large, open-windowed house; with the gasoline lanterns burning, Bob remembers thinking there were a thousand airborne bugs for every stationary human.

One council member pre-empted the meeting to harangue the North American visitors. The mayor apologized to Monroe that he was their lone Communist.
"Even my Spanish was good enough to understand: We were the filthy capitalist pigs coming down to take over what was rightfully the people's land. He shook his fist. Why didn't we go back where we came from, and stop trying to make the Ecuadorians our

slaves? The *jefe* (head man) smiled, and shrugged apologetically to us.

"After the meeting, the same little man, wiping his sweaty face, took me aside for a private word. I followed him around a corner in the hall, feeling more than uncomfortably wary.

"When we stopped, the Communist offered me a half-interest in his crystal mine for ten thousand dollars. He came with the deal: He would continue to work the mine for us, and share in the profits.

"His Communism wasn't deep enough to interfere with business. I thanked him, and told him I would let him know." It would have been a neat investment to hold onto into the New Age.

* * * *

The next morning, the survey party chartered a fishing trawler and headed the thirty miles down the coast to the oil concession. It was a gentle, smooth passage; the breezes off the Humboldt Current tempered the equatorial heat. Bob felt deeply pulled to the pristine white beaches and the mass of deep green jungle on the vessel's port side.

The crewmen trolled for a mackerel-like fish. They roasted their catch immediately over a charcoal brazier on the afterdeck. Later, they cut more of the same fish up and served it raw, spiced with a strong vinegar. Bob had never eaten *ceviche* before. Both the raw and the charcoaled fish tasted so good, he had eaten nearly a dozen by noontime.

The trawler's destination was Cabo de San Francisco. "A little after one in the afternoon, we dropped anchor just outside the offshore breakers. Right on the beach in front of the boat was a cluster of thatched huts.

"Three honest-to-goodness dugout canoes, each with two men paddling, came off the beach to meet us. A deckhand tossed a rope ladder over the side, and one of the men came on board.

"He was a small man, no more than 21 or 22 years old, naked to the waist, wearing ragged canvas shorts, no shoes. He was very dark brown and smoothly-muscled, very masculine and an extremely smart man as well. His eyes, unwavering and alert, told it all.

"He introduced himself as Juan, the *jefe* of the village. He was unusually young to be head man.

"Juan was very disappointed we had no doctor aboard, since there was a very sick child in the village who needed immediate attention. Still, we were *muy sympatico*, and we got along in my pidgin Spanish.

"He perked up, though, when we expressed our desire to see the oil seeps and the asphalt lake. I went over the side into the first dugout, with the scintillator—a piece of oil prospecting equipment—clutched to me, and carefully settled into the middle of Juan's dugout. My partner crawled gingerly into the second canoe.

"My canoe took one of the breakers the wrong way, and we rolled over. I lit, standing in shallow water, the scintillator still dry above my head.

"Juan led us about three miles into the jungle. We looked at the seeps and took samples. The asphalt lake was about half a mile in diameter, and there we also took samples, but for some reason, I couldn't get a reading on the depth of the deposit with the scintillator.

"Juan invited us to stay for a meal. Then he showed us the village. It had about a hundred and fifty inhabitants. Thatched roof houses built on poles. Juan couldn't read or write, and he'd never been away from home, but what he had done for that community!

"He piped fresh spring water in through a covered viaduct. Somehow, he understood refrigeration and had built a natural water-evaporation system to keep vegetables fresh. He grew *naranjilla*, a green orange which has a beautiful taste. He perfected an egg-and-food delivery system. No one in that village was undernourished.

"The village was isolated for six months during the rainy season. Then, when it dried, the people went by foot to the nearest market town, packing their coffee and rice crops with them. They averaged maybe seventy five dollars per head per year. They bought staples and brought them back.

"Juan had developed a system of true communality: He ran the store, and the people had credit there for their purchases. His most important stock was tin cans—not only for their contents, but as roofing material."

After Monroe had seen the village, in detail, Juan had delayed sufficiently, and the unscheduled meal was finally ready. Bob recalls it in fine detail.

"Juan took us to his house. His wife was behind a screen cooking; she never sat down during the meal. *Ceviche* of seafood; hot chicken soup in hand-made clay bowls, with carved wooden spoons. Their most prized possession was a glass pitcher with a broken lip. Juan poured drinks of *naranjilla* into coconut halves."

Bob noticed some fuzzy grey matter, perhaps a bug, floating in the green-orange juice. But he squelched his misgivings and courteously downed the drink at a gulp.

"They even had napkins of very soft leaves. And then the main course: Boiled chicken. Never mind that it was tough. Between the time we got there and dinner, Pepe's wife had killed, plucked, gutted, and boiled that fowl for us." Bob's voice, more than thirty years later, is still full of wonder at the hospitality they were accorded.

"When we got ready to leave, Juan was embarrassed. Shyly, he pulled a bit of soiled, creased paper out of his ragged pants pocket. 'Does this really exist?' Juan asked. His greatest wish was to go there.

"I looked at the paper; it was a flyer for Miami Beach! I bet he made it!" Monroe parted from his small friend with great regret. "We gave each other the big *brassos* [hugs]."

The survey yielded no promise of successful oil exploitation, which left Bob with private feelings of relief for the village by which he had been so moved.

* * * *

When Monroe got back to Quito, it was time to play. Bob phoned Chicho Estrada. Next morning he went to pay his hotel bill. The clerk said it had been taken care of: "Senor Estrada owns the hotel."

The Monroes flew south to Guayaquil. Chicho was waiting inside the terminal.

His father was "the Simon Bolivar of Ecuador." He left five banks to his four children, and they expanded their holdings in every direction. When Estrada learned that Monroe had fallen in love with Ecuador, it cemented a new and far tighter bond between the two men. Mary was content since she found a close friend in Chicho's sister, Tina.

Bob noticed that Chicho had adorned his wife with a necklace made from gold doubloons. In the weeks that followed, Estrada taught Bob to scuba dive, so he could search a sunken Spanish galleon for more of the coins.

On his first attempt at freelance salvage, Bob recalls, "I was tethered by a rope, but I felt myself being tossed around like a top, after I had gone two hundred feet." The Pacific cross-currents were too rough for Monroe to make the critical diving attempt. Chicho, a decade younger, goaded Bob, "Come on, Old Man, you can do it!"

Every time Bob psyched himself up to leave, the hospitable Estrada dreamed up new and tempting ways to keep him in Ecuador: Going on an expedition in search of Inca gold; or, "He showed me a mine where a guy went into a four-foot entrance and came out with two ounces of gold. I wouldn't have done it, but the guy came with the mine."

Bob's nimble mind dwelled on other possibilities: Minerals close to the surface, begging to be exploited. Liqueur from the millions of stems of bananas which were thrown into the sea each year, too ripe for shipment to North America: Chicho could make a distillation plant available at a monthly rental of one dollar.

Estrada offered Bob the exclusive sulphur concession for the Galapagos Islands—"and he could have delivered it, too." He showed Monroe a waterfall capable of generating "enough hydroelectric power for all of northern South America."

Once Chicho said, "You want that oil concession? I'll get it for you. The president's a friend of mine." To demonstrate, Chicho organized a presidential visit, ostensibly, to inspect a construction project. "He even had the workers lined up to greet the chief executive, just like a military operation."

Monroe suggested Chicho buy a helicopter for his far-flung operations. The idea tickled the Ecuadorian. The chopper was air-freighted in and assembled. The pilot-salesman who brought it took Chicho for a ride. Estrada came back and suggested he and Monroe take it up. The salesman protested that Chicho didn't know how to fly the helicopter. Chicho whipped out a checkbook, wrote a check and said, "Now it's mine. I fly."

And there was soaring. Chicho had a hangarful of sailplanes. Once, the pair of adventurers glided to Cape Salinas. Chicho signaled, "Follow me," looped, pointed at an airstrip and darted through a low cloud base. Monroe did likewise, to come out over water, land nowhere in sight.

The wind had shifted suddenly. Monroe was disoriented. He was losing lift in the glider. "I was dropping and drooping." At one hundred feet, Bob finally spotted the beach, and made a quick landing. "Chicho came down on foot, furious. He had to have the plane dismantled to get it back to the strip."

One of the high points of Monroe's life came when Bob and Estrada soared the Andes. They flew more than one hundred miles, along the crests of towering peaks, as high as sixteen thousand feet, with oxygen.

"But by now the New York office was cabling. I'd reply happily, 'Back next week'," and more time would pass in lotusland.

When Bob finally decided he had to go, Chicho took him to the airport, and emerged from the terminal triumphant. "There's a strike. See, you're not supposed to leave." Monroe accused his friend of organizing the stoppage, but discovered it was legitimate. So he stayed on for another week.

When Bob and Mary returned to the United States, Monroe sent four Siamese kittens to Chicho as a gesture of thanks. "I persuaded the pilot of one of the Panagra planes to take them in a cage behind his seat in the cockpit.

"Well, by the time those cats got to Quito, I bet that pilot wasn't very happy with me. Can you imagine a boxful of yelling Siamese cats all the way to Ecuador?

"Still and all, they got there. And today there's probably about a thousand Siamese cats roaming the jungles and the Andes."

For a while, Chicho wrote passionately and regularly, urging the Monroes to come back. Finally, the letters stopped.

"My Ecuadorean sojourn is one I'll never forget, and much of it is still fresh in my mind more than thirty years later.

"I've always had trouble with what I call pacifica. The tropical lifestyle holds a strange attractiveness I can't define. Instinctively, I know I could drop into it and forget everything else.

"If I went to the South Pacific, I don't think I'd come back. Either I've read too many books about it, or seen too many island movies—but I don't remember doing so.

"Or perhaps I lived on a tropic island somewhere, somewhen."

Why didn't Bob Monroe stay in the Ecuadorian paradise? All the material wealth he could ever have dreamed of was there for the taking. He would have operated under the patronage and protection of one of the benevolently-feudal princes of the land. But when it came to the crunch, he decided to return to North American reality.

"If my skin had been a different color, maybe. But I couldn't have kept up with Chicho's playing. And we had two small kids in school." The excuses sounded somewhat superficial.

"Well, there *was* something that pulled me back to the U.S. Some realization that the existence down there could not have provided the answers I needed."

Could it be that some power dangled a final lure, a temptation of sybaritic opulence in front of Bob, to see whether he would jump at the chance, rather than return to the uncertain future awaiting him in North America? Bob nods. "There might be something in that."

And, perhaps, something more. Perhaps the trip was a final, physical testing, too. The scuba diving experience, and being disoriented, then crash-landing the glider, bear remarkable resemblance to some of Bob's early non-physical sensations.

There was yet another indicator pointing to a possible pattern in his life.

"The year before I started to go Out-of-Body, I had a recurring dream which was exasperating. I dreamt I was taxiing my plane and taking off. I just barely got off the ground, but I was stymied by wires overhead. I'd fly along them, looking for a hole, but I couldn't find one. . . . I tried maybe a hundred times. . . tried to get free. Once I had my first OOB, I never had that dream again.

"Maybe that was the last barrier. . . trying to find the hole in that wire-energy network."

* * * *

One major turning point in Bob Monroe's professional life had been the sale of "Rocky Gordon" to NBC.

Another came in 1956. "When I left Mutual, I had several options. I really wanted to write books. . . and a play. I had enough money to support the family for two or three years."

The temptation was great. Bob had the plot already sketched out in his mind for "The Brownstone Novel," based on his hand-to-mouth days in Manhattan's West 50s, "I had a recognizable name. I had the story. I knew how to do it." And from the novel, he secretly wished he could develop a play. That was Option One.

"Option Two was to move to the West Coast, to get into film and TV production. It would have eaten up all my capital in one year.

"But I wasn't prepared to stay on in the cut-throat world of network programming. Network competition is *savage.* You find you really don't have one friend you can trust a hundred-and-one percent.

"If I had gone into TV in Hollywood, I don't know whether I would have survived physically. I had already gone through my ulcer phase in the 1940s. . . ."

Monroe isn't out to bite the hand that had fed him so generously. "Don't get me wrong. New York was very, very good to me.

"But the only thing I really wanted to do and hadn't done was to write and produce my own play on Broadway."

Bob had written, by his own reckoning, more than a million words. The novel-play would have been another outlet for the creative mind he now ached to exercise to the fullest.

With a disappointment still evident today, Bob discarded the idea of the play, and instead, went into radio station ownership.

* * * *

More or less by the way, Monroe had also developed, during the 1940s, a "covered motorcycle." It was a design which permitted a two-wheel, motorbike-rider to pull into a frame, clamp a plexiglass hood over his machine, then emerge with a small "car." In 1985, four decades later, they were becoming common in California, Bob says—but not his design.

As a young man, Bob built cars. "He was one of the first people to take seat-belts out of airplanes and put them in cars," says Dorothy. The cars, of course, had leopard-skin upholstery.

In the 1950s, Bob's horizons were grander: He built "The Rogue, with its nine-foot-long hood, longer than the Jaguar E-Type." He had to get a manufacturer's license so he could register the vehicle, which then stood proudly in front of the suburban Croton chalet.

* * * *

There is a photograph of the Monroe family on the occasion of Father's retirement from active teaching at Ohio State in 1957. The Professor bears remarkable resemblance to the Bob of the late 1980's.

Three decades later, Bob Monroe looks back on his complex, formative relationship with his Father.

"My association with him dwindled after that disastrous incident with the theatre company near Pittsburgh. After that, whenever we met, he was glad to see me, but never complimented me on my exploits, and I didn't expect him to.

"It was almost as if he assumed I would do something constructive, someway, somewhere. I heard from the rest of the family that he expressed quiet pride in telling others of the activities of 'my son in New York.' But I'm sure I was not out to please my father.

"I remember Dad very warmly and sympathetically. When the chips fell down hard, he backed me all the way. The fact that he thought it best is all that matters. His ignorance *was* a good excuse.

"What I learned from my father, knowingly or unknowingly on his part? The key items? Integrity. Consistency. No one is an authority on everything. Words are not enough.

"In the end, just being father and son was enough."

In his father's retirement photograph, Bob is what used to be called a spiffy dresser.

His keen, sharp eyes look beyond the camera. But that piercing glance is more than overwhelmed by a roguish twinkle which says, "I don't know where we're going, but we're going to have fun getting there."

By the spring of 1958, Bob Monroe, the prototypical pre-Yuppie was poised for the next and greatest of his adventures. He had rejected the material temptation of the lotus life in Ecuador; he had left the highly-paid slavery of Mutual, and was on the verge of becoming an independent operator; he was an innovator; he had expanded his mechanical engineering abilities; he continued his love-affair with the sky and the sea; he was certainly a card-carrying adventurer. Domestic circumstances forced him to drop his writing project, but his creative Right brain was constantly churning; he continued his addiction to music; he was separating from his emotional involvement with Mary.

What was lacking in his physical life was the philosophical ingredient. Bob knew he was different from other people, but had never paused to examine that distinction. And he was, as always, curious, about everything.

In 1958, Bob Monroe was set to accept a challenge to be dramatically different, after having proved he could successfully march to the 'Real World's' drummer.

Monroe pauses, from the age of seventy-two, to look back. "Don't forget, I was a hungry, Depression-time teenager. I know what that feels like.

"Oh, yes, I have been driven."

* * * *

Bob Monroe took a deep breath and buckled down to the field he knew so well, radio, but as an owner. He established a corporate office at 509 Madison Avenue, which ran properties in North Carolina—WAAA in Winston-Salem and WHKC in Durham.

There was one diversion from the norm of the radio business, which suddenly occurs to Monroe as he recollects. "Of course, we got into Biorhythm all the way back in 1958-59." Monroe unearthed the inventor of the technique, made a deal, and tried to market the process, but only after testing it on himself.

"We were the first to try it. It was quite convincing. But we didn't promote it enough. After six months, we dropped away from it. Now, of course, it's computerized, and you even can get Biorhythm on your wrist, to help you make decisions." Monroe shows no regret that he was, as so often, too far ahead of his times for the public to cotton to his innovation.

In Winston-Salem, Bob came to know Agnew Bahnson, the owner of a manufacturing company there, who was similarly ahead of his time.

"To give you an idea, Agnew made commercial air-conditioning units, but in the middle of his plant, he had a laboratory to experiment with anti-gravity, which was his passion." Agnew was also "a flying type" who introduced Monroe to the society life of Winston-Salem, "All the tobacco people," who helped make his monthly trips to North Carolina pleasant.

"Oh, sure, I was frustrated that the writing venture hadn't come off, but I found another outlet in writing musical bridges for the radio program breaks. We had the longest sign-off modality in radio—eight minutes. It was fun."

An elusive air of puzzled expectation hung over Bob at the time. Something seemed to be in the wind, but it was nothing he could define. He continued to search for a niche, apart from radio ownership.

Today, he says, "Obviously, I was trying to do something else. I was seeking new outlets, always. I made forays here and there, but they weren't structured." He investigated the concept of sleep-learning, but stopped his experiments in January 1958, "probably because of financial constraints."[1] The concept of 'sleep-learning' is also part of the pattern that led to the events of April 1958 and beyond.

"I wasn't necessarily challenging society's frontiers at that point."

Monroe catalogues his state of health: "In the late 1950s, I was athletic. I did scuba-diving, sailed a lot single-handed, flew gliders. I was very active, in good shape. But I wasn't a fitness freak.

"There was no physical system in my body that disturbed me." It is an engineer's appraisal of a useful piece of equipment.

"I hadn't had any illnesses to speak of. Oh, I had an appendectomy in 1940-41, somewhere in there, and I shot up to 160 pounds from 138 right after that. I had that ulcer which kept me out of the service in World War II.

"Well, there was one thing," which could be part of the significant mix of the time. "When I came back from Ecuador, I started to get a malarial-type illness. High fevers and cold, cold chills. I checked into the hospital in Tarrytown and they ran all the tests. I was shaking so bad, the hospital bed was rolling around the room. I discharged myself after a week.

"But it wasn't a malaria they knew of. I wasn't incapacitated.

"The fever subsided after I had been home for a week," to the general relief of those around him. "For a while, it came back about once a year." It was only some time later that Bob connected the fever with that mysterious grey mass in the cup of *naranjilla* juice he had drunk at the village on the coast of Ecuador.

* * * *

Bob's Mid-Life Crisis came when he was forty-two years old, but it took a distinctly different turn from the norm.

He leans back, both feet tucked under him in reasonable approximation of the lotus position. "I guess you could call it a gradual stage of awareness. I was my own worst skeptic. What I had was great curiosity. Nothing else.

"It was not evident to me that I had some great need for spiritual growth. I had no great desire to know about God." Bob pauses. "Well, sure, if someone had offered me a chance to explore the Universe then. I would have jumped at it, that's true.

"But I look at it an entirely different way. You can't describe it as coalescing into a fiery zeal. It was a dawning realization that I am not what I think I am."

Mentally, in early 1958, Monroe was opening himself to the huge adventure that was to come.

* * * *

Bob Monroe's first steps on his new path were uncertain, uncomfortable, fraught with terror. He had absolutely no conscious preparation for what was to take place. That it should happen to the successful radio executive seemed no more nor less likely than if it happened to, say, a Kansas wheat farmer. Yet the farmer might not have had the mix of ingredients which would have suited him for the adventure.

One night in April 1958, while Bob was still living in Croton-on-Hudson, it all started.

The run-up to Monroe's first involuntary Out-Of-Body's began on that Sunday afternoon in April 1958 which he chronicles in *Journeys Out Of The Body (JOOB).* "I didn't want deep emotional patterns in *JOOB.* That was purely a reportorial job." Now he is prepared to talk about the travail.

The recollection is still poignant. The first stage was sheer agony, "in the muscles below the ribs," says Bob. "I tried to look for reasons I was so sore! I tried to find a doctor, but they were all out playing golf." Late that night, he finally fell asleep.

"Then there was this cataleptic vibrational state. I went to Dick Gordon the next day. He was a show-business doctor. He said it was just tension, 'Don't worry about it.'

"But I did. I couldn't move any part of my body. I guess I had eight to ten seizures, till finally I stopped fighting them and said, 'I'm going to lie here and see what happens. If it kills me, OK, so it does.'"

That, in itself, was a remarkably cool approach, given the mysterious circumstances. "I made that decision and then I waited. The vibrational state came, but nothing else. It faded away after about five minutes. I was mildly disappointed.

"Weeks later, I was lying in bed on a Friday night, waiting for the vibrations to end. I was thinking the weather called for a good northwest wind the following day at Wurtsboro, where I was planning to go gliding, and how nice it would be to soar." Nothing could have been more coolly Monroe than that attempt at mental diversion in the midst of pain.

Then it happened. "The reason most of my medical and psychological friends give is that I was thinking of flying."

The first OOB's "really did scare me. They were spontaneous, of course, two or three times a week, always preceded by that vibrational state. The episodes usually happened in the first five minutes after I lay down.

"The first stage was getting over the fear. It was a process of trial and error. You can't imagine the state of panic those first experiences brought in me." It was a demonstration of the single-minded bravery which was to serve many thousands of people.

"I must have talked to Gordon five times about it. Dick was a friend as well as our doctor. Was it a tumor that was growing? He told me I was physiologically OK. He thought it was some kind of neurological state."

Bob discussed his experiences two or three times a week with the only person he felt he could really confide in, Foster Bradshaw. Bradshaw had an industrial psychology consulting firm. "He was a former dean at the University of North Carolina, and lived near us in Croton."

Bradshaw listened, in person or on the phone. "Sometimes he was bored. Sometimes he reacted. I didn't have any desire to share what I was going through with anyone else.

"You take the average person off the street, and put him through that experience—not knowing where to turn—to the degree it happened to me. . . ." Bob pauses and reiterates, ". . . to the degree it happened to me. . . .

"That whole process of trying to move from one place to another in space and time. Totally different from anything we knew. . ." The recollection, even thirty years on, leads Bob to frequent pauses, as he snaps back and forth between realities.

In *JOOB,* Monroe records the experience of checking in for a flight at Newark Airport in 1959, after the OOB's started. He boarded the plane with a vision from the previous night of a crash, but of his own survival. "I wondered whether I should take that plane, and I also wondered what the meaning of my survival was."

Bob suffered a heart attack after his arrival in Winston-Salem. He was hospitalized for three weeks.

* * * *

There occurred about this time a series of incidents which have led to confusion and misunderstanding of Bob Monroe on the part of some writers and their readers ever since.

Bob recalls the chronology: "There was an unusual side-effect to the heart attack. In the months prior to it, we had met Andrija Puharich, an M.D. who had conducted several ESP studies for a foundation up in New England. The meetings were quite pleasant, and Dr. Puharich was very friendly and personable.

"My wife, Mary, came down to visit me in the Winston-Salem hospital, and then returned to New York. She gathered together all the notes I had made on my OOB activity, made copies and took them to Puharich. She did it, she later told me, because he was a medical doctor who knew something about unusual states of consciousness, and because she thought he might know if the heart attack was related to or caused by my OOB's.

"Mary didn't mention it when I got back to New York. Not that she was hiding it, I'm sure. She simply forgot.

"Several years later, Puharich brought out his second book. By that time, our paths had taken us in different directions, not because we weren't friendly, but we were both busy.

"I was astonished to find a chapter on my activities in his book, thinly disguised. Most important, however, he had reworked my notes, moving parts entirely out of context, so as to convey that my Out-Of-Body's had begun as drug-related, the product of 'glue-sniffing.' "

In fact, the Puharich book devotes nearly eighteen pages to "Bob Rame's" notes and his own comments. "The key sentence in the author's introductory remarks is: "I have carefully checked the entire series of episodes and spent much time interviewing him. He writes as follows." The following text ascribes Monroe's early OOB's directly to "inhalation from a can" of liquid cement. [2]

"What had actually happened was that, in trying to figure out what was going on, I had gone back into my past and had recorded in my notes some sensations I had experienced while gluing a formica counter-top in a nearly-closed alcove in our house. This happened about a year before the onset of the OOB's.

"In his book, Puharich made it appear as if the two were the same event. He was heavily into reporting drug-related experiences; his first book dealt totally with such events.

"Mary was furious, and it was then that she told me how Puharich had obtained copies of my notes.

"He had used me in an attempt to tie the new book to the readership of his older work, in the opinion of those who reviewed the situation.

"We went to our attorney, Jonas Silverstone, to see if we could enjoin or sue Puharich. Jonas studied the case for several days.

"He said, 'We can start an action, and there's no doubt we'll win. But there will be a lot of publicity and the trial will not turn on the question of libel or slander, but on the question of your sanity.'

"I got the message and let it slide."

"When I finally encountered Andrija, his response was, 'I thought you'd like it.'

"It was one of the early events that led me to the firm conclusion that the woolly world of Consciousness Expansion does not necessarily include integrity, empathy, or honesty."

Bob still feels strongly on the point, because the Puharich publicity has dogged him ever since. A man of honor, Monroe still can't put aside the feeling of dismay the whole episode has caused in him. The fact that many other highly-respected and respectable people who today lead the serious Consciousness Movement started their experiences using drugs is not enough.

* * * *

It is nearly impossible to imagine the paradox of Bob's startlingly unconventional non-physical life in the late Eisenhower years, so devotedly intent on material well-being. It took someone as singular as Monroe to persevere, not only in the face of his own physical solitude, discomfort and fear, but in the atmosphere of the day.

Even a decade later, Bob's experiences would not have seemed all that untoward, because by then, the drug culture had made references to other realities and 'illusion' commonplace. But here was a straight citizen doing things people in the 1950s had not even dreamed of; or, if they had, they were probably frightened by vague thoughts of warlockry and witchcraft. Anyway, it all belonged in the netherworld of the Indian sub-continent, not to Croton-on-Hudson, USA.

"I was a conventional person, convinced of conventional reality. Whom could I talk to?"

The experiences were a challenge to the "conventional" engineer and innovator. Bob had himself as a research subject. "Luckily, I had that private company I could use for research and development, so we built a small laboratory with the first Chec Unit. Really, just a Faraday cage, a copper-screened cylinder which we charged with 100,000 volts. It hung from a rope.

"Eight months later, the situation hadn't changed. I could roll out, even with the charge isolating me."

"I developed some curiosity. I felt I was unique. At least I didn't know of anyone else who was doing the same thing. I looked in all the literature I could get my hands on." Monroe firmly believed he needed the information for his very survival and, as he later wrote, to "tame this unexpected wild talent.

"I was flat looking for help. I was still leading a 'normal life', doing business. I knew nothing about psi at the time, of course. I had only the vaguest idea of Eastern disciplines. I couldn't take the time to go to an ashram in India, which was the only place they were supposed to know about this kind of phenomenon. "

Many others did travel to the sub-continent and elsewhere to confirm what they had seen under drugs, particularly LSD. Bob was perhaps unique in the field, because he stayed home, and did his own exploration.

* * * *

Monroe sent an employee to look into ARE, the Association for Research and Enlightenment, which carries on the work of Edgar Cayce, the famous trance medium, at Virginia Beach. His messenger brought back some reassurance that at least someone else had had visions which defied "normal" explanation.

Monroe went to the leading parapsychological investigator in the country, J.B. Rhine, a professor at Duke University. He told his tale of extra-body exploration. Rhine listened courteously, then turned Bob away with the brief remark, "We don't work in that field." But a graduate student heard Monroe, and drew him aside to say, "I do it, too. Don't worry about it."

He visited Eileen Garrett, the only living OOB'er he knew of who was fully out of the closet. "Sure," she told Bob. "I do it all the time. It's handy to see if my slip is showing."

Bob says, frankly, "Some of the early OOB's took me to the full-fledged panic/terror stage.

"During the first ones, it wasn't so bad. I was in a familiar environment. There was the ceiling, the floor, the bed.

"I guess I thought I had it under control.

"But once, I was heading for Agnew Bahnson's lab in Winston-Salem. I'd done it before. No problem.

"A huge wind came up, like a tornado, and I went ass over teakettle, tumbling like a leaf, out of control. I was so confused...had no orientation...Tumbling an incredibly long time...." Bob voice's drops to nearly a whisper as he remembers.

"Then it was as if the wind went around a corner, and I was tossed off its flowstream, into a quiet spot.

"That wind wasn't seeking me out. I know it was a highly impersonal thing.

"Some people give it a religious connotation: The Devil's out to get you. Wrong. It was just a high wind, going somewhere.

"It happened three times over several years. It left me uncertain, disoriented.

"I had no idea where I was. How would I get back? I rubbed my physical fingers together, the system I normally used. It didn't work, so I just stretched and dove back in the direction of my physical body, and made it.

"But once I had done it, I had learned how to get back. The emergency technique." More stimulating things came along to investigate.

There was a block on Bob's progress he had to overcome. "Very early, I realized until I controlled the sex drive, I couldn't get more than ten feet away from my body. I was tethered by my need for sex, really. I had to divert that energy.

"I did so by what I call the Gene Autry technique. I'd tell my sexual urge, 'Not now. Later. But first....' It was a sort of delayed gratification."

"Once I got a handle on my sexual drive, it gave me a tremendous sense of freedom.

"The first breakthrough. The next problem was how to control the OOB's.

"I had some wild trips, looking for verification. I'd try to make runs down to Winston-Salem, where I might be able to check stuff. There I'd be, holding nicely over New York, and suddenly, bam, I'm sitting on the eaves of a house. How, why, I don't know.

"A woman looks up from carrying her laundry basket. She sees something on her roof, and she drops the basket.

"Now, what did she see?

"I was one hundred and two percent sure she actually *saw* something. But I don't know where I am, and don't have even a hope of finding out, so there's no way to check it.

"There was an awful lot of that kind of stuff....Lack of control. I'd be aimed at one place and end up in another."

Proof became very important. The memories are still deep-etched, thirty years later.

"I was trying to do a validation type of thing, and I'd get waylaid. I had no idea why.

"Once, I was aiming for a woman channeler in New York, by pre-arrangement. She even had a seat at her table ready and waiting for me. I made it, and got good documentation."

The only person he could talk to was Bradshaw, the psychologist when Foster had the time and the patience to listen. "He was at least interested, but he had no information. He would discuss what was happening rationally, but it was sort of like a boy saying, 'Let's you and him fight.' Egging me on. He wanted me to go and find out.

"It was an emotional loneliness.

"I didn't interpret the experience as mystical or religious. I wasn't out there visiting the angels and God, and I couldn't have accepted that interpretation, anyway."

* * * *

What was going on? In the late 1980s, he says, "I now know what was involved, but it's still very difficult to translate.

"I had found out it wouldn't kill me, but I needed proof it wasn't all hallucination.

"It took a year to convince myself that the reality I perceived was not an illusion. But I could only validate it to myself." It was deep into 1959 before Monroe found he could handle what was happening.

"Maybe it was the sixty-sixth well-validated event, somewhere in there. I just decided, 'I'll have to accept this.'"

He had long since started keeping a detailed diary of his journeys. "It's still around somewhere, probably down in all the stuff in storage in the barn. Foster Bradshaw recommended I do it.

"I kept on. It wasn't affecting my business life, this covert activity. Well, it did affect my family life, yes, but even that I covered up."

The frightening aspects of Out-Of-Body travel were often present, sometimes in new and startling form. "I met some savage beings.

"There weren't any fire-breathing, evil physical forms. Just a feeling of destruction. Dislodgements." The word sounds peculiar, but it's a Monroe-ism, covering deep disquiet, even today.

"Once, I found myself in a native village square, surrounded by primitive huts. There was jungle around the periphery. I tried to make friends with the natives. They backed away, and yelled among themselves, but I could understand them, 'Go get the ghost-catchers!'

"So the only thing I could do was shoot straight up and get out of there.

"I guess they were relieved when I took off."

Monroe recalls another episode. "Early in that period, I had four cats three of them Siamese, one standard brand domestic. One day, when I was in an OOB, here came these snakes undulating towards me. They were friendly, not poisonous. I pushed them away, and continued on my journey.

"From the other way, there came this striped snake. A rattler. I tried to wring its neck, and threw it away.

"Next morning, there were only three cats at home. My favorite, the striped one...I never saw her again. When you come to think of it, cats have such snake-like faces....

"I felt bad about that one for a long time."

Monroe regards these adventures as "part of The Learning Experience. I drifted into that type of situation almost to see what I would do. . .how I would handle it, but not of my own volition."

He turns thoughtful. "There are those who can synthesize that kind of experience for you. Now, I *know* that capability exists.

"At that time, I never would have thought so.

"We may, however, never truly see the whole learning experience.

"I'll give you an example: If I dress as a lieutenant in a Soviet Army uniform, that uniform presents me as a Soviet Army man. But I know that I am not, and it's always possible that I may be discovered not to be what I appear to be. That kind of thing."

Is human life a masquerade? A game which is part of the whole, greater Learning Experience? Bob leaves the question open for the listener to answer.

Agnew Bahnson, his fellow-flyer and close friend in Winston-Salem, was killed in a fiery plane crash. His corpse was so badly burned, the coffin was not open at his funeral.

"That's doing it the hard but quick way! I waited for three months after the accident, then I asked to meet his personality.

"I was escorted by a presence to a level surface and was told, 'Wait here.' Out of a vent a couple of inches in diameter in the floor, there came a whoosh of gas.

"It formed into Agnew. He excitedly told me of his new hi-tech activities. Then, the gas curled down into the hole again and was gone.

"I figured he had been in a reconstitution chamber under the floor, where he prepared to regain his physical appearance for me.

"When I saw him, he wasn't burned. He looked young and vigorous, just as I had remembered him."

And there was Dr. Dick Gordon, who went into a hospital, was opened up by surgeons and found to have cancer throughout his body. "He didn't tell anyone beforehand. I don't think he knew he was on the list." Gordon died shortly thereafter.

"Three months later, I went looking for him. I was assisted, again, and was accepted without curiosity. I didn't give it much thought by then.

"I was placed at a given spot, and an essence said, 'Doctor will see you now.' Just like that. There were a couple of guys standing on what looked like a stage. Then a lot of vibrations, and an eager guy rushed in.

"He turned and looked at me, hard. Sort of stared, and said, 'I see you.'"

Bob soon thereafter saw a photograph of Gordon as a young man. "It was exquisite. Just as he looked when I saw him in the OOB state."

Bob Monroe saw his Father, as he recorded in *JOOB,* but years later he had a different experience with his Mother.

"I sent her the manuscript of *JOOB.* She read it and said she'd like to talk to me.

"Several months later, I got a call from Emmett, who said she could only last a couple of days more. I flew to Sandusky that night.

"I wouldn't have recognized her, except for her bright blue eyes. I took her hand, and she rolled her eyes back, and said, 'Ooooh!' Her jaw was slack. It happened three or four times. Just 'Oooooh!' Finally, she said, 'That was very interesting.'

"She had waited until I got there. She had read the script and she wanted to show me she could do it—establish her beachhead before she crossed and made the landing. She had hung around long enough.

"That was on a Sunday. On Tuesday, I was driving to work in Charlottesville. Suddenly, I noticed a very profound presence in the seat beside me. It was very specific. Mother. She had come to say good-bye.

"I couldn't see her, but I felt her. She stroked my hand on the steering wheel for maybe ten seconds. Later I discovered, this happened about three minutes after she was pronounced dead.

"I looked for her later during OOB's, but I never found her. It puzzled me, because I felt sure I could, as I had found my father.

"Ten or twelve years later, I think it was, one of the Explorers [3] reported my Mother had already come back. A quick turnaround. She'd done it because she still had something she really wanted to do.

"She was a musician, remember, and she played the cello. She even had a family string quartet at one time.

"But she never really played seriously, or got any recognition.

"The Explorer gave me the name of a little girl in a village in Italy, and her birthdate.

"I never looked it up. The information is around somewhere in the tapes.

"Still, it's beyond a guess. I know that's where Mother went. To Italy. To live in music."

* * * *

By the early 1960s, Mary and Bob Monroe had little common territory.

"When I got into radio ownership, I went to Winston-Salem a lot." Sometimes, Mary came along on the trips; Agnew Bahnson gave the Monroes entree to the tobacco-and-hunting society of the southern community. Mary "enjoyed the horsey set, but she didn't ride."

Mostly, Mary stayed at home. She "never did get into the sailing run. I took her gliding maybe four times."

"She was busy with her own life, don't forget. She had the two girls to take care of. I left their upbringing to her."

Mary never told Bob why she hadn't made it to the top as a singer. She told him little about her first marriage. Or why she returned home to Boston after being the Chesterfield Girl and singing on The Perry Como Show. Mary's sense of disappointment over a stunted career may have been a factor in her increasingly preoccupied state.

In the early days of Bob's OOB's, Mary "doubted them very heavily. Oh, she wasn't contemptuous." Bob leans back, looks at the ceiling, strokes his fringe beard. "She didn't take part in them, although she did participate in the fallout from the early ones."

Mary witnessed some verifications, done by Bob, Foster Bradshaw and his wife, Linda. "I did some tests with them, by appointment. I'd tell them what they had been doing at a particular pre-arranged time.

"It was something different to talk about then, in Croton...a peculiar type of prestige. So, in the early days, she wasn't completely divorced from it all.

"And it began that a number of people were in and out of the house who were of interest to her. People who were a novel sideband entry into our lives.

"I guess you might say she liked to indulge in the notoriety of what I was doing.

"But...well, maybe it was resentment, which started to grow when others got involved. It was no longer just our secret to share with one or two other people. I guess her emotional requirements were too heavy."

Despite the dismay and emotional upset of the times, Monroe, the engineer, persevered with his exploration of the OOB state.

"By 1959, I had developed the concept of Focus 10." It is the state of Mind Awake,

Body Asleep that has become the first step in the Gateway program, familiar to thousands of Monroe students from the mid-1970s to the present day.

1960s

One Saturday afternoon in the late autumn, Bob Monroe sits, owl-eyed in front of the huge TV monitor he has hooked up to his word-processor.

"Let's change venues," he grunts, and he strolls over to the second room of his private refuge on the crest of Roberts Mountain. It is a sitting arrangement in front of a fireplace. In the corner, the electronic keyboards which will one day help Bob compose the Life Symphony. A few bookcases. A man's den, complete to well-worn furniture, and a watercolor of the Space Shuttle taking off.

Bob Monroe bought radio station WRGM in Richmond, and the Monroes moved from Croton to Richmond in 1961. He brought with him a lab assistant, his OOB lab equipment and the records he had compiled.

"I still had my love of the ocean, and I wanted to be near the water. I took a map, and drew a parallel from Lexington, Kentucky, because I liked the climate there. It crossed Richmond, so that was that." In 1964, Bob moved from Richmond to Charlottesville, and discovered the area which was to be his final seat.

Monroe managed to continue his covert life as an apprentice Out of Body explorer despite a series of business ups and downs.

He found the commercial atmosphere in Richmond unpleasant and puzzling. There was a lot of cut-throat competition. What was most baffling was that Bob had done big business on the strength of a handshake in the major leagues of New York; in Richmond, he had to have airtight contracts, and his debtors still welshed. There were times when money to pay the radio station's bills was tight.

Monroe got into Cable Television in a peculiar way. It began because he went to El Paso in 1962, to weight the acquistion of another radio station. Bob was accompanied on the trip by a media broker. On the plane back to the East, the broker happened to mention "CATV"—Cable-Antenna Television, as it was then called. The broker's casual reference alerted Monroe to the possibility of a new business venture.

"Richmond was too big. It would have required an investment of ten to twenty million, which we didn't have." He discovered he could get the franchise for Charlottesville.

Thereupon, Bob Monroe plunged into the new Cable TV industry. He sold the radio stations to raise cash for the venture. When the Charlottesville system was about half completed, nearby Waynesboro—an industrial rather than academic community—wanted Cable too. Monroe's company tried to oblige, but it's resources were stretched thin. "We had a situation, in time, where we had two systems, each only half-installed and half-operational. If you don't think we felt pressure from the people on one side of the street who didn't have it, when their neighbors across the way did, you're mistaken."

The solution to the capital problem? Sell stock to raise money to complete both jobs. "When I shifted from radio station ownership into Cable TV, I first had an insurance outfit in Roanoke as a partner. Shenandoah Life Insurance. The president and vice-president backed me. Real fine people.

"They put up four hundred thousand dollars. It was the company's largest single investment, and they were nervous. Cable was an entirely new deal to them. When we had to take on Waynesboro as well as Charlottesville, they didn't have the cash to put into our expansion.

"So we decided to put their shares and some of mine up. It was a very friendly parting. We never had a contract. Everything done on a handshake basis.

"The purchaser was American Financial Systems, a financial house." Bob's new partners in the Jefferson Cable Corporation provided the two-year bridging period necessary to complete the installations and sell the services to subscribers.

The Charlottesville system was finished in 1963. It was, says Bob, the second operational twelve-channel Cable TV system in the country. Waynesboro followed in 1964. Emmett Monroe comments of his brother, "His getting into Cable TV that early may have been another indication of his pioneering. Or his prescience."

Monroe's company remained for a while longer in Richmond, which had the innocent side-effect of leaving that city without Cable for years: Everyone in the business assumed Monroe had the franchise, when in fact, he had never been interested.

"Eventually, we built the company up to ten cities, as far south as Lafayette, Louisiana. Charlottesville was the hub.

"We bought a feature film package from a major film distributor, and we instituted one of the first 24-hour movie channels.

"Why, we even had the old Saturday afternoon matinee serials I'd known as a kid. We'd run one episode each evening before the news, then run the entire week's quarter-hours back to back on Saturday afternoons; we had the audience locked in. It was a big hit.

"To show you how far ahead of our times we were. . . . We had a small mail order channel even then. A call-in system. But it wasn't making enough money to justify the overhead of a live camera crew, so we dropped it.

"The Cable Business took a lot of time. It's not a stable activity. Especially if you're starting up. You've got to find the people, train them, buy everything, dig up the streets, string the wires.

"By about 1969, the Cable companies were operating very well. I worked at them daily into the '70s."

* * * *

Monroe also invested in student apartment complexes. Most of Bob's excursions into business other than the media involved a certain degree of idealism. But there was other reasoning as well behind his optimistic ventures in the late 1960s and early 1970s. It emerges slowly.

"I needed funding for my Out-Of-Body research. It was that simple. I went into the modular home business specifically to make money for the OOB activity. That was Monroe Industries (now Interstate Industries Inc.), which had nothing to do with the Jefferson Cable Co.

"I figured the cash flow would support the research, and I could spin Monroe

Industries into more R & D activities.

"I started out to build modular housing for students. The idea was, we would sell units to their parents, then buy them back when the students left the University, and turn them over again. Two-family duplexes, six miles south of the city. We used a three-box system of modules, which gave us flexibility in construction." Bob detours off in fond reminiscence of the technicalities of prefab house construction.

"But, well, we depended on a company in Charlottesville to supply the modules and it went bankrupt. We thought about it, and decided to build our own.

"Then we began to build rural housing for the Farm Home Administration: Poor farmers could get houses and pay only thirty nine dollars a month. It was a great deal for them!

"We got into something else, with a builder-architect." The aim was to build prefab housing "for the little guy, so he could live comfortably, but not overspend." That operation fell apart because Bob feels he misplaced his trust. Monroe was caught short of capital, and his partner refused to continue payments while local authorities haggled over zoning restrictions. By the time officialdom delivered its favorable verdict, it was too late; the business had gone down the drain.

Many years later, Bob's laconic statements mask that anguish. "The short of it was . . . . we lost the FHA contract because of some political upheaval in Washington, and we lost the deal with the architect because he had local political connections, and we didn't stand a chance in court. So we closed the construction business down. We didn't have much choice."

"Bob doesn't handle failure well," says Nancy Penn Monroe of that dismal time. "He's sensitive to the fact he's hurting people when things don't work. He feels he lets them down." The same sentiments had gnawed at him when he was working in Monroe Productions in New York, and a good number of people were dependent on him.

"The thing is that Bob snaps out of it fast. He says, 'We have to move on.' He's always looking ahead, not behind. But he was hurt by those housing messes."

There was an episode which underlines Monroe's aversion to drugs and alcohol, and shows Bob Monroe does have a temper, even if it flares rarely: "I got a phone call one day that the fraternity boys from the house next to our apartment complex had set fire to the new, palisade-type fence I had put in to protect our development. They were burning it down!

"I raced over, and I found myself confronting several football types, each well over 200 pounds. I said, 'OK, if you want to play tough, I'll play tough, too. I grabbed a beer bottle out of the trash, and broke its neck, then I waited, with that jagged edge in my hand. By now the fire engines were arriving.

"One of them said, 'That's not fair.' I replied 'You've got 100 pounds on me. It's fair, all right.' " Nancy still speaks with some awe of the sight of her husband in cold fury.

* * * *

By the mid-1960s, "I already knew major changes were coming into the pattern. I didn't mysticize it at all. If you hear thunder in the distance, you know there's going to be a storm."

"I was shifting into Cable, and writing *Journeys*. I was still a go-to-the-office type . . . .

Bob's voice drops. "I suppose my personal relationship with Mary really began to deteriorate at the time of the move from Richmond." The Monroes moved to Charlottesville in 1965.

By now, "Mary wasn't part of my OOB activity. At the house we had on Ballard Road, Charlottesville, I'd usually do OOB's in the middle of the night." But there was no longer even a hint of sharing the adventure with his wife.

The couple went to see a marriage counselor, a Roman Catholic priest, in whose parish they lived. Father Michael talked to each Monroe separately several times, then called them in, together. He said, "I have to tell you I give this marriage a ten percent chance of continuing." With that, he walked out of the room, leaving Mary, a Catholic, aghast. It was the closest a priest could come to suggesting divorce.

By the time they separated, Maria was in college and Bob had arranged to send Laurie to boarding school in Pennsylvania, because he knew what was coming and wanted their daughters to suffer the least possible hurt.

The memory surfaces as Bob sits in his four-wheel drive wagon. He props his elbow on the open window frame, cups his forehead in his hand, looks at bare trees and a crystal Virginia sky.

It had been a glossy-magazine 1950s marriage: The glittering couple near the top of the show business heap. Then someone dimmed the marquee lights, and the pair came down to the physical reality of making a day-to-day partnership work.

"Country club membership was important to Mary, but I didn't care about it." Bob circles the still-tender topic delicately. "Well, I did become a member of the local hunt club. When we were divorced, they detached me from membership. It would have been fun to have been a Ross Perot, and sued the daylights out of them for discrimination . . . ."

"In around 1967, the decision was made to separate. By 1968, we were living apart.

"She moved back to Richmond . . . . maybe three, six months later.

"For a while, I lived in temporary rentals. I had bought into that property-owning partnership in Charlottesville. I'd go to the general partner to find a place, and he'd say, 'Sure, I got one for you.' Can you imagine—living in a penthouse in Charlottesville! I did!

"Then, when Mary left, I moved back to the house at Ballard Road, and put it on the market. It sold quickly.

"My separation agreement and divorce from Mary required a financial settlement, not alimony. Mary was very cautious. She knew I was working on *JOOB*, of course, but she didn't think it would be a success."

Had he truly loved Mary? The answer was slow in coming. "No, not in terms I understand love to be today.

"She was an excellent partner, don't get me wrong.

"It is all unemotional to me now." A statement that has to be made, to keep up the pretense of the impervious male.

But then, Bob brightens, "Somewhere in there, Nancy came on the scene."

Nancy Penn Honeycutt first knew Bob and Mary Ashworth Monroe in Richmond in early 1961. Then her Marine Corps husband was reassigned for a three-year tour of duty in California. Nancy returned to Charlottesville because one of the girls was in school there.

Between them, Bob and Nancy have six children. Nancy has three daughters, Virginia Penn Holmes, or Penny, who lives in South Carolina; Nancy Lea Honeycutt McMoneagle, known around the Institute as Scooter; Lucinda Beale Honeycutt or Cindy, who lives in North Carolina; and a son, A.J. (Terry) Honeycutt, who lives near Hartford,

Connecticut. With Mary Ashworth, Bob had Maria, the daughter from Mary's first marriage. And Laurie was born to Mary and Bob in 1951. Maria is married and lives in Richmond, Laurie is in Tampa.

"When we came back from California, Nancy separated from her husband, and was waiting the full legal year for her divorce. I hired her as apartment manager, and she did an excellent job of it."

Nancy did not pursue Bob, after Mary left. It just happened. They recognized kindred souls in each other, and they shared some deeply metaphysical experiences, which remain highly personal.

With Nancy Senior came Scooter, who was to play a major role in Bob's future. Nancy Lea was born in 1952. Her mother, says Scooter, is "pretty psychic." At the age of ten or eleven, Scooter starting having dreams in which she flew—and then tried to prove them to her school friends by jumping off the living room couch.

Scooter's first memory of Bob Monroe is of the help he gave her mother—well before they were married—on a book she was writing. Although "Mr. Monroe" was formidable to the teenager, Scooter was intrigued by Bob, and started asking questions. "He never gave me a straight answer. He'd put a hook into me and drag the answer out. He was a great mentor for me," even then.

Soon enough, Bob installed one of the old cumbersome reel-to-reel tape decks by Scooter's bed. He made a special tape for her, which began with an affirmation she still remembers: "I choose to know and understand myself, to the extent that I can experience complete control of myself."

Scooter was also fascinated by the Monroe house on Ballard Road, which contained Bob's music studio, and was mostly gadgets. He had a piece of aluminum mounted on glass which gave off rainbow hues. He made glasses ring with tuning forks. It was magic. We experimented with names for him. Uncle Bob. Mo-Mo." Soon, Bob became Dad.

By the time she was sixteen, Scooter was a frequent Out-Of-Body traveler. On one occasion, she encountered Nancy and Bob, and painted a watercolor of all three of them looking at the Universe. Then she experienced an unsettling series of visions in which a goatee'd man with penetrating eyes appeared close to her face. He laughed "almost diabolically." Bob calmly advised the teenager to ask the man what he wanted, and that ended the apparition.

Scooter read everything she could find on metaphysics and parapsychology. Bob tutored her in ways of thinking outside the confines of conventional schooling.

* * * *

In Charlottesville during the early Cable TV days, Bob was so immersed in his mundane life, the OOB's dwindled to "quite sporadic." Then Mary left and Bob's life changed.

"When I was living in Charlottesville proper, we had a covert lab. I rented a basement room in the name of one of my companies, RAM Enterprises, a strictly legitimate commercial operation." But in the lab and with new circumstances at home, Bob quickened his development as an OOB explorer.

What precisely is an Out-Of-Body Experience? For the layman, there may be three acceptable definitions.

The first is the hallucinogenic drug trip, usually associated with LSD, but also induced by certain types of mushrooms, and other exotic, mind-altering substances. These drugs produce experiences which are similar to the non-drugged OOB.

The second is the kind of episode Bob Monroe at first endured, later enjoyed: The ability to separate from his physical body, observe it from close-at-hand, or later from a considerable distance, move his other self through obstacles; in general, to dis-locate from the physical casing, which then remains observable back at home base.

The third, and perhaps more common experience, is, more properly, what Charles Tart dubbed an Altered State of Consciousness, but is often thought of as an OOB: "A qualitative alteration in the overall pattern of mental functioning, such that the experimenter feels his consciousness is radically different from the way it functions ordinarily."[1]

Drs. Glen O. Gabbard and Stuart Twemlow came up with a composite: "An altered state of consciousness in which the subject feels that his mind or self-awareness is separated from his physical body and that this sense of self-awareness is more vivid and more real than a dream."[2]

* * * *

No one can, of course, duplicate Monroe's own dual life of the 1960s and early 1970s: outwardly, the respectable businessman, inwardly the night-time adventurer into a realm which was practically unknown. In New York, in the early days, there were Foster Bradshaw, and later, Agnew Bahnson in Winston-Salem whom he could visit and with whom he could talk, if he didn't get sidetracked. They understood, at least partially.

Bob could not share his images and visions with Mary, who was, by the time they were in Charlottesville, no longer interested. At about the same time, Charley Tart was a welcome and compassionate companion, but he, too soon left Monroe's immediate orbit. Now Nancy and Scooter came on the scene to give welcome relief from the loneliness and the feeling of apartness.

* * * *

Bob Monroe doesn't internalize; it's not part of the engineer's discipline. He reports, as in his books, but he tells little of what his feelings and his emotions were as he steadfastly challenged the unknown over the years, and pushed even farther out into seldom-glimpsed realms. What description he does give of the turmoil within him comes only haltingly.

To give a small approximation of what must have gone through Bob Monroe's physical consciousness, I can offer only feeble personal analogies. The samples are weak, because I have never had a negative trip—certainly nothing to compare with Bob's vivid experiences of downright unpleasantness, threat, and hostility. The best that can be said of them, as an illustrative device, is that I know I share them in common with other Monroe graduates as well.

At the Center, I do not hesitate in the slightest after embarking on any voyage. I feel cossetted and safe. At first, all of us in a Gateway Voyage are, perhaps, nervous, but we draw unspoken courage from the presence of others in nearby Chec Units. The trainers are at hand, and, in a real jam, Bob can come hustling down the mountain to help. Above all, we know we are only experiencing what countless others who have gone before have learned: It's new for us, and a marvel, but it isn't, really, like, say, Christopher Columbus sailing off to the brink of the world.

Practically everyone who has done Monroe exercises knows the feeling of being out there and not wanting to come back; even of resentment when Bob's taped voice gently calls you to return to physical reality. It's so enticing, warm, gentle, loving; who wants to re-enter, to face the nightly news, supermarkets, and phone bills?

So there is that fear: That if I do a tape alone, at home, I might decide or be persuaded not to come back to my physical, earthly body. There is, too, just a shadow of fear that I might get on a trip which was radically new, going into truly unexplored realms, just me, alone. I tell myself, repeatedly that my belief systems have changed. Now, *I know;* there is no fear. And then—no matter how much I may have benefitted from the Monroe courses I have taken—on the verge of an exercise at home, in bed, there comes just that little tug of doubt.

Is there really Someone Out There who's ready to help me? Can I truly believe all I have previously experienced? What is dream, what is reality? There aren't any comforting green route signs, and there's no automobile club to ask for highway information. I'm volunteering to go on my own. And apart from the companionship of physical life, I'm leaving all my comfortable, well-known, tangible surroundings, to venture to . . . well . . . where?

There is an element of hold-back in contemplation, too, of what I may find, no matter how much I have previously prepared myself and been cleansed; no matter how positive, beneficial, and constructive I think my motives may be. Are they really? There is the deeply-ingrained, post-victorian upbringing still in me. Aren't I violating some of the rules by doing this?

I affirm before I start my trip that I am open to whatever may come my way: Knowledge so shaking, I wonder whether I can handle it when I return to physical life, without someone else present to help ground me, and with whom I can immediately discuss what I have just learned. It can be as shattering as a Divine revelation to a devout Christian; the knowledge of a heretofore only-suspected role in life; future or past lives, some of them perhaps unpleasant and gory; it can be a vision of another planet, or of profound wisdom, perhaps the essence of Life itself. All of it pretty heady stuff, and tough for anyone to digest on his own.

I recall my week of racking tears at Gateway, when I had to unload what was happening to me on someone. I could not contain it within me, no matter how shielded by apartness I had felt throughout my life. None of it is threatening of itself, but it's pretty heavy baggage to carry alone.

Then there's the post-op syndrome. If I have such a shaking experience by myself, and then walk out into the everyday world, will I be able to conduct myself "normally?" Will my behavior remain consistent with my previous self? Will I stay sane? Will something happen to me out There which will unalterably change me Here?

Many of us hesitate to do tapes or go on voyages at home, even if there is someone around who knows what we are up to. And this, too, even though the Interstate has been well explored by Bob and others. These are some of my reluctances in 1988—thirty years after Monroe started doing his OOBs completely on his own. It's hard to imagine his fear, his loneliness, and his courage.

* * * *

Monroe had conquered his fear of the Out-Of-Body state by the beginning of the 1960s. Then he amends the statement, "Well, sure, there was still fear in it sometimes.

"More, I was seeking verification all the time. But there was no scientific authority which could give me what I needed."

There was one curious episode in the early 1960s which became part of the Monroe lore. "I was up in Hyannis, Massachusetts, and I went OOB one night. I got over a large house, and suddenly I ran up against some very, very tough non-physical guards. They made it unmistakably clear that if I didn't leave the space over the house instantly, they would wring my neck, or something to that effect. And they weren't kidding. They were bruisers. I left, very quickly."

It was only the next day that Bob learned by chance the President John F. Kennedy was at the Kennedy family compound in nearby Hyannisport.

* * * *

In late 1965, a couple of years after Charles T. Tart got his Ph.D. at the University of North Carolina, he came to the University of Virginia to teach medical residents about hypnosis and to do research under Professor Ian Stevenson, a parapsychologist. Bob says, "Charley got in touch with me and we immediately became close friends. We had a lot of fun together." Tart has remained part of the Monroe scene ever since.

Charley Tart is today one of only a handful of full professors of psychology who also study parapsychology in the Western world. He is a member of the Monroe Institute's Board of Advisers, and is Senior Research Fellow of the Institute of Noetic Sciences; he writes prodigously, runs seminars, gives lectures: He's a man in full flight at all times, and much of his effort is bent to making the world of psi more acceptable to the populace. He wrote the classic *Altered States of Consciousness*[3] and the recent *Waking Up*.

Tart is today firmly lodged at the University of California, Davis. That, in itself, seems an unlikely perch for a world-class parapsychologist, since Davis is far better known as a pioneer in agricultural research and, indeed, used to be solely an agriculture school. Tart says loyally, "It's an outmoded stereotype. Davis has been offering everything for twenty five years. Our Psychology Department is in the top ten in the country in terms of publication in scientific journals affiliated with the American Psychological Association." Davis suits Tart to a 'T' since the university has given him tenure and the freedom to do what he chooses.

One of the first bonds between Monroe and Tart was that Charley had worked his way through college at radio stations. At age eighteen, he had an FCC Class I engineer's license.

Along the way to lasting friendship, the two men designed and built what they called "Lori Lights," named after the ancient sea sirens. Some are still around the Institute: Globes which reflect and throw off kaleidoscopic colored light patterns as an aid to meditation—or just for fun. They were never mass-produced because Monroe and Tart did not have the start-up capital to get the venture going.

On first encounter, Tart gives the impression that the visitor has abruptly wakened him from a nice snooze in the hayloft of the barn, but he's immediately more than cordial, and his mind is never anything but incisive: Charley is a rustic, jeans-clad man with a bicycle pack, his hair semi-long and untended. He has an elfin face which registers constant, amused, but gentle and hopeful amazement at what the "real" world does to itself.

Tart says, simply, of Bob, "I liked the guy. He was a genuinely decent, friendly person. We'd bounce ideas off each other...wild ideas...."

In late 1965, Bob was stretched thin by the demands of the Cable company. Charley comments today, "I have often had the feeling he was on the brink of financial ruin, but especially at that time."

But despite his preoccupation with business, "Bob always found time to talk about the really interesting stuff. He was glad to have someone like Judy (Tart) and me to talk to. I could give him some scientific perspective on what was happening to him."

Over the centuries, there had, of course, been psychic literature on OOBs. In the 1920s, academic interest in the phenomenon died out. Hornell Hart did some exploration of the spontaneous OOB phenomenon in the 1950s at Duke University.

Tart remembers, "There were a couple of other parapsychologists at UVa who had not been interested in talking to him. He understood they were specialized, but it bothered him intellectually that he was shut out."

Tart, for his part, was, "particularly happy Bob had no background in the field. He was a metaphysical virgin.

"At the time, he didn't talk to me about fear. He did talk about his aloneness. It was one of the things that brought us together."

Tart recalls, "It was quite clear this guy wasn't making up his stories. He was reporting too clearly. They were definitely OOBs. The question was: Did that mean he was literally at a particular place? That's what we wanted to find out.

"He had doubts, and I did, too. We shared a body of acceptance and skepticism. Over the years, what research in the field had been done indicated some OOBs may be dreams or imagination, but that others were real.

"Was he really going some other place?

"Conceptually, we could come up with a precise definition of what we were talking about.

"But the actual experience...that's something else."

Charley was now set to pioneer a new field of scientific inquiry on deliberate Out-Of-Body Experiences. He was the first academic to take Bob seriously, and to devise lab tests which attempted to measure what was happening during Bob's OOBs.

Typically, "Bob was curious. He wanted to see if he could do an OOB under lab conditions. He was disappointed the results weren't unequivocal...that we couldn't consistently prove something psychic was happening. But he felt he didn't look so odd."

In The Cabin on Roberts Mountain, Bob Monroe recalls the first, benchmark Tart experiment.

"He didn't have any official sponsorship that I knew of." In fact, Tart adds he did not need sponsorship to conduct the Monroe tests, which fitted in with his official research program.

Monroe continues, "Charley initially suggested doing some stuff at the UVa sleep lab, because I didn't have any EEG [Electro-encephalogram] equipment available.

"I don't know how many times I spent the night there, attempting willfully to go OOB, and read some numbers on a wall in the control room." Bob reports the experience in *JOOB*. "They put electrodes on my earlobes, which were at first an annoyance, then I got used to them.

"Finally, I was able to roll out. It was pretty profound. I was so excited I was able to do it under those conditions! I was dog-paddling along the floor of the lab, out through the door to the control room. I wanted to tell the girl who was supposed to be monitoring in there, 'Hey! Look! I can do it!'

"But to my utter astonishment, there was nobody there. I looked around, and there she was, down the hall talking with a guy." The ever-chivalrous Monroe hastens to add that the woman wasn't necking or doing anything improper. Just standing there talking. "Maybe with a boyfriend," he adds.

"I tried to attract her attention, danced around them. I was totally unsuccessful.

"It was 1:00 a.m. or so. All the doors were open. I went back into my body, and called out, and she came running.

"I told her about what had happened. It would have been impossible for me to have seen what I saw in the physical state.

"I simply couldn't have detached the electrodes from my ears, and then put them back on. I was wired up and plugged in.

"It was an evidential piece of data. I had been there and seen her. I described the guy perfectly.

"She maintained at first she had been in the control room—where she was supposed to be. Then she confessed she had been talking to the guy, after we told her she wouldn't get into trouble."

Tart reported the tests with academic dryness:

"Mr. X was monitored for nine sessions at various times between December 1965 and August 1966. Eight of the sessions were in the evening, generally from nine to midnight or later. I ran the equipment for the first four sessions; a technician . . . for the later sessions. In addition, a full-scale clinical EEG report on Mr. X was obtained from Dr. Lever Stewart of the University of Virginia Hospital. . . .

"Further work with Mr. X is needed, and in the future, I hope to be able to continue this sort of study with better physiological recording techniques. . . .

"I would like to point out that the most important aspect of the present investigation . . . is the demonstration that OOB's and similar 'exotic' phenomena are not mysterious happenings beyond the pale of scientific investigation . . . if these studies should encourage other investigators to work with people who have such experiences rather than automatically dismiss their experiences as 'weird,' they will be making a lasting contribution." [4]

Monroe recalls other experiments with Tart that followed. "He put me in a group in his house in Charlottesville. I spent all day listening to Oriental music. Around one in the afternoon, a great "Ah Ha!" hit me.

"From that point on, I appreciated Oriental music: It was a musical interpretation of people having a non-verbal conversation! Their individual personalities were expressed by the instrument that was used, instead of by a voice. The conversation was the harmonic, melodic pattern.

"I still get enthralled when I hear it now. It's real for me."

It was the period when psychedelic drugs could still be legally used in clinical experiments. Dr. John C. Lilly, Timothy Leary, Richard Alpert (Ram Dass), and even Bill Wilson, the co-founder of Alcoholics Anonymous, experimented under lab conditions, especially with LSD, before the drug was withdrawn from the market.

"Charley Tart thought he'd like to see what effect drugs would have on me. He gave me some mescaline. It was a Saturday. About nine in the morning, I swallowed a pill. Charley sat there, looking at me expectantly.

"An hour later, he was still staring at me, looking into my eyes. I didn't feel anything.

"Around one, he gave me another. It only made me vomit. The only other thing was, it seemed to enhance my hearing. Otherwise, blank.

"A month later, I went back to Charlie's house. He had a gleam in his eye.

"He said, 'This isn't street stuff, it's lab stuff. Pure.' It was LSD.

"I felt very comfortable with Charley as an objective monitor. He was very empathetic.

"He gave me a dose. Maybe 200 micrograms; I'm not sure. Anyway, it was huge.

"We sat and talked and not a single thing happened."

"Charley was disappointed. He said, 'Go on home. The stuff has absolutely no effect on you.' I didn't feel any after-effects either. Nothing."

At any rate, there had been some progress in verification. After a couple of years, Charley Tart left UVa to take the better position at Davis.

When Tart left Charlottesville, Monroe says, "He passed the word quietly to two assistants in the department. Those two guys started to help us surreptitiously and voluntarily. We became a release point for them, an escape from the confines of academic discipline."

Resettled on the West Coast, Charley Tart started to write of his findings with Bob Monroe in learned journals. Bob remembers the articles had a semi-comic side effect. "People began to call the university in Charlottesville, asking for me. They thought I was attached to the University of Virginia in some official capacity. It made the academics very uncomfortable.

"In fact, the Psychiatry Department became downright angry. They told me I had no right to claim I was part of the university.

"People got through to me eventually, and told me the UVa people had been caustic and rude. I telephoned the chairman and said, 'What's going on? The last thing we want is to be known as associates of UVa.' We had lunch and smoothed the whole thing over."

Later, Bob wrote Ian Stevenson, the chairman, suggesting some radical experiments. "I proposed they explore planes of anaesthesia without the pain and anxiety of surgery. For instance, when an anaesthesiologist gives you a shot, you go through various stages.

"Back in the old days, surgeons used alcohol, and to knock a man out was a very dangerous thing. If you gave him too much, he could die; the margin between unconciousness and death was very thin. Then along came ether and chloroform. Each better than the last.

"The anaesthesiologists could reel patients out through the various planes, more and more, under control. They led, of course, to present-day anaesthetics.

"We thought of using all forms of anaesthetic to explore the states of consciousness.

"We wanted to converse with volunteers as they were going through the planes. It would still be a fascinating study, if anyone would do it."

Not surprisingly, perhaps, "Stevenson didn't like the idea, but it gave him second thoughts about human 'experimentation.' "

* * * *

Tart leans back, comfortable in his nest of papers, posters and odd pieces of equipment, and reflects on the mid-1960s.

"It's not very scientific, I know, but can one speculate....

"Here was the one scientist in the country who was doing research into OOBs; who just happened to come to Charlottesville; and who happened to become friends with Bob Monroe.

"Bob is one of the rare people in the last fifty years who made himself available to be measured in this field."

Charley Tart defines the puzzlement of the Out-Of-Body Experience: "Our society calls everything we experience during sleep 'dreaming.' Ninety-eight percent of the world's cultures distinguish between OOBs and dreams. But many people go OOB every night. That's their subjective reality, but it's not an objective one.

"In our culture, we have the physical—'The Real'—and the unreal, nothing in between. There's no middle ground for the true spiritual experience, for instance: There's no way to check it."

"Someone can say, and believe, 'I was somewhere else. My mind was alert.' Then society asks him to prove it, which he can't do. And he starts to ask, 'Where am I, really?'

"That person could be quite mad by society's standards, but genuine in his 'madness': He wouldn't be putting me on."

Tart and others in the tiny group of parapsychologists face the same problems in their efforts that the maverick scientists of Chaos have had to contend with in their disciplines.[5]

Many people in the American Psychological Association are vehemently opposed to research in the field of parapsychology at all. Tart himself gets grudging recognition: He is invited to read papers at prestigious scientific meetings, but the academic trade union feels uncomfortable with the paranormal.

The reasons aren't hard to determine: If every parapsychological phenomena were proven, members of the psychological establishment—as many others—would be embarrassed at having missed the boat for so long.

There are perhaps two or three dozen full-time parapsychologists in the whole United States. The Psychophysical Research Laboratory, an independent facility at Princeton, not affiliated with the university, faced closure in 1988, for lack of funds. "If it goes, one of the few set-ups of its type will disappear," remarks Tart sadly.

Arthur Koestler endowed a chair at Edinburgh University, but other than that, the field is too controversial for the public to support wide-ranging research. Tart estimated research funds available in the field at half a million dollars in 1977. Today he muses, the figure might have doubled. Tart thinks the Soviets might be spending fifty times that much on parapsychological research.

* * * *

Throughout the mid-to-late 1960s, Bob Monroe was devoting considerable energy to writing *Journeys Out Of The Body*, even despite the fluctuating and often distressing pressures of his business and personal life.

"Remember, I had spent a lot of the early 1950s writing hack stuff."

"This time, I figured I had something really worth writing about. I had the mass of notes going all the way back to the beginning, and I figured, maybe. . . ." As so often, the soft voice trails off.

"I'm not sure exactly why I did it."

"The OOB's were a fairly lonely run. I had a great deal of trepidation. Revealing the covert side of my life . . . I had no idea what the effect would be.

"I didn't really know if it could be written about. Or whether it would be acceptable for publication. I said so in the first paragraph of *Journeys.*"[6]

"I had gone through so much intense trial and error... I guess I thought if nothing else... if someone else had gone through something similar, and it helped them, it was OK...."

It was something very, very deeply felt.... That ongoing loneliness...."

From the very beginning, the engineering-trained Monroe literally dropped back into his body from an OOB, rolled off the cot in the shack at Croton or in the Charlottesville basement, and sat down at his typewriter. Those instant-replay notes help to explain the clarity and color of Monroe's reportage.

Charley Tart doesn't remember whether he encouraged Bob Monroe to write *JOOB,* but he did play a key role in the publication of the book. Monroe sent him a copy of the script. Charley recalls today, "Bob also sent a copy to an agent. He waited, and waited, and didn't hear anything. I took it upon myself to send my copy to Bill Whitehead, my editor (for *Altered States of Consciousness*) at Doubleday.

"Bill took it home, and read it till four in the morning. He told me he stopped at the 'How To Do It' chapter, because he was afraid he might have an OOB."

Monroe was sitting in the Cable company office in Charlottesville, when Bill Whitehead called to say, "We'd like to publish the book." Monroe asked in genuine puzzlement, "What book?"

The man who handled the New York legal side of the publication negotiations was a close friend. He was also one of the few people with whom Monroe had shared some of his early experiences, Jonas Silverstone. "He was very sensitive. He knew I was sane. He believed me, because he knew me.

"When we were still in Croton, Jonas and I would take walks in the country, and he'd just listen."

"Jonas was a big man. I grew up where men shook hands, but here was this guy who hugged me every time we met. Gave me a *brassos.* It was disconcerting at first. He was the first man who taught me men could embrace without being homosexuals. I also learned if I was going to be around a female, I'd better shave."

After he swallowed the news that the book was to be published, Bob had to face another decision—whether to use his own name or a pseudonym. He was concerned that going public with his OOB activities might jeopardize his business standing.

Bob reluctantly decided to use his own name for several reasons, and probably with the "Bob Rame" experience clearly in mind: A pseudonym might imply he was ashamed of that activity; then, too, hiding behind an assumed name might open his material itself to question; finally, he used the names of real people in the book, therefore it seemed inconceivable to him that he would not use his own.

Having given talks in California—at the University of California at Los Angeles (UCLA) and elsewhere—with no backlash, Bob assumed the book would not penetrate the business world. He was only partly right.

* * * *

Tart says, "*JOOB* is still the best book on Out-Of-Body's in the past thirty or forty years.

"Basically, its audience is parapsychologists like myself, then, those people who have had OOB experiences, most of them well-educated; and then, also, the people in the 1960s and 1970s, and even now, who have had experience with drugs.

"Bob probably didn't think of the book that way, because he was in Virginia, but I did, out here in California."

Charley Tart moved to California while *JOOB* was being written, and as drugs became part of the everyday scene. Not only did the University of Virginia escape much of the drug culture of the period, Bob Monroe, except for rare brushes with student-neighbors at his apartment complex, had little knowledge of the depth to which drugs had penetrated American life.

Charley continues, "The book showed the drug culture they could get there without using drugs."

Bob Monroe never became connected with the Movement of the 1960s, or its subsidiary academic offshoot, the transformation movement. Monroe has never been a political character; he does not seek short or longterm reform of the American system or the society, as did and do many of those whose names were associated with the hippies, SDS, humanistic psychology, and the myriad reformist groupings that had their zenith during the Carter Administration.

Monroe was a businessman; he knew many of those involved, but he kept his distance from the dervish dance of the decade.

1970s

Bob Monroe seems almost purposefully vague about what drove him to drop all his business interests and throw himself totally into exploration of the world of Supra-Consciousness. Somehow, Monroe recognized—or was told—there was purpose behind his OOB's.

Much later, Monroe reflected to one of his associates on the early days of all-out OOB work. "There are often times when I think what happened was that a door opened. I still don't know if I should have gone through it."

"Maybe it hinged on the decision to publish *JOOB.* It's very hard to pin down.

"I guess I experienced a slow takeover, as opposed to a revolutionary change.

"It was time for me to repattern virtually my entire way of life."

Part of the "repatterning" was his marriage in 1971, to the very supportive Nancy Penn, and the acquisition, six months earlier, of a gentleman's estate outside Charlottesville, called Whistlefield.

Some of the change may also have had to do with Bob's second major health setback, in 1971, when he had a coronary and subsequent carotid artery surgery. It was a renewed, unwelcome reminder that his physical body is mortal and can let him down.

Bob hired an ex-radio announcer to manage the Jefferson Cable Company, which, by now, "had become a store-keeping operation. By about 1974, I was still making the nine-to-five run, but he was handling the major part of the business."

After the illness, "I began to suffer from vertigo. I couldn't take the G load in flying, and I blacked out at times." It was a severe blow to Bob to have to yield his pilot's license. The cause was also extraordinarily ironic when contrasted with Monroe's OOB flights.

* * * *

Another peak moment in Bob's life came with the publication of *JOOB* in 1971, although, "It didn't seem like much at the time." There was little reaction; reviews were scarce. The world seemed coolly indifferent to the startling adventures of the former media executive.

"A couple of weeks after the book was published, we had a meeting of the directors of Jefferson Cable at Pier 66 in Fort Lauderdale." And, although he was now an out-of-closet OOB artist, "I was still president of the company, and it was a multi-million dollar company, understand.

"After the board finished its business, we boarded the chairman's seventy-foot yacht. As we cruised up the inland waterway to where we were going to have dinner, the wife of the chairman came up the companionway, with a copy of the book in her hand, and said 'Would you autograph this for me?'

"Without turning around to look at me, her husband said, 'That's a pretty good book. I never make any business decisions without consulting her psyche.'

"No other board member ever mentioned the book. Only one guy used to kid me. He'd call and say, 'Why do we have to use the phone.' Or ask for a stock market prediction. He was the nephew of the chairman.

"But the beauty of the moment was, here you had a successful businessman who consulted his wife's psyche. His principle was, 'If it works, use it.' He didn't care what it was."

Charley Tart reflects on *JOOB:* "We never envisioned the success the book would have. Not only its sales, but the hundreds—thousands—of people who have directly benefited from reading it."

Journeys has been translated into eight languages; more than four hundred thousand copies have been sold since publication, in all its editions.

Tart continues, "And then, look at what Bob has built as a result of it: The Institute and its buildings, and the continuing stream of people who pass through and get exposed to him."

Much to Monroe's surprise, appreciable numbers of letters started to come in shortly after publication. And still they come, from all over the world. "The first surprise was, there were so many people who routinely had the same kind of thing happening to them.

"I began to feel this problem was far more important, culturally and human-wise than I had anticipated." The tone of the letters has remained consistent to this day. "It's almost always, 'Thanks. I'm glad to know I'm not crazy.' " Monroe still gets "about 200 or 300 letters" each month.

JOOB has had even more of an effect, as it has rippled steadily through a substratum of society over the years. Charley Tart notes, "People now are inclined to say, 'Hey, you're not weird; you've got a talent.'"

Tart adds, "Bob has had a big impact on the public. Don't underestimate the value of the reassurance he has given people. He has probably helped keep some people from going crazy, and a lot of people from enduring useless agony and unnecessary medical expense."

Many of the letters arriving at the Institute beseech Bob's help in dealing with OOB's. "We feed them some information which may help. The great bulk of them are highly conventional people who have encountered this particular phenomenon: Not people who actively attend New Age seminars and workshops.

"I wasn't a participant in the Consciousness Movement. I had no idea there was this covert side to so many people."

Why do *JOOB*—and Bob Monroe—have such enduring appeal. "I guess it's the stance I take. I don't assume responsibility for people. I don't counsel them as such.

"I don't believe in cultism. Cults require a leader, and the leader has to be omniscient. I know I'm not omniscient. That's a constant for all humans.

"The matrix for each is different, purposefully different. Anyone is wrapped up in his own beliefs. Everyone has his own limitations. We are a nation of followers, but we don't have to be.

"My experience is different from yours. Both yours and mine are of equal value. So how can I make a value assessment of you and what you do?

"There are no exceptions to this rule.

"I take that position.

"Sure, I have fun trying to bait people....to shock them out of their lethargy and consider other realities.

"What's my appeal to people who haven't had OOB's? I'm pragmatic. I may talk about other realms and realities, but I take a very phlegmatic pattern.

"I say, 'Don't take my word. Go look for yourself.'

"And one other point which may help people understand what I'm about. I don't use New Age jargon. I attempt not to attach mystical labels to things."

* * * *

After *JOOB*, there was a shift in Bob's approach to his Out-of-Body excursions. Sometime later, he wrote an informal paper he headed, "Preview Excerpts from *Far Journeys*,"* which is worth quoting here.

"In the Spring of 1972, a decision was made that...the limiting factor was my conscious mind. Therefore, if the decision what to do (in the OOB state) was left up to that part of me, as it had been, I would remain just as I had, going nowhere. What would happen if I turned this decision-making process over to my Total Self (Soul?), who was purportedly conversant with such activities.

"Believing this, I then put it into practice. The following night, I went to sleep, went through two sleep cycles, woke up and remembered the decision. I detached from the physical and floated free. I said in my conscious mind, the decision to *do* is to be made by my entire self. After waiting for what seemed only a few seconds, there was a tremendous surge, a movement, an energy in that familiar spatial blackness, and there began for me an entire new era in my OOB activities.

"Since that night, my non-physical activities have been almost entirely due to this procedure.

"The results have been of a nature so far removed from anything that my conscious mind can conceive of that a new problem arose. Although my physical here-now consciousness is always a participant in such activities, better than ninety percent of such events seem to me impossible to translate into the Time-Space medium. It is as if one were trying to describe music, such as a symphony orchestra with choir, and do it in words without the use of technical descriptions...One can use such words as nice, compelling, frightening, awe-inspiring, warm, loving, beautiful—and be nowhere remotely near the actual description...You do the best you can."

* * * *

The good times were now beginning. "In the early 1970s, we had a very dedicated group of people working. All volunteers. Very diverse people. They weren't flakes. Most of them local. Tom Campbell, a physicist, and Bill Yost, an engineer, among others." They gave up whole weekends to work on wiring the lab, first in the basement of the office building in Charlottesville proper, later at the Monroe's new country estate, Whistlefield.

Yost, Campbell and another engineer, Dennis Minnerick, worked at a government facility in Charlottesville fulltime. But the excitement and the intensity of Monroe's quest was such that the trio gladly surrendered their free time to help pioneer.

* Far Journeys *was published in 1985.*

"They were the heart and guts of the period," says Monroe. "It was a magnificent team effort.

"We were playing it by ear. All of them were very bright in their fields; solid Left-Brainers in hi tech." Bob told them what was needed in the way of equipment—wiring circuits, control boards and the like—and the trio would figure out how to do it. They were also devoted scavengers—a practice Bob continues today.

* * * *

Biofeedback is a term which occurs often in discussion of Bob Monroe and those in similar fields. Elmer and Alyce Green at the Voluntary Controls Program of the Menninger Foundation, and Dr. Art Gladman of Oakland, among many others, have for years used biofeedback instruments to monitor autonomic nervous system activities, such as hand temperature, muscle tension, and brain wave activity.

The set-up is similar to the polygraph lie-detector, except that instrument reports are fed back to the patient, so he can recognize the rapid changes in his physiology. The patient learns that, with concentration and practice, he can control his body, and can function in a more relaxed fashion. The holistic system allows the patient, says Dr. Gladman, to be "no longer a victim. He is in charge." Biofeedback is thought of by most MD's as, at best, an unconventional system of healing.

Bob Monroe is frank to admit that he borrowed from Biofeedback techniques, although his processes were distinct developments on their own. Bob's early lab equipment was an outgrowth of Elmer Green's work. "We started with the GSR (Galvanic Skin Response) monitor, and we made it even more sensitive, until we cut the power to it off completely, and then we were monitoring pure body voltage.

"We pasted the electrodes on people, which was not the way they were designed to be used. Conventional methodology said you couldn't do that and get good GSR results.

"In other words, we had a good technical base, but we made changes."

So began an exciting if laborious process. Bob and his fellow engineers combined the biofeedback monitoring concept with Monroe's earlier theory that audio signals can effect changes in consciousness—and perhaps do far more. Monroe sought to perfect a system no one had dreamed of; it simply took time and stick-to-itiveness. What came out of countless hundreds of painstaking, enervating hours of concentration, by Bob and the volunteers was, eventually, the binaural Hemi-Sync system.

The development came through a series of tests: A volunteer on a waterbed in the lab at Whistlefield, a monitor (usually Bob) at the control panel feeding audio signals into the ears of the subject, to see what happened. It could have been very scary, and at times was, as the innovators blipped frequencies into willing human minds.

Anything that was risky was first undertaken by Bob himself. The process had to be painstakingly slow: who knew what would happen, as each new threshold of tolerance or discovery was reached?

Eventually, the right combinations of signals were found to help people get to Focus 10, then to 12. It took more time to develop Focus 15 and 21.[1] Other applications followed in time. Bob made tapes for many uses—each of which represented hundreds of hours of lab work and months of recording and editing. With time, Bob's fledgling Mentronics Systems, and later the Monroe Institute of Applied Sciences, produced designer Hemi-Sync tapes for pain control, surgery, various forms of sleep, golf and tennis improvement, concentration, meditation. [2]

Hemi-Sync, a registered trademark, has been used most often to help students at the Institute achieve the Altered State of Consciousness. Its applications in education, psychology, medicine are still, at the end of the 1980s, disappointingly limited, partially by fear, partially by the reluctance of the various establishments to accept anything not of their own making, and partially because Hemi-Sync does not lend itself readily to scientific testing. The Monroe Institute is still trying, in its own way, to overcome these obstacles.[3]

* * * *

In the early 1970s, Bob Monroe says, "I was giving occasional talks about our experiences and the lab work." One who heard him very early on was Raymond Waldkoetter, a psychologist with the U.S. Army, who has been associated with the Institute from a distance ever since, and who has done much to explore the practical applications of Hemi-Sync. "I first met Bob at a Harold Sherman ESP seminar at Hot Springs, Arkansas in 1970. As one of the featured speakers, he was tremendously effective in communicating with the audience. As I look back now, he, in essence, laid out a plan then for creating his Center and the research program which he has since been following."

Bob was also traveling. He and Nancy visited Jane Roberts in Elmira, New York, the author of *The Seth Material,* and channeler of the non-physical entity who called himself Seth. Some notes from *The Nature of Personal Reality* describe the events:

Session 653, April 4 1973
9:23 PM Wednesday

We were visited over the weekend by Robert Monroe and his wife, Nancy; they live on a farm in central Virginia. Bob Monroe is the author of Journeys Out of Body, *the book that Jane and I regard as the premier work on the subject. Among many other things, he wanted to tell Jane about the research complex, tentatively called the Monroe Institute—or System—that he's building on his farm. It will be used 'by just a bunch of guys' to study various phases of psychic activity. These 'guys' then will be doctors, parapsychologists, psychiatrists and members of other scientific disciplines.*

(Seth came through Sunday night, April 1, in a long recorded discussion with the Monroes. We were all to meet again late Monday. Beginning Monday morning, however, Jane began experiencing another strongly surging burst of creative inspiration. . . .

. . . . (No session was held Monday evening. Instead, Jane used her 'own' abilities to tune in on the diagram of a machine that Bob Monroe drew; he had seen this in one of his OOB journeys. Questions involving physics arose—the Fermi gap [having to do with the movement of certain electrons], and so forth—and Jane ended up drawing diagrams of her own. She enjoys using her abilities this way.

(She gave her notes and drawings to Bob. On Tuesday, then, besides writing about her transcendent [above] she wrote an account of Monday evening's discussion, and reconstructed the notes and sketches for her own records.) [4]

* * * *

Monroe had been working in the lab for some time when, suddenly, "There came the invitation, in 1973, to do two workshops at Esalen in California. Mike Murphy (one of the co-founders of Esalen) gathered in the participants. Bill Yost went out with me to do one at Big Sur, and the second in San Francisco, over two successive weekends. Both of the sessions were full—about forty people in each.

"Neither of us knew much about conducting workshops. We weren't worried about the people as much as whether we would appear competent.

"We developed the Gateway Affirmation so we could have something appropriate to use in the workshops out there.

"Really, we had to have something we could expose to strangers—people who hadn't been in the lab, who weren't the selected subjects we had been dealing with until then.

"We had to devise something to get strangers into a different state of mind."

Charley Tart might have played a role in that landmark invitation to Esalen. Charley doesn't remember clearly. "It's ninety-nine percent probable I suggested to Mike Murphy, that he have Bob come out. Esalen was *the* prestige entry to the humanistic psychology movement of the time."

* * * *

Dr. Elisabeth Kubler-Ross had her first involuntary Out-of-Body experience in Santa Barbara in the mid-1970s. It caused her to do some research on the subject, and she found a copy of *JOOB,* which led her, in turn, to Bob.

Monroe invited a select group to try some informal tape-training over the Fourth of July weekend, 1976. Alyce and Elmer Green's daughter, Patricia Norris, was there. Dr. Kubler-Ross was present, as were Drs. Stuart Twemlow and Fowler Jones, Shay St. John and her then-husband, Bob Ellsworth, many of them names which have now long been associated with Bob's. Someone remembers Ram Dass and Elisabeth Kubler-Ross, on a later occasion at Whistlefield, sitting on the folded roof of a convertible, as Bob drove them around the farm.

Dr. Kubler-Ross had breakthrough experiences over that Independence Day weekend which were so poignantly moving, they have lived with her ever since. She described the experience to a writer for *Human Behavior* magazine; *Cosmopolitan* picked the interview up and reprinted it in February 1980. Elisabeth has retold the story for other audiences from time to time since and intends to use it herself in a forthcoming book.[5]

The Human Behavior reporter was impressed: "I sat spellbound as she recreated for me a remarkable experience that she seems herself to view with a combination of matter-of-factness and still-lingering sense of amazement and awe. She touched my arm often as she spoke, as if to make sure that I was still 'with her' on her journey."

Dr. Kubler Ross's experience was this.

When I decide to do something, I do it wholeheartedly, and one great asset I have is that I am not afraid of anything—or almost anything. But Bob Monroe didn't know that; so when I had my first (lab) experiment, I went too fast, and he interfered when I was just at the ceiling. He called me and I went kerplunk back into my body. I was mad as could be.

It was the first time I was able to do it on command, and it was a big thrill that it actually worked. I was like an excited child, but just as I was getting to the ceiling, bam. So the next time, I thought, "I'm going to beat him to it. . . ."

The moment we started, I said to myself, "I am going so fast that nobody has ever gone that fast, and I am going further than anybody has ever gone." And at that moment when I said that, I took off faster than the speed of light. I felt like I must have gone a million miles, in my language. But I was going horizontal, instead of up.

"You understand that in an OOB experience, there is no space and no time, but you are so conditioned in your thinking you think you have to go up or otherwise, you will hit a wall or something.

I switched and made a right-angle turn, rounded a big hill and went up. And then I started to experiment. It is incredible to get to a place where there is no time and space. . . .

And I went to a place so far that, when I came back, something incredible happened:. . . . The best description I can give you: I felt like a source of light that could illuminate the darkest corner of the world. I can't describe it any other way.

When I walked out of the laboratory, everybody stared at me, but I had no recollection—I could not remember or tell them where I (had been)."

Dr. Kubler-Ross continued in *Human Behavior*:

All I knew was that something so absolutely incredible had happened to me it was beyond description. All I could remember was the words Shanti Nilaya, *and nobody there knew what that meant. They tried every gimmick to get me to remember, but nothing worked—I know now. . . . It was too sacred to share with a bunch of strangers.*

That night, the sleeping arrangements were such that I ended up sleeping alone in a very isolated guest house and I was in a sort of conflict, feeling that if I actually should go to sleep there, something horrendous would happen.

Dr. Kubler-Ross stayed at the Owl House on the Whistlefield property. This guest house seemed ominously "crowded" to her, so much so that she would not take a shower, and even piled furniture in front of the door. She thought of getting up in the night and going over to ask if she could sleep in the main house, or even go to the nearby Tuckahoe motel, where a comforting "group of scientists" was quartered.

I thought of. . . asking to be in the presence of other human beings, but the moment I contemplated my alternatives, I knew that I had gone too far and could not back out. I had to finish what I had started. . . .

She had presumptive evidence that something not of the ordinary was taking place when she found the Owl House door unlocked after the first night. The second night,

I went into that house, and I knew the imminence of something horrendous—not horrible, but horrendous—that something horrendous would happen.

I couldn't sleep, and I couldn't stay awake. I wanted to sleep to avoid it, but I knew at the same time that I could not avoid it. I didn't even bother locking the doors any more, but I kept a night-light and the porch light on, (knowing that I would have) an unsurvivable experience. . . .

I was delirious, fighting to sleep, wanting to sleep, but knowing I couldn't fight it much longer. . . . And then it hit me like lightning." She fell asleep about one-thirty.

And then I had one of the most incredible experiences of my life. In one sentence, I went through every single death of every single one of my thousand patients. And I mean the physical pain, the dyspnea (labored breathing), the agony, the screaming for help.

The pain was beyond any description. There was no time to think, and no time for anything except that I twice caught my breath, like between two labor pains, like for a split second; and I pleaded, I guess, with God for a shoulder to lean on, for one human shoulder, and I visualized a man's shoulder that I could put my head on. And a thunderous voice came:

'You shall not be given.' Just those words. And then I went back to my agony and pain and dyspnea and doubling-up in the bed.

I mean, it wasn't a dream. I was reliving every single death of every one of my dying patients—and every aspect of it, not just the physical.

Then, about an eternity later, I begged for a hand to hold. My fantasy was that a hand would come up on the right side of the bed and I could hold it. And then again, this voice.

"You shall not be given." Then, you know, there was the whole self-pity trip I went through.

I've held so many hands, and yet, I'm not even to have even one hand in my own hour of agony—that whole thing. (She laughs.)

I didn't have time to think of all this, but it was all part of the agony. For a moment, I contemplated whether I should ask for a fingertip—a fingertip I couldn't hold onto, but at least would know the presence of another human being.

I said, 'Dammit, No! If I can't get one hand, I don't want a fingertip, either!'

That was my final outpouring of rage and indignity at God or whoever. . . . It was something like anger or defiance, but also the realization that in the ultimate agony, you have to do it alone—nobody can do it for you.

Once I realized this, I said in almost a challenging way—and, again, this is not in words but in experience.

"Okay. Give it to me. Whatever it is that I have to take. I am ready to take it." I guess by then the agony and pain—and this went on for hours—were so great that ten thousand more deaths wouldn't have made any difference. . . .

But the second I said "Yes" to it, and really meant it from the bottom of my heart—the moment I felt the confidence I could actually take whatever came—all the dyspnea, hemorrhage, pain and agony disappeared, and out of it came the most incredible rebirth experience.

It was so beautiful, there are no words to describe it.

It started as my belly wall vibrating, and I looked—open-eyes, fully conscious—and I said, "This can't be!"

I mean, anatomically, physiologically, it was not possible. It vibrated very fast. And then, everywhere I looked in the room—my legs, the closet, the window—everything started to vibrate into a million molecules. Everything vibrated at this incredible speed. And in front of me was a form.

The closest way to describe it is like a vagina. I looked at it, and as I focused on it in utter amazement—there were incredibly beautiful colors and smells and sounds in the room—it opened up into the most beautiful lotus flower. And behind it was like a sunrise, the brightest light you can imagine without hurting your eyes. . . .

At that moment, the light was full and open, like the whole sun was there, and the flower was full and open.

The vibrations stopped and a million molecules, including me—it was all part of the world—fell into one piece. It was like a million pieces falling into one, and I was part of that one. And I finally thought, "I'm okay, because I'm part of all this."

I know that's a crazy description for anybody who has not experienced this. It is the closest I can share with you. It was so incredibly beautiful, that if I would describe it as a thousand orgasms at one time, it would be a very shabby comparison. There are no words for it, really. We have very inadequate language.

And then, the next morning, as I walked outside, it was incredible, because I was in love with every leaf, every tree, every bird—even the pebbles. I know I didn't walk on the pebbles, but a little above them. And I kept saying to the pebbles, 'I can't step on you because I can't hurt you.' They were as alive as I was, and I was part of the whole, alive Universe."

As Dr. Kubler-Ross walked lightly downhill from the Owl House, she saw Bob Monroe sitting on a bench, waiting for her. He knew that she had had her peak experience.

It took me months to be able to describe this in any halfway adequate words.

And then somebody told me it was an experience of cosmic consciousness. I have had many experiences like this since, always spontaneously, when I least expect them. . . .

But Shanti Nilaya *means the 'home of peace,' which is where we all end up one day, when we have gone through all the hell and all the agonies that life brings and have been able to accept it. This is the reward. . . .*

Today, Dr. Kubler-Ross emphasizes, "What you have to understand is that my experience at the Bob Monroe farm had nothing to do with Bob Monroe, or even his method, as I did my own experimentation and the time was simply right for me to have such an experience." She is, of course, absolutely right, and it is not to detract from Elisabeth in the slightest to point out that her experience did take place in surroundings which were perhaps conducive to life-changing episodes.

* * * *

Dr. Kubler-Ross's visit to Whistlefield coincided with the invasion attendant on the convention of the American Parapsychological Association at Charlottesville. Everyone who was anyone was at the meeting, but Bob was not. A sympathetic Tart and others explained to Bob he could not have been invited, under the ground-rules of the Association, because his academic field was not parapsychology, and, in fact, he was not an academic.

Nancy Monroe says, in riposte, "But they all came out to Whistlefield. The Greens stayed with us. Hal Puthoff, Russell Targ, Stanley Krippner, Ed Mitchell (the astronaut who founded the Institute of Noetic Sciences). All of them. Sixteen people slept at Whistlefield. I was serving breakfast in three shifts, and made dinner for forty-seven one night!"

Charley Tart came down to the main house the first evening, saying, understandably, "I don't want to sleep up there in the lab." Nancy said Tart could only sleep in the main house, if Scooter agreed to move in with a sibling and let Charley occupy her room.

In the exhilarating days of the mid-1970s there was a constant stream of visitors. Many, undoubtedly, looked at Bob's tape technique as an Open Sesame—the legal successor to LSD. They and others wanted to see if what they had glimpsed in the hallucinogenic state could be reproduced, enhanced, above all, confirmed, without drugs. What was there, out There? For the young students and practitioners of the paranormal, it was a realm that cried for investigation.

A sober-sided Bob comments: "What we had was all new and exciting, then. Ours was one of the few places, maybe the only place, where they could come and do their own thing, informally."

* * * *

In 1969, another institution got off the ground, in mid-Kansas, and it has become legendary in parapsychology-paranormal-metaphysical circles.

Alyce Green bluntly tells the story of how the deceptively-named Council Grove Conference on the Voluntary Control of Internal States got started:

"Elmer (Green) and I had organized the first Council Grove in response to the decision of a group of eight people brought together through the efforts of Helen Bonny. The group included Helen Bonny, John Lilly, Kenneth Godfrey, Stanislav Grof, Pauline McKririck, Walter Pahnke, Elmer and me. We were professionally concerned that the accelerating search for 'expanded consciousness' might be getting out of hand. People in all walks of life, and especially young persons, were acting with abandon in their use of such things as psychedelic drugs, marijuana, hypnosis, and sensory deprivation. Aside from danger to users, the group feared that public reaction would adversely affect scientific research in these areas.

"We gathered at White Memorial Camp, Council Grove, Kansas. . . . The Conferences cut across cultural boundaries, discipline boundaries and religious boundaries. . . . Zen Buddhism, Tibetan Buddhism, Integral Yoga, Sufism, Mystic Christianity, hypnosis, Autogenic Training, sensory deprivation, psychedelic drug experience, and biofeedback training." [6]

Attendance is limited to ninety-six people, all of them invited by Elmer and Alyce Green.The meeting takes place annually in the Council Grove collection of fieldstone buildings, "with no reporters present. Nothing is recorded. We say it like it is. There's no one around to quote or misquote us," says one man who has attended over the years.

Elmer Green is an amazing, modest, energy-laden scientist who began life in physics. At the age of forty-four, he shucked his career as a guided weapons specialist-supervisor with the U.S. Navy at China Lake in the Mojave Desert, and went to the University of Chicago to obtain another degree, this time, a Ph.D. in Biopsychology, "because I decided human beings were more interesting." His wife, Alyce, meanwhile, got a B.A. in Psychology. For reasons which border on the mystical, the Greens almost immediately thereafter went to the Menninger Foundation in Topeka, Kansas, to help develop what is now known as Biofeedback.

"Since then, I have been studying human potential." Dr. Green bounces around his office, unable to contain his enthusiasm for his subject, reels off quotations from Western and Eastern metaphysical sources, patiently explains basics to a visitor: The epitome of the practical academic who lives and breathes his subject, whether it be tangible and demonstrable, or in the realm of unprovable faith. But mixed in with the theory and the unprovable are the hard experiences of the intensely-practical engineer and administrator.

Elmer Green is a living legend on the frontier between the Conscious and the

Supra-Conscious. He and Alyce have been deeply involved in the metaphysical world for half a century. They are scientists who conscientiously dodge headlines and TV lights. Had the Greens chosen to be, they might well have become the Western gurus' gurus. But Elmer and his wife envisioned their role otherwise. They are master healers, and of quiet counsel to many, in many fields.

Elmer Green invited Bob to the first Council Grove Conference in 1969, in itself a resounding form of recognition. Elmer recalls, "We talked, and he told me what he was doing. It was before *Journeys Out Of Body* was published.

"Then, a couple of years later, *JOOB* appeared. We invited him to another Council Grove." Monroe thinks he attended his second Council Grove in 1975. The discussion was on the scientific validation of Supra-Consciousness techniques.

Dr. Art Gladman of Oakland, who has been a longtime friend of Bob and is a member of the Institute Board of Advisers, met Monroe at Council Grove in 1974 or 1975. Word got around before the meeting that Monroe had some new tape techniques; "Everyone was dying to hear the tapes. Here was a chance to get to an Altered State—without drugs!"

Chris Lenz, later a key figure in Monroe operations, recalls a disagreement between Bob Monroe and Elmer Green at that Council Grove. "Elmer said that, while he certainly wanted the training to continue, he wanted to see a more scientific approach, more experiments separating out the suggestive effects of the tapes, and the influence of the trainer's personality."

Bob remembers his second encounter with Elmer Green in much the same way. "When we went public with the tapes, Elmer felt there should have been more testing.

"There was a big to-do. We had just started the M-5000 Program, which was the predecessor to Gateway Voyages. Elmer was part of a brisk discussion. They were talking about all the mind-expansion techniques of the time, est and so on. But not us, we were too small.

"I wanted to get up, but then a psychologist who was sitting behind me beat me to it. He said that all the techniques might not be valid scientifically, but, he asked, 'Why do people attend those seminars like est? People are parched for this kind of help.

"'You want to wait twenty years, to sample and test the water, and make sure it's absolutely pure. Meanwhile people are dying of thirst.

"'People will happily drink the water, now, even if it's tainted.'

"What he said turned the meeting around, and he certainly spoke what I had on my mind."

Council Grove is designed to provide an information exchange for unorthodox treatments, for instance in skirting the American Psychological Association's laborious protocols for scientific research, which, one of its members privately calls "hogwash."

Then as now, what those who attended Council Grove were doing was outside the pale of recognized establishment practice; the practitioners needed the reinforcement of knowing others were out there with them.[7]

A doctor realized, for instance, that if he believed in the treatment he was administering, he could convince the patient it would work. "But if you try to talk to the profession about your success, you won't get anywhere. You don't have scientific proof. You can give someone aspirin, and convince him it will cure his headache. But that's not satisfactory scientifically."

Only if the patient transfers the doctor's or practitioner's belief to himself does he have a chance of success. Council Grove gave many the confidence to proceed with unconventional healing methods.

The same doctor uses selected Monroe tapes. "I set the patients up to have a relaxing experience," by explaining Hemi-Sync. After the tape, the patient gets thirty minutes of Biofeedback treatment. It's a technique for "people who would never go for therapy. The term Biofeedback is misleading. The chart's needle simply shows what's bothering you."

Although Bob Monroe is regularly invited to attend, he usually has representatives cover the Council Grove meetings for him. Monroe has not changed his view over the years that his mission was to bring Hemi-Sync sound into practical use. Others—like Green and Stuart Twemlow—now agree that his course has been partially correct, since the body of experience shows many people have benefited from Monroe techniques, even if they are not scientifically demonstrable.

Elmer and Alyce Green eased their previous position sometime in 1978, when they came to Whistlefield and spent a week listening to tapes made by Shay St. John, Rosie McKnight, and other of the Explorers. "These have to get out to the public," the Greens urged Bob, who at the time had no plans for dissemination. The result of their enthusiasm was the Explorer Series of tapes. Elmer Green is, however, still sad the Monroe techniques have not been applied to more classic laboratory experimentation.

* * * *

Dr. Stuart Twemlow is a burly New Zealander who came to the U.S. in 1971, "because I had to be here." He qualified as an M.D. in his native country, then went to Australia to get his "certificate of sanity" so he could train as a psychoanalyst and psychotherapist at the Menninger Foundation in Topeka, Kansas. Stuart was, in his own words, "a shitkicker" as a young Kiwi—a member of a radical collection of anti-Vietnam protesters who challenged the New Zealand establishment. But Twemlow is today as deeply American as any Midwesterner—perhaps even more so, because, as is common with immigrants, he values the good in this country more than many native-born citizens. Today, he speaks with deep sympathy and understanding of the farmers who are his neighbors in rural Kansas, of the tragedy of foreclosures and suicides. He is, as he says, "at home with kings and with paupers."

Twemlow is a devoted practitioner of the martial arts—a Black Belt in Kaju Kempo Karate and in the Okinawan Kobudo (Weapons) System—as well as a follower of Buddha. Stuart is a man of appetites and humor, robust and outsized in many ways; a man of large girth and broad horizons. It is little wonder that there have been clashes in his relationship with Bob Monroe over the years.

Monroe and Twemlow first met at Council Grove in 1973, although there is some mutual vagueness about the year. "Exploring the Supra-Conscious was part of my residency training at Menninger. I was tired of guru trips by then. Fed up with all that garlic breathing. Once I was told to eat 'Baba's lunch,' which I discovered had been regurgitated by the guru at that workshop. I realized that kind of stuff was crazy.

"I participated in Stan Grof's LSD training. It turned me on to the other world. I never came back, really. My whole view of things changed.

"At that Council Grove, Bob was looking for people who were interested in his system. I went to Whistlefield, with Fowler Jones (a Kansas colleague) and Elisabeth Kubler-Ross, for an informal workshop.

"I had an OOB. Actually, more like a combination of an OOB and a Near Death Experience. There was a high-speed roaring, like in a wind-tunnel. I ended up at my home in Topeka. My wife was lying on a couch. Then I saw her washing the dishes, and I looked in a mirror, but didn't see anything of myself.

"Bob helped me come back, re-entered me. I was seeing double, triple. When I got back to Topeka, my wife had a priceless expression on her face. She told me there had been a chill in the room, then she saw a translucence, and felt a shadow standing over her.

"It was this experience I described in a *National Enquirer* interview for an article they did on Bob. It brought hundreds of letters.[8]

"Bob and I hit it off. I was interested in the investigative side of his work, not the religious part of it."

Monroe was invited to Topeka in 1976, where Twemlow ran a number of tests with Dr. Glenn Gabbard and Dr. Fowler Jones, a psychologist at Kansas University Medical Center. The tests took place at the Menninger Clinic, at the Veterans Administration Hospital in Topeka, and privately. They led to a full psychiatric profile.

Monroe told Twemlow he thought he could go Out-Of-Body while under observation, a step further than the Tart experiments. Twemlow and Jones hooked him up to a polygraph in the lab, and watched Monroe through a one-way mirror. They were getting no GSR reading on Bob, so they entered the chamber, and checked the electrodes.

Immediately thereafter, the experiment took a dramatic turn.

Twemlow recalls, "It was almost as if he were dead. His breathing was spasmodic." Suddenly the two scientists noticed a "heat-wave-like distortion" around the upper half of Bob's body. He was blinking rapidly and rubbing his eyes. The heat-wave distortion disappeared shortly before Monroe announced he had returned to his body.

Gabbard and Twemlow came to some conclusions about Monroe's Out-of-Body state: "Clearly, Monroe was in a state of deep relaxation. In addition, when in his OOB state, there is a frequency slowing, with an interesting shift in power to a 4-5 Hertz range, the theta-delta transitional zone. This electrophysiological borderline state correlates closely with Tart's findings . . . ."[9]

Gabbard, Twemlow, and Jones produced a major breakthrough in the acceptance of the OOB state as a reality in the academic and medical worlds.

The work with Bob led to a series of studies on reported cases of OOB's. The trio succeeded in placing three papers on the subject on the agenda of an annual convention of the American Psychiatric Association in the late 1970s. Even though the papers were delivered at 8.00 a.m., the hall was filled to capacity.

Their presentation was sponsored jointly by the University of Kansas Medical Center and the Monroe Institute. It was the first recognition of any kind by the establishment that the Institute even existed.

Bob remembers the tests were not all fun. "The most painful of it all was the strobe flicker system they used. It was a flashing light effect, testing with an EEG to see what your responses were. They shone the strobe in your eyes.

"One frequency triggered a near-epileptic seizure: It was like them hammering a knife into my brain.

"There they were, the doctors, sitting behind the light, watching the results, saying,

'Oh, isn't this interesting!'

"And there I was, screaming, 'C'mon fellas, get me out of this!' Talk about torture chambers!"

But still, Bob Monroe comments, "That was a great day, when I reported going Out Of Body, and it coordinated with the EEG readings! They actually saw a hazy substance emerging from me!" The tone of wonderment, tinged, perhaps with a bit of pride, hasn't diminished, well over a decade later.

* * * *

One late autumn afternoon in 1987, Bob Monroe is feeling restless, cooped-up, hemmed-in by a mountain of paper. A lot of trivia has upset his day. Abruptly, he says, "Gotta go pick up some smokes." He clambers into the four-wheel drive, and heads down Roberts Mountain. First, a detour to chat with Morrie Coleman and Linda Jackson, a New Land couple who raise llamas. A pause at the office to glance at the mail and sign some books for sister Dorothy. A grave consultation with a county road crew which is surfacing the approach road to the Institute. Progress with Bob Monroe through his domain is never rapid.

As he meanders along back roads, Bob abruptly hangs a sharp 'U' turn. "Let's take a look at Whistlefield."

He drives a few miles north, towards Afton, and branches onto a byway. "Had to fight the county to get it paved. They finally agreed," he comments with some amusement. Around a sharp left-hand bend, and down a slope, past a spick-and-span Full Gospel church. Bob gave the knob of land on which it sits to the congregation's pastor. "He goes into an Altered State regularly during services. Good man."

All along the road, Bob points out houses belonging to people he once knew well. "I wonder if he's still there?" or, "Now there was a nice person!" He remembers a family with thirteen kids which was burned out in a fire. He gave them a replacement modular unit. It's the first time in three years he has driven the road.

Monroe pauses at a junction of sparkling white wooden fence. Just ahead, on a slight rise, is a serviceable, brown-colored prefab with a sharply-sloping, nearly-gabled roof. "That's the old lab," Bob says simply. Hardly a New Age building out of a Spielberg movie.

Bob Monroe wheels the Blazer onto Whistlefield's driveway, past the furlongs of sentinel fence which stretch like exposed white veins over the hillocks of the property. He slows at the barn-stable-cattle pen, and points to a rusty gas pump. "That was a constant source of trouble. Never mind we put a lock on it; every month, we'd encounter a two hundred gallon deficit. Hell of a rate of evaporation!"

His eye turns hesitantly to the main house of Whistlefield, on a knoll facing the Blue Ridge. A long, stately, white brick building which speaks of warmth and comfort, now deserted and stark.

A real estate brochure published when the Monroes sold Whistlefield depicts everything to which gentry could aspire: "432 acres, heavy forest 60%, pasture 30%, croplands 10%. Six drilled wells, two spring-fed lakes, streams and other springs. Six bedrooms, five baths...den and a 'pub' game room with an enormous fireplace ...The Meditation Garden has twelve-foot box bushes...Farm Manager's House. Tenant House. Stable. Price: $725,000."

Buying Whistlefield was a nerve-wracking operation. Nancy Penn later said, "From the moment I saw it, I knew the house was my dream. Bob knew how much I wanted it." He made an offer, which the owners accepted. "But then their lawyer got into the act. He told Bob the offer wasn't good enough." Bob called Nancy at the apartment complex she was managing for him. "If I knew you could get away and leave the kids, I'd say, 'Let's fly to New York and have dinner tonight.' It was his way of saying how sorry he was the deal had fallen through."

The sale was consummated about six months before Bob and Nancy were married. "Sometimes we needed all that space, if all of our kids showed up at one time. Horses, cattle, a small pond which had good fishing and was good for swimming." Today's owner, who has made a number of improvements, including roads, is asking "about three million" for Whistlefield.

Now, on this fall afternoon, it doesn't look as if anyone is around. Only the trees stand sentry. Some stubborn leaves droop from them sadly, reluctant to join the carpet below. Bob says, "I guess it would be all right if I drove up there." Slowly, the Blazer climbs the rise. Bob stares straight ahead. He scans sightless windows, identifying the rooms behind them; the porch, "The new people glassed it in. Best place there was to meditate."

Bob does not tarry. He heads the vehicle down another hill, past a pond where a young black girl drowned, trying to jump into a rubber ring. "She couldn't swim. I rushed down from the house with fins and a snorkel mask and dove for an hour, trying to bring her up, but I couldn't find her. The county rescue squad dragged the lake and finally found her body. It was very sad."

On past a couple of tenant houses, and more stretches of gleaming white fence, to a flat, overgrown clearing. "Used to have a one-acre greenhouse there. Chrysanthemums. But we had to take it out as a condition of sale." He points to tennis courts and a swimming pool. "Well, he put them in where I suggested."

There's a weighing silence. Finally, Bob breaks it. "There's a lot of nostalgia in this place. There was a lot of action here. A lot of very vivid memory patterns." A man, isolated in his thoughts, cocooned in memories of unique adventures with a collection of unique people.

* * * *

Nancy and Bob Monroe's marriage in 1971 was unusual. The civil ceremony was performed by a county clerk, then the couple returned to Whistlefield for a reception lunch. Nancy remembers, "I was fairly elegantly dressed up, but we ducked out. I got muddy getting in the truck. No one knew where we had gone."

They went to the house of the Catholic Monsignor who had become Bob's close friend. A fire roared in his pot-bellied stove. Father Michael awaited the Monroes—in mufti. "I can't give you any form of religious ceremony, dressed in the cloth. This way, I can give you a spiritual blessing." He proceeded to do so, simply, movingly, reading carefully-selected writings of profound meaning.

"It was our spiritual marriage," said Nancy—who does not shy away from using the word Bob so often avoids.

Bob and Nancy returned to the reception; shortly thereafter, the Monsignor arrived, now in clerical garb, to show Bob's children that the marriage with Nancy was acceptable in his view.

Nancy Penn has her license as an interior designer, and she's a former English teacher who chooses her words with care. She glories in such delightful Southernisms as "H-E-two-sticks!" She recalls with pained amusement the embarrassment of uninvited callers looking for the Center when the Monroes later lived at the Gate House, close to the entrance to Roberts Mountain Farm. Once, a businessman wandered into the couple's bedroom, bag in hand, to find Nancy in her nightdress. The confrontation was brief, courteous, and definitive.

Nancy is a Lady of the Old School's Roanoke branch, though no retiring wallflower. She has memories of excursions to her grandmother's farm—a humble establishment which had no indoor privy, nor running water. But where it was *de rigeur* to dress for dinner, at which generations-old family silver was laid on the table.

* * * * *

A *Penthouse* magazine writer who visited Monroe in 1976, wrote:

Tall and heavy.... He drives an old Valiant.... to the site of 'Green Meadows', one of three suburban developments being built around Charlottesville by his construction company, Process Builders Corporation.

He ambles around the five houses already plunked down on the bulldozed red dirt, his hands thrust deep into his pockets as he chats with the carpenters. He does not look like a man who has been popping out of his body for the past seventeen years....

He has the salesman's and storyteller's trick of pausing in the middle of phrases for suspense, and sliding the end of one sentence into the beginning of another to keep the listener hooked.... Even his cats enjoy talking to him. [10]

Bob Monroe doesn't worry about the view from *Penthouse*, but does remember the time. "I was still involved with cleaning up the mess of the construction venture. The modular company was about to close down. We had built a sample house. I thought it might make a good lab, so I brought the boxes out to the farm, and eventually we added some wings. The Lab there had three Chec Units—the forerunners of today's Black Box—copper-sheathed isolation booths. There was a control room and a debriefing area." It also had some Biofeedback instruments and a larger room where five people could be hooked onto a tape simultaneously. And there was room for expansion: A door opened onto nothing, only a three-foot drop to the ground; another modular unit could be hooked on, should it be needed—or affordable.

Several years after the acquisition of Whistlefield, Bob Monroe made the conscious decision to withdraw from the business world entirely and devote the rest of his life to research into, writing about, and propagating the findings of his OOB activity. Despite the modular housing fiascos, it must have been no easy shift.

Bob was approaching 60. "At that point, I knew what I had to do. Whistlefield became the double center of my life."

The deserted estate resonates to Bob in its stillness. He drives slowly to the lab building, pauses, turns away quickly. He glances over his shoulder, and says, "Back there. That's the Owl House." Another simple, modular structure in a clump of trees, where Elisabeth Kubler-Ross had her shaking, dedicatory experience.

The early core group that gathered here around Bob was composed of, "Pretty mature, experienced people. No long-hairs or drug-users.

"It became an avocation with them. I didn't solicit their help.

"The mystery is, I don't know how they got to Whistlefield. I draw a blank.

"They just seemed to materialize. None of them knew each other. Charley Tart didn't know them.

"We were generally pretty covert about it. It peaked in the 1970s."

Monroe says, "The Explorers began to develop their own OOB efficiencies." The other Pathfinders, as they were sometimes called, of the time were Tom and Judy Campbell, Scooter, who brought in an entity called 'Sol,' and Nancy Monroe.

* * * *

Rosalind McKnight comes from Dayton, Ohio, got a degree from Union Theological Seminary in New York, and now teaches parapsychology at a community college near Lynchburg. She is an ebullient woman with swept-back hair, a ready smile, and a glorious singing voice who radiates her love for the world and for Bob, despite the ups and downs they have gone through over the years.

Rosie first heard of Bob from a psychic while she was living in New York. When she moved to Virginia in the early 1970s, she got in touch with Bob. "He realized I could type, and I went to work in the office at Whistlefield, as a part-time secretary."

Rosalind remembers, "I had done some trance work before, but I didn't know anything about Hemi-Sync. At the time, Bob was experimenting.

"He would grab anyone who happened to be around. 'C'mon out back,' and we'd have a session in the lab. I'd just go in and do my thing, which was the thing dearest to his heart—exploring." Rosalind may be the best known of the Explorers because of tapes the Institute has issued of some of her sessions, identified by the initials ROMC.

"I didn't have any definite purpose, just going along with the flow. We never knew what would happen. I think the first time I went in, I fell asleep.

"Then the Guidance started to come through. At first, it was philosophical."

She channels a quartet of entities which Bob Monroe dubbed "Ah-So," and also a whimsical nineteenth century musician named Alfonso Pincinelli. In the first "Ah So" appearance, Rosalind perceived four hooded figures lifting her out; one of them, the spokesman, entered her body. Bob quickly established that entities don't like names, hence the soubriquet. "The four entities worked to cleanse me. They were there for my benefit, always for me," she recalls.

"Anything else was incidental. If good tools came out of the sessions which could be useful elsewhere, Bob used them.

"Bob wanted a question-and-answer format since he was interested in getting information on new techniques. Sometimes the sessions lasted as long as a couple of hours. I did two or three a week.

"It was all low-key, experimental stuff. The Guidance always seemed to have something pre-planned."

After Exploring for two years, and receiving consistent guidance, Rosie McKnight relates, "We finally began to realize what we were getting was structured. We just hadn't recognized it at the time. For instance, the Resonant Energy Balloon*: The entities were trying to teach it to us. Bob took me through the Rebal several times, until he understood what the Friends were saying. Bob followed the instructions—he always

* The Resonant Energy Balloon, or Rebal, is Monroe's protective construct for Altered State explorers.

does—and then it became part of Gateway.

"Bob was incredibly patient. He would wait for something to happen; he loved to talk to the Guidance, and he always knew how to tune in, ask the right question.

"Sometimes, he would do an experiment, tell the Guidance, 'I'm thinking of something. Can you tell me what it is?' They could always pick up what he was thinking."

Apart from her technical instructions, Rosie McKnight's adventures became legendary around the Institute. The four Light Beings, as she refers to her Guides, showed her and explained the nature of plant and animal life, voyaged to the core of the planet, explored life and after-life, relationships, and went to look at the year 3,000. "They took me through all levels of Awareness." The title of Rosalind's unpublished manuscript is *Journeys Through Consciousness.*

"After a session, we'd go up Skyline Drive to the Howard Johnson's and sit for hours in philosophical discussion.

"I feel very close to Bob in a spiritual and very special way...He has helped more people to grow than anyone realizes."

Bob Monroe reflects on the days with Rosie. "Real exciting stuff," he smiles. "I wouldn't have done what she did. She built up what we call a 'full faith and trust' relationship with her entities. She felt fully safe with them."

Rosalind wanted to visit a spacecraft "which was in the vicinity." Monroe was monitoring that memorable session: "Rosie said, 'They want to take me in there. I'm all right...They're putting me on a table...They're putting a band on my head...I'm all right.' "

The entities decontaminated her in a tube, and took her into a control room. The occupants accepted the presence of a human being as nothing unusual.

"Ah So took her into the spacecraft and let her look at the banks of lights. They saw different ships in different dimensions. " Bob did not interrupt, since he knew Rosie had confidence in her Friend. Rosalind relayed descriptions of where each spaceship unit was at any time. Some were in physical, others solely in energy form. One bore the designator KP-25. They had different colors. When Rosalind asked whether the occupants of the control craft were male or female, two stood up—one dominant Male, one dominant Female. She couldn't see any difference.

"The entities told her to remember an incident from her physical life. She did, and, bam, it was projected on a screen. That was very interesting.

"But she never exhibited any fear. Rosie was under their protection, not mine."

In the mid-1970s this was all very new and very exciting stuff at the Institute. Even today, with the plethora of Ufology lore, the firsthand account can easily raise goosebumps on the listener.

* * * *

Bob Monroe tried to explain what was going on to *Penthouse's* highly skeptical writer in 1976. Having attracted the attention of his Helpers, David Black wrote, Bob "is learning to become a god."

Monroe sits in the Blazer, his eyes and mind on those distant days of the mid-1970s.

"We were trying to figure out what were the right frequencies for the Frequency Following Response. We were doing bio-monitoring, spending hours in the Black Box, listening to signals." There's a tinge of wistfulness for those days of discovery and excitement in Bob's voice.

"Up to that point in the early-to-mid 1970s when our volunteers came together, I had felt fairly lonely. But now, my sense of loneliness was past.

"We had the group. I could be free with them, trying to find out what was going on. We were happy.

"They began to explore the Universe for me. We were looking for intelligent life, and we looked to hell and gone, but couldn't find any.

"The Gateway Affirmation changed it all.

"A month later, the Explorers began to meet intelligent beings all over the universe."

Could The Affirmation have been channeled? Bob pauses for a moment, and gives an oblique reply. "There was a woman, Mary Jane, who was a psychologist in the Social Services, making a big salary. She didn't go out, but she would meet a third party, which was far better than channeling.

"She'd tell us, 'Hans says...' and then she'd report. Neat, quick, straightforward.

"Beautiful, beautiful things came out of it.

"All of those people were selfless. They were family, not ego-bound." It was only later that the "crabgrass syndrome" began to appear in Bob Monroe's operations.

The combination of the Esalen imprimatur in 1973 and the Gateway Affirmation set Monroe on the course on which he has expanded ever since.

"The Esalen workshops were certainly successful, to judge by the word-of-mouth. Friends of those who were there got in touch almost immediately, asking when we would do more. In the early days, most of the people who attended were seminar-hoppers, workshop-junkies, that kind.

"Six months after Esalen, the demand was great enough for us to start offering the courses regularly."

* * * *

Bob continues to drive the Blazer slowly over the looping roads of Whistlefield, so-called for the quail whose piping tones are a part of its soundscape, deep in recall of the early days. "We had the basics in the 1960s, but we didn't name it Hemi-Sync till later. Our fundamental was there: Mind Awake, Body Asleep. Focus 10. We figured, if we could establish that in people, we had something valuable. Then we started playing around, to see what else would work. What would mix."

Bob's easy, casual phrase belies the hours of repetitive, enervating work, checking frequencies, to find just the right combination to open up the Supra-Consciousness.

"There was a lot of groping going on. I was working on it nightly in the lab and the control room, looking for the Hemi-Sync type frequencies in my Out-of-Body state and with the group.

"Oh, yes, there was a form of Guidance involved. The Explorer team was asking questions all the time of the non-physical sources.

"If we had a master plan, I wasn't aware of it on the surface.

"When it came to additions to the program, we asked three sources directly: Miranon, channeled by Shay St. John; Ah-So, who came through Rosie McKnight; and the

No-Name entity we called 'Hans,' who talked through Mary Jane."

* * * *

When it started, Monroe called his flagship program M-5000. It later became the M-5000 Gateway and, later still, simply Gateway. The M was for Mentronics; 5,000 was the maximum number of people Bob thought he would take through the course to form a wide statistical base.

The first announcement, inevitably undated, but probably issued in late 1973, simply offered the Monroe Auditory Guidance System (MAGS) M-5000 Program, which included Stress-Tension Reduction; a Management Executive Training Program and several other courses. The Executive Program never really took off.

Bob explains, "Back in 1976, Ned Hermann invited us to bring our EEG equipment to the General Electric training college at Croton." Monroe demonstrated his technique to forty-five GE executives and submitted a proposal which would have cost the company $3 million—but been worth a $180 million to them.

"We hooked the equipment up and were watching changes in the brainwaves of a volunteer, The Rev. Gabe Campbell." The minister, an old friend of Bob's, was listening to a special tape—put together by Monroe for the occasion— on which frequencies changed every five minutes.

Dr. Art Gladman recalls that his associate, Dr. Tod Mikuriya, asked Bob what frequencies he had used to produce Campbell's brainwave pattern. Bob answered vaguely. "Either he couldn't or wouldn't tell," says Gladman, shaking his head. Even when his techniques stood everything to gain from open discussion, scientific scrutiny, and acceptance by an industrial giant, Bob Monroe was elusive.

At the time, Monroe and Gladman drove past Bob's old house at Croton. Today, Art muses, "That house in Croton!. . . .The pyramid-shaped copper roof over Bob's bedroom!. . . ." It was that roof, some speculate, that was the final element in enabling Bob to become an OOB traveler: The pyramid shape as a focal point for the concentration of power, and copper as the most effective conducting material.

The executive program was rejected by GE. It was, inevitably, too far ahead of its times. But Ned Hermann, who subsequently retired as manager of GE's Management Education Operations, to this day rents the Center in Virginia eight or more times a year for his own week-long management creativity-training seminars.

* * * *

By the mid-1970s, Bob Monroe's stepdaughter-protege, Scooter Honeycutt, began to play an increasing role in the nascent Institute.

Nancy Lea's parents were divorced by the time she finished high school, so Bob Monroe undertook to pay for her college education. At first she thought of Antioch, in Ohio, but it was too hippy-like for her more conventional personality. Instead, she went to Wittenberg, also in Ohio, which Bob remembered from his university band days. After starting with a psychology major, Nancy Lea switched to an unheard-of Major in Honors, with the connivance of a maverick faculty adviser.

In 1972, she studied for six months in France but it did not appeal to her ("I got hit on a lot"). Then she went to Japan, where she studied the language and did some Zen Buddhist meditation in a monastery: "I felt like I had come home." When she got back to the United States, she decided her days of foreign adventuring were over. Scooter was graduated cum laude from Wittenberg in 1974.

Then in her early twenties Scooter quickly became "Secretary, trainer, and jack-of-all-trades to Bob, who became my mentor." She painted "miles" of fences at Whistlefield. The relationship blossomed because Bob recognized in the young girl "a doer," the kind of person he most respects. "She was participating in the whole process, from an early age."

Scooter started traveling, giving early Gateway courses in California and the Midwest.

One of the students, and a longtime figure around the Institute, with whom Scooter became involved, is Ruth Domin, a quiet-spoken hospice worker from Chattanooga who was, if anything, more active with Monroe in the years before she died in early 1989, than when she attended the first-ever Virginia Gateway in the winter of 1976.

In those early days, Ruth Domin recorded her feeling that Bob Monroe was "a man with a vision. He has tremendous persistence, tenacity and patience—just what it takes to get a new concept going. With his sunny outlook, light touch and easy way with people, there is just no way of stopping him, no matter what goes wrong. I was impressed by his search for productive uses for the tapes.

"He was very easy to get to know. He always made his concepts easy to understand, and yet I never felt I understood all he meant when he talked to us. There seemed to be a depth his words hinted at. I never could quite figure out what puzzled me. Sometimes I wondered if he had a hidden agenda."

* * * *

Meanwhile, the scene at Whistlefield became at times circus-like. Scooter recalls, "We had hippies who would come here with their guitars and camp out," until Bob moved them along. Whistlefield harbored for a time a homeless man who alleged Edgar Cayce had said he was the bona fide physical incarnation of both Alexander The Great and Thomas Jefferson. His girl friend had been Jefferson's wife. When the visitor was put in the Box, he flunked the credibility tests. "When he came out, he said he got too scared, because there were so many enemies waiting for him, if he went out."

There were Ph.D.'s who came and stayed to write their theses. One man was working on "The Tone of the Universe." He knew the sound of the astrological signs, he claimed, and he wanted to develop harmonic chords to mix with Hemi-Sync.

Around that time, a Swiss doctor named Frank Lang became part of the Monroe family for a while. Lang was urbane, cosmopolitan, a contrast to the rough-and-ready, informal Americans. He captured the hearts of all the women around Whistlefield.

Lang acted as consultant on a film, became fascinated with the movie business and gave up medicine. He came to Virginia to shoot a documentary on Monroe, with a five-man team, mostly Germans. He sat beside Bob in the lab control room, and had a soft, winning, "bedside manner." Bob asked Lang if he would stay on and use his eight languages to make tapes for distribution abroad. Lang had other commitments, and departed with his crew when the film was finished.

Later, the Monroes met Lang again in Los Angeles. They were staying at a posh hotel, and had Elisabeth Kubler-Ross with them. Before descending for dinner at the notable restaurant to which Lang had invited them, Dr. Kubler-Ross dragged Nancy

Monroe into her room: "Mommy, what should I wear?" she cried, as she pulled crumpled dresses out of her duffel bag. Nancy remembers, "When we got downstairs, Lang apologized for already having ordered a drink without us. But then we were a bit late due to the hilarious choices we made in Elisabeth's final dinner dress."

It may have been during that trip or another to the West Coast that the Monroe's spent some time with Dr. John C. Lilly, the scientist who is most famous for his work with dolphins, but who has also made substantial contributions to understanding human consciousness.[11]

In *The Center of the Cyclone*, in 1972, Lilly mentions the parapsychology work of "youngsters" Charles Tart and Carlos Castaneda, and continues: "The naturalistic approach to our own inner nature is progressing. . . .Monroe's (*JOOB*) is a talented inner naturalist's report on the flora, fauna, geography and terrain of some of the inner territories." Although Tart, Werner Erhard (of est), Joan and Stan Grof (of the Transpersonal Institute), Burgess Meredith and Jerry Rubin all recorded their flotation/isolation tank experiences later in the 1970s for Lilly, the Monroes did not do so.

Penthouse took its skeptical look at Bob Monroe. David Black led the 1976 piece predictably: "There are, it seems, lewd possibilities in journeying outside the body; and although Monroe resisted the temptation to turn into an astral Peeping Tom. . . .he has enjoyed astral sex, a casual frictionless flash. . . .

"In September 1963, in some random, OOB dimension, Monroe stumbled across a group of astral inhabitants who formed a line and as he walked from one to the other, stepped forward and zapped him with astral sex. . .Monroe describes astral sex as a merging of energy fields, 'an invisible, rigid state of shock.'"

David Black's *Penthouse* piece may be the source of a persistent whisper among people who attend Monroe Institute workshops that Bob meets ladies while Out of Body. Monroe smoothes, "No, there's a lot of legend about that, but I never have.

"It's an interesting commentary on David Black. He came to our lab facility at Whistlefield somewhere in the mid-1970s, and presented himself as a researcher from a Midwestern university who was driving south and decided to stop by.

"We welcomed him openly and discussed our activities freely. I myself spent considerable time covering many areas of the OOB state with him. I'm sure I made only casual reference to sexuality as it relates to my own participation in the OOB.

"We had a very pleasant meeting, I thought.

"Some months later, we were astounded when someone made us aware of the *Penthouse* article written by Black, now apparently a magazine writer.

"I don't know that we would have treated him any differently had he represented himself as a writer; it was simply the fact that he was deceitful in his approach."

Black's skepticism appeared to be mirrored by *Newsweek*, which devoted space in its May 1, 1978 columns to "Life After Life." The piece aroused some ire at the Institute because it stressed that some fourteen hundred Monroe students had reported or achieved OOB's. Monroe's Explorer Bulletin commented pithily: "This figure was in error in that it confused the number of former participants of the Gateway program with those that reported OOB's."

Monroe continues, "Later, Black came out with a book covering Out-Of-Body experiences, in which he made several derogatory statements about the authenticity of the material in *Journeys Out Of Body*.

"I let them pass, feeling sure others would consider the source.

"Years later, Scott Rogo used the Black statements in a column for *Fate* magazine.

That was taking it too far. I challenged *Fate* and Rogo with a potential law suit if they didn't print a retraction.

"I supplied *Fate* and Rogo with verified data that showed Black had indeed made severe mis-statements.

"Subsequently, Rogo carried a retraction and apology in his *Fate* column and the matter was closed.'"

But, unhappily, not quite closed. The printed word has a survival quotient that is not always predictable.

In 1983, Rogo published another book, *Leaving The Body*[12] which underlines the author's skepticism. Rogo summarizes Bob's OOB techniques, then makes comments.

Rogo stresses the importance of the Twemlow-Gabbard-Jones work. "All these tests and data are certainly suggestive, but this is not to say that Monroe's credibility is unimpeachable. . . ." From this comment, Rogo proceeds to rake over the Andrija Puharich material, and Black's story. Black, "found the Virginia businessman evasive. . . .

"My own opinion is that Monroe probably does have the ability to leave his body, but has exaggerated and romanticized his accounts. His writings about the OOB certainly contain much understanding and insight about the experience, leading me to believe that he has much personal knowledge of it. But how much and to what extent must remain a mystery."

Rogo's comments damn with faint praise. They overlook several key points.

Bob Monroe has gone far out of his way over the years to subject himself to laboratory testing. The simple fact is, science has not devised a way to prove that Bob's experiences are what he says they are, and this has been a major source of frustration to Monroe throughout his Altered-State life.

Secondly, as has often been repeated and not only by Monroe supporters, it makes little difference how Bob started going OOB. Glue-sniffing was an analogy gone wrong and seized upon and repeated by skeptics.

If one accepts the world of Consciousness at all, one accepts some or all of the work of a number of people beside Monroe, many of them names now legendary in the worlds of psi, parapsychology, altered-state exploration, psychotherapy, psychiatry, and so on. Many of these academics, scientists, even doctors got their first inkling of There using drugs in one form or another, then determined to examine the world they had seen in a clean and sober state. They have done so for the rest of their productive lives, and have won some grudging recognition from the "straight" disciplinarians of their various fields.

It is also obvious that Monroe's experiences, and those of other Western discoverers, are strikingly parallel to the teachings of the various Eastern religions and philosophies, but have been achieved by methods far different from those traditionally used in the East.

The Monroe Institute goes out of its way to stress there is no guarantee of an OOB in the Gateway or any other of its programs. Bob says, bluntly, on the first evening of a Gateway, "If that's all you came for, why let's have a pleasant evening, and we'll refund your money and cheerfully take you to the airport tomorrow morning."

Gateway is far more than merely "local traffic" OOB training. There are very, very few people who emerge from a Monroe Institute training who are not willing, even happy to state categorically that they have gained a richness, an understanding, and a view of life from it they might not otherwise have. They also say they could have found the same experiences elsewhere—Monroe makes no claim to exclusivity; but they, for the most part, will defend Monroe passionately as the quickest, most stirring and most effective way to comfort, in an Altered State of Consciousness. Additionally, it's a lot of fun.

Stuart Twemlow and Charles Tart, among others, point to the large numbers of people who have benefited dramatically, and whose lives have been unalterably changed, as a result of Bob Monroe's experiences and the training methods he has devised.

Finally, it must be added that, just as there is a growth industry in New Age products, techniques, gimmicks and the like, there is also a small but thriving business in debunking, conducted by a few practitioners for their own reasons.

The sad fact is that Puharich, Black and Rogo are in circulation and are, from time to time, seized upon by analysts who look no farther. Their views of Bob Monroe are so colored by this unfortunately-focussed series of writings, they thereafter regard Monroe with suspicion, and completely ignore Bob's notable positive achievements, which go far beyond the fulfillment of the OOB-wish.

* * * *

The Institute began to expand as it went public with Gateway. The days of exciting experiment and exploration in the isolation of Whistlefield were closing.

In 1976, the Institute sent out invitations to some five hundred Gateway grads to join in an exercise at a precise time. It was called "The Fly-In." The participants were given assignments to perform on their astral arrival at the Center.

Monroe had kept the Explorers separated until the Fly-In, when they were all brought together to help deal with the number of Gateway Voyagers expected to check in.

Bob and his colleagues devised a double-blind method to check the volunteers' veracity. Three monitors were stationed in the control room. All of them were overwhelmed by the non-physical response: "Hi, I'm Jane, what do I do?" The monitors literally could not stand being pulled at so many ways. "We had to break it off. . . We didn't get the (clinical) results we hoped for. It was just too successful," recalled Bob Monroe long afterwards.

Monroe by now felt he had to bring in seasoned businessmen as marketing people and managers. Scooter was still only in her mid-twenties, but she was expected to break the new administrators in. "There were communications difficulties," she says succinctly.

For a while, the scene in the office was the Institute's version of the revolving door. One administrator would depart, another would come. "Their ideals and expectations were not met; and Bob's ideals and expectations weren't met, either," says Scooter. She felt she was left the job "of sweeping up behind. Picking up the pieces." She was still traveling and training the new program, called at first M-5000, later Gateway.

The strain told. "I wasn't just Bob's step-daughter. I had something to say." At the end of 1978, Scooter left the Institute for an extended sabbatical. At first, she sold textbooks and solicited academic manuscripts for Prentice-Hall in northern California. "But I was lonesome, the work wasn't meaningful to me. I always tried to guide the conversations around to OOB's." In time, she was transferred to a new division of the company in Richmond. When that operation folded, she went to work for John Wiley & Sons. "I stayed in touch with the family and the Institute, of course," which was easy because she found a house only six miles from Roberts Mountain.

"I was still burned out from training; answering the same questions over and over, at each course. But I had a growing sense, bookselling wasn't what I was supposed to do."

Bob Monroe says Scooter "broke loose. It wasn't an easy route to take. But she earned her freedom. She helped conduct the early Gateway programs on the road. She was pretty young to be put under that kind of pressure. After a while, she realized that sales was a dead-end. I figured she had learned a sense of reality, and offered her a job. She took it." Scooter returned to the Institute fold in 1983.

* * * *

There came another turning point: The decision to leave Whistlefield. The Monroes started looking for the right place as early as 1976. Bob, sitting in his four-wheel drive, looking over the lawns and paddocks which were once his, tries to define what had pulled him away from established comfort to the raw, red-clay farm of Roberts Mountain. "I still don't have a handle on it. It was a wrench to leave, and to pioneer. It was a different part of the forest, put it that way.

"Looking back now, it doesn't make much sense. Very strange. I was uncomfortable with the 'Man in the White House on the Hill' label. I was expending a lot of time and money. It was presumed ostentation. I had an image with the local population.

"We sneaked the lab in as a research facility. But my rationalization to move was, we needed a place big enough to do research and conduct classes." There was no room for seminars at Whistlefield, and it was extremely doubtful that the image-conscious county authorities would have granted the necessary building permits—quite apart from what the hunting folk would have said.

"I had to sell Whistlefield in order to complete the Institute. I had a certain mental set."

At Whistlefield, it cost two hundred fifty dollars a month just to manicure the lawns. The property is pictured in "Estates of Virginia," The Guide to The Places to Live in the Old Dominion. Neighboring Nelson County, with a population of less than eighteen thousand, is one of the less well-to-do.

On the drive back from Whistlefield that autumn afternoon, there's a straight-line rainbow over the Blue Ridge—although no sign of rain in the gathering clouds. Bob gropes to phrase his explanation, "I'm trying to reconstruct that time. By then, I knew I wanted to start a school. The neighbors were capricious. All sorts of social obligations held sway.

"I just didn't feel right in Albemarle County. Whistlefield represented a way of social and cultural life which wasn't computing for me any longer. I had difficulty belonging to it, even though I had lived in it for years."

Bob seems to reflect that his remark is judgmental, so he produces other reasons for the move. It was a time to trim the Monroe sails: The modular construction business had collapsed; the Whistlefield lab was operating at a considerable loss.

Departure from Whistlefield, "wasn't financial necessity, but it got expensive to live here. People were always coming and asking for the loan of money, which they never paid back.

"And the bedroom leaked air whenever there was a wind."

Back at the Gift House on Roberts Mountain Farm, Nancy adds, "We looked for another place for about two years. When we saw the "New Land," it was mystical. Can I tell the story?" Her husband nods. "Why not?"

"We were out looking with a realtor, and we pulled up on a hill where we could see Roberts Mountain. I like trees. That's basic. When the real estate man told us the price, our spirits dropped. It was far too high for us to consider, so we pigeon-holed the idea.

"Then, one day, a psychic came to Whistlefield. He said he usually didn't do readings for people who smoked, but he would do us. Bob mentioned we were looking for a place. The medium said, 'You've already seen the place, but you have not considered it.'

"Very early one morning, it came to Bob that the land we had seen but had not considered was the beautiful property that was too expensive.

"So we'd drive over, up a crazy road which was the only access at the time, and walk way up to the top, and picnic, and dream.

"Oh, we thought it all out, even then."

Now, however, things began to click. Nancy continues, "We went over to the Nelson County Clerk's office and found the title. The property belonged to a Florida real estate developer." Bob and Nancy continued to search for a new location all through 1976.

Then, Nancy happened to pick up a day-old newspaper ("Which I never did"), and saw an advertisement for Roberts Mountain Farm.

"Bob said, 'Now we call him.' It was a man named, of all things, Warren Harding, in Sarasota. When Bob got him, he said he was too busy to talk, but he'd call back.

"A couple of days later, he did. He asked, 'Are you the Robert Monroe of *Journeys Out of the Body*?' Bob said he was. After Mr. Harding had read *JOOB*, he spent four years looking for Bob.

"He said he had just been on a plane to Phoenix and read an article about Bob.

"Anyway, he came up to Virginia for a week, and mostly we talked about metaphysical stuff.

"Maybe it was on the Thursday, he said, 'Well, it's time to do business. It didn't take more than twenty minutes.' We were amazed. Bob thought we were in for a long haggling session. Harding's original asking price was tremendous.

"But it was easy." The deal was made, literally in minutes. An exchange of some property on Whistlefield plus cash for Roberts Mountain. " 'See, I told you it would go quickly,' Mr. Harding said."

Bob Monroe adds softly, "A great sense of approval came through from the nonphysical Friends. They had kept me busy, thinking of all the reasons I should leave Whistlefield."

The Monroes finally bought the New Land in 1977. It is thus named, because while they were at Whistlefield , they always said, "Let's run over and look at the New Land." A family named Roberts lives on the other side of the mountain, but doesn't use the name in their farm business. Thus Bob's property formally became Roberts Mountain Farm.

The deal done, Monroe was land-poor for a short while, until he was able to unload the rest of the Albemarle County estate. And then the problems on the New Land began, in earnest.

"We sold the Charlottesville apartments quick. I was down to a third mortgage on one of the complexes, and that's kind of a thin place to get.

"I sold my interest in the Jefferson Cable Corporation, too.

"Of course, I didn't realize what I was getting into. It was a revolution in lifestyle. I mean, going from living in something over 6,000 square feet to less than 1800!"

Would the Monroes do it again—split from the life of the gentry—if they had the option? "That's debatable. Now, I tend to think we could have achieved it all without moving away from Whistlefield."

* * * *

The actual move to Roberts Mountain Farm came in 1979. Once, in the early days, Emmett and Alice Monroe visited the New Land, and Bob typically and grandiloquently told his brother, "Well, I'm going to dam that stream and make a lake there." Emmett thought nothing further of it till his next visit—but there was the lake.

With the decision to buy the New Land, another phase of Monroe operations started to compute. The plan was to build an impressive center for the Institute, but before that, roads and other infrastructure had to be put in on the wild, undeveloped farm. A period of intense activity of a very physical nature ensued, to parallel the metaphysical.

Bob pauses for a moment to do some mental computation. "I guess you could say we sunk at least six hundred thousand dollars (at late 1970 prices) into Roberts Mountain Farm in land purchase alone.

"My total investment, in building the Center and the Gate House and the Gift House, must be around two and a half to three million.

"The jury's still out on whether it was right.

"One reason is that the Center is a compromise; it's not what I wanted it to be. It's a building someone else started. It's not my design, and we had to jury rig it to get it going. The same with the Gate House. We had to take over empty shells.

"Then, I've had to accept the realization that many things I contemplated doing here probably won't come to pass."

There were grandiose plans for the Center, at first. Bob had designed what Nancy Penn still considers a superb building: A glassed-in dining room, a wraparound deck. A donor who remains nameless, came forward and offered to fund the construction, but insisted that the plans be changed to make what amounted to a VIP dormitory. Building started. Suddenly, the philanthropist stopped paying the contractors, and left Bob with a bill for more than seventy thousand dollars. The donor had lost his discretionary money on the stock market, he said.

"The funny thing is, he came back to us in February 1980, and made an offer of $1.2 million for the entire farm and buildings," Nancy continues.

"It was just another example of Bob being badly burned by people whom he had given his trust. He just can't bring himself to ask for a person's financial statement before he plunges into something.

"He has been burned to the bone by 'Consciousness People'—more so than he ever was by the hardcore Wall Street and Madison Avenue businessmen. When he got down here, he thought the Consciousness People were more moral, more Godly, more honest than the New York wheeler-dealers. Now, he's backed off. But I can't say 'I told you so.' It hurts too much."

* * * *

One of the most thoughtful observers of Bob Monroe over the years is the deceptively-young-looking Chris Lenz, who worked at the Institute in a variety of capacities and, even when not associated with Bob Monroe, has maintained a watching brief. Lenz is not hesitant to make blunt comment on Monroe, but through his remarks shines a deep affection for the man and a respect for his work.

Chris is a student of mystical history and Oriental faiths, particularly yoga. He grew up and went to college in Michigan, migrated to Hawaii, became a tour guide, and eventually led tours to the Orient. When he returned to the mainland, he went to work on a Ph.D. at the California Institute for Asian Studies. His Indian professor delivered the final lecture in the course and died the next day. There was no one else who could guide Chris through his doctoral thesis on the chakra model. Lenz abandoned his studies.

Chris had raced through *JOOB* at one sitting several years earlier, after his father tossed it to him one night. He first met Bob Monroe when he attended the 1975 Council Grove with the California Institute dean of students, Dr. Hilary Anderson.

Thereafter, Chris and Hilary took a Gateway course trained by Scooter and Tom Campbell at the Westerbeck Ranch. Then they rounded up a group to train at a retreat north of Santa Cruz. At the last moment, the cook cancelled out. Lenz asked an acquaintance, Karen Malik, if she would cook for the thirty students. Karen agreed, and therewith started another long association with the Institute.

Scooter came out to the West Coast again, watched the Santa Cruz seminar closely, then certified Chris and Hilary as qualified to train Monroe material at weekend courses. Three days later, Lenz had an OOB.

Somehow, Chris recalls, Monroe scraped together enough to pay him a survival salary; Chris put together a few weekend groups in California. Hilary Anderson bailed out of the program: "She was disappointed at the lack of philosophy. She felt that people undertaking this level of exploration needed a solid intellectual grounding from which to interpret the experience. Bob, thought as he does today, that the experience was far more important than a doctrine: That each individual has his own needs. . . . that each person would draw from his experience to create some sort of philosophy in this, human level of reality. He regarded the process as the truest form of human creativity, as well as a reinforcement of the whole consciousness. From my own experiences in meditation, I agreed with him. Now I'm not so sure."

Chris Lenz continues, "Anyway that left me alone on the West Coast. I was it." "It" became the Monroe Institute West.

"I was a natural for it. I had the historical side of mysticism behind me. I had developed my own philosophy." Tour-guiding gave him the confidence to stand up and talk in front of groups. "I could explain myself."

Chris discovered a new building at 42 Miller Avenue in Mill Valley, Marin County, north of San Francisco. In a stunning setting of redwoods, it had been designed primarily for medical offices, but contained a large ground floor room with mirrored walls. The building also had a sauna and the other gadgetry of a spa. It became a cherished address for Monroe-ites, and was later the home of the Explorers Club—a group Lenz organized to do weekend tape excursions.

* * * *

Bob Monroe presided over the first full-length Gateway ever given in August 1977 at the Feathered Pipe Ranch near Helena, Montana. The accommodation was primitive; it even snowed during the course, which was a ten-day affair. But the material was so powerful, people remembered it clearly long afterwards.

Feathered Pipe kicked off a period of intense activity for the Monroe Institute of Applied Sciences. Brochures of the late 1970s carry imposing lists of seminars, workshops, weekend refreshers sprinkled liberally across the country, from Seattle to Boston.

Immediately after Feathered Pipe I, Chris Lenz moved to Virginia. Karen became Chris's successor, took over Lenz's apartment and got stationery printed: Monroe Institute, Western Division, 625 Fifth Avenue, San Francisco. Karen's territory was "anywhere west of the Mississippi." She organized mailings and workshops. In the summer of 1978, Scooter came out to train a Gateway in San Diego. Bob was present, "to lend moral support." They told Karen, bluntly, "You'll have to train." Feathered Pipe II and III followed, into 1979.

Karen found that selling Monroe on the West Coast was mostly by word-of-mouth. "We didn't have the money to do any advertising. I would start to meditate well in advance of the course, and put out to the Guides that the right people show up, that enough come so we could keep going." Monroe West did have to cancel some workshops, because of insufficient enrollment. Karen says, "I never tried to sell anyone who really resisted. It was really a soft sell. Monroe is not for everyone."

In 1979, the Institute participated in a "Holistic Life" Eastern Mediterranean cruise which featured a number of the serious New Age leaders of the time, including Elmer and Alyce Green, Jack Schwarz, and Patricia Sun. The enticing flyer for the metaphysical odyssey—including a summer solstice celebration at the Great Pyramid—advertised the participation of Bob Monroe, but in the event, Chris and Karen pinch-hit and conducted back-to-back Monroe workshops on board, between shore excursions. "It was a picnic, but a lot of work," Karen recalls.

Many of those on the ship were Feathered Pipe graduates. During the cruise, Elmer Green said he would recommend Monroe training only if Chris Lenz or Karen Malik were the trainers, because they brought a spiritual base to it. Lenz continues, "Art Gladman thought that the approach of the trainer and his way of interacting with the students was seventy percent of the course. I was surprised, because to me, the power of the course rested in the tapes. I thought of myself then as purely a tape jockey."

* * * *

Not only is Monroe not for everyone, as Karen Malik commented: By 1977, he was sufficiently well known to attract adverse publicity from a predictable quarter. Until *JOOB*, most of his metaphysical work was "covert." But that the book had some impact, may be judged by the following.

An organization called the "Spiritual Counterfeits Project"(SCP), in Berkeley, California, specializes in debunking cults and in countering threats to what it perceives to be Christianity. In the April 1977 first edition of its new quarterly Journal, the SCP weighed in at length against a trio composed of Elisabeth Kubler-Ross, Dr. Raymond Moody ("Life After Life"), and Robert A. Monroe. The article, entitled "Thanatology: Death and Dying," appears to be based primarily on a Joan Kron piece which appeared in the 1976 year-end edition of *New York,* but the writers Mark Albrecht and Brooks Alexander weave their own interpretation of Ross-Moody-Monroe's work. The criticism of Monroe and the others in the mid-1970s is judgmental, stinging, and dogmatic.

The critical link between factual research, theoretical interpretation and overt occult involvement in thanatology is provided by Robert Monroe, who is—

paradoxically—the least known of the three. . . . (JOOB *is*) *an incredible book which reveals that the focus of his work is away from the center of academic credibility and well toward the fringes of psychism, necromancy and the bizarre. . . .*

The practice of mediumship (or necromancy, i.e., divination by contact with the 'dead,' especially through the agency of 'familiar spirits') is dealt with extensively in the Bible, which gives it the worst possible notices. . . . The mediumistic involvements of Robert Monroe find their most direct outlet to 'thanatology' through Dr. Kubler-Ross. . . .

Kubler-Ross serves on the board of advisors for M-5000 and occasionally (if not regularly) refers clients to Monroe. She has herself undergone the OOB training twice, reportedly getting out of her body on both occasions.

The Journal article goes on to quote an unnamed attendant at a Kubler-Ross lecture, during which Dr. Kubler-Ross talked of meeting her spirit guide, Salem, and two of his companions, Anka and Willie. The writers comment:

There are several things to note in this account. The first is that what is described here can only be classified as a form of concourse with the forbidden spiritual realm (necromancy) and therefore bears the full weight of the relevant biblical warnings and judgments. The second is. . . . a considerable belief-commitment and surrender of will to the spirit(s) involved.

And, later in the article:

As we have pointed out. Moody, Kubler-Ross and Monroe all are involved in mystical experiences and have a vested interest, emotionally, ideologically and financially in the acceptance of their views. . . .

If we are to take the teachings of Jesus seriously, we must also take Satan and his forces seriously. . . .

It is perhaps not surprising that the conclusions of Moody, Kubler-Ross and Monroe are finding an increasingly enthusiastic audience in a 'post-Christian' society. . . .

People like Monroe, Moody and Kubler-Ross are very available and influential pawns in a cosmic chess game. Kubler-Ross hinted at the objectives of at least one party to this conflict when she shared her hope that "in the decades to come, we may see one universe, one humankind, one religion that unites us all in a peaceful world" *(Journal's emphasis).*

In any case, we seem to be dealing with forces and concepts that have been forbidden and opposed by God and His people as far back as Moses." [13]

* * * *

Chris Lenz moved to Virginia in the fall of 1977. "Scooter needed a break away from the family. Bob watched me at Feathered Pipe, and that was that." He first stayed at the Owl House at Whistlefield, later helped with the transition to New Land. Lenz wrote some of the first Gateway manual.

Lenz takes stock of Bob Monroe as he prepared for another major turning in his life. "Gurus attract us by implying they can satisfy a need we have; they then act as midwife to a new state of consciousness that reduces or cancels the need.

"I think Bob realized this role most of the time. But the internal and external pressures of the time and his energy swings would sometimes put him in that anxious, sad, fearful, depressed state in which all the negatives in his life were so apparent to him.

"Or that state would cause him to view in a highly colored and distrustful way his own tendency to love, trust the Universe and delight in the deep sharing with others. He recognized these swings and handled them as responsibly as he could, but he felt sorry that the confusion inside himself caused dismay in those around him.

"When Bob's 'on,' he's perfect. He uses all his radio training to great effect. He's a showman. He's one of the best communicators I've known—if he really sees the necessity. His ability to give the large picture, with all its sub-levels, is amazing. When he has to do a TV tape, he needs only one take to get it right."

With Lenz's arrival in Virginia, and the increasingly "professional" approach to Monroe's work, Tom Campbell remarked, "The fun went out of it." His comment hit Lenz hard, "because what we were doing should have been the essence of fun, not highly-pressured."

* * * *

Once he made his full commitment to the Institute and the New Land, and worked out his remaining other-world business problems, Bob adapted to a new routine. He was still the driving force behind the Institute courses, and he put in regular appearances wherever they were held. But much of his time was now spent in supervision of development on the New Land: First, the Gate House, which was to serve as housing for the Monroes and office space for the staff; then, gradually, the Center, David Francis Hall, and the new lab building. There were financial pressures, too, as money from outside sources dried up and Bob had to scramble to provide funds from his own resources. Operations closed down for the winter of 1978 through 1979, to permit the construction to proceed.

The Institute became an entity in itself, began to take on a troubled character of its own, and became part of what is sometimes called the Monroe Group. There were, too, throughout the period, the series of disappointments in his relationships with others that were left unattended as Monroe prepared to withdraw into his contemplative period.

At the time, he was beginning to think about *Far Journeys*, still some years from publication; the germ began to flourish as Bob continued to travel the Interstate ever farther, using the facilities of the Whistlefield lab as long as it was available, thereafter exploring in the privacy of his own quarters.

Somewhere in the boxes of Monroe Institute papers are some photographs of the site where The Center was taking shape in the first half of 1979, on the crest of the gentle hill, overlooking the meadows of Roberts Mountain Farm. What is startling about the pictures, says one who has seen them, is that shafts of light emanate from the excavation.

Soon, the framing of the Center was in place, but little else. The contractor was new at his calling; he was a man more accustomed to working behind a microphone or on camera, and he still has a TV program in Lynchburg. After the first financier pulled out, a second well-wisher offered to pay for completion of the building, but then also reneged. Monroe was only able to finish the Institute's main building by taking out a third mortgage on his property. But he had to cut back on what Nancy calls "his unbelievable design," and draw the plans yet again, to produce what is today's Center.

"Bob had everything to do with the building of the Center, which a lot of people don't realize.

"He pulled the chestnuts out of the fire," says Nancy Penn. "But Bob doesn't rue the day he had to scuttle his plans. He never says, 'If I could just have done it as I wanted to!' He's just glad he came out with something that turned out as well as that building."

Just two weeks before the first Gateway at the Center, Bob Monroe was in the county seat of Lovingston, appearing before the Supervisors to get the necessary permits. "They didn't understand what this new educational institution was all about, but Bob was persuasive, and we got the go-ahead."

What followed immediately was the Maiden Voyage—the first Gateway at the Center, in 1979. It was chaotic. Not only had the necessary permits only been forthcoming at the last minute, but the innards of the building itself were not complete. Participants in the Maiden Voyage remember carpet being laid, wiring being installed as they checked in. The course actually started two days late, and it was a very bumpy voyage. Some students rebelled; Bob Monroe called a meeting, and offered any who wanted it, their money back. It's a policy that's still in effect at the Institute.

* * * *

In San Diego, Barbara Collier, who attended the first two Feathered Pipe Gateways and the Maiden Voyage in Virginia, recalls the late 1970s on the West Coast. "In a way, those first and second courses in Montana were depressing. Everyone began to talk of survival. We were thinking a lot about getting away from the cities, because a lot of people were getting dire images of the future." At both, Barbara's friend Mary White had visions of a world in devastation.

Such fears led, in part, to the meetings that kept the Montana group closely-knit. There was much talk of an attempt to buy a rural retreat and survival center.

Around 1977, an Explorer at Whistlefield came up with some grid coordinates. Bob Monroe located them on a map and asked Chris Lenz, who was then still in California, to "go see what's there." Lenz reported, with some excitement, that the coordinates matched a beautiful ranch in Kern County. Lenz learned the ranch was for sale at a reasonable price. It seemed obvious Monroe West was destined to move there. The place had everything the Californians needed: Hot springs, buildings, a temperate climate in the Sierra foothills.

The Monroe Institute, of course, had no spare money. At the second Feathered Pipe Gateway, Bob Monroe mentioned the prospect of the California property. It became known as the Rainbow Ranch Project. John Biggs, a real estate developer in the Bay Area at the time, developed a two-year game plan. Biggs formed a limited partnership for would-be investors. With Chris Lenz now in Virginia, Karen Malik and Biggs visited the ranch often, and even flew over the high Sierra grazing pastures with the spread's owner. Karen explained the work of the Monroe Institute to him carefully.

On one occasion, Bob Monroe met the owner at Burbank Airport to discuss the deal. The two got along well together, but the California Monroe-ites needed signed, bankable agreements which would give them operating rights in the West. "We almost had it several times," Karen says delicately. "But the lawyers always raised more difficulties."

The ranch has since changed hands. Karen has an indescribable feeling that "it is being held by the new owners for us. There's such wonderful energy there...Such a place to do healing....I sort of think it has been placed on hold. People just weren't ready for it back then."

From the San Francisco office, Karen Malik organized a schedule of activities, up and down the West Coast, primarily among the redwoods in Marin County: "In 1977 and 1978, we did a lot of weekend workshops in Mill Valley. We formed the Explorers Club. Just get together and do tapes." Eventually the Explorers' activities moved to Oakland. The group sometimes gathered at San Luis Reyes Mission, near San Diego.

The San Diego women volunteered to help staff Monroe booths at New Age expositions as part of the push to get the Institute into the popular consciousness.

"It was funny. We could always tell when someone was hooked. About one in ten would listen to a demo tape on the headphones, and his eyes would start to roll in the middle of the hubbub of the New Age fair! He'd come out of it, glassy-eyed, and say, 'How many can I buy right now? I've got to have them all!' ", says Barbara Collier.

Then, on top of disappointment over the Rainbow Ranch project, and, according to Karen, just as West Coast Gateway operations were beginning to pay, Bob abruptly closed the San Francisco office to concentrate all Institute activity at the new Center in Virginia.

* * * *

In the summer of 1979, Charley Tart issued a plea for the investigation of spiritual phenomena and beliefs, by scientists trained in achieving an altered state of consciousness. There was a note of desperation in his paper, born, no doubt of the frustration Tart had come to know so well as a result of his professional colleagues' hostility to the paranormal. The paper is brilliant, and saddening. A key paragraph is:

> *"....We are not operating in a vacuum, but in a world that is rapidly deteriorating and where civilization may collapse, not simply through economic factors, but because of a lack of shared values that would enable us to put cooperation ahead of separatist, individualistic values....*
>
> *"How much in-depth knowledge of d-ASC's (discreet Altered States of Consciousness), and the longterm effects of experiences in them, do we have to have before we begin (training people in d-ASC's to promote) value experiences, versus the very real pressure that if a sufficient number of people do not have these kinds of values above all else, there may be no world left to continue our investigations in?"* [14]

It was a stern, strong end-of-decade call from a man of vision whose ideas were taking shape when he first met Bob Monroe, more than a decade earlier.

1980s

Well into the late 1970s, the Explorer volunteers shared Bob Monroe's enthusiasm, and worked long hours to give him much of the information he needed to perfect today's Gateway, Guidelines, and latterly, H+ programs. But the Explorer core group members disbanded, in the way of humans, and not of their own volition.

There is a theory sometimes voiced in the outer circles of the Monroe Institute that the original Explorers drifted away because Bob no longer monitored them personally. Any hope of the return of Miranon, one of the cluster's most productive sources, dissolved when Shay St. John moved from Virginia. [1] The intrepid Tom Campbell transferred out in the course of his professional life, as did Yost and Minnerick. In time, Bob and Rosalind McKnight stumbled on their own differences. All remain friends and visit Bob when they are able to.

Other people came into Bob's orbit, although most of them not as Explorers. And not all were as selfless as the early core group. To the contrary, in Monroe's eyes, too many of the newcomers wanted to take Bob over, to exploit his potential in the marketplace, and manipulate his technology for purposes diametrically opposed to his and his non-physical Friends' intent.

Bob became even sadder than he had been in the Richmond business world that commercialism, materialism, and matters of mundane power and prestige intruded in surroundings that should, by his measure, have been pristine. He was, in the words of Nancy, badly burned, too many times, and he withdrew into himself even more.

One of the last of his giving friends was David Francis, owner of the coal mining opertion in Huntington, West Virginia. Francis first made contact with Monroe by phone, then attended an early Gateway. From then on, the two men became more than ordinary friends. In time of need—of which there were many—Francis made donations, none of them probably more than five thousand dollars, but nonetheless useful at critical junctures. Typically, however, it wasn't the money that endeared David to Bob: It was the meeting of minds. The kind of open, non-demanding relationship that Bob could treasure. Francis was available at all times. He could understand what Bob was about. He talked Bob's language, and understood what Bob was going through.

David Francis had an illness, which led to diabetes. He died in 1985. David was, in Nancy's words, "One of Bob's last friends." A stalwart, quiet supporter and confidant.

Bob's gesture of thanks was to name the lecture and classroom building which contains Institute offices and the auditorium "David Francis Hall."

Now, the Monroe Group split into the present constellation of companies: The non-profit Monroe Institute; Interstate Industries Inc., which makes and sells tapes and is the commercial arm of the enterprise; International Training and Communications

Center, basically, the board-and-room aspect of the Center; and Roberts Mountain Farm, which runs cattle and maintains the farm.

* * * *

The most famous of the Explorer tapes issued by the Institute is the Patrick Rescue Mission, which took place on August 22, 1981.

Rosalind McKnight (ROMC) was the Explorer-channel. She recalls, "I had done some rescue work of souls earlier, in New York, but Bob never had." That day, Rosie, as so often in the past, yielded her body and vocal chords to Ah-So, spokesman for her cluster of four entities. Ah-So told Monroe what lay ahead.

"When the entities described what they wanted Bob to do, his jaw dropped."

Bob Monroe remembers, "They said they were going to put Patrick in Rosie's body. I was very concerned. I wasn't sure we could get Patrick back out so Rosie could re-enter.

"It was as if they were patting me on the hand, to tell me, 'We've done this hundreds of thousands of times.' "[2]

Several times during the operation, Ah-So asks for a pause to check on Rosie's well-being, wherever he had parked her for the duration of the mission. "There was a very macho guy standing watch in the control room during that episode. It blew him out of his mind," says Bob.

The Patrick Rescue is the "live" drama of Patrick O'Shaughnessy, galley-cook on a coastal freighter out of Oban in Scotland, in the nineteenth century. Patrick was lost at sea when the ship caught fire and sunk. Bob, as monitor, is put in touch with Patrick by Ah-So, and guides the sobbing, querulous chef to the knowledge that he is dead, that it is time to go Home to his waiting mother.

Rosalind says, "When Bob gets into it, you can hear his Left Brain at work on the tape, trying to establish who Patrick is." Bob's voice ever-so-softly probes the lost sailor, bobbing around in the black, Irish Sea, for identifying information; data which could later be checked, to lend credibility to the event. "Once he got that information, he shifted, his Right Brain took over, and he handled it very well," says Rosalind.

Monroe's efforts to trace Patrick in "real-world" history yielded nothing definite: the Oban parish records contain a proliferation of men with the same name at about that time. There is, however, plenty of corroborating information that the kind of event could easily have taken place.

Bob Monroe has been known to describe the Patrick episode with mock-diffidence as, "The worst bit of ham acting I've ever seen. But I had to believe it because I was part of it." The Patrick tape is today required listening in parapsychology courses worldwide.

Monroe speculates the drama might have been "staged for our benefit. I tend to consider that whole operation was a synthesis, just to show us something. I *know* 'they' have the technological capability."

* * * *

In 1979, the Institute conducted four ten-day Gateways. In 1980, the basic course was cut to eight days, and only four were held—far fewer than the fourteen or more given annually by the end of the 1980s.

After Chris Lenz's departure, Melissa Jager became the director of training. Melissa, according to an acquaintance, is "brilliant; a true student of the occult."

But Melissa insisted on conducting lengthy post-tape philosophical discussions, and interjected her own beliefs into the format of the course. In some cases, the bull sessions, which those who experienced them say were absolutely fascinating, ran nearly through the night.

Students were leaving Roberts Mountain, their heads crammed with a lot more than pure Monroe; Bob began to hear complaints. He felt people came to the Institute to learn *his* techniques, not to attend a school in comparative mysticism. The two gifted people, consciously or otherwise, steered a collision course.

"Bob had absolutely nothing against any other method, but he didn't think it was proper they be taught during Monroe courses," says Nancy Penn Monroe. The upshot was inevitable. In 1983, Bob heard Melissa express violent anger, while students listened in the background, and asked her to resign as director of training. Melissa did so, but her anger persevered.

"The funny thing is, if Melissa walked in here today, Bob would give her a big hug," says Nancy Penn.

* * * *

One of those who came to Virginia went on to become a growing figure in the New Age. Meredith Lady Young attended a Gateway in April 1980 with her husband, Jim, then a vice-president of CBS, and later wrote about it in *Agartha*.

> *I agreed to go along on what I was sure would be just another of (Jim's) intellectual exercises on consciousness. . . .*
>
> *Although I did not know it then, this workshop would forever alter my conventional existence, changing what had always been. It was called "The Gateway Program," a term which later proved to be entirely prophetic. . . .*
>
> *I was expecting nothing, and Jim was expecting everything. . . The people who came to this workshop were mostly serious researchers, not neophytes like myself. . . .*
>
> *My visions grew in intensity with each new session until I lost count of the days, the time and even what Jim was doing. . . .*
>
> *The memory of the experiences glowed within me, and I laughed, cried and rejoiced in my discoveries. . . . It was as if a dam had broken within me and a sense of renewal flooded into my life. I was free. . . .* [3]

* * * *

Morrie Coleman, the California businessman who came in as one in the chain of administrators, and stayed on independently to breed llamas on the New Land, convinced Bob to ask Nancy Lea to return to the fold.

Scooter recalls the 1978 parting from Bob "had not been easy. I was trying to be something more than the little daughter. I wanted to understand what was going on. And then, we both like to be right. We were butting horns a lot." But now Scooter knew, "the time had come to return," and she became administrator on August 4, 1983. She also immediately trained three Gateways in a row.

The office atmosphere was uncomfortable. "I was thirty-one by then, and there was a feeling that my return was nepotism." Some more staff changes were made. Martin and Rita Warren, who had settled on the New Land, volunteered to run the Explorer program.

Stuart Twemlow and Bill Schul came to Virginia from Kansas periodically, but, with Melissa Jager gone, there was no permanent training cadre. With her usual, remarkable energy, Scooter compiled a list of requirements for trainers. The Institute literature at the same time was poorly produced. Scooter designed and printed the first new brochures. "We added structure."

Scooter reflects, four years after her return, "There are too many things here which we do outside of standard operating procedure for the Institute to be orthodox. We have an incredible amount of flexibility.

"It's Bob's baby. To work with Dad, you have to know how to let go, especially let go of your ego attachment.... Letting go of 'how I think it should be.'

"Working with him is a real educational experience. It can be a lot of fun: He's an entrepreneur, but he's also an idea man, and he goes off at a tangent a lot. Or he'll say, 'I don't want to hear the details; just take care of it.'

"All of us have done a lot of changing. He has let go of a lot of small decisions. He realizes things are going very well. He doesn't come down to the office very often, and he's not switching things around every whipsnitch."

* * * *

There is a strong international aspect to Monroe activities. A steady stream of Gateway Voyagers, Guideliners, and H+ apprentices, comes across the Atlantic. There is even a trickle from the Pacific basin. The foreign participants usually get to Monroe the same way Americans do—by reading the books, occasionally by word-of-mouth. They generally come individually, and are from Britain, a few from Germany, and sprinklings from other countries. In mid-1987, a wave of interest started to gather in Australia, the result of an article in a New Age journal there, and the arrival of *Far Journeys* from its British publisher. Almost immediately after the magazine piece, a phone call from a Melbourne bookstore held out the possibility of at least three back-to-back Gateways in that city.

Operations in Europe itself ticked over at a comparatively low rate. A young professional psychic and psychotherapist named Harrald Wessbecher read about Monroe in a German magazine in 1984, and felt drawn to Virginia. He did a Gateway and stayed on to do some Exploring in the lab. Thereafter, he visited the Institute several times a year, learned to be a Gateway trainer and translated and voiced the tapes in German. Harrald operates his own "Dynamis Institut fuer Metaphyschologie" in Karlsruhe, and he saw an opportunity for the Monroe curriculum in conjunction with his other activities.

Wessbecher started to give Gateway in England, with seminars at Newmarket, attended in each case by thirteen people. But traditional British reserve over new techniques presented a stumbling block. Monroe was not a well known name in Britain; expenses were high. After the three sessions, Wessbecher withdrew from England.

More recently, the informal activities of Jill and Ronald Russell, and their "Monroe Outpost," in Cambridge seem headed towards establishing a more solid Monroe presence in Britain. The Russells' operations are discussed elsewhere.

* * * *

Why has Bob Monroe had so much difficulty with people over the years, at least some of whom have come to the New Land genuinely wanting to help him? Why have almost none stuck with him more than a short time?

Bill Schul was around the Institute intermittently at the time: "It's only my opinion, but I think Bob was torn between two worlds—whether to stay Here or not. Personally, he would have liked to have moved on. He felt more at home There.

"But it was his and his Guides' decision that he stick around and finish things. That period of decision before the issue was resolved, maybe it affected the programs.

"All of this trauma, this internal scanning... Our life Here focuses us to look through different windows. If we're complacent, we don't.

"That period gave Bob the time to make acquaintance with himself, to learn where he was going. It's part of the 'integrals' of decision-making."

Bob's comment on some of his deep disappointments is straight-from-the-shoulder. "People attach expectations to me. They expect things I neither promised nor offered. Because those expectations aren't fulfilled, they feel I have let them down.

Some time ago, a representative of the Institute "spent thousands of dollars without my authority and then tried to bill me for it. I flat out refuse to pick up the responsibility for other people, unless I have a contract which specifies my responsibility."

Someone else was "an independent contractor. I wasn't responsible for his debts. He was exquisitely casual in his bookkeeping. It took months to get his reporting. He's a pretty good predator."

Another business associate openly said he was learning the business at Bob's expense, before branching out on his own. "It was six months till we got any accounting. When I got it, it was a P & L statement mixed in with a balance sheet. It was a scam. In fifteen months, we didn't get a nickel out of the deal.

"I'm antithetical to the idea of people taking big bites out of me and running away to chew them. We spend twenty years developing something, and they make money without giving us a return!"

Another source of disenchantment has been outright copying of the Gateway program. "One man dubbed the Gateway tapes and tried to open up in Florida. Another copied the tapes through his Chec Unit and tried to set up in Michigan."

In contrast, Bob cites his dealings with the American Finance Corporation in the cable company expansion: "I never had the first controversy with them, or any contractual disagreement. They brought one thing into the company, capital, I brought another. Their business was money. I learned a lot from them.

"I operated my own business, not unsuccessfully, for years. I didn't make a hundred million, but I didn't starve.

"The moment I got involved in the consciousness field, I did have problems.

"The consciousness people may not be any less ethical than anyone else, but you *expect* them to be better.

"It's as if they're saying, 'What's Bob's is mine and what's mine is mine.'

"That was a dull, dull surprise."

"It seems as if I never learn. These days, I'm becoming a little arbitrary. I put things on paper."

Bob shifts gears. "I'm not New Age. They're like kids playing with toys, using stuff that has been around for centuries, in some cases. But that doesn't make them valid or useful.

"Crystals are crystals are crystals. Scientifically, we don't know about their effectiveness in healing. There's not one solid shred of evidence.

"It's not to say that crystals aren't effective. But I wouldn't bet my life on them.

"I'll bet my life on H+. If I can find a way to use crystals which I can respect, I'll put it in the H+ program.

"I'm hard-nosed when I look at various things. They've got to produce results I can see objectively.

"I can be mystical all over the place, but it helps to have a little knowledge.

"Maybe I should be a hard-nosed guru, after all."

* * * *

One of the persistent rumors among people who have had contact with Bob Monroe is that he has been approached to do work for the CIA. Bob flatly denies that any overture has ever been made, although, he says, "We've had moles come to the Institute to attend the Gateway courses, posing as reporters." "Agents" who have taken the Voyage arrive ostensibly to learn, but, in a number of cases, have been so thinly covered they have become embarrassed, especially as the power of the experience hit them.

Bob Monroe's view of the use of Hemi-Sync techniques for espionage is an amusedly tolerant one. "If Joe and Ivan were Out-Of-Body and met, say, over Iceland, they'd probably get together and take off from there to have fun."

The Soviets have, indeed, made gestures to Monroe. The first was in the form of a postcard, signed by an individual, asking for information which was publicly available in Bob's books. Bob had the individual's identity checked through some of his government friends; it turned out that the Soviet Institute from which the man was writing was of interest to the American intelligence community.

* * * *

In 1983, the news services carried a story which led to considerable trouble for Monroe. It dealt with stress-management in battlefield troops in any future war, and was picked up by *Omni:*

> *One possible way to get troops to sleep on command is a technique developed by Bob Monroe of the Monroe Institute. . . .*
>
> *Monroe's system recently underwent a trial at Fort Benjamin Harrison, where Army officials say all the results aren't in. "We're going slow with it," says psychologist James Caviness, chief of the soldier-performance division. "Our job is not to laugh at the possibilities, but to try them."*
>
> *Caviness says the (Monroe) technique appeared successful when tested with a*

comparatively small group of twenty subjects, and more trials are under way. All who wanted to were able to go to sleep, he says, and none found the sleep-inducing tones unpleasant. "None of our students ever thought, 'Oh, my God, I'm going to sleep,' and fell into a zonked-out state," he says....

Caviness says other combinations of tones from Monroe's tapes appear to increase alertness. Continued success in research might someday lead the Army to issue psychological support gear as well as guns to men headed for the front. [4]

Ray Waldkoetter amplifies the story: "From September to December 1982, I used Bob's advice to design research with the Defense Department Information School (DINFOS), Fort Benjamin Harrison, to learn whether Hemi-Sync in audio training materials would enhance learning.

"Bob's consulting role and training of a small Army research team led to a successful experiment using basic broadcasting students. While the students did not necessarily learn 'more,' they significantly learned more readily, with less attendant stress.

"I've seen Army researchers convinced in the past, even though they had expressed reservations about the FFR (Frequent Frequency Response) and Hemi-Sync.

"An Army Science Board sub-group met at the Monroe Institute circa July, 1983, to address emerging technology affecting human behavior and performance. Although the Board did not endorse the Hemi-Sync technology over others, it was extremely important that the Monroe Institute was chosen as the meeting site."

The publicity on the DINFOS test came to the attention of congressmen. The Army dropped the project with unseemly haste, under the political pressure.

* * * *

In 1984, Bob was finishing up *Far Journeys*, which was not easy to write. Sometime in late 1983, he put together a flowchart headed, "MIAS (Monroe Institute of Applied Sciences) Vision." Among the contents of its neat little boxes are the following, in unmistakable Monroe terminology:

Purpose: To keep funds flowing in for further R & D and overall operations. Keep in profit margin. All bills paid with abundance in all accounts.

Tapes: Being main product of MIAS, new product will insure growth and expansion. Produce new experimental music and prof. research tapes. Four new tapes a month, with at least two being salable. RM to teach another the art and science of making tapes; RM making tapes; Get ideas from Prof. Members, Gateway participants, staff.

Research: To discover and use more of a man's mental abilities to enhance his understanding and control of his life. R&D on greater scale thru Explorers, Prof. members, outside research facilities. Ongoing NVC with Hi-Tech established. Stat. reports on how Hemi-Sync affects brain. Emerging new applications. Develop a profile to determine talent of potential Explorer. Find Explorers.... Getting already-established researchers to do research on bio-effects of Hemi-Sync on brain and body.

Programs: To disseminate our methodology; to help fund MIAS. On-going development of Gateway, etc. One full Gateway a month at Center. Three-five Graduate Gateways (Guidelines) a year. Five West Coast Gateways a year. Through Gateway participants, find out what is and isn't working and adjust. Train more facilitators. Set up West Coast operation. Seek new applications for program such as prisons, nursing homes, orphanages, etc.

Distribution: To make Hemi-Sync available to as many people throughout the world as possible, to aid man in understanding and controlling his life. Making H-S a household term through marketing. *(Emphasis added) Internationally known. Large sales. Get background research needed (e.g., statistical reports on effectiveness of H-S process); Get professional marketing association to handle advertising and distribution; Direct mail; bookstores*

Education: To integrate H-S into all levels of educational systems. Have H-S process in school systems (elem-college) across the country. Have H-S in all elementary schools in Wash. from Edrington work. See expansion of above to all elem., secondary and colleges throughout the country. Follow thru with Edrington's work at elem. level in Wash. school system. Distribute Super Learning pkg. @ elem. level, branching out thru prof. marketing. [5]

Medical: To upgrade present barbaric medical practices, e.g. overuse of drugs and consequent habituation; to aid in psychiatric treatment; to speed up and enhance healing process. To see H-S used effectively in hospitals, clinics and private practice. Continued reports of successful use by patients. Start with prof. members who are MD's, psychiatrists & psychologists who are using tapes on patients. Get H-S into hospitals, clinics, thru prof. members. Get in hospitals, clinics, private practices through prof. mass marketing.

There is much to ponder in the above outline. It is not the business plan of a man bent on making millions. The emphasis, right up front, is to make enough to pay the bills and have some left over to maybe buy a prime rib dinner now and again.

It is also the plan of a man with far visions and the conviction that he can help, if given the chance, in a number of key areas of human life.

The plan reflects, minimally, Bob's setbacks to date, but it is optimistic they can be overcome in the future with the goodwill and efforts of Monroe enthusiasts.

Finally, Bob sees his Hemi-Sync technology broadly available in the mass marketplace, which is an approach he had heretofore not made explicit.

* * * *

In 1985, Bob Monroe's near-mystical second book *Far Journeys*, appeared, after the usual lengthy period of gestation. With publication, Bob Monroe headed into his contemplative period—the home stretch.

Charley Tart, reviewed *FJ* for readers of his now-discontinued newsletter, *Open Mind*: "It is a moving, complex, fascinating story of the kind of experiences that are prominent in mankind's spiritual heritage."[6] Tart expanded: "Lucid dreamers may be inclined to believe that people who claim to have OOB's are merely misinterpreting their dreams. People who have OOB's are inclined to think that those who talk about their lucid dreams may be too readily dismissing what may be actual OOB journeys to other realities. I suspect both are right sometimes.

"Monroe has told me that his OOB's are easily distinguished from lucid dreams because he can't work 'magic' in them. He finds himself in places that have their own reality, and he cannot change them by mere acts of will. Further, the other worlds he visits in OOB's show the stability of ordinary reality. . . .The out-of-this-world places Monroe visits in OOB's maintain their principal characteristics from visit to visit. . . .

"*Far Journeys* will be difficult for many readers because the journeys are not local, they are interstate. Monroe (and The Explorers) experience other worlds and communicate with beings in them, and there is no way we can evaluate their reality by ordinary criteria. . . .Again, I strongly recommend reading (or re-reading) *Journeys Out Of Body* before tackling *FJ*. . . .These books will stretch your mind in some very useful ways."

As Tart anticipated, many people have had difficulty fathoming *FJ*. Chris Lenz once remarked to Monroe it was "an analogy of an analogy." Monroe looked at him piercingly and said, "So you understood that, did you?" Chris comments today, "*FJ* is almost jejune science fiction, a most creative work. Those for whom it was written got a rare and delightful twinge of recognition. *Far Journeys* was an attempt to lead people to There. He needed to take a certain number of people with him."

There is, however, enough solid material in the book to have whetted the appetite of a good number of people to explore Bob Monroe's world further.

Where *JOOB* had run its course, *FJ* took over to stimulate interest in Monroe's work, and, incidentally, renewed sales of the earlier *Journeys* book. *FJ* went into paperback in late 1987.

One of the other books of the mid-1980s which expanded the appeal of the Monroe Institute was Michael Hutchison's *MegaBrain*, dealing with "new tools and techniques for brain growth and mind expansion."

Hutchison winds up the section on Bob Monroe's work with this: "There's no doubt more research needs to be done. Meanwhile, there's a certain amount of research that can be done by anyone. The goal of the research is to answer certain questions: do the binaural beats of Hemi-Sync produce an altered state of consciousness in the user? Is this state experienced as beneficial, useful, or pleasant? Can one learn to produce these states at will? It's not like experimenting with genetic manipulation of radioactive material, requiring billions' of dollars worth of equipment and advanced degrees in microbiology or nuclear physics. Nor does it require belief in OOB's, whatever they may be, or in Bob Monroe's arcane gnostic gospel about the spiritual values of 'graduating' from physical reality to higher planes, no matter how charming and exotic these beliefs may be. All that's required is a bit of curiosity and a tape player with headphones. You can do the research at home, alone, in your spare time. The tools are available. Go find out for yourself."[7]

In 1985, the Institute finally began to pay its own way. Soon thereafter, the Explorer program was temporarily curtailed, so the lab would be free for work on the new technology computerizing some aspects of altered-consciousness voyaging. The Institute also became a separate legal entity and a registered non-profit organization.

One of the recurring problems the Monroe Institute faces, in common with other educational outlets, has been the selection of trainers. The Institute's selection from volunteers who are prepared to invest their own time and money in the programs, until certified as trainers, has produced a crop of instructors of uneven talent. The best trainers are those who remove themselves from the substantive guts of the course, and who simply guide the student on his path of exploration—those who provide the form, and leave the content to the initiate. Not all trainers have been able to do this. It has not been unheard of for an instructor—or, as they prefer to be called, a "facilitator"—to tell a student he is wrong, when there is no right and no wrong in Monroe exercises. This failing seems to have been corrected with an innovation in late 1988.

Three "core trainers" were named, and they are the three best and most selfless the Institute has—Dave Mulvey, Darlene Miller, and Stephen Bladd. Every course will be led by one of the trio, assisted by another, outside person.

In 1988, the Gateway program again had a five-to-six month waiting list. Guidelines was in fair shape. The forecast of courses for 1989 included fourteen Gateways, four Guidelines, five H+ intensives, GO (Gateway Outreach) training seminars, a Gateway graduates' retreat and the Professional Seminar.

Increasingly, too, there was a need for some sort of national structure, to keep the expanding network of Monroe people in touch not only with the Institute, but with each other. Of the thousand members, a figure which astonished Bob, two hundred of them were "solid professionals."

The Gateway Outreach (GO) program of weekend introductory courses by resident trainers around the country was introduced in 1985; they might become regional focal points for Monroe activities in the future.

Gateway programs also were held at Joy Lake in Nevada and at the Hawaiian International Conference Center. In the last eight months of 1987 alone, the office staff doubled. A marketing manager came on board. The Gate House offices began to bulge. Soon, the apartment below would have to be commandeered for desk space.

* * * *

By 1987, "trance-channeling" had become big business. J.Z. Knight's Ramtha attracted network TV attention. Shirley MacLaine's books were bestsellers and prompted her autobiographical television drama. Consciousness crept out of the closet, despite, or perhaps because of, the materialism of the Reagan years.

Channelers seemed to materialize out of nowhere, some to cash in, others to perform acts of service modestly. In June 1987, Bob Monroe took a stand of sorts on the subject in the Institute's Bulletin.

"The process is not a new development in human consciousness. . . . It has always been a part of history under various guises, reaching back into antiquity and pre-Biblical eras. . . . The Spiritualist Church. . . . The fundamentalist Christian 'speaking in tongues'. . . . Prophecy, meditation, hypnosis and certain dream states, all bear a remarkable resemblance to the basic phenomenon.

"The Institute. . . . can and does investigate seriously *any* aspects of human thought and behavior beyond the parameters of conventional acceptability, i.e. the 'babies thrown out with the bathwater.'

"The Institute learned quickly the reason for such rejection: Few if any at all could be studied, measured and replicated by applying orthodox methodology. Trying to drink water with a sieve as a cup is a good analogy. A few drops are left on the rim which tantalizingly increases thirst. . . .

"The Institute first encountered assorted versions of what is now labeled channeling as early as 1975.[8] Since that beginning, it has conducted over eight hundred experimental sessions directly or indirectly related to such awareness states, utilizing a total of one hundred and fifty-six subjects.

"A number of such subjects have subsequently moved of their own volition into private and public practice of information gathering/dissemination via altered states of consciousness, long before the current trend...It may be that the Institute has been inadvertently one of the progenitors of the current wave of interest in the channeling process....

"At the very least, the Institute *can* affirm that measurable physiological changes did occur in those who produced successfully such phenomena in the Institute laboratory facility....

"Without exception, each (lab-channeled) 'entity' has as an original purpose the well-being and growth of the living human individual through whom the contact was made. If others benefited from such counseling, this was incidental and relatively unimportant. None had as an avowed purpose or intent the delivery of a vital message for humankind in general. It was only through adroit and persistent queries by Institute monitors that a great mass of raw data/information was generated....

"From our perspective, the public channeler faces one of the most difficult tests imaginable. Because of the nature and profundity of the material transmitted, great attention is focused on the transmitter, the 'television set' as it were. The problems engendered are monumental in terms of the human ego. When the difference between program and set become blurred, the quality and performance of each declines...More questions than answers.

"The Institute does hold that there may be many benefits arising from the wide and growing interest in the channeling process. More and more individuals are discovering that they, too, can 'channel'; in so doing, each can become his own authority with his own source."

Bob Monroe takes more than a casual interest in the sayings of J.Z. Knight's Ramtha, and Mafu, who is channeled by Penny Torres. One afternoon, he sat in the Blazer, musing. "If I listen to Ramtha and slow him down just a bit, he's identical to Mafu, and I've heard both.

"I'm supposed to be on the leading edge of this kind of stuff, but I don't understand it. I know all the processes a director uses to obtain characterization and performance from an actor.

"You can't train a person to be an identical clone of another. For a few minutes, perhaps. But in an ad-lib or extemporaneous situation, week after week? I don't know of any actor who could do it, or a director who could teach him to perform that identically."

Bob shrugged, when considering a theory that J.Z. Knight was elaborating on memory of her early contacts with Ramtha, but that the spirit had left her when she turned commercial. "Possible. But when you get past the razzle-dazzle...." And his voice drifted off.

"As for Mafu! I was all set to meet him (at a public gathering). But he just came up to me and said, 'This is the moment you've all been waiting for.' And hugged me. I got in one bland question, and was ready with the next, but he turned away."

The Institute informally monitors some of the content of both Mafu and Ramtha readings. Despite the lack of substance in the interchanges between Bob Monroe, on the one hand, and Mafu and Ramtha on the other, each of the three, as well as other, less public figures, is basically receiving much of the same information.

* * * *

Musing in public in 1987, Bob Monroe said, "Now we're heading toward more scientific research. We're walking the very narrow line of the orthodox and conventional. The Institute transduces the orthodox. It has a reality of its own."

One afternoon, Bob went to David Francis Hall to see a film brought by the first resident New Lander, Joseph Chiltern Pearce, author of *The Crack in The Cosmic Egg*, and other books. It was a fascinating exposition of the art of "cinemorphology"—the application of computer technology to medical science to produce images: A learned filmed treatise, full of technical jargon, underlining the scientists' true lack of knowledge of the function of the brain.

The movie was not concerned with Right Brain-Left Brain synchronization in the slightest. At the end, Bob leaned across the table, his voice full of ingenuous wonder: "What a piece of engineering the brain is!"

Later, Monroe used the dry, clinical film to illustrate the direction conventional science is headed, mapping parameters, rather than examining content.

It was almost an agonized plea for understanding and courageous initiative; what good was knowing the structure of the brain without investigation of what went on in it?

"Can we not perceive penetration from There? For example, the placebo effect works. Spontaneous remission exists. Belief affects Belief.

"Some massive changes in consciousness are badly needed....Till the fear of 'Have No Body, Will Travel' won't exist any more."

* * * *

In the early 1980s, Professor Charles Tart spent some time examining fear of psi, especially among his colleagues. Some of his comments are apt, when one considers the establishment's reaction to Bob Monroe:

"(Even) positively oriented, pro-psi believers....when they seriously consider psi actually working well, instead of being an infrequent, weak, spontaneous event....a level of fear and realization of negative potentials comes." [9]

Tart issued another plea for acceptance of the altered state of consciousness in 1986, and even though his paper happens to talk of the dream state, it applies to Bob Monroe as well: "In World 1 (waking consciousness), I and practically all of the other ostensibly, independently-existing beings I experience...have convinced (our)selves that only World 1 experience is real and worthwhile, and that World 3 (the dream state/altered state) is useless, unreal, and totally delusory! Why? Because it is not consistent in the way that World 1 experience is, and because it does not accurately mirror the regularities and events of World 1.

"I, a being who knows nothing directly but my own experience, have convinced myself that part of my direct knowledge—direct experience, which I know just as directly when I experience it as any other kind of direct experience—isn't real.

"This dismissal of dream experience as unreal and delusory is, of course culturally relative....(It) goes hand-in-hand with a mainstream rejection of the reality of altered states in general." [10]

The rejectionist point of view was reflected in a short, sharp exchange of correspondence between Elmer Green and a man in Omaha, Nebraska whose topheavy letterhead billed him as an "Independent Consultant: Comprehensive Operational &

Project Consulting. International, Hospital & Clinic Consulting Services. Biofeedback & Stress Management."

The Omaha correspondent said he was writing a book, queried the usefulness of Biofeedback in general, then attacked Green for "'supporting a 'mind-training course,' namely Robert Monroe's Institute of Applied Sciences." (The writer referred to one of the 1977 brochures for the old M-5000 program, which he had kept in his files for the ten intervening years.)

The exchange is instructive for the light it sheds on the 'outrage' of people who cannot accept that others should be allowed to venture into the unknown and find alternate answers.

Elmer Green was told that Monroe was a pure "salesman" with a media background, yet Green had given his "stamp of approval to Monroe's mind-training course....total support to Robert Monroe....Conflict of interest....Both you and Robert Monroe were supporting each other at this time (1977)....Quite a profitable move for you to 'scientifically validate' Monroe....Perhaps you received some form of 'payment'...in a 'consulting fashion'...an honorarium?"

Dr. Green replied calmly to the various threats contained in the lengthy letter: "...My connection with Robert Monroe was as a researcher. I was willing to be an advisor on research, but when he began marketing his program, I did not support it, because it seemed more research was needed, first. If you had called me....you would have found out that my name does not appear on promotional literature. I am not listed as an advisor, and have not been for many years....

"As far as your suggestion that some kind of conspiracy may be afoot to get clients of Robert Monroe into the Menninger Foundation, as a result of our collusion, this is totally untrue and unfounded....

"My advice (to you) is....to expose some of the groups which find parapsychology, consciousness research, and the development of Human Potential a menace to the status quo."

More and vituperative challenges to Monroe from many directions could be anticipated as *Ultimate Journey* came into circulation.

* * * *

It was the Monroe Institute of Applied Sciences until 1985. Then the title was shortened, because the 'Sciences' caused some raised eyebrows among people Monroe wanted to convert to believers, then knowers.

Regardless of the disdain of the scientific and academic communities, there can be little doubt that Monroe's techniques work. There is increasing doubt that scientific method has all the answers.

The simple test for many who question institutions and establishments is whether Monroe actually helps people. The unsolicited testimonials that pour into the Institute, would be dear to an advertising man's heart; they contain ample personal, if anecdotal, proof that Hemi-Sync and Monroe exercises do provide users with anything from relaxation and calm during illness, to healing, and satisfactory explanations of metaphysical life. These experiences are often the main ones that concern the individual. He cannot get the answers he seeks from academia, science, or religion. He may well have experimented with other metaphysical techniques and found them wanting.

The main consideration is that Bob Monroe does not arrogate to himself the power to control men's lives. He leaves the individual in charge, to find his own Guidance... And to choose to return to physical reality after a trip elsewhere.

* * * *

With *Far Journeys* out of the way and the Institute finally making progress, Monroe perhaps for a while thought he could settle back to enjoy putting the finishing touches on the Gift House, putter around the farm, write a few novels, devote time to his music, and to the other projects which have always flooded his mind.

The Gift House nestles on small plateau under the crest of Roberts Mountain, and has a sweeping view of the surrounding foothills and valleys, sometimes wreathed in magical mist. It is at the top of a steep, graveled road which, with ice or rain, is slick and treachorous. It's not a manor house nor yet a castle, but it is very much Bob and Nancy Monroe's redoubt. "It's as if I had seen it before, the way it was supposed to be," Bob says.

The exterior, at least, was pre-ordained, even to the seventy-five-year-old box bushes installed in the winter of 1988, to break up the lines of the facade. The Gift House and its grounds give the feeling they are in a snug compound without the presence of walls or a gate.

It's not a bare hermit's lair. As long as Bob Monroe is stuck in the physical life, he is determined to enjoy it insofar as possible. The house reflects many hours of discussion to achieve a happy balance between the couple's aesthetic and practical needs. There is a waterfall which tinkles over and through the artfully-shaped stone wall in the living room. The dining room is large, formal, ante-bellum. The kitchen-den-TV arena merge into one. "We designed each room so we could change mood, just by walking from one to another. It took two years to build that house. It's the nicest place I've ever lived." especially after the seven years of cramped camping-out in the Gate House, at the entrance of the farm.

The Monroes finally moved in during the summer of 1987. On occasion, Bob waxes lyrical over his retreat:

"It was indeed worth it. A wonderful and different view in every direction. In the summer we live in a forest. In the winter, with the leaves off the trees, the big sky feel. We can see Bear Den Mountain, eighteen miles away. We watch sunrises that are both familiar and different each day. Sunsets in the garden room. We play a little music on the piano, in a room acoustically designed for it. Music in every room in the house, piped from the audio-video center in the den. We can relax at night to the wind roar—deliberately deflected from the house...Lying in bed if we wish. Then to sleep in peaceful, quiet solitude.

Occasionally, a young doe or two come to graze on our new grass, pleasantly surprised to find it in the middle of their territory. Rabbits also drop by and shop around to provide excited frustration for Steamboat, our small dog, who can never quite catch them. A flock of some seven wild turkeys becomes insulted regularly when we insist we must use the driveway. We've seen one black bear, but he took off and didn't come back. And overhead, the turkey buzzards and the hawks pass by, riding the ridge lift on their way up for the big view...And when it rains—the thunderstorms! Unforgettable—they're around us, not overhead. Then the heavy, thick clouds that softly envelop us and our home in a strange gray world. Mornings, when the fog is in the valley below, and we look down on an island-filled grey ocean...."

The sylvan peace of the Gift House is broken uproariously by a couple of dogs whose periodic, meticulous grooming doesn't compute with their facetious efforts at ferocity, nor even with the mud in which they prance.

The animal population of the premises is enhanced by the inevitable core of cats. Bob says, "Blackie always knows when I'm going to eat breakfast, too. She's only missed twice in fourteen years. She was dumped on the road and left for us by her mother."

It's called the Gift House for good reason. When Bob and Nancy thought they had money enough to start construction, the available funds were needed to build David Francis Hall.

But, Bob says "In 1985, we decided if we didn't start building, we would never do it. We got land loans on the farm, but we didn't have the completion money.

"Then, every time we ran out of money, something would happen." Monroe ticks off some of the events:

In two years:

a) Subsidiary rights to *JOOB* unexpectedly sold. Royalty checks in February and August 1986 doubled.
b) A lawyer closed an eight-year-old escrow account on the sale of Whistlefield. His letter contained a check for $18,000.
c) The Social Security Administration re-evaluated Bob's file in his favor. Back payments, plus interest brought in another few thousand dollars.
d) Roberts Mountain Farm produced more calves than usual; simultaneously, the price took off.
e) In March 1986, Bob's insurance company converted from a mutual to a stock company. Monroe took the stock. He then sold the shares in a rising market for $34,000.

"These are only a few of the unusual events...The lesson is...if you want to build a house, start it."

* * * *

The Monroe lifestyle is far from ostentatious. Nancy uses the family silver when the occasion calls for it. But she also zooms off enthusiastically to a Richmond discount emporium, and returns with a carful of mundane supplies. Many of them end up in a pantry which looks as if it has been stocked for earth changes.

Nancy Penn Monroe is slim, handsome, silver-haired and elegant. Except if she's caught by unexpected visitors with her hair in curlers, when she shrieks and runs for cover. She claims she merely cooks and keeps house for Bob, which isn't quite true, although her life is devoted to his well-being. Inevitably, she lives in Bob's shadow as far as the public—and even many New Landers—are concerned. But she is very much her own vigorous person, well aware of the benefits of appearing to be an ineffectual Southern belle when it suits her purpose. Nancy humors Bob, and is humorous about him, but only about the inconsequentials, and even then, with great love and devotion.

Nancy has been mystical since childhood, when she talked to minnows in a pond and often felt "the onrush of something from Nature." She has a concept for a book which she is shy about writing. The idea came to her in an altered state of consciousness: She was simply told, "Build a city not made with hands." It took her some time to fathom the sense of the message.

Bob keeps telling her to get down to the book, let her creative juices flow. But then there are the two dogs and a fluctuating population of cats to be fed, or shopping to be done, or, as Nancy cheerfully says, "Anyway, whatever. . . ."

Nancy sits at the table in the Gift House, far from the "higgy-piggy" formality of Whistlefield, and talks of her man. She could easily reflect wistfulness that she met Bob only after he deserted New York's fast track, and retired to the calm of Virginia, but she shows no trace of envy.

Bob's contentment in his marriage with Nancy is not a commentary on his age. The truth is that Nancy is the first woman in Bob's life who has grown with him, in many—if not all—aspects of his complex personality.

One of the difficulties of living with Bob Monroe is "his crazy time cycles." He gets up around 4:30 in the morning, and treasures the early hours. Nancy is almost reverent, even in the recounting: "It's a form of meditation. Often, I want to get out of bed, but I've learned not to interrupt his quiet time."

Sometimes by 11:00 a.m., Bob's fatigued, so he takes a nap to recharge. Meanwhile the Institute office has opened and needs decisions, there are telephone calls from all over the country and overseas. "I had a lot of trouble learning to fib for him. I'd say he's out, or he's working.

"Now, I don't bother. He's who he is. I don't justify his naps any more. He has plenty of things to do with his time which don't concern me or others. But he hates to be awakened from his sleep."

He has strong views on alcohol, because of its effect on people. "Bob says, 'You don't need booze. You're loving. That's enough.' " The Monroes avoid cocktail parties, especially on weekends. "Bob says, 'Why can't people be like that on Monday morning?' He would prefer we not drink here. But can you imagine a dinner party with no wine?"

"He won't use profanity unless it's to prove a point. I didn't like the four-letter 'f' word in *Far Journeys*, but it proved something."

The Monroes don't belong to the local country club, because Bob considers that style of life too phony. "He says to me, 'I've reached the point where I can be what I am.' He can't stand triviality; he'll get up and go somewhere to sit quietly instead of listening to gossip."

Monroe voluntarily dons a suit (and, in cold weather, one of several knit vests Nancy bought him at Harrods in London) for an evening's appearance at David Francis Hall. He also dresses for the occasion if he has to visit the local bankers. Otherwise, he clothes himself in what can best be described as shambollicking casual style.

Nancy has given up chiding him to pull his shirt down over his paunch. His comfortable belly strains the waistband of baggy trousers, one leg of which is often caught in a sock. For some reason, one sock usually seems to be high up on his calf, the other down around the heels of his tattered canvas deck shoes. Or he wears slippers which even the dogs disdain. He's a cap freak, who enjoys a collection of lids—from the USS New Jersey cap to a brown leather crush bonnet; and they're often in place indoors as well as out.

"He looks so nice when he gets dressed up!" says Nancy with mock despair. "But that's because he's doing what people expect of him."

Nancy continues, "Bob won't let me buy a status car. He would give me one, if it was right for the job, but not just for the name."

Bob once remarked he didn't revere antiques for their age. The precept was, "If it's old and it works, fine. But just because it's old doesn't make it good.

"Of course, he's a techno-nut. Any gadget has to be the most technologically advanced that's available." Which keeps Nancy jumping at Christmas time. "I have to watch the music magazines and things like that. But his attitude is that a toy for the sake of a toy is not satisfying. He immediately asks, 'What can it be used for? If it's constructive, then go for it!' "

Nancy mutters, "Of course, he's a chocaholic. He sneaks sweets. He just can't stay away from them.

"He won't diet."

It is a surprise to those who have formulated rigid visions of Bob that he regularly slumps on the couch at home, shirt and trousers agape, to watch the evening news, "Wheel of Fortune," and "Jeopardy." At times he comments on the production of the quiz shows, and recalls techniques he used to insure that a popular participant got a big prize. ("We didn't rig the shows, but, well, there are ways you can help influence the outcome. Just make the question easy.")

He retains firm control of the TV zapper, and switches from channel to channel, checking out a new antenna which brings in two new movie stations. Nancy, puttering in the kitchen, soliloquizes, "He has to find out who won The War." Autumn Sunday afternoons, Bob makes firmly clear, are reserved for the pro football games, and metaphysics be damned.

One evening, Nancy Monroe brings a supernatural epic from the overflowing library of paperbacks and videotapes in the basement. Bob and Nancy sit cuddled on the couch, absorbed in a film they have seen often before. Occasionally, Bob turns to comment—not on the convoluted plot, but on the film's musical score.

Of course, Monroe is human enough to make excuses for his unthinking time. He "has to" watch the news and the quiz shows to keep in touch with the Culture. Football mayhem is also a barometer of the workings of the public mind, but it's a heartbreaker if the Redskins lose.

The sight of Monroe glued to the television points up one of many paradoxes in the man. Bob was in the forefront of molding the public taste as a broadcaster, an early producer of quiz and entertainment shows in the 1940s and 1950s. Yet now he leads his own rebellion against the enforced mentality society dictates, buttressed by the media monster he helped create.

Another paradox: Bob's manners are post-Victorian: he is courtly to women, whom he still tends to put on pedestals; his attitude towards casual sex is stern (no hot tub at the Institute); he is dead-set against alcohol and drugs. Monroe lived through the social revolution of America's 1960s and 1970s, but they have barely affected him. Conversely, he has taken a quantum leap into spheres that make our customs seem oddly inapplicable.

Bob made some special sleep tapes for Nancy some time ago. They were so powerful, Nancy starts to drift off while listening to Bob's voice in public. "It's so persuasive! I hear just a few lines, and I am gone." Nancy no longer uses those tapes.

But Monroe has to be very careful in his relations with other women. He never holds an embrace with any woman very long. At an evening in David Francis Hall, women "sometimes hear me say something and they think it's directed at them." Bob is aware of the idolization, but is puzzled by it, and probably unaware how much excitement his gentle, understanding, completely male ways arouse in women.

* * * *

The continuing action which swirls around Bob Monroe in his contemplative years centers on the Cabin, across the driveway and up a small incline from the main house. On at least one occasion, the path to the Cabin was a mixed blessing: In February 1988, Bob slipped when the surface was slick and broke an ankle bone. The good news is that he recovered in two-and-a-half weeks, using self-healing, instead of the four weeks the doctors estimated.

The Cabin was hard to build. Bob took the old, hand-hewn chestnut beams from a ramshackle two hundred fifty year-old barn on the property, beams which had been used in three or four earlier structures. The hard wood shows the scars of ancient axes on its surface. It was hard to shape the chestnut to the demands of his blueprints. The insulating chinking between the beams is a special, non-cracking material of which Bob is technically proud. It, too, was very difficult to work. "I can assure you, we wouldn't try to do it again, building a house out of old logs such as these. Some of them weighed as much as seven hundred pounds. But it was worth it."

The internal pine planking was left over from the Gift House construction. Carpenters' pencil marks are still clearly visible, a sign that the construction money for completion has not yet quite materialized.

It's a thinking, creative man's dream hideaway. Not forbidding, but the visitor instinctively knows he must request permission to enter.

The Cabin office is as cluttered as one would expect: a couch, Bob's totally unruly desk. His battered office chair, its stuffing spilling out. Close at hand in the next room, an eight-track reel-to-reel tape recorder, sound-mixing panel, three musical keyboard synthesizers. Then there's the word processor, and the huge monitor screen. He hunches, cap on head, in the nest of the chair, composing *Ultimate Journey*. Memos, letters, flow-charts, reports, policy and planning directives and other papers strew the desk and nearby tables.

Bob is fully aware his material comforts are purely transitory pleasures: "I'm past owning anything. I like the Cabin. I get the use of it. But I don't care who owns it. . . ."

He uses the snug refuge during physical life, and it is a joy to him, but when he is finished with it, it can self-destruct for all he cares.

The "normal" human being in his position might be sorely tempted to insure that his aerie be preserved as a shrine or a monument to himself and his work. But for Bob, the physical appurtenances are passing illusions or props, divorced from true Reality.

The snatch of conversation recalls to mind a haunting phrase spoken by Rolling Thunder: "We Indians are the keepers of the land. We don't claim that we own the land and nobody else does either. . . . The Great Spirit owns the land, but it was delegated to us." [11]

* * * *

Bob Monroe has always had a somewhat cavalier approach to physical health, fairly typical of the generation which matured before aerobics and jogging and fiber foods were mass-marketed. The theory of his generation went roughly to the effect that if you fed, watered, serviced, and rested the physical parts reasonably—but otherwise ignored them—they would do their job routinely, until they wore out in the natural course of events.

In fact, into middle age, Monroe was probably as physically-fit as many of his contemporaries. He knew he needed his reflexes to fly and to glide and sail; he was a scuba-diver. He points to these signs of health with some pride today. He ignores the fact that he smokes, but hastens to add he does not inhale. He also tends to overlook the ulcers in the early 1940s, the later heart attack, and the post-Ecuador malarial siege of his early-to-middle years.

Since his OOB adventures started, Monroe has, not surprisingly, been even less than fully concerned with his physical well-being. Today, he reflects petulance that his body lets him down: His mind continues to soar, but the physical cage inconveniently shows signs of wear and tear. The body is still a necessary vehicle for his earthbound functions, but he still does not treat it with undue reverence; it's merely a physical appurtenance, a means of worldly locomotion, and a sign of his fairly uninteresting physical existence.

Monroe's sleep pattern, especially, is by most people's standards erratic; and even though he no longer drinks at all, he continues to live on a diet which appalls his medical friends—heavy on red meat and coffee (although no butter), and, of course, the continuing addiction to snatched sweets.

* * * *

Nancy frowns, "When he's sick, he's a roaring bear. I do what I have to, then get out of his way. But really, he's mad at himself for being ill to the point of being in bed."

Monroe has had four major surgeries since he and Nancy met and married. In 1970, with a week intervening, he had two endartarectomies at Baylor University in Texas. In April, 1981 he underwent a bypass operation of the sub-clavian artery. Nancy itemizes: "Those two carotid artery operations at Baylor were very painful. He swears he won't have another arteriogram." In March, 1982 he was notified of an aortic aneurism and again underwent agonizing surgery, which "ripped me open from stem to stern."

Nancy continues, "In his last two surgeries, he came to, on the operating table, and if you don't think that gave the anaesthesiologist a shock! He throws off drugs. His local traffic body can't handle local traffic drugs."

Someone asked him why he didn't go OOB during surgery. Bob answered, "If I did, I'd never come back to this cauldron of fire."

The 1982 siege "was the hardest operation, believe me. What kept me going was the knowledge that this was part of the experience.

"That awareness was the only thing that held me through the exquisite pain." It is a remarkably philosophical, calm statement covering a truly traumatic passage.

"That kind of pain only programs you for the same kind of pressure you feel in other realities."

"There are other kinds of things you feel at a different level, which prepare you, so you can handle situations as a non-human does."

Bob Monroe's heart misses a beat at times. "When the skip-beat first started, it caused me some concern. I'd sit there and wait: I could feel my blood pressure and circulation going down. I'd say to myself, 'When is it going to beat again?' " Now, Bob pushes his physical self into a jump-start: "I say, 'Go!', and it goes. If it's going to start up again, it will."

God or spirit? "You can call it a 'god' or a Superbeing, Supra-Consciousness. I prefer to call it the Total Self."

Rolling Thunder has some experience of pain, too. "These things are the price we have to pay, sometimes. Nothing comes free. It's my choice, and sometimes I have to pay heavy....

"I'm also interested in how to handle these things....Every case of sickness and pain has its reason. And it's always a price that's being paid, either for something past or for something future. But that doesn't mean we're not supposed to do something about sickness and pain. The important thing is to know how these things work. Modern doctors—most of them—don't seem to understand that. A medicine man's job is to look into these things. We know that everything is the result of something and the cause of something else....Sometimes, a certain sickness or pain is meant to be because it's the best possible price for something; you make that go away and the price becomes greater. The person himself may not know it, but his spirit knows it....Physical troubles have all kinds of reasons....but they all start on the spiritual level...." [12]

Monroe's comment is complementary: "You may be subjected to an experience which seems to be destructive or injurious, but, in fact, is constructive and beneficial, because of what you learn from it. It can be a physical or a mental trial."

His last bout of surgery is among his Peak Moments: "I don't think I've ever recovered from it.

"I make no excuses. I'm a product of the culture. I may have eaten and done the wrong things. But it has been worth the price."

The experience was a reminder. "That operation was a change in a sense. I realized how mortal this part of me is.

"So I said, 'The hell with anything else.' " Monroe took a close look at his priorities. Top of the list was *Ultimate Journey*. He was told it was OK to be comfortable. He decided to enjoy life, and to ease out of as much day-to-day responsibility as he could.

His brother Emmett, and other medical men who know and care for Monroe agree Bob should not, by their standards, still be alive. Dr. Stuart Twemlow comments on Bob's habits with genuine concern.

Dr. Art Gladman saw Monroe in July, 1986, and noticed he looked exhausted. Gladman asked, "'Bob, what's going on?' I felt I had to point out to him that he looked incredibly stressed."

Soon thereafter, Art called Bob to check on him. Monroe said he had fallen asleep the previous night, and had, in the altered state, discovered what the source of his stress was.

In June, 1987, Gladman and Monroe met again at Reno, where the Monroes were staying while a Gateway Voyage was being given at nearby Joy Lake. By then, Bob looked in far better shape than he had the previous year.

As long as he is Here, Bob Monroe would like to be inconvenienced as little as possible by his physical casing. He has long known the time has come for urgent maintenance, if he is, indeed, to hang around the physical for a while longer.

November 17, 1987 was very important for Monroe. At 8.00 a.m., he had a date at the lab, to guide Nancy through the H+ Preparation Tape.[13] During the following hour, Bob himself went into the Black Box isolation chamber, to have the initial H+ step imprinted in his own mind. He fell asleep. One of the senior monitors, Rita Warren, watched the dials as Bob listened to the tape, and found herself gradually breathing in unison with Bob, so strong was her empathy with him.

Monroe emerged overjoyed. The fact that he had slept proved to him he had accepted the Access Channel for the H+ exercises he feels he needs. He had worried that his familiarity with the contents and his critical ear would so preoccupy him, he would reject the imprint. Henceforth, he felt he was clear to absorb and utilize functions he felt were vital to his well-being, and some which he had specifically designed for his own use. "Now I can do it, too!" he grinned with utter delight.

Bob immediately started to employ some of the H+ exercises. By winter, he reported his eyesight was vastly improved and, he also seemed to feel various unspecified afflictions were on the mend.

* * * *

Where is the Institute going? There is, of course, some criticism from those who have gone through courses, which is more valid than derogatory comment from outsiders who have not experienced the Monroe techniques.

One such comment is that Bob has hit his peak and is now in a holding pattern: Of the more than three thousand hours of taped Explorer sessions, little is available to the public. Much of the material is verbose, tortuous in syntax, difficult to comprehend, and repetitive. A critic cites the "clarity" of Ramtha, for instance, and asks,

"What has happened here? Why is there no more information coming into the lab? The Institute was clearly in the lead. But now. . . ." The critic says the information that has come through has been held too closely and has not been released as it should have been.

"Once the Institute gets back on track, everything will be fine again," the critic says, without specifying what that track may be. "It may well turn into a major center for Earth communication with other intelligences."

The comments are superficial. Bob has been deeply involved in his own voyages, and is putting as much as he can formulate into words into *Ultimate Journey.* The formal shutdown of the lab and the curtailment of the Explorer program was for a technical overhaul of the facilities. It was completed, and the lab resumed normal operations in late 1988. There is no lack of new Explorer candidates coming out of the Gateway program. Some second or third generation Explorers continue to channel new information to the Institute.

* * * *

One place the Institute does not have a public relations problem is among the rural Virginians of Nelson County. A young man who worked at the Institute and doubled as a bartender in outside civilization heard his customers discussing Monroe's: "Oh, sure, they do routine brain transplants there." Someone who stopped in a roadside watering hole listened to locals say: "That's the place they exchange souls."

Bob Monroe thinks such comments are deliberately made within earshot of 'furriners', and are a sly reflection of Blue Ridge humor.

The Institute does lack a broad PR program, in keeping with Bob's theory that the "right people" will somehow automatically find their way to Roberts Mountain. Some at the Institute might add, "with a little bit of judicious help, not to say hype." Only in the spring of 1989 did the Institute at last publish a set of handsome, four-color brochures.

Where almost every institution today is well aware that its image starts with correspondence, Bob Monroe chronically refuses to answer mail, especially when he is involved in a major project. Bob has no full time secretary. At times, this absence of response makes those who have troubled to write wonder just how far one has to go in excusing genius.

Until mid-1988, when B. Dan Reynolds was appointed, the Institute had been without a marketing executive. Since then, the Institute staff has expanded rapidly.

Jim McMahon, a Florida advertising and marketing executive, took a Gateway in 1986, returned for Guidelines in 1987, and became close to Monroe. At Bob's suggestion. McMahon conducted "goals-and-vision" meetings with practically everyone on the Institute staff, and made a series of recommendations. McMahon's main concern was an expansion of the Gateway program: "There really isn't any clear focus on just what the long term goals ought to be. We max out at less than eight hundred people a year, without any promotion, and there's a waiting list.

"I see the first order of business being to increase capacity. But even before this, everyone would have to agree on objectives, timing, responsibilities and so on."

McMahon also thought a new Center was needed, at a cost of one or one-and-a-half million dollars, which could accommodate three or four Gateways simultaneously; he even earmarked space for a new building in the meadow below the Gate House, at the entrance to Roberts Mountain Farm.

Although the non-profit Institute seems to be on the verge of a major expansion, it has no income except from fees for its courses and donations. No foundation has stepped forward to contribute hard cash to the Monroe way of expansion in human consciousness, perhaps for fear of being publicly associated with a bunch of kooks.

The financial bind is, however, not peculiar to Monroe: As Charley Tart earlier underlined, research funds for paranormal activities are lacking everywhere.

Bob and Scooter have more modest plans than Jim McMahon's for expansion of the Center. Ground was broken in December, 1988 for a new wing which will add more bathrooms, and provide a staff dining room. The expanded Center will also have a glassed-in observation tower, to look at the moon, or the wild-fowl, or just for peaceful meditation. There has been talk of building time-share apartments and housing for visiting researchers.

Bob Monroe muses about the future: "I'd like to see Hemi-Sync out in the marketplace. But it would take a strong project manager who could raise a million or two million dollars to set it up.

"One of the surrogates we need is a whole-brained administrative type with a lot of experience in the business world. And with integrity. If I knew one who was available, I'd have him here tomorrow morning."

There are two particular Institute projects which Scooter hopes to develop. One program close to her heart is that the Institute help paraplegics, particularly veterans, to live useful lives. Married to a man who has more than served and suffered for his country, she feels ex-GI's are owed a better deal than purely vegetating in Veterans Administration hospitals.

Scooter describes the second, "to develop ways of using Hemi-Sync to deal with the practical concerns surrounding death. The sense of loss. And how do you tell a terminally-ill patient he's dying?" The idea she is considering is "similar to the Institute's Star System, but for the survivors, so we can deal better with the fact. We need more understanding." AIDS is her prime example.

Scooter has come a long way from the brash youngster who asked Ruth Domin why she wanted to contact people who were in comas, in the mid-1970s.

Not all are sure the Institute can long survive after Bob's passing, which Bob insists, is not imminent. There is the magnetism he exerts, by his presence of an evening, and simply in the knowledge he is just up the road, atop Roberts Mountain.

Scooter confidently rebuts the dubious: "We have so much of Bob on tape and video, it will be almost as if he were there with us in one form or another."

There is, however, anxiety in the minds of some that, without the new metaphysical input to date provided only by Monroe himself, the courses will become warmed-over, outdated and less attractive, as time wears on.

When asked directly if he will return to guide the Institute after his departure from physical life, Monroe says, categorically, "No. The Institute's processes and impetus are established. I hope it will continue to expand and grow."

* * * *

Monroe shows little sign of slowing down, although his physical being may require more rest than it used to. Mentally, however, he surges ahead at what, for anyone, at any age, still amounts to a breathtaking pace. One day in the Cabin, he mused about the priorities he had established for himself after the last surgery.

One of the practical toys that Bob Monroe cherishes is the Lowrey Orchestron—that microchipped organ on which he has composed Metamusic themes. It takes only a little bit of gentle persuasion to get him to move from the cluttered Cabin desk to the Orchestron in the next room, to fiddle with a bewildering variety of stops and buttons—and produce themes evocative of the ocean, or France, or space. All of the sounds can be recorded, amplified, woofed and tweeted on an imposing bank of nearby electronic gear. And if the Orchestron doesn't have enough sounds, there are the synthesizer keyboards racked conveniently to its left.

"I may sound immodest, but I'm pretty good musically. I know what's effective." Of the twenty-five Metamusic tapes issued by 1988, only eight are pure Bob Monroe. Most of the others are the results of a collaboration with a young musician, since dissolved.

Bob's favorites among the Metamusic tapes are Forest Teacher, Blue, and Soft and Still. ("A single flute against a natural background.")

Monroe speculates with a familiar gleam in his eye, "I have a feeling we could really move with Metamusic. You see, I've got about five hundred of my old scores out in the barn.

"You take and send them to Hollywood, get a film music composer to work on them. Emotion by music. That's what they do anyway, only they would be producing it to another specification.

"So much desert sound. So much ocean. Excitement. Tranquility. Passion. You name it.

"It's non-directional music. It doesn't bring back a memory, like 'The Last Time I Saw Paris' does, but it would bring forth something new in your mind.

"I give them the score-sheet. It's like a storyboard for a film. We bring their tapes back here to Virginia, and we lay Hemi-Sync in them, and sell through one of the big distribution companies.

"Only, I need a project manager. I've got too much else to do.

"There's music which is demanding to be done.

"The Life Symphony is one of them." There's not much to describe the Symphony, yet. It's just something that will be, if Bob has the time to complete it. His musical statement of human existence.

After the Symphony, there are, of course, the three novels, including the Brownstone story, he has had blocked out in his head for years.

And then, of course, there's the Wave of Change sculpture, which is to be embedded outside the Lab at the Center. The concept is vintage Monroe:

The Barn down near Miranon Lake contains, among its other artifacts, a mountain of obsolete electronic gear, bought, joyfully, at auction at the University of Virginia. ("He's a pack rat," says Scooter flatly.)

Bob recalls with a note of pride, "I got a genuine laser for five dollars once." The catch is that the five dollars also paid for a pallet-load of other stuff, which had to be carted away as part of the deal.

Little by little the frames and control panels are sorted through or cannibalized, then they end up in a pile in the mud outside the barn—which also contains original fifteen-inch tape reels from the 1950s, a harpsichord, and who-knows-what-else.

The problem has been what to do with the accumulation of electronic detritus. Thus, the Wave of Change, which will be a concrete sculpture depicting a cresting wave, running, maybe "Oh, forty feet or so." In the crest will be embedded the remnants of the electronic gear, face out—"flotsam from another era," says Bob. The whole project reflects another Monroe characteristic: "If I think about something, 'it' often becomes real, here and now." And he cites the Institute, the Center, Miranon Lake on the farm, the Gateway and H+ programs, "just to name a few."

As ever, a fusillade of schemes rains down from crest of Roberts Mountain in 1988. They are, for the most part, more of Bob's fun ideas: The possibility of syndicating a startling new concept in FM radio; storefront locations in suburban shopping malls to offer a variety of Monroe programs. ("How about a sign saying, 'Stop by for your ten-minute Relaxation and Recharge'?")

Or super-Chec Units, akin to the Black Box, in which lunchtime mall visitors could take trips from Focus 21 out into the cosmos. The possibility of giving Gateway in a converted bus, touring throughout the land. Publications, audios, and videos. The new concepts reel out, constrained primarily by lack of seed money, and by people to carry out the programs. [14]

Monroe thinks he has fulfilled his role as teacher or physical-life guide. His legacy is in the courses and the other material at the Institute. He has consistently recorded accounts of his OOB's since 1974. The tapes are stored and are available for dissemination under certain conditions. ("I wouldn't want them to be the basis of a comic strip.") Transcription and publication, especially of such a volume of readings, would be a huge undertaking, far beyond the Institute's current or foreseeable capability. The Institute needs a grant-writer to put together a proposal for money to catalogue and transcribe them.

* * * *

The physical Monroe risked his life in physical feats as a younger man, often, it seemed like daring death to take him: Life was often the high adventure of his early radio series.

Then, when he started to go OOB in 1958, he at least thought he was truly facing death, until he decided to accept what was happening—to go with the flow. Over the decades, he had many threatening experiences; and he came "to know, not just believe, that death is no more than transition."

About 1985, his altered-state voyages seem to have expanded and taken a different turn. *Far Journeys* recounts his travels on the Interstate, but those excursions ceased with the publication of the second book. The Interstate itself probably became something akin to a platform or a springboard, maybe a catapult. Bob took off and went into the jetstream, soaring far over local highways and expressways, into The All.

Most of Monroe's early OOB's happened during naps. Now, they may come at any time—the early morning "downtime," around three o'clock, is a favorite hour; or during an afternoon "recycling" snooze. They are involuntary. "I don't work at them. They just occur."

The sheer terror of going Out-of-Body was a characteristic only of Monroe's early OOB experiences. "I haven't pushed the panic button in years."

Monroe's explorations have taken him to realms far beyond death, well beyond the belief system of inculcated human institutions, beyond conventional imagination and beyond ordinary human understanding.

Out of the recent OOB activity has evolved a series of visions—a philosophy—which Bob has woven into *Ultimate Journey,* his explorations "beyond Creator Concepts."

It is a subject on which Bob is reticent. Partially because, as this book was being prepared, Monroe was assimilating and summarizing his findings for inclusion in *Ultimate Journey;* and partially because the substance of his experiences is so moving and so deep, it defies description in our language.

There were times, when talking of his most recent discoveries, that Bob—who can choose his words with precision when he feels so inclined—lapsed into pauses. At other times, he simply stopped talking. His eyes misted, his vision switched to a realm only he could recall and was then, perhaps, beginning to understand.

Beyond Creator Concepts and *UJ* are not angry or pitying. They are not deliberate provocations or gauntlets thrown down to the institutions of our society, particularly the organized churches. They are complex statements of fact, as perceived by their enunciator.

Bob Monroe, as ever, reports his findings with a minimum of personal interpretation. His attitude is, "Take it or leave it, but this is what I have seen. Go ahead. Find out for your individual self." Monroe is the insouciant revolutionist, happily prepared to help deflate pomposity and belief encrusted by millennia. *Ultimate Journey* might just as well be entitled, "Ultimate Iconoclast: The Philosophy of Robert A. Monroe."

He is equally happy trying to get people to think for themselves, and delighted if they will scour all sources available to them in their searching.

* * * *

Monroe looks at his physical existence with detachment. "The loves and emotions of this life are already stored There, in that other Me. They're part of a thousand other memories.

"I won't forget the love and experiences of this lifetime, but I'm not going to hang around Here just to see what happens.

"Some day, I'll wake up from this dream, and I'll ask, 'What's next?' Maybe I'll work in Central Casting for a while."

Book Two

His Work

The Gateway Program

A bunch of people in various stages of informality sprawls on the floor of the paneled, subterranean room in a lodge bedded in the red clay of Virginia. A retired insurance broker. An elderly librarian. The vice-president of a company which stages consumer expositions nationwide. The manager of a couple of upscale sporting-goods stores. A British commercial artist who designs record-jacket covers, and an art teacher, also from London. Two Germans, a Venezuelan. The head of training for a public utility. A practicing psychiatrist. Two hospital administrators. An art museum archivist. A housewife. Median age, probably around thirty-seven or thirty-eight.

It's Gateway Mark VI. The F-type, or the Silver Cloud version of the program that Bob first offered in 1973—with Scooter Honeycutt McMoneagle as "first trainer, driver, secretary and bottle-washer."

When asked on arrival what brought them to the Monroe Institute, the participants often glance at the floor and stammer, "Well... his books sort of jumped out at me from a shelf. And then I picked up the phone, and, well...." Some can't offer much more explanation. Their trainers and fellow students nod, knowingly.

These people who have gathered in Virginia are usually among the estimated 60 percent of the population who have had parapsychological experiences, and who are cautiously coming out of their closets. Some hope Bob Monroe's techniques can help them control their involuntary experiences in the metaphysical world. Others come to have their first experience of higher consciousness, usually drawn to Monroe by his matter-of-fact, technological approach to the Altered State.

It is precisely the low-key approach of the Institute that pulls mature, serious searchers to the hinterland of the rolling Virginia countryside. The Institute appeals to skeptical nuts-and-bolts people: Those who otherwise would never dream of attending metaphysical confabulations. Part of the lure is the Progenitor, the solid, business-wise citizen of 'the real world'—whatever that may be.

Practically everyone who gets to the Institute is sure there is a reason for his or her presence at that particular Gateway.

The other side of the coin, as Monroe casually says, is "We don't know what the pattern is that gets people here. But we do know there is a pattern." The only discernible one is that a majority seem to be of above average education, and high intelligence; they are often successful in their fields of endeavor, and they are of inquiring mind.

The majority of students now are men, often professionals. An increasing number of businessmen also conside it important enough to take the time and to let their facades drop—at least in private—to examine the Inner Self. Students also come to

Virginia precisely because they know there they will find people with whom they can talk of experiences better left unmentioned outside.

The wait for Monroe's basic Gateway course is generally four to six months. Price keeps some potential students away: Gateway costs nearly twelve hundred dollars, including bed and board. The graduate Guidelines class is one thousand dollars for five days of instruction.

A number of people take the Gateway Voyage at home, using the tapes in a series of six cassette albums which cover much the same ground. The disadvantage is the lack of group-energy, of feedback, as well as the absence of Bob Monroe himself from the participant's living room, and the missing encouragement of the Institute trainers.

Those who take the Voyage get a set of keys to inner awareness. They progress from the psychic equivalent of county highways to zoom along the Interstate, when the Left Brain is finally able to unify with the Right, and the supranormal becomes commonplace.

The objectives in Supra-Consciousness are of each individual's design. Some want to apply Monroe's techniques in their working lives, others come to Virginia in search of spiritual enhancement.

During the course, Monroe intruduces the concept of the Learning School: That we have come Here to learn about being human. Everything, absolutely everything that we do here has value "somewhere else." That other place is for the explorer to discover for himself. The discovery might come in the Gateway Voyage.

By about the fourth day, even the most rational pragmatists acknowledge, with something approaching awe, they have come to regard the course primarily as a spiritual experience. Monroe's adamant stand against any discussion of spiritual matters has led to open friction, as in the Melissa Jager case, and muted criticism in the past. Some Gateway graduates feel strongly that Bob should allow discussion of the missing metaphysical ingredient, in order to round the course off.

One alumnus says: "It doesn't prepare you to integrate the spiritual experiences you receive during the week, into your daily life. There should be some effort to line you up with physical reality, so you can combine your metaphysical life and your daily life, after you return home, with your new spiritual experience."

* * * *

A fascinating side-note to the Monroe experience are the findings of Dr. Kenneth Ring of the University of Connecticut and the International Association for Near-Death Studies (IANDS). Ring's two books on the subject contain accounts of what happened to Near Death Experiencers (NDE'ers), remarkably similar to the events envisioned and participated in by Gateway and Guidelines students.

Here is just one example, drawn from Dr. Ring's analysis in his book, *Heading Toward Omega*. He describes the sensations of the "core experience" shared by many NDE'ers:

> *The realm that the NDEer enters at the time of the experience is one of timelessness, infinite space, and total freedom. One feels enormously expanded in all ways and filled with divine love and knowledge. Usually, with all one's heart, one desires to remain in this state forever.*
>
> *Suddenly, there is a pulling back. One's footing in this blissful realm begins to give*

way. Paradise, having once been attained, is about to be lost. Awareness of the journey back may or may not be present, but the return itself is all too real. . . .

One has returned to the old world of time and space with its legion of restrictions. One's consciousness has once more contracted so as to live within the tiny confines of the ego. Seemingly, everything that one was and could ever have yearned to be has been lost. . . . Who could ever begin to understand what one has left behind. [1]

There are at least two highly noteworthy points in Dr. Ring's description, above: The first is the remarkable similarity in experience between the Near Death Experiencer and at least some of Bob Monroe's Gateway Voyage graduates. I, for instance, know precisely what Ring is describing. This is not to say that many others who have meditated or searched in other ways have not undergone the same transcendent experience, merely that Monroe is one easily available way to achieve it, and to remove fear of the unknown.

The second similarity is the relatively high incidence of spiritual experience in Ring's NDE sample, which is, again, consistent with the feelings and knowledge of many Monroe-ites.

Much more could undoubtedly be said on this subject, and it could well be the subject for fruitful research. Suffice it for the layman that there seems to be an astonishing correlation between the experience of the involuntary NDE and the voluntary entry into Higher Consciousness brought on by Bob Monroe's Hemi-Sync process.

The unchallenged consensus of graduates is that their Gateway experience changes their lives, often in dramatic form, as has NDE changed the lives of many of those who have experienced it. Is each, then, a method made available to humankind for very specific purposes? There is considerable food for thought here.

* * * *

A Gateway graduate returning to the low building on the ridge at Roberts Mountain Farm immediately snaps back into the state of bliss in which he left. Maybe it's the smell—of untreated cedar. Or recollections of such concentrated emotional release, cleansing, knowing, seldom achieved elsewhere.

Gateway is the first bridge novices cross into Bob Monroe's world. Bob no longer guides students personally, with at-times whimsical, live voice-overs from the tape-control-room of the Center—although he is perfectly capable of telling his trainers to substitute a different tape for the scheduled exercise. Now, he comes down Roberts Mountain evenings, fondles his cup of coffee, and talks softly of his past, his hopes, and his final missions, renewing the tone of the week as it progresses.

Bob keeps a gentle finger on the pulse of each Gateway. If he hears the class is moving too slowly, or hasn't gelled as a cohesive group, he makes an extra effort to inspire or guide the novices. His past as a master showman is evident in the modulation of his voice, and in his stage-presence. But what he has to say and the evident truth of his conviction are not artifice.

The Institute today has a staff of sixteen mostly-nonresident trainers (never "instructors"), two of whom lead each class through the sessions. The trainers' role looks absurdly easy. The pair usually seem merely to sit around casually and encourage discussion, or tell jokes. In fact, their responsibility is far more complex. They should be as near ego-less as possible, and subtly as well as obviously—often late at night—go out of their ways to help the querulous or baffled student, in selfless, non-judgmental ways.

Karen Malik, who has been involved with Monroe since 1977, and is one of the most experienced Gateway trainers, starts preparing a month before she arrives in Virginia.

Once the seminar has started, "I feel responsible, but I have to get out of the way. We have to see how Gateway is affecting the students. We can help them to integrate what they're getting in their daily lives."

* * * *

The standardized Gateway format was not developed until 1983; by then the Institute realized Gateway would not stop at five thousand students.

Some of those who attend are startled to find there is not much correlation between the Gateway program and the experiences Monroe recounts in his two books. They do not automatically start to communicate in Monroe's outer-world vocabulary of "rotes" and "curls", "smoothing" and "blanking."

There are interesting questions which arise after Gateway graduates have had a chance to digest their experiences. Women sometimes wonder whether they have more difficulty than men in letting go of "empowerment" - i.e. their encultured innermost defenses block their smooth progress in Gateway. Conversely, men also encounter problems in dumping their image—macho or otherwise—and standing innocent before the adventures that await them.

Gateway offers the novice a chance to divest him or herself of all ties to society. The device is a simple one: the Energy Conversion Box, an imaginary container in which the participant can place all his worries, anxieties, ego-factors, images, material attachments, even the thinnest bond to physical life—anything that might hinder him from having a successful exercise.

Some are disappointed they do not immediately soar Out-of-Body in as dramatic fashion as Bob's books recount. The Institute, in its literature, and the Gateway trainers in person, deliberately discourage anticipation of Out-of-Body experiences. But many still come with expectations.

How many people actually do go OOB during a Gateway? The answer seems to have to do, in some mysterious way, with the makeup of the course. In some classes, a majority of students succeed in going Out-Of-Body—or say they do. In others, the number is small.

It is also a matter of definition. Probably not very many do travel OOB in Bob Monroe's sense of the phrase, hovering above their physical bodies, or suddenly learning they can visit friends while their minds are awake, their bodies asleep. But very few do not experience at least a taste of Altered States of Consciousness. Some people sleep through many of the exercises. A few skeptics who don't launch into the wondrous trips they have programmed for themselves may think Monroe isn't really all he is cracked up to be.

The fact that Gateway and Guidelines are truly inner voyages is not explicitly stressed in the introduction to either, but this is, perhaps, as it should be, in keeping with Monroe's thesis that he provides only the tools: What you experience is your own design.

There are about thirty tapes in a week's course; the usual exercise consists of "Resonant Tuning," the Gateway Affirmation and the voyage to other awareness itself.

Each exercise is carefully dovetailed to build on the previous one in understanding and experience of advanced consciousness.

The novices' first contacts with their Inner or True Selves are often disquieting, sometimes overwhelming; then, as they gradually overcome Fear of the Unknown, the students become familiar with There. Few, having fully sensed the serenity of Greater Life, want to return when they hear the remote foghorn summoning them back across time and space, even to the tranquility of the Institute, much less to the hurly-burly of existence on this planet. At the end of Gateway or the advanced Guidlines programs, students are no longer sure the Virginia soil they tread is red—or real.

Some decide, even during the courses, to make radical alterations in their business and personal circumstances. It is not rare to hear of someone who, during his stay at the Center, decided to change career, sell his house and move elsewhere, alter personal relationships. For others, it is a slow comedown from the high of contact with their Supra Consciousnesses, and a measured assimilation of what they have learned into their daily lives.

Post-course results can be funny as well as useful. Some graduates use Monroe techniques to find parking spaces in crowded cities. One participant mentally protects himself against highway speeding tickets, and reports total success, at 85 MPH. Some search for and find missing objects. Others tap sources of information long-forgotten, or not theretofore available.

One Gateway alumna awoke at four o'clock in the morning to find her partner sitting bolt upright in bed, ice-cold, terrified. She listened to disincarnate voices coming through him and realized they were the cries of humans who had died suddenly—a Vietnam casualty, then the victim of an automobile accident. Hastily recalling the technique she had heard on the Partick Rescue tape, she gently guided the beings to release their physical selves and accept the fact of their deaths.

Many find it nearly impossible to continue practicing Institute tape techniques once they re-encounter the pressures of their "normal" existences. A good number report no obvious change in their lives—at least, not on first return to the humdrum world; perhaps their expectations were too high, or their skepticism too great. Monroe nods quietly when he hears such reports, and says, merely "Wait and see."

In fact, some rather startled Gateway graduates have reported their lives have changed, inexorably, even though they were not consciously working with the tapes or continuing Monroe exercises after they left Virginia. The change may not be noticeable quickly, but nonetheless, it makes itself evident.

One evening, a couple of the women who work in the Center's kitchen reflected on the students they see over the weeks. In broad Virginian, one commented, "They're all highly intelligent, and I think they're here because they've got to get away for a while." The other, less vocal, merely added, "Those people sure have more common sense than a lot of folks."

There have been times when Monroe wanted to close down the course, because he wasn't getting anything except more bills out of it. "But then," he says, "Someone would report a remarkable event in his or her life, and, well, we'd just keep on going."

The final night of any Gateway course is a continuing Peak Moment in Bob Monroe's life, a cheerful one.

"You have to see the transformation in those people as I can see it. It gives an exquisite sense of the constructive change that has taken place. It's not euphoria. Some are contrived, sure. But twenty of the twenty-four have done what I hoped they would do: they've had fun and they've experienced a quiet, knowing joy. It's contagious. What a difference from the opening night!

"By the closing, they've melded and merged. Completely different people who have shared a deep experience."

There's something about a Gateway Voyage which releases a creativity. Almost every course produces some form of poetry, song or pageant—usually humorous, almost always, however, full of gratitude to Bob Monroe. The wonder is that the students find time to compose anything during the jam-packed and highly-emotional week; but they do, often sitting up until late at night to do so.

The following, designed to be sung in the style of Woody Guthrie, was written by a Bob Rosenthal, a Philadelphia psychiatrist—during a session in November 1987, and it particularly pleased Bob for its perspicacity and wit. Some of the terms in the poem relate to Bob Monroe's writings, particularly in *Far Journeys*.[2]

Now I'll tell you all a story-y
'Bout a man named Bob Monroe.
It started on this earthly plane
Some thirty years ago. . . .

Well, Bob he rested in his bed
But little did he know
That out from his ole body
Soon his consciousness would flow.

He bumped right through the ceiling
And was really off the wall.
Fifteen feet above the ground
And still he did not fall.

He went to see his friend, the shrink
To find out if he's sick,
And get him a prescription,
Bring him down to earth right quick.

The doctors had no answers for him,
Left him on his own.
And so this lonesome traveler
Had to find his own way Home.

Now, he's a-cruising on the astral plane,
A demon form appears.
Confronts him in an instant
With his mortal body fears.

"Before you pass this way, yon soul,
Your Ident I must know."
He smoothes and tosses back a rote,
"My name is Bob Monroe."

"In that case, pass right by my friend.
In these parts you are known.
We understand your purpose
And your lonesome journey Home."

Now he's told us all 'bout astral sex
Other worlds and times and more.
Into these realities
He's opened up a door.

Now Bob, he runs a pumping station
In the Blue Ridge hills
And the people they come from miles around
Their consciousness to fill. . . .

So when you climb aboard your Chec Unit
Of your earthly cares be rid.
Just dump 'em in your Conversion box,
"And close the heavy lid."

Now maybe we're all Guernsey cows
And the loosh production, it's slow.
But Moo spelled backwards is Ooomm,
So why not let your Energy flow?

Well, Bob he's had a revelation
Changed him to this day,
While traveling with his Inspec,
He's discovered he's AA.

And now for all you listeners
Some advice that you might heed
To lighten up your travels and
Your Out-Of-Body deeds:

As you tumble through the Universe
In Focus 33,
You just might stumble on some rote,
Reminds you, you're BB.

Guidelines

Bob Monroe's Guidelines program is the graduate course for those who have gone through the Gateway Voyage. Guidelines is the least-known, and perhaps least-appreciated course in the Monroe curriculum.

It is not, strictly speaking, a continuation of the basic seminar: Gateway gives the student some methods to explore the Inner Self, smash ego, overcome fear—techniques which enable the graduate to integrate his physical being with the world out There.

Monroe describes Guidelines thus: "It gives you the tools to communicate with consciousness not ordinarily available during the physical waking state." It is sometimes thought of as a course in channeling, or as Explorer training. The emphasis is on practical communication from everyday life to the guidance and wisdom available in the philosophical-metaphysical realm. Guidelines lets the student contact and explore hitherto hidden aspects of Self or the Conscious, to a further degree than Gateway allows.

* * * *

Kaye Andres attended Guidelines in June, 1987, six months after her Gateway introduction to Monroe. Even during the initial course, she knew she had to continue with the Institute. One of the main reasons was that she needed, "Something parallel to my sensory system.

"Our language is painfully inadequate to explain what happens There. I, particularly, encounter great stumbling blocks trying to use language to convey my meaning.

"Gateway gave me the symbolic language I need, like a wonderful abstract painting. But I cried with pain that I couldn't express my thoughts.

"Guidelines was my elevator. It immersed me in expressing my consciousness. I let the feelings flow through me."

* * * *

During my own Gateway in the spring of 1987, I felt an inexorable compulsion to continue further with Monroe, and I signed up for the next Guidelines while I was still at the Center.

I had a curious introduction to the course. Those who come to the Institute from afar often are forced to spend the night before a class begins in Charlottesville, the victim of airlines' idiosyncratic scheduling. I inquired at my motel's reception desk for other Monroe-goers.

I ended up dining very pleasantly with a quiet Canadian who told a dramatic story of using Monroe's techniques in some remarkable self-healing. My dinner companion was also a firm believer in communication with trees.

The next morning, with more time to kill, we strolled near the hostelry, in search of good trees to embrace. Somewhat skeptically, I went into a grove and found a likely-looking oak. I approached the fine trunk, wrapped my arms gingerly around it as far as they would go, and—in effect—prayed, or yielded to the power of the tree. To my surprise, I was immediately rewarded with an image of utterly sublime Energy coursing through the trunk and branches. My new friend returned from a quick shopping expedition, to find me nearly blissed out.

"See what I mean?" he said. I nodded, thoughtfully, and we caught the van to the Institute.

That Sunday evening before Labor Day, I once again listened to Bob Monroe in David Francis Hall. "This is your flow, no one else's. I'm the mechanic and security base for you to truly explore from. We'll begin with some reinforcement. . . Then the action begins." The last statement made, once more, with relish: The Ultimate Adventurer offering us a chance to join him.

"You don't have to be dealt with as neophytes. We can be totally relaxed. . . This is an extremely fun deal. I'm just here this evening to give you a huge welcome.

"Guidelines people don't have many questions.

"We don't say what we expect of you. This is a step beyond Gateway, but we let you find that out for yourselves. Anything goes in your exploration.

"It's intensive. You're a smaller group than at Gateway.

"I wouldn't even want to tell you the experiences of Guidelines graduates. . . that would be suggestive.

"It's that step beyond Gateway: To have it all Here, not There. It takes a lot of releasing, and a lot more acceptance. Then it becomes automatic. The key is, you do it yourself.

"You'll learn to report physically while you're There. Don't edit what you're getting. Don't worry about the source. Just talk what you're getting into the tape recorder. Let it flow.

"We're not out to make you channelers. What you'll do is not necessarily channeling.

"I don't know what it is. But it is a major process to make contact, whenever you want, with your Inner Self, your Guide. To gain useful information. To enhance your perceptions. To realize the magnitude of the human state.

"Just let it come. And have a good time."

And we were off. First a brushup of Gateway techniques, with new emphasis on reporting what we were experiencing during the tape exercises, into the gooseneck microphone in our Chec Units.

A group of seven men and eleven women, a handful of whom had gone through a Gateway in Florida together, and who formed a compact inner core within the class, led by the trainer who had instructed them.

There were several problems I experienced at Guidelines. They were subjective but, because others felt a certain dismay as well, they are worth mentioning.

One of the intangibles which contributes enormously to the success of a Monroe workshop is the constitution of the group and the amenability of the trainers. Those who know their business feel it takes a couple of days for the group to form its own consciousness. Skill, delicacy and sensitivity are required of the instructors to promote this group spirit.

Our chief trainer misread the group. Perhaps she felt uncomfortable dealing with the older people in the course; at any rate, she played consistently to her core of friends from the Florida course, and made little effort to extend her warmth to others. She also tended to speak in the jargon of psychoprattle: After the first day and a half, I waited eagerly for her to "give me permission to be myself", for instance. Had she done so, the rough edge of my tongue would have lashed back. (In justice, I must add that the same trainer was also at my subsequent H+ course, and by then had revised her vocabulary.)

Concurrently, the August, 1987 Guidelines was less than a successful group experience because the age level was considerably below that of many Monroe intakes; the median was probably somewhere in the early thirties. Those of us of riper years were happy the younger souls were present; but their concerns were considerably different from ours, and those, too, were catered to by the chief trainer.

The second trainer was curiously apathetic and preoccupied by major developments in her own life which were a direct result of her Monroe experiences. The third was Stephen Bladd, a former rock musician with a wild sense of humor. But since Stephen was still an apprentice, he rarely opened his mouth. [1]

A final brake on a successful group experience was interesting: Several of those present at the course had taken their Gateway in the do-it-yourself home album version. Their experiences were, of course, different from those who had already been at the Center.

These comments aside, Guidelines was still a fascinating, shaking, revealing experience for me. The power of Bob Monroe's exercises overrode my dismay at the constitution and conduct of the group.

In the early tapes, I immediately saw people who were close to me, got guidance on problems I was facing, felt renewed confidence in my ability to explore, was reminded that my Guides were loving. It was reassuring.

By the afternoon of Monday, we were beginning to travel. One series of images came because someone in our group remembered Bob, the inveterate pilot, yarning about a place out There where space vehicles flew at five thousand miles an hour. Monroe commented he had enjoyed the trip so much, he had been reluctant to ground himself and come down to David Francis Hall for a Gateway evening.

I reckoned if Monroe could visit the place, I could too. I came into "Planet Green"—which also had some magenta mixed in—through arches of energy and was met by a green friend who, I intuitively knew, was a pilot. Boss Green bade me welcome and telepathed, "This is what you wanted to see, isn't it?"

I went on a tour, looked out a window on the galaxy from what I suddenly realized was a green orb of creativity: A font of words and music and graphics, to be tapped at any time.

In the next session, we traveled to Focus 15 (F-15)—a level for which tapes are available only at the Institute. In F-15, the level of advanced consciousness where there is no time and no space, I wanted to discover the history of the mystical Christian group I had had some altered consciousness indicators about.

I got views, at first swirling and confusing, later clear, of a cloistered, heretical brotherhood in a monastery in Germanic central Europe. The dating was difficult. At first, I placed the scene in the Dark Ages, but later was shown a guild town which seemed to date the experience around the eleventh or twelfth centuries. The Grey

Brotherhood, as it was called, was antithetical to the Church hierarchy and was eradicated, probably by the Inquisition.[2]

Monday evening, with a feeling of physical weightlessness, I went soaring to another space. The voyage was totally out of my control. I started tumbling, counterclockwise. A large hand steadied me into a gentle, deliberate roll. I met some familiar beings, had a mantle of light thrown over my shoulders, was told I still had problems of ego and pride and apartness to take care of, and then revisited the Hall of Love, found tranquility and reassurance that all would be good. Too soon, Bob's voice bade me return to the physical.

Next, I asked to view other lives I had lived which might have a bearing or influence on my present or future tasks, Here and There. I was given a series of vistas, from the time of the Creation, through African pre-history, Mayan Central America, a Tibetan meditative cave in which an oil lamp flickered; on to Biblical times; on, again, to the medieval brotherhood. This time, I was a member of a guild as well as of the underground sect, and was in danger. Then, a scene involving what I took to be an Australian aborigine—an old, old woman; an American Indian surviving the Ice Age; a British Army lieutenant in World War I, leading a charge over the top of trenches, knowing his duty was suicidal. A transition period of service in The All, and a final, future, life—I think—in what might be China, at any rate an agrarian, vegetarian society.

After this panorama, I fell into a period of non-productivity, and became disconsolate. I talked that lunchtime with a fellow-student who had noted my difficulties.

"Why don't you," he suggested, "stuff all your reportorial gear in the Energy Conversion Box. Your tape recorder, your typewriter, notebook. Everything." I did, in preparation for the next exercise, and also disposed of my journalistic image.

Then I stood, naked, exposed and—I hoped—innocent, to await the next journey. The advice of my friend worked. I took part in a vision of beauty and light which was beyond imagination.

* * * *

Other vistas followed as the exercises continued to unroll. I traveled in a space vehicle; journeyed to the center of the earth—where, to my surprise, I was not burned by the intense heat I felt—and looked at "the control room," which charted all the planet's life systems; played and talked with a pod of dolphins. The visions were endless—and joyous.

By Tuesday night, I had met my newest Guide. The two of us bounced around on an unseen trampoline for a while, but I was tethered by what appeared to be a nylon cord. A soft voice said, "Know this is serious."

In the calm that followed, I learned my Guide was my alter ego, my second self, the inner voice who would always be with me as a conduit for the Universal Consciousness.

After we got over the heavy stuff, my new non-physical Friend asked, as any schoolmaster might, "What's the capital of Ecstasy?" Without hesitation, I replied, "Bliss, of course."

My alter ego and I met again on the Wednesday morning. It was face to face—a mirror imaging. We found new names for each other, and my twin dictated rote. We have been together since the Creation, alternating physical and non-physical roles. We have shared previous life experiences involving considerable wealth and the exercise of power, by choice; and from those, we learned lessons. This life—and my earthly alcoholism—has been a final training. But we will always have a choice of which path to take.

Together, we examined the New Medicine, a concept which had arisen at the Professional Seminar several weeks earlier. It is love, and self-healing. "First, one must heal oneself mentally, so that he can grapple with the new consciousness. Only a healthy mind can deal with the altered state. The supra-awareness that comes will, in turn, make the individual capable of monitoring his own Energy flow, so he can direct his Energy where it is needed."

There came a revelation that we are all One, a concept I had trouble accepting, and still have difficulty with. My guide said, "Yes, dummy, it's about time you learned. You are interchangeable with anyone and anything else. You can be anyone you want." I resisted the symbolism, but it gave me much to ponder.

We had some time left on that tape, before Bob called us back. It was playtime. Myself and I did some inter-galactic skiing, then hopped aboard a stellar roller-coaster, and returned to our trampoline.

Wednesday evening, Rosie McKnight came into David Francis Hall to talk about her experiences. She brought with her not only Ah-So, but also Alfonso Pincinelli, the nineteenth century musician who has been known to give impromptu transpersonal concerts for enthralled Institute students. Someone brought a portable keyboard, but Alfonso didn't feel like playing that evening.

Pincinelli is irreverent about "Mr. Monroe": "He creeps into (David Francis Hall) to check on what's going on. Don't pay any attention. You paid your money. . . I sometime enjoy slipping in on one of his seminars. But I don't want to tell him. He might send me a bill."

"Oh, we have a lot of fun together," Monroe says. "He's a quick man with a throwaway line. You know, he even times his delivery. He waits for the laughter to die down when he's performing for a group in David Francis Hall."

That night, I accepted Alfonso's invitation to attend a concert over There. It took place in a roofless structure with a pink stucco facade and an entrance hall where colored light fountains played a cascade of music I had never heard before: Crystal light chords, chimes, music of far different worlds.

Thursday morning, a mediocre session, by my new standards. Then came "Superflow", the penultimate trip. I impulsively jumped Bob's taped instructions, glided easily over the colored levels up from F-15, right to Focus 21—the borderline between Here and There. I pictured the Guidelines group, holding hands in The All, swooping, circling in formation, reminiscent of the flock of migrating geese which tacked by the Center at dawn, in the early Virginia autumn. We cartwheeled, where they held their V-formation.

Gradually we split into distinct entities and went our separate ways. My alter ego and I met all my previous family guides at a staging area, and took off, waved on by my loving family-reception committee. We went to my home planet, which bears the designator XT (As in IBM, I suppose) 79. It is also made of liquid, as was Planet Green. Innumerable entities waited in a wispy circle to greet me.

"You are our delegate to the School of Life. Carry on with your divine task for us. This is Home. We will welcome you back when your assignment is completed."

I received some detailed instructions and another confirmation that I was on the right path. There was a prickling, tingling sensation in my right foot which I knew was an infusion of their Energy. [3]

Bob called us back to Focus 15. I stopped, waited, and was once more in the Hall of Love, where exalted beings reaffirmed that I was doing what was wanted of me. I felt myself again being charged with Energy to a point I knew was close to overload. A piece of quartz I had picked up during a stroll in a nearby meadow, and had been using as an Energy battery, became fiercely heated. The symbol I wear around my neck felt incandescent.

As a final act, I put all my worldly possessions—all my "appurtenances" in Monroespeak—in the Energy Conversion Box, and sealed it in a cave, leaving a chink in the wall so I could get at what I later needed. I again stood naked, now innocent, ready for whatever might come. I had come as close as I could to the Know System.

Thursday afternoon, we took a silent walk, as part of the integration process—using what we had learned in Guidelines to associate with the world of grass and flowers and trees and cows.

The finale was a straight channeling exercise, projecting out fifty years. I delivered a running commentary of what I beheld into the Chec Unit microphone.

To this day, I do not know whether what I was saying was "channeling" in the usual sense. The voice is mine, though slightly lower and softer. The material I speak on tape could be the vision of a disincarnate entity; or it could be a deeply-logical extrapolation of information I have run across in many forms, over a period of years. Who's to tell?

I remain skeptical that I am a channel; that I am, indeed, anything more than a being who has been freed enough to think and speak those shielded thoughts we normally don't allow into our conscious mind. Or, perhaps I'm speaking with my alter ego's voice. Those who have listened to my rare adventures along this boulevard can't make up their minds, either. Is it for real? Is it purely imaginative? Who knows?

It was Friday morning. Time to blow off steam. Russ Russell and another man dressed—or undressed—and did a ceremonial American Indian dance in turquoise Indian dress and loincloth—sort of. We reluctantly put our watches back on.

Our Guidelines group, never as closely-knit as the Gateway bunch I had been with, split.

* * * *

On the Thursday evening, Bob Monroe made his farewell appearance at Guidelines, his balding pate shining in the spotlight. "Just look at all you hardcore people there.

"OK. What's the goal of Guidelines?" His voice boomed.

"INTEGRATE!...Integrate what you have learned into your daily conscious lives.

"I'm always struck when people do this course. You're well on the way to something other than what ordinary humankind is...whatever that is.

"Nothing but constructive patterns seem to emerge from Guidelines. Answers and solutions you didn't anticipate. A week ago you might not have accepted them. But now, you say, 'Oh, Yes!'

"It's what I call an 'Ah, So!'

"You have come to know your own best ability."

But, Bob quickly adds, "Not that this is the only place this can happen. There are thousands and thousands of other environments....

"But now you don't have to read any other books. You don't have to go anywhere else...It's all inside you, now.

"The goal is not necessarily notoriety or public acclaim.

"We have far different goals. People from Guidelines never exhibit what they really are. Nor do they emerge and stick their personalities up. The doing is the game. It's ego-less.

"You can have fun, but not ego-gratification on the path you are likely to travel."

The Canadian hesitantly told of the disappearance of his brain tumor, due in large part, he felt, to his practice of Monroe techniques.

Monroe sat entranced through the recital. Then hands clasped in the familiar baseball gesture, he whispered, "Very good. That's great!...all you have to do is remember how you did it."

Very slowly, once again, "Remember how you did it.

"You've done it once. Do it twice. It's learnable...Thank you so much for sharing."

Then, some advice for neophyte OOB travelers. "Right after a sleep cycle, in the mist of coming awake, take a deep breath. Click. Roll out. You're gone. Just say, 'I'm ready. Let's go!'

"Well, it doesn't always work that way. Sometimes one makes as many as eighteen attempts."

Then, the wind-up, and the significance of Guidelines to a suddenly very humble Bob Monroe: "It took me a very long time, but I finally understood.

"Everything we do here has application elsewhere in altered form. The blend of conscious and autonomic is of intense value."

Monroe lifted his coffee cup, and stared at his arm's action. "Even this. Every human act has application in a non-human way. I don't know where, and I don't know how.

"The synchronous energy you have learned here has its use. None of your experiences here in physical life are wasted. It is all of exquisite value."

The time for a quick farewell had come. "I never said it would be easy, the integrating process. It's vital, but not easy.

"You will be faced with inescapable decisions. They will change certain textures of your life pattern.

"And if that doesn't work, well, there's always H+.

"I'm going to go eat dinner." Bob Monroe waved and strode out of David Francis Hall.

* * * *

In truth, a number of those who attended that Guidelines did have difficulty in re-entering the outside world. I spent the following four weeks in a state of utter, querulous turmoil, wondering where I was going, what I was doing, unable to work satisfactorily.

I called a fellow-student who burst forth on the phone, "Boy am I glad I'm not the only one." Reports trickled in from others, telling of feelings of disassociation with daily life, disorientation, questions which loomed larger than life, and answers which were slow in forthcoming.

It must be added that this Guidelines came hard on the heels of the Harmonic Convergence observation of August 16 and 17, 1987. Many students participated in that observance in one form or another, and felt they had been part of an event which could also cause change in their lives. Perhaps the Harmonics and Guidelines together were a double whammy.

I had barely four weeks to assimilate Guidelines, before going back to Virginia again. About the only thing that remained constant after I left Monroe's that Labor Day weekend was the sure knowledge that my private, onboard consultant was with me at all times, ready to share advice and nudge me in directions which I—down deep—knew were correct, but may have been reluctant to accept.

* * * *

That very engaging British couple, Russ and Jill Russell, enlivened the proceedings at Guidelines, as they had at the previous Professional Seminar. After their return to England, Russ turned out the following tongue-in-cheek 'explanation' of their most recent visit to the Monroe Institute. [4]

The Way We Live

So, you enjoyed your trip to America?

Yes, very much

What about this seminar—this conference—you went to?

Well, some of it was about death and dying.

Sounds a bit morbid.

No, it was fun, actually. This little doctor was terribly funny about the time she was accused of having VD and couldn't walk straight.

Oh... really. What sort of people were there?

Doctors, psychologists, businessmen, therapists. There was a leading Canadian astrophysicist who said he was an Extra-Terrestrial.

A what?

Comes from another planet. And there was a chap from the United Nations who's a shaman, he says.

United Nations, you say?

Yes. Then there was a woman who sees inside people's bodies and tells them what's wrong with them.

What else did you learn about?

A lot about different uses of Hemi-Sync.

Hemi....?

Hemi-Sync. You play different frequencies into each ear and they produce a third frequency which puts the left and right sides of the brain into synchronization so you can become more imaginative, more creative and more relaxed.

What's it sound like?

You don't actually hear it. It's sort of embedded beneath specially-composed music. On tapes.

Oh, I think I see... How does it operate?

I'll tell you later. We attended a course on that. Oh, and we divided into groups for different purposes. One group created a group mind.

A....?

Group mind. Any one of us can use it if we need it.

Where is this group mind?

In a room at the Conference Center. We created another one, too, a few days later.

What happened then?

Well, this was the Harmonic Convergence.

The Harmonica what?

Harmonic. Not Harmonica. Convergence...It's a time predicted by Mayan astrologers when the stars were in a specially auspicious situation relative to the Earth, and....

Excuse me. I'm not quite understanding you....

Never mind. Anyway, we had a group meditation in the morning—at dawn, actually. We stood in a circle and said words around the circle, and then meditated, and then we all huddled together and created a group mind.

Where is this, now?

Outside someone's house. He refuses to pay taxes to buy arms.

Anything else happen?

Well, one night between the seminar and the course, we went out to dinner with Bob and Nancy. Vietnamese restaurant in Waynesboro.

Bob?

Monroe. He founded The Institute. He goes Out-Of-Body most nights. Well, he used to, but doesn't, anyway not so often, any more. Oh, I've told you about him before. He gave us The Message as guidance for our lives last year. You know.

What message?

$6N + L (R^2 + 5)$ over $T + 2P = STC$.

What does it mean?

We don't know. STC might be Spiral of Total Consciousness, we think. But maybe not.

It doesn't sound very useful. When was your course?

A couple of days later.

What was it like. What did you do?

There were eighteen of us. Very interesting.

Who were the others?

Lots of girls. One teaches regression and rebirthing. Another came from Disneyland. A third is a healer working with crystals. There was a swami from Arizona. There was a lapsed Baptist minister who runs a computer consultancy. One man makes rainbows over harbors, and he made one with a hose on the lawn...All sorts...

What about the course?

We spent most of our time in our Chec Units, in the dark, lying down and listening to the tapes—like we did last year, you remember. Only this time, we learned how to report what was happening.

What did happen?

Hard to say. Everyone had different experiences.

Tell me about yours.

Well, Jill experienced being crucified and looked in on the Last Supper. Russ sang a hymn he hasn't sung for fifty years. His left hand got very hot, too.

What does that mean?

We don't know, but it may be very important. He also had some sort of revelation.

Really? What did you do in your free time?

Oh, we swam every day in the lake. Jill blew up a rubber shark and floated around. In the evenings, we had talks from channelers.

Channelers?

People who channel entities from somewhere else. One is called George, and Alfonso is another. They told us lots of interesting things... and on Monday, we flew home.

Good trip back?

Oh, very. There was a seat for Michael. He didn't have a ticket, but no one minded. The Customs man at Heathrow just smiled at him.

Michael? Was he with you at the course?

Sort of. He's a white bear. Friendly, but not familiar, if you follow me. A lady gave him to Jill.

What else did you bring back?

Oh... A large kite. Several clowns. A blow-up globe. An airship. Some posters. A set of chimes. Just stuff, really.

I expect you're glad to be back home?

No... not really. We can't wait to go back to Virginia. In fact, we're going to another course next year. Wouldn't you like to come? [4]

Bob Monroe and the Professionals

The scene is, once again, the auditorium in David Francis Hall. It's daytime; usually the hall is used only at night.

Today, the room is jammed with a collection of more than fifty sweltering doctors, psychologists, educators, therapists, scientists. It is the opening session of the Monroe Institute Professional Seminar, in August, 1987. The theme is "Death and Transformation."

Bob Monroe is at bat. To the surprise of many who know him only slightly, he's wearing a suit and tie in the 90 degree/90 percent humidity of the stifling Virginia summer.

Monroe stands in front of his professionals, balling his hands, grinning broadly. He says, "My job is to get you to conceive of something you might not have considered before." And he's off again, with a joyous rallying cry to unconventionality.

"What we're talking about...So much of life is controlled by anxieties and fear. Man's fear of the unknown. Fear of change. Fear of the predators beyond the circle of fire. It's the only game in town....

"Here is afraid of There. We don't have enough data. We've got to find a way to let people who are near their exit cross over, take a look at the beachhead before they make the landing.

"That way, they won't have fear of dying. It's a question of Knowing, not Believing.

"Death is not what the culture and religion have told us it is. It's the Knowing that counts.

"That's why we're here today. We've got to work on converting Belief Systems into Know Systems."

* * * *

In the early 1970s, Monroe grudgingly came to terms with his rejection by the broad population of scientists. First there was the lengthy, wearying lab work that led to Hemi-Sync; then the expanded case-study project, Mentronics 5000, and later Gateway.

In the early 1980s, the Monroe Institute Professional Division was founded. It is the clearinghouse and monitoring device for the work being done by others to expand and explore the use of Hemi-Sync techniques in fields other than self-expansion. Until 1985, the Professional Division existed in a hit-or-miss fashion. Then, the emphasis changed to developing empirical evidence and proof of the efficacy of Hemi-Sync.

Monroe has given up active pursuit of scientific validation. The obverse, and very satisfying, side of the coin is that a trickle of open-minded engineers, doctors, and scientists are veering to a holistic view of their fields; some attend Monroe courses to see for themselves what Bob is all about.

* * * *

All the technology developed by Bob Monroe and his companions has come out of a laboratory. The first was the semi-covert operation at Croton, New York. Considerably later, it was in the modular house at Whistlefield that the lab became a major part of Bob's life. With the move to Roberts Mountain, the lab building became part of the Institute.

The man who presides over the wires and meters that make up the lab today—and does far more—is Dave Wallis, a happy, enthusiastic former researcher at Lockheed in California whose specialty is electromagnetic fields. In 1979, Dave was restless in his job. He came East on vacation with his wife, Jean, who was the first director of the Professional Division, and now gives beneficial massages to Institute students. The couple "happened" to come to the Institute, where they met Bob.

Driving around the property with Monroe, Dave explained his work. Bob exclaimed. "Boy, have I got a job for you!" Monroe proposed that Wallis take over responsibility for designing and building the technical aspects of the lab. Dave went back to California, quit Lockheed, and has been with Monroe ever since. Because the Institute operates on a tight budget, Wallis makes his survival money as consultant, primarily overseas, working on hi-tech communications systems.

Dave's enthusiastic speech bursts out, machinegun-like. The non-technical listener has to beg him to slow down. Kindly and patiently, Wallis complies, as he leads the novice through the mysteries of the lab.

It is the outgrowth of the earlier ones, where the pioneering work was done in Exploration, and in the thousands of hours it took to develop Hemi-Sync. Today's version is a collection of rooms. In one, there is a water bed, now seldom used. The control room looks much like the monitoring part of any sound studio. It is a collection of every type of tape recording device imaginable, interwoven with mixing and control boards, digital equipment: an array of dials, panel faces, meters, switches which only initiates would dare to touch.

Some of the equipment centered in the control room is used to produce the Hemi-Sync patterns which are at the heart of Monroe Institute operations. Dave calls it "triple-layered sound; or more."

Wallis moves on to point out a Mind Mirror, which he calls a "Bilateral EEG" machine, and which is today often used in monitoring Explorers. The Polarity-Sensitive Voltmeter is its "Physiological Indicator."

From the crammed control room, Wallis leads the way into a larger room, much like an old fashioned radio studio, which is equally crammed with a jumble of equipment. Over in one corner is the Booth, or the Black Box: the earthly home of the Explorers.

* * * *

The basis of Bob Monroe's contribution to the exploration of consciousness is his Hemi-Sync process, the binaural technique which links the two spheres of the brain.

While still a vice-president of the Mutual Broadcasting System in the mid-1950s, Bob toyed with an idea well ahead of its time, which he called "Companionate Radio." The scheme was, "The network would feed an overnight program of soft music to affiliates, playing songs just for you. It would be radio being your buddy—well ahead of the trends in today's FM broadcasting." Mutual didn't bite, but the thought led Monroe into his first experiments with Sleep Learning.

An offshoot of the Companionate concept was that the network would give courses to listeners while they were asleep. "It would have been rote learning. We experimented with the multiplication tables from thirteen to twenty-four, since most schools stopped at twelve." And, as always, Monroe was his own guinea pig.

From Companionate Radio and Sleep Learning, it was an easy theoretical hop to Hemi-Sync, but far from an easy technological accomplishment.

After years of dogged research, Frequency Following Response (FFR) and Hemi-Sync emerged. The FFR technique received patent No. 3,884,218, under the name Mentronics in May, 1975, assigned to Monroe Industries of Charlottesville. "As outlined in the patent, the method includes generating a familiar, repetitive, pleasing sound and generating a second signal with a waveshape characteristic of the electric activity in the brain during periods of sleep. The two signals are blended to produce an audible sound to which people can listen, presumably becoming drowsy."[1]

Monroe says, "We do know Hemi-Sync works. There have been sixty or seventy thousand applications of the binaural process over the years. We have discovered some, but not all of the reasons why it works.

"Somewhere, someone will find out why. It establishes a coherent brain pattern which accesses human consciousness at many levels. perhaps even down into the cellular structure." Hemi-Sync was registered as a trademark in May 1984.

Gregg Carroll is a talented musician and musical educator from the University of North Carolina at Greensboro. His view reflects the frustration of others who are convinced Hemi-Sync works, and that it offers much promise, especially in education. Carroll commented at the 1987 Seminar: "To date, there are no journal publications that discuss this particular technique. The National Research Council's Committee on Techniques for Enhancement of Human Performance has recently initiated a two-year study of Hemi-Sync."

Ray Waldkoetter, the psychologist who works for the U.S. Army at Fort Benjamin Harrison, probably reflects the feelings of many professionals who have dealt with Hemi-Sync, know its value, but find themselves frustrated in attempts to push applications: "Many rigid scientists say Hemi-Sync should be modeled after physical sciences and related experimental procedures. But the Hemi-Sync technology does not fit the traditional research mode.

"It is not frequently debated that the Frequency Following Response cannot really affect and effect human behavior.

"Bob repeatedly has said the effects of Hemi-Sync 'are all in the mind.' This suggests a belief system that is at work and can be utilized by the practitioner. However, I have taken naive subjects (children), exposed them to the therapeutic Hemi-Sync sound and then watched them relax and sleep. I have also used it as a hypnotic adjunct, where, with the relaxed state, I have presented organized learning tasks to be performed later. This procedure was very effective.

"Hemi-Sync must be studied in the larger context. That is: What effects are related and how they are induced. As a concerted program of research is developed, some breakthroughs can be expected, even if the original purposes are not always on target.

"As the Institute has also taken to exporting Gateways and other experiential programs, it may also gravitate toward some special consulting efforts for education and science."

* * * *

In keeping with Bob's general approach, the Institute has no concerted campaign to sell Hemi-Sync to any profession. The Institute thinks of its Professional Division as the leading edge of the wave to introduce Hemi-Sync into the culture, based on demonstrated success. Most of the new applications come from word-of-mouth advertising—and anecdotal proof that it works. The Institute has no salespersons.

One of the key figures in the continuing development of Hemi-Sync is Skip Atwater, a chunky, drily humorous researcher, who discussed the technology at the 1987 Professional Seminar. [2] Atwater and Wallis are working on the possibility of feeding the EEG brain waves of gifted subjects automatically back to a computer and thence to Hemi-Sync equipment. Atwater's research into the brain is a key to the Institute's research efforts. Bob Monroe calls the idea a "very profound" expansion of Hemi-Sync.[3]

Dave Wallis has spent some time trying to get technical help from non-physical sources to help solve the problem, using one of the current Explorers as a medium. A certain amount of guidance has been forthcoming but the three-cornered system of communication—Wallis-to-monitor-to-Explorer and vice-versa, into and out of technical terminology—is probably just too cumbersome.

Wallis "is being teased," says Rita Warren, one of the volunteer monitors in the lab. "They say, 'You expect us to do all your work for you.' " On the other hand, an M.D. asked an Explorer for specific technological information on a drug and got very technical replies to his queries.

Rita adds, "As far as we can determine, there is very little scientific and technical information coming through channels anywhere, at all.

"Maybe this scarcity is a problem of vocabulary. Or the concepts of the Explorer's mind and his categories of knowledge are limited. Maybe it's the monitor's vocabulary which is lacking."

Monroe hopes the new work will lead to a "Graduate Program in Consciousness," with the Institute acting as an arm of a college or university.

The Institute had received eighteen applications to do graduate work on the premises by the end of 1987. Several Ph.D. candidates have actually come to Monroe to do research for their dissertations, but the Institute's existing equipment is not sufficient to provide the type of physiological measurement the researchers need. Two new Ph.D. theses are in the works, one on developmentally-disabled infants.

Applications of Monroe Technology

Peter Russell and a number of other Consciousness thinkers, Western and Eastern, have, in the way of philosophers, inched more and more confidently to an unprovable spiritual or mystical hypothesis, based to some extent, at least, on their own metaphysical experiences. Greatly oversimplified, according to this theory, the human brain is but one aspect of the Mind. The Mind, in turn, is part of the Collective Consciousness—of mankind, the planet, and the Universe. Man and the Mind are also reflected or duplicated in the physical Earth and its environment. What we, as humans, do is registered by the living Earth (or Gaia), and the Earth, or the Universe, responds in like measure.

It is this phenomenon that has led us to the global retaliation we now face, evidenced in the warnings of AIDS, and devastation the planet is now issuing in such forms as the Greenhouse Effect, depletion of the ozone layer, drought, desertification, earthquakes and volcanic eruptions, floods, even hurricanes.

But the message of Russell and others is hopeful. There may yet be time to minimize the effects of humanity's greed. The way is through the healing of expanded Consciousness. Some of the tools we have to achieve Consciousness are the techniques perfected by Bob Monroe.[1]

If you asked a representative sampling of the American public to list the country's priority problems, many would immediately respond, the "Economy." But an appreciable number, at least, would probably answer "Education"; others would cite "Health"; In these two fields alone, Hemi-Sync could have major impact. It is hard for the converted not to be overly optimistic, on the one hand, and despairing, on the other, that the promise of Bob Monroe's technology is so scorned by society's rigid establishments, so little understood, and so little used.

* * * *

In the March, 1985 issue of "Breakthrough," the Monroe Institute reported, hopefully:

"Pilot tests of the Hemi-Sync Synthesizer are nearing completion in several schools in the Tacoma, Washington area. Because of the positive results so far, it has been introduced into several other schools throughout the United States...

"Since 1978, when the research started, several thousand students from elementary grades through graduate school have utilized Hemi-Sync for cognitive and effective learning enhancement....

"Several persistent themes dominate the history of consciousness enquiry, one of which is that humans use only a small portion of their mental capacity. Estimates vary, but there is agreement that most of us use less than ten percent, and some researchers say that figure is more on the order of one-tenth of one percent. The obvious question arising from this observation is, 'How can we tap some or all of the wasted potential?'

"The question has not gone unanswered, and in the past fifty years, the answers have varied widely. But a careful examination of the answers given in the last ten or fifteen years reveals a common thread. The thread is the conviction that optimal learning takes place when the learner is in a certain state of consciousness. The state is not one of intense arousal, as when one is anxious, excited, hyperactive, or fearful. Nor is it sleep, as some people thought twenty years ago."[2]

One solution is, at least according to the late Devon Edrington and some others who have used Hemi-Sync in the classroom, the Monroe technique; the same people, however, would hasten to add that Hemi-Sync is merely one way of achieving an optimum learning state, but it is here and available, so why not use it?

The reply they all-too-often run across is a variation on myopia, or outright hostility to changing the system. Devon Edrington's work on Hemi-Sync applications in education stopped with his death in 1986. His papers were distributed among his close associates. One of them, a school teacher, found it expedient to stop using Hemi-Sync in her school when the political makeup of the school board swung conservative. The woman who inherited Edrington's own work was so distraught over his death, she has not carried on.

The Montgomery County, Maryland, Department of Instructional Resources recommended Monroe's Progressive Accelerated Learning tapes for use in that district's school system, according to "Breakthrough" in June, 1987, but then the program ran into political opposition, and nothing further was done about it.

Fear is a motivating factor which prevents acceptance of Monroe techniques. It can come guised as board members' sanctimonious righteousness, politicians' charges of 'brainwashing,' even the opposition of teachers to a new technique.

Yet Hemi-Sync is an available, inexpensive technology which could help the United States out of the pathetic doldrums into which its educational system has sunk. Certainly it would require further testing before its introduction on a broad basis, and the appropriation of money for such research would take courage at whatever level of political responsibility it was made. But President Reagan's Secretary of Education, William Bennett, consistently warned of the shortcomings in America's educational system during his term in office. It was a warning to which many non-doctrinaire educators privately subscribed.

* * * *

Biofeedback had proven, by a mass of experiental data, that humans can control at least some of their bodily functions by voluntary, guided effort. Bob Monroe based his first lab work on Biofeedback equipment. The Institute today is working along parallel, but possibly more advanced, lines.

There are innumerable stories around the Institute of accelerated healing, pain reduction, minimal-stress surgery, using Hemi-Sync tapes. But they are just that: stories, anecdotal, word-of-mouth, not correlated and above all, not scientific. In the case of the Canadian's disappearing brain tumor, for instance, the doctors were at a loss to explain what had happened.

That story and many others underline that there is a quiet, small revolution going on in public and professional attitudes to, and acceptance of, the expense, risks, and failures in the practice of conventional medicine. An appreciable minority seek alternates to the established system which is so epitomized by the rigidity of the American Medical Association. Acupuncture, shamanism, holistic medicine, homeopathy, self-healing, medical clairvoyance, even crystal power and pyramid power have gained acceptance among a tiny minority of the population because they have produced positive, notable results to the patients' demonstrable knowledge and satisfaction.

Dr. Art Gladman is the distinguished Oakland psychiatrist, whose specialties are biofeedback and psychosomatic illness. He is a leading exponent of the use of Monroe techniques in medicine. Gladman has been a member of the Monroe Institute Board of Advisers for many years.

His long career has brought him from being a World War II psychiatrist and flight surgeon, to state and national distinction in his field. Despite the weight of impressive practice and recognition, Gladman looks and acts like a cheerful elf, who has a saucy tongue with which he makes light of his year's seniority on Bob Monroe.

Gladman and his colleagues in a joint practice and at the E.A. Gladman Memorial Hospital in Oakland treat some patients who come to them for stress-related disorders, using Gateway Discovery album tapes. "When we determine that they have some ego strength, we ask them if they want to come in forty-five minutes before their scheduled appointments, and listen to a tape here." Gladman quickly adds that not all patients respond positively to being told what to do by Bob's voice.

Art reflects on his own experience of Monroe's tools. For years, he suffered severe pain in his feet. A number of diagnoses proved nothing useful. Finally, a colleague correctly identified Gladman's ailment. He went into surgery, and "didn't remember anything for the next three or four days—I was that heavily doped." A year later, he still had no relief from the pain.

Gladman needed further surgery. He decided to try Monroe's Emergency Treatment tapes. Art approached Dr. Bob Roalfe, a Bay Area anaesthesiologist to see if he would go along with the unorthodox procedure.

"When I told him about the tapes and my intention, I knew I had a prospect." Roalfe gave Gladman considerably less anaesthesia than usual. The operation lasted three hours and twenty minutes. Art was fully awake and alert when he came out of the operating room. That afternoon, he was on the phone, talking to his wife. He left the hospital in five days, rather than the ten it had taken to recover from the first surgery.

Since that experience, Gladman has compiled a number of other, similar histories. The enthusiastic Bob Roalfe, continues with the technique in the Bay Area, and has, alone, logged over one hundred cases.

Why can't such a beneficial procedure as the Emergency Treatment series find general use in surgery? Why not make it routine operating procedure?

Art Gladman replies, "You have to look at the sociology of a hospital. There are four different teams involved in surgery. You arrive in the morning, two hours before the operation, and are handled by the pre-op people. Then the surgical team, itself; the recovery room people; and the floor team. They are four separate entities which do not communicate with each other.

"To do the Emergency Treatment series right, you have to have someone who will stay with the patient throughout the whole procedure. It could be a family member, or even a hospital-insider who's responsibility it is to carry the patient through the whole chain of events."

In order to get the Emergency Treatment series of tapes into general medical acceptance, documented tests have to be carried out at length, preferably in a small general hospital—of about seventy-five beds—where the program can be introduced to the entire staff. Gladman and his associates are looking for just that hospital.

* * * *

Medical clairvoyance, although a rare ability, is not unknown. Edgar Cayce is probably the most famous example of a diagnostician who worked, in effect, by remote-viewing. Meredith Lady Young (*Agartha*) and others practice a similar form of analysis-at-a-distance. It appears possible that at least one such practice may be subjected to objective, scientific scrutiny.

When Teresa Pope attended her Gateway in 1983, she was working in the office of the Virginia attorney general as a paralegal. Almost immediately, she became an Explorer, and adopted the name "Winter," by which she is today best known at the Institute. Even in her early Exploring, Winter gave rudimentary diagnoses. Right off the bat, she told one woman the cause of some physical pain, and told her she would be a healer.

Winter's life changed with that Gateway. She moved to Providence, Rhode Island, and started to do medical clairvoyance with Albert Dahlberg, an M.D.-Ph.D. and a well known scientist and researcher in biochemical-genetic engineering at Brown University. Dahlberg has held numerous National Institute of Health grants.

Winter "read bodies" under conditions controlled by Dahlberg, which were as strict as he could make them; by summer 1987, the pair had done about ninety diagnoses, including the amendment of verdicts by other physicians, during Winter's altered state of consciousness, and had prescribed treatments.

Word of Winter's gift and the team's success rate spread among "straight" medical practitioners who kept open minds. The beginnings of a medical underground seemed to be developing. In the summer of 1987, Winter and Dahlberg were interviewed by a panel of distinguished doctors at the National Institute of Health, who were searching for candidates for the Institute of Noetic Science's "Exceptional Ability" program.

Winter thought the interview would be a one-on-one session, not a committee appearance. She was frightened, but as soon as the questioning started, "a male voice came into my head, which turned to a thought." The august committee members, at the end of their screening session said, probably to their own surprise, "This should be tested. It cannot be closeted any longer."

Dr. Al Dahlberg, a member of the Professional Division, says, "Bob Monroe has had a very important influence on my life, for which I am most grateful. Many of the people with whom I now associate I met directly or indirectly through the Institute. Bob has worked hard to get the results of the Institute's work out to the 'real' world. It takes time, but the benefits are and will continue to be enormous."

* * * *

One of the most controversial fields in which Bob Monroe is interested, and that on which he has taken a rare, philosophical, public position, is death. Elisabeth Kubler-Ross has had more than her share of trouble and rejection from the Establishment for her views. In *Ultimate Journey*, Bob makes his own attempt to demystify society's ingrained fear of dying.

Would it conceivably be possible that anaesthesiologists could put into practice one of Monroe's more revolutionist ideas: Taking patients out to the "beachhead" of There, and letting them look, before making their exit, through death? Or, in Bob's words "reeling them out, and then reeling them back in."

Dr. Art Gladman shakes his head emphatically, and ticks off the barriers to such innovative procedures. "Malpractice. Find a hospital that would go along with it. Convince the hospital administration.

"You have to justify everything. There's no chance it could be done under our existing system."

Ruth Domin, of Chattanooga Hospice, had been working to ease the transition that is death for well over a decade. After she attended Elisabeth Kubler-Ross's workshop in Connecticut in 1975, Ruth wrote Elisabeth, "If I could ever learn enough to become part of your Star System program, I would be supremely happy!"

The Monroe Institute issued a terse description of the Star System in 1976:

> *The Star System program offers intensive training for a physical life of predicted short duration. It is operated on a one-to-one basis under the supervision of a local physician or psychiatrist.*
>
> *The training program includes all phases of preparation, exploration of transfer point, and interim activities. It must be used with an M-5000 Representative.*
>
> *Volunteers handle individual one-hour exercises once or twice weekly for six weeks in their local home areas.*

A friend wrote Ruth, "The Star System sounds like the very thing you have been looking for. Although the practitioners are volunteers now, surely they will be paid workers when it becomes recognized as an indispensable part of adjusting." Twelve years later, Ruth Domin penciled a note on the letter, "It still isn't recognized, but maybe we're on the way with the Professional Division's Life Transitions Group."

Mrs. Domin was, in her own way, an Explorer. She did precisely what Bob Monroe preaches: took the tools he provides and put them to work, totally selflessly, to gain information about the act of dying she could then use in her Hospice practice.

After her first Monroe course, the M-5000, in February, 1976, Ruth worked with Bob's tapes. She exulted in her journal after a Focus-12 exercise, "A beautiful, beautiful trip. Inquired about people whose bodies are in comas. Where are they? What is it like for them?

"Was standing on the edge of an enormous black hole. Should I go down? (The answer came) 'Yes.'

"I went down, down. . .stopped somewhere. There were sides. Darkness, but I could see a little. Confinement. Not unhappiness. Just nothing. 'Is it like this?' I asked. 'Sometimes,' was the answer."

Ruth persisted. She used a Focus-10 tape. Her journal records, ". . .In bright light. Then in a room. Someone is sitting on a stool—like in a kitchen. I tried to talk. Did talk. But couldn't converse, because the person (male? female? I don't know) couldn't hear me.

" 'Is this person in a coma?'

" 'Yes.'

" 'Then they sometimes have trouble here?'

" 'Yes.'

" 'Is there any way someone from the Obstructed Universe (the physical world) could help them?' I was quite puzzled. Surely there are people here to help them.

"Then a strange thing happened. A person appeared—I think it was a man, but it mostly just seemed like a person—smiling, loving, radiant. He said, 'We can work together.'

"I started to cry. I really hated to leave. I knew he would come along if I wanted. I asked. He came back to Focus-10. I still hated to leave. Still crying.

"Am still crying, though I know he's here. The sadness will go away soon. But I have never known anyone so beautiful, or any place I would rather be than Focus-12."

Ruth's years-long interest in the subject finally led her, at the Professional Seminar of 1987, to organize the Death and Transformation project, whose aim is "to develop and test a package of Hemi-Sync tapes which will support patients/clients, families, and health-care providers who deal with life transitions to facilitate and ease these transitions."

Several months later, Ruth had a Hemi-Sync'ed pilot tape which is now being used on a trial basis by volunteers. The script for the tape was written by Ruth, who was helped in her writing efforts by one of her terminally-ill patients. Bob Monroe found time to voice it; Harry Shay, a retired merchant marine captain who works with AIDS patients, copied the cassettes and sent them out in early 1988.

* * * *

One of Bob Monroe's pet projects has been and may yet again be Metamusic, the trade name of a series of tapes marketed by Interstate Industries. Metamusic is a series of non-directional melodic tape cassettes which have a Hemi-Sync bed beneath the music. The music is primarily designed to be an aid to relaxation, although some people use the tapes as meditational background. The titles of the cassettes give an indication of the type of response they evoke: Nostalgia, Sunset, Pacifica, Midsummer Night, Back Room, Outreach, Downstream, Eddys, Random Access, and others.

Metamusic has not been an entirely happy experience for Monroe. Bob feels that some of the tapes are successful, but not all. He hopes to return to the project in the future, to build up a comprehensive Metamusic library.

Psychotherapists probably are the most frequent users of the music tapes. But Metamusic pops up elsewhere as well—in a lawyer's office, for instance, or on all eight tracks of the audio system in one dentist's chair. (The same dentist started using Hemi-Sync in his waiting room, to ease patient tension; he discontinued it when he realized his staff was too blissed-out to perform effectively.) A plastic surgery group practice in Phoenix, which treats forty outpatients a week, is using the music to reduce tension.

A relatively new field of application for Hemi-Sync is in business, especially in Organizational Development training for managers, where one of the buzzphrases is "unleashing creativity."

One couple uses Metamusic for a style of New Age brainstorming in management seminars. They say to the executives, "If you're afraid of this, it's your loss not ours," and claim they will walk away from the job if they meet too much resistance. Organizations, the couple says, must envision their own future, consciously and responsibly. Executives are slaves to their emotions: They "feel" corporate decisions.

A Charlottesville consultant who grew up next door to Rube Goldberg, and thereby started life as a cartoonist and Walt Disney animator, now promotes creativity in corporations and Hemi-Sync's his workshops. He has given seminars at the U.S. Government's Federal Executive Institute in Charlottesville. He calls his practice "Safe mind-stretching" or Whole Brain Thinking. "This is an idea-friendly time."

Since the early 1980s, the Institute has operated the program called Gateway Outreach (GO), designed to take the basic program out of the Institute and around the country. GO is given by people who are trained in a week-long special course at the Institute, then return to their homes and try to promote Monroe techniques. About a hundred people have been through the GO training course, of whom some sixty are active. They have a tough job, not only to introduce Hemi-Sync, but to establish regional networking centers, and to make their own operations financially viable.

* * * *

In Britain, the energetic Russells say, "We'd like to get the Monroe people in the United Kingdom together. . .make this an outpost of the Institute, based in our house. We've converted a large room. Bought a hi-fi. It's now the Monroe Room.

"Jill is using Metamusic and (the Hemi-Sync) Surf tape while working as a therapist. She does her work in a different state of consciousness. Whatever she's doing, it certainly benefits the patients. . . .

"A maternity hospital in Gloucestershire: A midwife became interested, now the nurses have asked to use it.

"A school in Cambridge. . . .

"A hospital for adult mentally-retarded (mental level less than five years). Very calming.

"An art therapist. . .working with subnormal children. . . .

"We're gathering a store of experience.

"We had a gathering of local yoga teachers and played them Metamusic tapes. . .they said they were the best relaxation tapes they'd ever heard.

"We're planning a once-a-week, eight-week course. Relaxation, stress-management techniques. . .for nurses and teachers, especially, maybe even a salesman, using Metamusic and Bob's tapes.

Consciousness and Science

Talking of professional exploration of his work, Bob Monroe comments: "The scientist is curious, but the ordinary researcher is limited by time and space." A scientist would do beautifully if he could accept the reality of Monroe's Focus 21. "He'd exclaim, 'What's this vibration that makes my being resonate with joy?'

"That's when *you* become God. You can go beyond Focus 21 and explore on your own. There are no limits."

Bob was talking before the new science of Chaos became known to the general public. But even with the discoveries of the new field, few name-brand scientists can accept that there is a reality not governed by laws of their own making. It is a subject which has, on the one hand, saddened and frustrated Bob Monroe; on the other, typically, he has sought ways around, over or through the obstacles strewn in his path by the various establishments.

After he decided to live with his persistent Out-of-Body excursions, Monroe, the engineer, did the logical thing, for him: He sought proof that what was happening to him was real. Some of his early demonstrative attempts were in the experiments with the sympathetic Charley Tart, and are recounted in *JOOB*. But the Tart lab sessions didn't really demonstrate to Monroe, much less the nation or the planet, that here was a novel, certified-if-not-unique, physical-world experience. He had been checked and evaluated by Stuart Twemlow and his colleagues—and the scientific evaluation of Bob Monroe thereupon stopped, cold. All Bob could do was to cultivate contacts as they came to him, look for open minds willing to explore, and hope for the best. Scientific validation has been elusive.

Dr. Stuart Twemlow, the psychiatrist who studied and practiced at the Menninger Foundation, observes Bob Monroe from the point of view of a sympathetic professional. He devoutly hopes Monroe will forget the credibility issue.

Twemlow says, "In a nutshell, we don't have the methodology to examine what he does; not only Bob, but other people who work in an altered state of consciousness.

"The scientist says the world of thinking and the world of physical objects are independent of each other. If you grant that assumption, how can you use the method of this assumption to test it?

"Look at the teaching of geometry in school. It's based on the four Euclidian principles: assumptions that are unprovable but are essential to geometry. You have to accept them.

"Thus, every answer can be countermanded. The enquirers' biases will be proved. You make your own answers. The voltmeter used in schoolrooms to 'prove' Ohm's Law is based on Ohm's Law!"

Twemlow echoes Peter Russell, whose *The Global Brain* is a passionate but closely-reasoned plea for expanded consciousness in our physical world: "Today, the philosophy of science is really more important than the result." But Twemlow feels the philosophy hasn't caught up with the reality that a pioneering minority recognizes.

"In 1976, scientific philosophers told a group of metaphysicists, 'You people can't even describe what you're studying. We'll talk to you when you get your act together.' A weight of anecdotal confirmation is not the equivalent of a thermometer in a vat of molten steel. Immanuel Kant led the way with his view that, 'If you ask a question, you must be sure there is an answer.' In the world of the supraconscious, there is no such surety."

Twemlow reflects on Bob Monroe's work. "The results he gets in people using the tapes are not independent of the person doing the tape itself. Investigators try to separate the binaural beat from the rest of the event. Bob is experimenting with untestable things.

"There's no doubt the tapes can be helpful, even transformative. But double-blind control studies will never work with his tapes. Those tests depend on things which, in Monroe's work, cannot be controlled.

"All of us..." Monroe's pioneers as well as students of other metaphysical disciplines, "...have seen or experienced the altered state."

Even Charley Tart's early experiments with Monroe are open to skepticism from the scientist. Twemlow adds, "It is always possible that the numbers Bob saw in his Out-Of-Body state were known by someone at some point. The computer from which they were drawn was programmed by someone.

"It's just not possible to arrange a test without some human experience in it. So it is also theoretically possible that Bob achieved his results by some form of telepathy or ESP.

"The only hard and fast proof of the OOB state is if someone can be absolutely proven to have been in two places at once."

Bilocation, as the phenomenon is called, is, as of now, only rarely encountered. Bob Monroe has a friend who bilocates involuntarily, to the astonishment of witnesses, and of the subject, himself. He once repeated a purchase in the same store on two successive days, but had no recall of the first occasion, despite confirmation by witnesses. The man *knew* and could prove he had been elsewhere at that time on the first day. On another occasion, he was observed emerging from an outdoor privy when he should have been sitting at a picnic table. As soon as his absence from the table was noticed, he reappeared, and the second figure coming out of the Portakabin vanished.

Although it is not a case of bilocation, the tale of the Eastern Airlines flight crew-member killed with all others on board a plane near Miami, then reappearing numerous times, in uniform, on other aircraft, is analogous. Painstaking analysis seemed to indicate the dead engineer materialized on flights made by planes in which parts cannibalized from the crashed plane had been used.[1]

Until more people who bilocate come forward and submit themselves to rigorous scientific examination, Stuart Twemlow's criterion for this kind of absolute, laboratory-tested proof will remain a wishful thought. "The scientific establishment will not accept Bob's work until and unless they have empirical proof of his claims."

Philosophically, as opposed to scientifically, Twemlow continues, "The idea that we live in a participatory Universe, where Observer and Observed are separate entities, is a false assumption.

"Nothing is wholly independent of all else.

"One way of testing is to apply Abductive Research. The Americans apply the

Hypothetical Deductive Method. The British use the Inductive.

"In the Abductive Model, you apply what you think is happening to a situation, and see if it works. Then you fiddle with it, fine-tune it. If it works again, you accept that it works.

"One possibility is studying one subject over a period of time. You challenge the subject, then he does a tape; You challenge him again; he goes back and does the tape again. If you get the same response, it's a pretty strong indication the tape works.

"That's what Bob is doing, in the absence of absolute, conclusive proof.

"He is changing people's lives. He's demonstrating his techniques work.

"But he'll never get anywhere with the Hypothetical Deductive method, even if he spends a million dollars on it." Twemlow shakes his head as he cites investigation of engineering anomalies at the department of applied sciences at Princeton. "They did some five hundred thousand trials to prove that psychokinesis exists.

"They used that amount of energy to prove something *I know* exists! But some still won't accept their results."

Perhaps it is high time to work for a shift in consciousness which will allow scientists to override their narrow disciplines.

And perhaps enough mavericks have strayed from the herds that a broader range of professionals might see in Monroe something more than just a peculiar old man living on a hilltop in Virginia.

* * * *

At the 1987 Professional Seminar, Bob Monroe addressed himself to a limited target—or, perhaps, Bob-like, he was using an allegory. The target was conversion of the Belief System to the Know System about the relative unimportance of death. But Monroe's logic may have been: If we can get this message across, the rest will be easy.

Another speaker, "speaking parenthetically," was Skip Atwater, the researcher, who boldly asked, "Why does the magic work? Why do we want a six-pack of it?

"Hemi-Sync is a fine line in the human consciousness. . .The difference between Believing and Knowing. . .Four mixed and layered binaural beats which allow the programming of the Belief System.

"You are creating your own reality. The impossible becomes possible. You set aside society's rules.

"You're saying, 'I brought my camera with me (my brain)—with a different focus, lenses, and filters, to preserve reality.' Each person has a different camera. A different reality set."

Monroe constantly reiterates that his is not the only way. But his tools are there, nearly free for the taking. They permit a fast passage to Supra-Consciousness, that feeling of oneness with the Universe, and the boundless information available from it. A basic in the Gateway course is the eradication of fear of the unknown, and therewith, fear of death. If anyone wants to explore farther, why that's fine, too.

The Explorer Program

From the late 1960s until the mid-to-late 1970s, Bob Monroe was assisted at Whistlefield by the small band of enthusiastic Explorers—ordinary folk, who simply appeared from the surroundings, seemingly at random. As the original Explorers drifted away to other locations, new candidates emerged, especially after the Gateway program moved into gear.

Monroe muses, "The Explorers of the 1970s all went through profound changes.

"At Whistlefield, the Explorer program was pure research. But a funny thing happened on the way to the store."

It was all new and very exciting, but Bob, their leader, felt responsible, and was concerned about the Explorers' well-being. It was as much this concern as the approaching workshop at Esalen that led to the collaborative composition of the Gateway Affirmation.

'We had nine Explorers in 1973. Right after we had the Affirmation, all of them made contact."

The early days were exhilarating but frustrating. There is a pause, as Bob Monroe recollects. "Just sitting there, listening to it all. . .For instance, you can't check what Miranon was bringing through. It's just uncheckable. But the power of the material. . . .!

"Oh, you could ask him cosmic questions, and he would answer. But Miranon was there primarily to help Shay St. John," the Unity Church minister, who has now left Virginia.

Miranon gave Bob a storehouse of useful information about the cosmos. He is the source for much of the knowledge Bob has interwoven into his own explorations and writings—for instance, on the levels of being beyond Focus 21.

An attentive Nancy Monroe, who was herself an active Explorer at the time, adds, "Miranon wanted Shay to know these things. He tried to give Shay the knowledge and asked Bob to pass it on.

"Each of the third-party non-physical Entities has a very, very special prime purpose which he states unequivocally.

'It is to help that physical person through whom he speaks. It's just that. He couldn't care less about the rest of the world."

The Ah-So cluster of four beings channeled by Rosalind McKnight has shielded and protected her. Another Explorer, Marie Coble, has been told the information she channels from "Friend" is primarily for her use, although whatever others may do with it is fine as well. One current Explorer is referred to by her entity as "This dear and beloved being." Martin Warren calls in "Magellan" when he sets off on a car trip so he will be sure to arrive, and can devote his attention to other matters while driving.

Tom Campbell, another of the early Explorers, had a physicist's scientific approach to channeling. Bob says, admiringly, "He was a great investigative reporter, fearless. He'd get into situations and boldly ask, 'Who are you?'

"He knew he wasn't perceiving what he was perceiving.

"Tom wanted badly to understand the Time-Space Illusion on Earth, and how it works. The Friends in the non-physical group offered to teach him, to make him understand, in his terms. But the simple facts of his own Time-Space Illusion—the requirements of his job, to be precise—prevented it." Campbell had to move away from Virginia before the concentrated inquiry could be launched.

There was Judy Campbell, Tom's wife in the early 1970s. "She was a left-brained executive, very successful in her career, efficient.

'Judy went into the future. She was emotional, but not afraid, when she made her trips. She was on the verge of sobbing all the time."

Monroe's close associate, and his son-in-law, Joe McMoneagle, is one of the nation's leading professional remote-viewers (seeing psychically at a distance), with a "hit rate" of about 86 percent, when using Monroe techniques.

McMoneagle, a stubby, tough, former Army man, had a Ufo experience in the Bahamas in 1966 and a near-death experience in Europe in 1970. As a result, he gravitated to Monroe, and started working with Bob on his own time, while still in the military.

Joe was involved in the emergency predicting of a possible crash site for the damaged Skylab. He first worked at Stanford Research International (SRI) in California in 1978, and is one of the remaining active members of a SRI remote-viewing panel which includes such other well-known viewers as Ingo Swann and Keith Harary.

Monroe recognized in McMoneagle a gifted subject. The pair worked thirteen months together developing a special Hemi-Sync tape for Joe. Where previously, McMoneagle did not travel with his body when he remote-viewed, he now occasionally goes OOB to be present at the scene on which he is reporting. The OOB cuts through "this fog we call living." His "cooling out" time after an Explorer exercise used to be between one and three hours. With the tape designed by Bob Monroe, Joe has cut cooling-out, in some cases, down to five or six minutes. Joe succinctly calls the tape "very effective."

McMoneagle frankly admits that a remote-viewing Explorer has many failures, and collects much useless information. Sometimes it can be a matter of mood. "It's very much like learning a new language."

At the Monroe Institute Lab, McMoneagle has traveled through time and space to give accounts of the birth of Jesus and other events. He is the reporter on Tape Number 27, "Origins of Man." Another Explorer has covered the genesis of the Universe and has voyaged to the center of the Earth.

These days, Monroe does not even listen to new Explorer material. His reasoning is simple, and self-protective. "It's about the most addictive stuff you can imagine. You can't wait for the next chapter. I've got other things to do; I have to watch my time."

* * * *

Over in the corner of the main studio in the Lab building stands the Booth. It's the pioneer model of the Chec Unit, and affords the occupant a great deal of sensory deprivation. The legs of the copper-sheathed chamber are embedded in sand. The

Explorer mounts a few steps, and enters a darkened room whose walls are thickly carpeted. The Booth contains a waterbed, video camera, microphone, and is wired for the electrodes to monitor the subject. The head of the bed as well as the booth itself are firmly pointed towards magnetic north. A lone chair and a small desk, and a wastebasket complete the furnishings. Once the individual is hooked up and settled, the monitor switches on the control room tape-recorder and regulates the flow of sound into the Booth which keeps the Explorer in a relaxed state throughout.

The monitor, usually assisted by a technician, remains in the control room of the Lab building. In sessions where the Mind Mirror is used, it as well as direct electrical current readings may be recorded on video. The session itself is audio-taped from start to finish.

The technician makes physiological and Mind Mirror measurements, handles all the recording, and keeps the monitor informed of any changes in the Explorer's condition while he is in the Altered State.

The monitor guides the Explorer into the early stages of the trip, to Focus 10 (F-10), then to F-12, F-15 and perhaps beyond, to F-21. The monitor listens to the voyager's progress in the Altered State. He must be sensitive to the subject's reactions to what he is experiencing, able, if necessary, to reassure the Explorer about his safety.

A novice Explorer can easily fall into a state of ecstasy so intense that communication ceases. The monitor holds the Explorer on track, to help gain helpful information systematically. He acts, in effect, as a constant physical guide or conductor, to take the Explorer out and bring him back to physical reality grounded, safe and secure.

When the voyage is finished, the monitor takes the Explorer into the control room for a debriefing, which includes any comments additional to those he has recorded on tape during the trip. The monitor logs the session, notes briefly the content matter, and files the tape.

* * * *

My own experience may or may not be similar to that of others.

Martin Warren hooked me up and closed the door on the darkened booth. His voice checked my comfort on the intercom, and he switched on the tape. As the signal gathered in strength in my ears and brain, I felt the presence of my Friend, an accustomed and comforting companion. Then came a sensation of buoyant weightlessness, as my mind detached effortlessly from the restrictions of my body.

I began, slowly at first, to soar with a feeling of unfettered ascendancy. For an incalculable moment, I registered a sensation of roaring, gathering speed as if a booster were thrusting my unlimited being into a realm beyond the pull of gravity. (Some Explorers liken their experiences to deepsea diving rather than celestial voyaging.) Then all was calm. Part of my mind tried to grapple with what was happening.

I knew I was elsewhere. I knew, also, that I was moving, yet I felt stationary. I glanced around me and felt rather than saw, orbs passing by—planets, I supposed, of no particular color or luminescence. Bored with hovering motionless, I suggested to my protector that we maneuver, and we went into a series of gyrations, whirls, dives, spins, and climbs that made a rollercoaster pale in comparison.

The sensation of traveling slowed, as if airbrakes had gently and noiselessly been lowered. We came into a slow glidepath, drifting down tenderly—the sensation was that of a soft parachute landing—to my destination, the green, liquid planet I had visited before.

I was greeted by a circle of energies—friendly, warm, more than hospitable. My Supra-Conscious knew I was one of and with them. We exchanged information non-verbally. Then one energy emerged from the cluster. I had the sensation that he unrolled a parchment document—much in the manner of olden town-criers—and read a proclamation which concerned me and my responsibilities.

Too soon, my Friend signaled it was time to depart. I had no desire to leave the green planet, even though I knew I must.

I anticipated by what seemed only a short instant Martin Warren's voice from the far distant control room, telling me to prepare to re-enter physical life. A wave of resentment at Martins's intrusion swept over me and was instantly gone. My companion and I floated back to our rendezvous point, where we parted, although I knew intuitively that my Friend remains with me.

Martin ever-so-softly started talking me down. At one point, I thought I was re-entering physical reality too fast, and I took over the countdown myself. I landed, back on the waterbed, in the quiet fulfillment of the Booth, breathless, nearly stunned by the experience.

* * * *

Since February, 1984, the Explorer Program has been operated by three volunteers, Rita and Martin Warren, and Darlene Miller, to all of whom Bob Monroe is quick to acknowledge a deep debt of gratitude.

Rita's soft-speaking manner is a cloak for her agile, incisive mind. She is a white-haired, kindly 1961 Ph.D. in psychology, with an extensive background in the study of the causes of crime, particularly among young people. Her list of books, book-chapters, and learned-journal articles is impressive. She has served as consultant to various university and state bodies, a presidential commission, and Canadian organizations. She was "Correctional Psychologist of the Year" in 1974, and is listed in *Who's Who of American Women.*

Her husband, Martin, is a retired California social worker. He has the forthright features of his Texas origin. On closer acquaintance, however, Martin turns out to be among the most gentle and compassionate of men.

Darlene Miller, also a psychology Ph.D., is the Gateway trainer who, in 1988, also became the ombudsman—psychologist-on-call for students who wanted to discuss their adventures in more depth than the busy trainers are able to give during a course. Thereafter, she was named to be one of the three "core trainers" at the Institute.

Martin Warren has his own view of the process of measuring and pinning down the non-physical friends. "You know," he says, leaning back in front of the bank of switches and dials which monitor events in the Black Box, "They literally just plain defy human analysis. They don't want to let themselves be explained by human science.

"Every time we think we begin to detect a pattern, that pattern shifts. The correlations we have collected disappear.

"We call the effect, 'Cosmic Laughter.'"

Part of the Institute's continuing enquiry is to concentrate on the operational side of Exploration. The monitors try to find out how information is available to the source (the communicating entity), his choice of language and ideas, and the nature of the Explorer's experience.

The Institute has developed a bio-monitoring technique which permits the Lab to ascertain with reasonable certainty whether a person who goes into the Booth is actually in touch with an entity, or merely wish-thinking what he or she channels. Only if satisfied, will the monitor accept information coming in through the Explorer as actually originating in non-physical realms.

Bob Monroe says, "The surprise is the individual you think is a phony. Often, he isn't." There was a woman who claimed she was in touch with an Indian chief, which sounded just a bit trite and predictable. But, when she entered the Black Box, says Bob, "Thirty-five volts of negative polarity!" Normal body polarity is one and a half volts-plus; when an Explorer goes through the Null Point, and his polarity shifts to negative, a reading of four and a half is a fair norm.

"It's a simplistic measurement system. It tells us something is happening, and the degree to which it is.

"Some have gone so high, it has made me nervous. I didn't know if they could live. But they'd been doing it already without us, so I let it go.

"Some day, someone's going to do a study of the Null Point phenomenon, and find out what it really is."

The wish-thinking process is called "aspecting." The word "aspect" in Institute usage connotes physical-life attachment or substance.

Rita Warren comments, "People may be merely drawing information from their Inner Self, Higher Self, Inner Truth. There's nothing wrong with it; it's just that they're getting the information from themselves, not from another entity.

"They're certainly doing something different from ordinary consciousness." The phenomenon is also referred to as the Inside/Outside Discussion.

Aspecting is the most puzzling, intriguing, and baffling conundrum which anyone who has ventured into the Altered State faces: "Was that a deeper Me talking, dredging up information I am not consciously aware I know?

"Or is what I have just heard/seen/reported, knowledge from a distinctly different, non-physical source?"

"The question," says Rita, "is more important to some people than we think it should be. You can use any name you choose for a disincarnate being. But does it really make any difference?

"In and Out are purely physical dimensions; perhaps they are irrelevant when we discuss non-physical entities. Some of them tell us it doesn't matter. 'As above, so below,' is their reply."

Bob Monroe says, "With one or two exceptions, the Explorers' 'communicators' refuse to give names. A name would latch them too tightly into physical reality."

Rosalind McKnight's Alfonso Pincinelli, the humorous musician from the nineteenth century, is one example of an upfront entity. Otherwise the names familiar to thousands of Monroe-tape listeners have been made up by the Explorers.

Rita Warren says, "Several of the Explorers have told us their entities are unlimited, and can't be 'boxed in.' Some sources have deliberately refused names, or say, 'Call us what you want.' We call one entity 'Friend,' but even such a concept is too limiting."

Rita notes it is almost impossible for humans not to think hierarchically. We automatically assign ranks or importance to people, and we carry the same practice over into the non-physical world. The entities, however, do not think in terms of precedence.

The Explorer monitors feel that some energies they have listened to are "purer," i.e., not so much filtered through the Explorer's ego. Likewise, they feel if an Explorer is able to diminish his ego requirements, he may be able to call on additional sources which, although not necessarily at "higher" levels, appear to provide information on a broader scale.

If a direct-voice connection to a non-physical energy is the definition of channeling, "What we do in the Lab is not channeling, really.

"It's hard to say what it is. The Explorers don't develop their own public personalities."

Rita Warren expands, "I guess you could say we do not believe channeling is rare; nor do we believe that truth and wisdom are available to only a few, special gurus or famous channelers.

"Our lab program has made it clear that many of us can tune in to our own expanded type of information-gathering capacity."

The difference between the Explorers and the better-known channelers is that Monroe's conduits do their thing in private, and—to the extent possible—set their egos aside when they go into the Black Box.

There is one variation in Monroe Institute procedure which is not common to public channelers. Public channelers, and some Explorers, vacate their bodies, to yield their vocal chords to non-physical entities. But when other Monroe Explorers are asked questions, they say, in effect, "Just a minute, I'll have to ask," or, "Let me go see if I can get that."

In such cases, the Explorer goes to the source of the information—for instance, the Library (or what Edgar Cayce called the Akashic Records)—queries it, and returns to report. Monroe himself prefers this three-way method because he feels the monitor has more control over the episode, and also that there is less ego-involvement in it.

Rita Warren adds, "Although many of our Explorers start out reporting via the three-party system, it's difficult to keep them that way. Whether it's because direct channeling has more pizzazz, or because channeling is a more efficient way of communicating with the monitor, I don't know.

"To what extent can you get the conscious mind out of the picture? Even the person with the least ego doesn't want to sound foolish.

"We try to get the purest, clearest channels we can, but some degree of personal interference—given our enculturation—is almost inevitable."

The public channels of today such as Ramtha, Mafu, and Lazaris use more complicated vocabularies than those of their physical-life spokespersons. Mafu, for instance, has said he draws words from the thoughts of audience-members at his sessions.

The language non-physical Friends use is often convoluted and abstruse. Why can't they speak more clearly? Monroe has a ready answer.

"Let's look at Rosie McKnight's Ah-So. He's very repetitive. He keeps saying, 'This is a tree. A tree has roots. This is a tree. A tree has bark. And so on.'

"What he's really doing is trying to work around the limitations of our language, translate into our physical reality, yet make his meaning absolutely clear.

"We can't get any perspective without Time-Space. For the Friends, there are no such things. They're trying to find our words to bridge the Time-Space Illusion. It's a conversion process for them—a quantum leap. It's awfully difficult for Ah-So, even after all these years of practice with Rosie."

Overcoming this difficulty is one of the main objectives of the Guidelines course: Accustoming the participant to verbalize complex 'rotes,' in Monroe's book terminology. It is an even more complex problem for novice Explorers, because the information they receive comes in images rather than words; they have to train themselves to report in language, for it to be of use to others than themselves.

The Exploring done in the Institute Black Box is not usually an Out-of-Body experience, in the sense of Bob Monroe's own exhilarating OOB trips.

Rita Warren comments, "This is a main point. It's interesting that we have never in our experiences in the Lab as Explorers or monitors gone through the exiting and re-entering of the body described by Bob and others. Rather, in the Booth, the experience seems to be one of simply releasing awareness of the physical.

"The difference may be because some experiences outside the Lab are spontaneous, whereas those in the Booth are planned and controlled."

* * * *

The Explorers' discoveries are taped and stored in the Lab, barely indexed, their contents perhaps now to some extent out-of-date, but still a treasure-trove of metaphysical information. An accumulation of some three thousand hours of Monroe's own tapes is locked in a tape vault at the Institute, largely unedited.

Could there be any hope the Entities themselves would help to arrange publication of the vast volume of information? Bob Monroe answers, quickly. "It's not their department." Could "other departments" be called in? "They're more *laissez-faire* than you think.

"I've done several sessions on this with the Friends." The possibility of publishing their information on Here-and-Now Earth "is sort of like jumping in a Concorde to get to Faber," the nearby railroad-crossing hamlet which is the Monroe Institute's postal address.

* * * *

When Rita and Martin Warren started to work in the Lab, they formulated a standard set of questions for Explorers. "It sounded like a neat plan. We thought it might be a reliability check," says Rita. "But in practice, it doesn't work. Just like in any interview, the monitor ends up following the lead of the informant."

There is at times an intriguing hint, or perhaps even evidence, of similarity in answers to the same question from different sources. The instances imply a vast, unanimous oneness out There. Rita comments, "A source may say, 'We just told you that yesterday, why are you asking again?' When we are dealing with two different Explorers. It raises questions about our research strategy."

The most consistent type of information that comes through the Explorers is in the broad spiritual or philosophical category. In general terms, it deals with the nature of the Total Self, with attitudes toward physical existence, and with the limitations of our belief systems.

Some of the information the Institute seeks is designed to be useful in exploration at levels beyond the human. The Institute's interest goes to what has been called "the perennial philosophy," or spiritual wisdom.[1]

The Explorers have covered any number of topics in their years of reporting, among them: The nature of God; death of the physical form; purpose of sleep; dreaming; illness, health and healing; guidance and masters; time; other lives; other universes; Earth-origins; human origins; the energy of human thought.

Monroe's intent in asking for some information is primarily pragmatic: data on alternate forms of energy, transportation using less fossil fuels, and dealing with food shortages.

The Institute takes no position on the information the Explorer program provides. On the urging of the Greens, some Explorer tapes, for instance, have been published for sale, without comment; the listener is free to make his own judgment on the veracity or credibility of the content.

* * * *

The Lab closed formally in late 1986 for a technical overhaul, although it continued in informal operation. Martin and Rita say, "Many people who come for a Gateway or Guidelines would like to go into the Booth to have us study their experiences, and in some cases, we do a session with them."

Marie Coble is a petite, southern-spoken lady who peers at the physical world through huge spectacles. These days, she works in the Institute office. When she first attended a Gateway, Bob asked her kindly, "What are you doing here?" Marie replied, quaking, "I want to be an Explorer." Bob replied suavely. "Come back in six months," and moved on.

Marie practiced with the home-use tapes daily, and with fervor. She came back for a second Gateway, as she had promised herself, half a year later, to the day. As Bob again proceeded around the hall, he came on her again. "And what are you doing here?"

"You told me to come back so I could be an Explorer." Bob was impressed by her persistence. There were technical holds and other delays, but two-and-a-half years later, Marie Coble was and remains today, an Explorer.

The procedure is that someone who feels gifted may ask for a Lab session. In extraordinary cases, Gateway trainers will recommend a student to the Lab monitors. This is usually the case only when someone in a Gateway has had experiences of a really startling nature. Unless specifically requested to explore, people who enter the Booth pay a Lab fee, to help underwrite costs.

Explorers and would-be Explorers are men and women of all ages, all levels of education, as well as of Right or Left Brain dominance. Over the years, more than one hundred fifty subjects, most of them Gateway and/or Guidelines graduates, have gone into the Black Box. Those who have become active Explorers have shown talent in achieving the Altered State, and in reporting experiences which are not aspecting.

The Institute has logged more than one thousand sessions with subjects since the Warrens came to Virginia, from a single appointment to more than two hundred with one individual. Eight 1980s Explorers have done more than thirty sessions each.

In 1987, three new Explorers suddenly moved to the Institute of their own volition, and began intensive reporting. Marie Coble, who had been traveling up from North Carolina for Lab sessions for some time; Teena Anderson, who attended a Gateway in 1985, gave up an important job in the mental health field in Boston, and moved to Virginia; and Ria Erickson, who came from California. Bob says, with some mystification, "They flat-out came here on their own hook. They all quit good jobs to come here. Were they directed to do so?"

Exploring is, as Bob says, addictive. Sometimes, an experienced Explorer is so eager, he goes into Altered State as soon as he steps over the threshold of the Lab building. Others are off, voyaging from the Booth, as soon as they are hooked up, and before the monitor can scramble back to the control board. Explorers often don't want to come back from their trips, any more than do Gateway voyagers.

'It's the lure, the knowing," says Monroe; they become too ecstatic over the incredibly beautiful things they behold. The monitor is there to ground them gently, skillfully using the Hemi-Sync signal.

Rita Warren says the Explorers "do not run into evil energies while they are out there. We don't know why; maybe there aren't any such things."

She tentatively ascribes this security to the Explorers' consistent use of the Gateway Affirmation, and to the belief system which most Explorers have adopted.

"When they go out, they may be in awe of what they see, but they're not in fear." Some have run up against the Barrier, which takes various forms, and which bars progress until the Explorer himself has overcome his limitations. But the Barrier is not a source of fear.

What happens when you "go out?" Rita describes the experience: "An Explorer may observe a non-physical guide, or may not. It is usually a presence which can speak to you directly or take you to a source of information. Some say they are guides and have been in physical life previously; some are part of a soul cluster and may move on beyond.

"Other Explorers go directly. There are all sorts of energy nodules in the energy stream. It's difficult to conceptualize and describe.

"There is an unlimited number of forms in which energies can come through. We try to get the Explorers not to linger with the first ones they run into.

"Bob thinks a lot of them are there, on planes close into Earth, to expunge their own guilt." One Explorer encountered an entity who had been a chemist under Hitler's regime, and wanted to pay his debt to mankind.

There appear to be two types of energies which are channeled to the Institute. Those which are 'fixed' and are always available to a particular Explorer, and the type which can only be described as the "Energy Flow," a limitless source of knowledge and wisdom. The second category is available to all who can make contact.

Rita says of the latter, "It seems that whenever you tap into the Energy Flow, what you get is appropriate for that time and place and person.

"There are various kinds of aspective energies available, and we can tap into any of them. We can get over-identified with some aspective energies, to the exclusion of others.

"Mothers, for instance, sometimes find it difficult to lead a full life without their children. Alcoholics become addicted to that aspect. Ideally, we would use aspects to improve ourselves, but we can't always manage to do so."

* * * *

There is considerable thought being given to the future of the Monroe Lab. It will reopen when the new, computerized equipment has been brought to prototype stage, and at that point, experienced Explorers will once again be needed to perform exacting test runs.

Beyond that, ideas spin out from various fertile brains. The business-minded envision the possibility of as many as six booths, available to fee-paying clients as the core of a new branch of the Institute—a self-healing and learning center which would specialize in development of the Whole Person. Such an innovation would, of course, require a larger trained staff of monitors and technicians.

Others foresee the Institute, after Bob's departure, as, perhaps, a major communications center linking Here and There—a metaphysical ground station.

Explorers will continue to play a role in any future Institute developments—at least until the process of information retrieval from There can be totally computerized.

New Land—The Dream

Bob Monroe's personal attempt to promote synergy and to evolve a collective consciousness foundered on human nature. Although, in the scheme of things, it is a tiny example, it may yet be a symbolic underlining of the nature of humankind, and of the difficulties humans face in attaining Peter Russell's Fifth Evolution.

That major disappointment in Bob's life and work, which he only reluctantly discusses, is the failure of the New Land experiment in "cooperative self-sufficiency, a survival modality; communal productivity."

Bob recalls examples of his original plans for the community from the disabused vantage point of 1988. "There's a full acre of greenhouse lying down there, unassembled. If it were in place, it could feed fifty families. The lake was going to provide fish, but no one's maintaining it. There's a manifold in the base of the dam at the lake to provide water and hydroelectric power.

"I envisioned people donating money and work. But no one would put the time and energy into building it. There was only one other person who helped. David Francis.

"As far as I can see, it's never going to happen," he sighs.

"Yes, it's a disappointment." He is reluctant to acknowledge that the New Land was an idealistic dream, based on a faith in the goodness of humanity, and that "The Right People" would automatically find their way to Roberts Mountain Farm, to buy property and build their houses.

He trusted it would turn out right, just the way the hidden selection process for Gateway Voyagers works. Bob lays no blame for the failure nor the back-biting that has ensued. Still, it hurts.

* * * *

The concept was simple and very appealing in the querulous late 1970s. When the Monroes found and subsequently bought Roberts Mountain Farm, it was only logical that it would serve the Institute and also become the refuge for a number of like-minded people who would be guided to its sylvan peace.

The September, 1978 issue of the Explorer newsletter announced the New Land project, and continued: "If The New Land will become the closed eco-system we all hope it to be, it will need the shared energies of all of us. Our needs are many and valid. Those who have lots of physical energy to give, we welcome you. The New Land will be built by shared energies." People who came and purchased lots on the property were expected to be self-supporting. There were to be no paying jobs at The Institute. Payments for goods and services provided by the community would be in U.S. dollars, or in Ergs, a notional currency issued in return for the amount of work a resident donated.

An early memorandum went on to distinguish between the New Land and "the many group/communities that are forming...growth in New Land as a group/community is more demanding, more difficult than thousands of seemingly 'similar' groups...due to the requirement of self-discipline, without patterns of rules...."

The "Original Principles" said the New Land was "a place for the gathering of individuals and families who wish to revise their lifestyles into more meaningful ways, means and ends; where permanent roots can be set down as securely as possible in a turbulent world; for the appreciation of natural pastoral beauty, relatively pollution free, yet incorporating the newest of modern technology; that offers a haven when all else may fail, from whatever cause—a 'safe' place; where learning and personal development may continue, be it creativity, awareness or other constructive growth; where competition, strife, and conflict are discarded upon entering the main gate, to be replaced with quiet serenity and understanding."

The property would operate as a cooperative. The New Land Association would rent land from Bob Monroe at a nominal cost to operate "a seasonal vegetable garden; a solar greenhouse; recreation areas; pasture land for horses and livestock; areas for eggs and poultry-growing; woodlot for firewood; processing plant for alcohol; association water supply; a twenty five-acre lake for recreation and fish supply; a methane generating plant...One of the aims is indeed self-sufficiency, especially in relation to the culture in which it exists."

By 1981, when the "Charter of New Land Community of Virginia" was published, the dream had solidified into formal, if quaint, verbiage: "We, the undersigned in this year 1981 ANNO DOMINUM, as time is measured in this continuum of physical matter, do hereby act as Founders and First Elders to establish and form in the service of our Creator....

"The PURPOSES of New Community....

...To establish operate, maintain extend and expand a Pathway into all realities and energy systems along which human Consciousness may proceed at an accelerating rate....

...To gather, classify, disseminate and preserve in its archives the Knowledge and Experience related by Seekers along the Pathway....

...To distill a consensus...to act upon the pattern...thus emerging, both as a coordinated and melded Whole and as individual participants therein...."

Attached to the declaration was a list of "New Land Basics" which outlined the expectations of the founders that members would contribute to the common good. "Be prepared to live 'on' the land, not 'off' it. You must be able to support yourself financially...You must give to (the New Land and the Institute) rather than take from them...."

The declaration was utopian. Perhaps it harked back to Francis Bacon's "New Atlantis" of 1627. Perhaps Bob Monroe should have learned from similar experiments in the past century, or, even since the 1960s. The idealistic dream was shortlived. Erewhon didn't happen in Nelson County, Virginia, sadly. A stream of advisories, cajoleries, reminders issued from the Gate House as people bought lots, settled on the New Land, and showed they were still very physical human beings, with egos and expectations to match.

"New Land represents a site, a gathering place, a refuge, a seed-bed, a point of focus where those from all walks of life (expression) may integrate into a living Whole...Each shall incorporate *noma agape* in daily application: To give to another without expectation of reward other than self-knowledge, most significantly, without the knowledge and awareness of the recipient."

The New Land dream disintegrated into an unhappy reality. Chris Lenz says, "Many of the people were attracted by the security, the self-sufficiency, by their fear of the coming chaos as predicted by some of the Explorers." Lenz has in mind the fever of survivalism which gripped many people who were consciously attuned in the mid-to-late 1970s, and which has reasserted itself in the late 1980s.

"Bob was prey to this, too....Many people saw Bob as the wise old man who was a key to satisfying their deepest needs for connection in the Universe. By living near him, they could better insure their participation in this wonderful opening. Bob felt this way, too.

"For him, it would be a warm, self-supporting community of people who could learn to 'travel' and be his long-sought companions, while making an end run around the coming trials. But the details of their interaction and the clarity of expectations on both sides were never, and probably couldn't ever have been made explicit."

Bob made a gesture which he undoubtedly thought would help coalesce the New Land community: All owners were offered a free Voyage in 1981, and the offer was repeated, probably in 1982. Gateway-Unity, as Bob called it, was the beginning of "a change in pattern," after it had become apparent that the early schemes for an integrated, productive community would not materialize. The precise incidents of unraveling in the fabric of the dream-settlement are lost in time.

Bob followed up on the Unity course with these instructions to residents: "As New Landers, you have made a major commitment so as to be in or very near the generating energy of the Institute wave, at the point where the resonance is strongest, at the origin.

"So be it. Each day, work with one exercise until you have perfected it and have incorporated that particular process into your daily mental and physical activities. When you do so, a second will be provided by the Institute, and a third, etc. Each accomplished exercise will move you closer. Each week, a growth session will be held on a Saturday or Sunday afternoon at the Center, only for New Landers. Here, new processes will be experienced, considered and evaluated. The melding of the group will occur at another, non-physical level.

"Further, upon completion of the Laboratory, you, as New Landers, become the first of a new breed of Explorers...You will be the first to try many new avenues of interest, under conditions never before available in our research...."

It was the closest Monroe came to calling upon the New Land settlers to become active, formal disciples of the Institute. The Gateway-Unity idea seems, in retrospect, to have been a logical outgrowth of the original Explorer concept at Whistlefield.

He overlooked the obvious: That the people who had come to New Land had come for reasons far different from those for which the Explorers had gathered around him, and even that the times had changed. The push for self-sufficiency was not as urgent in the early 1980s as it had been in the 1970s. People's priorities had changed.

On March 21, 1983, Bob issued a letter which reflects several abiding aspects of his philosophy.

To Fellow New Landers,

The Monroe Institute has been blessed with moral and material support from many individuals, both on and off the New Land.

We New Landers have an interest that goes beyond that of Offlanders. All of us have made this our home and our future lives, for reasons beyond the beauty of the locale. We might all put it in different words, but basically it would come down to wanting to be a part of the philosophy and future work of the Institute and the (New Land) Community.

Each of us has something to offer to our common goals or we wouldn't be here. Each of us has a differing ability to afford the giving and any judgment based on that "ability to afford" would be faulty. There should not, or must not, be any measurement of giving. It must be a fact that there is satisfaction in giving.

It is our birthright to be human and exhibit human frailties. It is also our birthright to exhibit our virtues. It must be our hope that we can as a whole define the virtues.

I would suggest that a basic virtue of our new lives be that a gift given never be mentioned again. We have had too much of individuals decrying previous gifts that have not been appreciated or rewarded.

I promise you that what I freely give will be enjoyed by me and forgotten. I promise you that I will never measure your gift against mine. Let us all promise the same.

Our policy from this moment on should be to accept no gifts of time, effort, or material that are not given on the above basis. It is the prerogative of each of us to decide for ourself what we can and want to give. Let no one do more than he or she can afford.

In retrospect, Monroe made the obvious mistake of mixing his role as businessman-developer with personal friendships and associations. He has since learned there is good reason to separate church and state, as he puts it.

As a result of his proclivities, Bob wearily catalogues, he found himself "being blamed for the dust floating off the gravel roads, for the smell and sound of cows from nearby pastures, for the logging trucks driving through the property, for failure to provide adequate jobs for New Land owners, for strangers walking along sub-division roads. . . just to name a few."

In a letter to one owner who complained about the traffic on the private, single-lane gravel road 200 feet from his house, Bob wrote:

'Hey, Wake up! A 'nice place to live' and 'quiet enjoyment' are relative terms. There always will be commercial traffic using the road in front of your house, and there is nothing you can do about it: Delivery trucks, construction trucks, farm trucks and tractors, repair trucks, utility trucks, UPS trucks, even logging trucks and

many passenger vehicles. There is absolutely nothing you can do about the airline traffic overhead, which amounts to some 300 aircraft daily, because of the Montebello Omni radio beacon twelve miles southwest of here.

'If you can't tolerate this level of interference in 'a nice place to live' and 'quiet enjoyment,' I don't know where to suggest you move in satisfaction of your needs.'

Bob adds he has "loaned New Landers money, provided jobs when they desperately needed them, given year-long moratoriums on land payments, given help and counsel when asked, provided the service of the farm crew without recompense—all without any evidence of appreciation of thanks. Just as if it was expected of me.

"The problem has been the fact that dissatisfaction lay in a small-yet-vocal minority. Most New Landers are happy to be where they are. However, the latter remain silent during any such accusations—which implies agreement." The point distresses Bob deeply: When he looks around for help and support, "No one stands up to be counted.

"One of the original ideas was that the New Landers and the Gateway people would get together on the final evening of the course. Here you'd have the world literally coming to them. A really stimulating bunch of people.

"Instead, we get complaints that the Gateway people are walking on New Land roads, or swimming in the lake."

One of the residents wrote a memo for a New Land Association meeting in November, 1986 which noted that, "Fear and distrust have become prevalent (in the outer world)...I have seen the same change in the New Land in the last four years. Bob Monroe had a dream and I believe every one of us on the New Land shared that dream to a great extent.

"In those four years, our individual egos have clouded and obscured our vision... The result has been a community that questions everyone else's motives and intents... We are not much different than any of our previous environments...If we cannot attain our original goal of a closely-knit community of dear friends, we must certainly try to eliminate any smoldering resentment."

At that meeting, the situation deteriorated to the extent Bob felt compelled to issue another memorandum.

To: All New Landers

It is quite apparent from the last New Land Association meeting that my attempts over the years to provide direction and leadership to move a subdivision into an evolving community have failed.

I recognize that only a few were vocal in the adversarial positions taken....

To 'change the pattern' (yet again), as I so often advocate, and to insure that I remain good and supportive friends with you, I am taking the following steps immediately:...I am divesting myself of any direct participation in the affairs of...the Association. From this point forward, I will consider New Land as simply a nice place to live, which was the original intent (sic)... My personal love and friendship for you remains of course unaffected. I will continue to do what I can to help you fulfill your individual needs and desires. The fact that I am with you infrequently does not alter this.

However, when (Nancy and I move to the Gift House), I expect to enter more and more into what I like to think of as the contemplative period of my life. The first step in the process is to delegate daily any minor decision-making to others. This memorandum is the beginning of the change. And then there was the familiar, scrawled signature, and the date of 11/15/86.

Part of the problem on The New Land has been confusion about Bob's role. He isn't the New Land resident guru, although some property-owners still expect him to be: They feel he got them into the New Land, somehow, just by being Bob Monroe, therefore he is responsible for them. On the other hand, he is also the Developer, the symbol of capitalistic greed whose every step must be watched closely. Those who cavil over Bob's actions or inactions in making their lives more pleasurable usually tend to overlook what he has given them outright—and often never mentioned.

Monroe found the spot, established the ambience, planned the development, created the lake which at least some enjoy. For this he gets and expects no thanks.

"Now, I'm out of it. There are some residual installment purchases, but most of them are being handled through the local banks."

Sometime later there was need for another sign of dismay: "There is a serious imbalance in us, both individually and as a group. It shows in many ways—the petty has become profound, the transitory an immutable truth, the brother's keeper a judge, as examples."

Martin Warren, the Explorer monitor, withdrew, at least temporarily, from the New Land Association in July, 1987, but, he did so with a statement of reason. For four years, Martin wrote in a circular letter, he had tried to get the New Landers to agree on a statement of common purpose, but without result.

> *My affirmation would go something like this:*
>
> *We deeply desire to join consciously with the powerful loving forces which we know to be at work in the currently-accelerated growth and evolution of human consciousness. We invoke the cooperation of these energies to help us in our joined seeking for solutions...overcome our obstacles to the achievement of harmony, peaceful relations, with roads well-maintained and dust-free as possible at a price we can feel good about, quiet homes where we can be alone in happiness or entertain our friends in comfort and freedom.*

Martin's statement was a long retreat from the joyous and free goals espoused by Bob Monroe eight years earlier, and it showed how drastically the aims of one community member had been reduced.

In July, 1987, another memo issued from the Monroe's temporary quarters in the Gate House. It was headed, *New Land Renaissance.*

"After exposure to many indirect allegations and innuendos over the preceding months regarding my development and administration of our New Land Subdivision, resentment of me by New Land residents, and most important, the obvious deterioration and fragmentation of what unifying spirit and purpose did exist on New Land, I believe it vital to all of our welfare and growth that I begin to change to a new direction. I do this in the understanding that I at least may have been one of the factors that brought you here."

There followed several pages of what Bob called "clearing the air"—his version of the Gateway Network debacle, the touring Voyage scheme operated by two New Landers which Bob abruptly shut down; hassle over roads; a case-by-case detailing of personnel problems at the Institute which had led to ill-feeling. Finally, Bob reiterated that he was withdrawing to the seclusion of the top of Roberts Mountain because he had much to do in preparing the H+ program and writing *Ultimate Journey.*

One New Lander says, "A lot of people came because they thought they'd find a core of others who had their shit together. Instead, they have discovered a lot of other people who are working through their shit here. Bob says it's a group learning to be a community and he's right. It's an ongoing workshop."

Bob's formal explanation of the New Land at a Gateway evening glosses over the strife and the personality clashes: "It's an experiment in trying to learn how to become a community. It's an expression of freedom. You can be social or be a hermit, do anything as long as it doesn't bother the others.

"Trouble is, we have too many chiefs, and no braves. We're all highly individualistic.

"People should do their own thing. That's fine. But whether the group here can coalesce...the jury's still out."

Bob has turned over most dealings with the Association to Joe McMoneagle, the retired Army officer. It's a role Joe is not too happy to play.

One night, the New Land subcommittee discussion was, as so often, on maintenance of the network of gravel roads that threads the property. There is an element of probably less than one-third of the residents who feel that Bob owes them, possibly to recompense them for their pioneering spirit in moving to the "wilds" of Virginia or for loss of the 1970ish dream which he has not materialized for them. An activist was sure to vent some personal spleen against the Developer and to interpret the ownership covenants in a way which suited his purpose. Joe sighed and prepared to enter the fray. New Land meetings take place five or six times a year, Joe said, "And they almost always digress into argumentative profiling."

* * * *

One evening near Thanksgiving, 1987, some fifty New Landers and Institute office staff combined to stage a surprise George Durrette Day. George is the farm manager who has been with Bob since 1971. They first met while George was cooking at the Howard Johnson on Skyline Drive. An immediate by-product of their meeting was the improved quality of hamburger Monroe got at HoJo. Then George started to do odd jobs for Bob.

Over the years since, George has built fences at Whistlefield, dis-assembled the one-acre greenhouse there and moved it to Roberts Mountain Farm, raised calves, maintained roads, played a major role in the construction of all the Center buildings and the Gift House.

That evening in David Francis Hall, Bob worked through a list of accomplishments scrawled on pages and pages of yellow legal paper. "Auction caddy; piano and organ mover; airport driver; builder of dams...."

George was embarrassed at the outpouring of love and respect for him. At the end, he shuffled his feet. "I'm not a big talker, especially in front of a lot of people. If I'd known about this, I would have figured some way to leave work early.

"I was young when I came here. If I wasn't, I don't think I would have made it. But I made it this far, and I enjoyed it." There followed a series of embraces from the women present, but none from the men. They weren't part of George's sense of what is proper.

It was more than just a token evening. Bob Monroe and many of those with whom he has disagreed, and who have contributed to the destruction of the New Land dream, could at least unite on one thing—giving credit to a humble man who had done so much for all of them.

If the work of George Durrette is all the New Landers can agree on wholeheartedly, that is at least something. Looked at as a microcosm, the New Land is no greater success than the planet as an experiment in coexistence. No matter how many people at Roberts Mountain Farm feel they have achieved a higher state of Consciousness, the symbiosis-synergy Peter Russell postulates is necessary before the next step to evolution can take place remains elusive as it does in the world outside the New Land. And yet, something is at work there, as elsewhere.

Human Plus (H+)

In the late 1980s, there appeared to be a sudden, spontaneous surge in Western metaphysical circles aimed at expanding Man's ability to accomplish extraordinary tasks. Do-it-yourself workshops proliferated. One program billed itself as "The Mind Revolution: Three Steps to Personal Power.... Turn fear into power by walking across burning coals—barefoot." A prominent channeled entity offered a series of excursions around the world which would place participants in situations of considerable challenge or even danger, to show that a mortal can discard fear by calling on hitherto unknown resources. The Institute of Neotic Sciences sponsored research into and a quest for people with exceptional abilities.

Bob Monroe was aware of all these efforts when he introduced a new program which tries to show people how they can dramatically improve their personal performance in areas which have heretofore been closed to them.

"H+" is the name Bob has given to his newest learning system. It stands for "Human Plus," and is a trademark. Monroe's friends thought Bob was going senile when he started to concentrate on H+. It seemed to them he was trying to "inculcate superhuman traits" in otherwise, well, normal citizens.

Bob describes his new course officially in these terms: "A System of Planned Evolution:... The difference between what can (and cannot) be achieved is our belief about what is possible. *Know how* is the problem—a belief isn't a known until you understand how to make it known....

"H-Plus is a different kind of pathway to new levels of freedom. You can become more than you ever could be—one step at a time. The process builds on three well-known concepts:

"A) Any human function that has been performed more than twice is learnable, *without exception.* The more a function is performed by separate individuals, the easier the learning becomes, not only for the participant, but for others....

"B) The greatest resistance to significant change is inertia. It is nearly impossible to move an entire mountain in one massive step. However, if the one-shovelful-at-a-time process is employed, the major goal is achieved.

"C) *Revolution* often produces chaos and requires a long period of adjustment and adaptation. *Evolution* absorbs change in an orderly manner with a minimum of stress. *Planned evolution* can place the entire process under personal control and direction.

"H+ achieves planned evolution at the individual level, using taped 'Function Exercises.' "

H+ seeks to free the individual to govern his own life by imprinting a series of techniques in his mind, to be called upon as the need arises.

By early 1989, the available tapes included exercises on various types of sleep; programming dreams; public speaking; de-habituation; reduction of pain; synchronizing mind-body coordination; instant but short-term increase in strength; caloric-intake control; body insulation from heat or cold; improved circulation; increased energy; optimizing potential; contemplation; programming a day; speeding-up thought processes; memory recall; body de-toxification; higher or lower sex drive; improvement of individual senses; betterment of the immunity system; letting go; dealing with physical emergencies; numeracy improvement; maintenance and improvement of heart, brain and lung functions; "wings on your feet" for joggers; empathizing; body-healing.

Monroe says, "We run the software, then we leave the rest to you." The H+ tapes are different from Gateway and Guidelines exercises. Human Plus uses a new "Access Channel" which Monroe has named Focus 11. The concept is not original with him, but the tools are definitely Monroe.

Anyone can do an H+ function: one side of the tape cassette is the preparatory exercise, which opens Focus 11 and readies the listener to have the function imprinted in his brain. The second side actually implants the function and teaches the learner how to implement it instantaneously when needed. The whole procedure is literally childishly simple, and devoid of mystical input. Some functions are "designed to be turned on or off as needed or desired." Others are permanently in place, for example an exercise to improve vision or circulation.

To call up the function, the H+ initiate simply holds his breath, repeats a phrase he has learned and expels his breath. "There's a crossover point. The autonomic system functions automatically, as in breathing or eye-blinking. Holding the breath accentuates the autonomic. The H+ encoding reaches down to the "reptilian" in the human psyche.

"Another thing we are learning is that effecting change in one system or another may have side effects in the same system you didn't bargain for. The more precise the instruction, the better."

There are and can be many more functions, which Bob frankly admits he is unaware of, as yet; just as there can be many more fields of application than the Institute has yet come across.

H+ is a new and growing program which depends to great extent on the resourcefulness of its participants. By the end of 1988, there were about fifty exercises in the library of H+ tapes. Seven intensive H+ workshops were planned for 1989. The program was also expanded to include two-day workshops away from the Center in Virginia, and an "In-Home Training Series" of two four-cassette albums.

* * * *

Bob Monroe had the first inklings of his newest course probably in the early-to-mid-1970s: wisps of visions, tantalizing teasers. He codified the images with the shortlived learning-enhancement series of tapes used at Fort Benjamin Harrison. After the media got hold of the story and blew it sky high, Bob recalls with merriment that some reporter dug up a Houston psychologist to say, obligingly, "What! Silly little sound waves can't do anything."

It just happened that H+ made its debut in the autumn of 1987, about the same time that the various other human-expansion programs were getting into gear, with considerably more publicity. The program had been in active development for about five years.

Monroe reflected on his new baby shortly before the first course, when talking to the Professional Seminar: "H+ takes the pragmatic approach. It's not going to hurt you. It's a recognizable bridge. It gives the participant self-activated evidence."

Bob likened the beginning of H+ to the introduction of pneumatic couplings between railroad cars: Once they were hitched together with buffered space between them, it was a lot easier to get the cars in the train rolling. He could just as easily have drawn an analogy to Rupert Sheldrake's morphogenic resonance.

* * * *

H+ is designed for all, not just for people who have attended other Monroe courses. Even after it started, there was no clarity at the Institute about how H+ would be implemented or made available. The general intent is that the program will ripple out to the population slowly, mostly by word-of-mouth, and primarily anonymously, for good reason.

"What do people need most? Modification of their belief system.

"Suppose you could obviate or control the physical needs of your body? We knew they could be changed, using Biofeedback.

"H+ is a learning process which provides control of the Self from within. H+ bypasses the environment to achieve 'normal functioning.'

"It's freedom from the usual needs of Man, learned at all levels of consciousness."

By August, 1987, he was saying, "It's the Quiet, Knowing Way. A Concept of Service.

"Basically, we're taking away the enculturated prohibitions.

"It is designed to endure for one's lifetime. You could call it a formulation of resonance.

"Gateway brings intense knowledge of Self, but doesn't pay much attention to the daily needs of the individual. It gets the Ego under good control.

"H+ asks: 'What would I really like to do?' It's a crib sheet, that's all. It's not to be taken at one huge bite. But in little pieces.

"It's sort of sneaky: It gives you control of your options. In developing H+, we looked again at Hemi-Sync.. We don't know how it works, of course. But we want to separate individuals from their habituation. First from their physical needs. Secondly from their emotional needs—their mental enculturation. Avoiding temptations, not evading them.

"If one can control one's physical, mental, and emotional self, there can be an amazing transformation.

"We looked around and found that the main obstacle was inertia. The more awesome the concept, the more humans tend to procrastinate. Call it laziness if you will.

"Becoming more than you ever thought you could be, improvement in every part of life.

"We need prudence in its use." Awareness of possible antagonism from the estabishments was a frequent sub-theme in the early days of H+.

"It's open-ended. What is needed is you. What you can see as fundamental applications.

"Critical mass in H+ will be achieved when the individual no longer needs anything."

There are no criteria for participating in H+. "Everyone is ready for it. It is not a sequential learning process. You select what you want to learn.

"Our Belief System is constantly being attacked by advertising. That's nothing new. We're modifying the Belief System, just as the advertisers do."

Such was my introduction to H+: An amalgam of references, dotted throughout previous Monroe sessions.

* * * *

In early October, 1987, another group gathered at The Center. We were the charter H+ course. Monroe's people referred to us as passengers on a maiden voyage. We tended, rather, to feel we were guinea pigs. As was the case with other early H+ programs, all of us had taken at least one Gateway.

The first H+ class was diverse in all respects. Despite the modest Institute publicity announcing the aims of the program, most of us came to deepen our contact with our Higher Selves, a goal which is more properly the province of Gateway or Guidelines. One participant was interested in the possibility of learning how to regenerate his body tissue. Some, inevitably, were not quite sure why they were there.

That Saturday evening, we assembled in the familiar surroundings of the David Francis Hall auditorium. Bob Monroe slipped into his accustomed chair, wearing the familiar USS New Jersey baseball cap, and his red knit vest from Harrods. He smiled broadly.

"I am acutely aware we're in the process of launching a new kind of journey.

"You're in on the very beginning. It hasn't begun till now.

"Understand one thing. Somewhere in H+ there is a beginning for you. Not necessarily the same as for someone else, but for you.

"How meaningful it is to me personally to see the beginning. You're the small beginnings of a generation. No one can say how far it will reach: individual; family; group; tribe?

"You don't all have the same growth pattern. It depends on who you are, what effect H+ has on you. The option is yours. No one else's. There is no compulsion.

"Those who use the functions will begin to experience true freedom during their physical lives.

"H+ has no hidden agenda built into it. It's not pie-in-the-sky. This is all about—truly—Here.

"We're giving you a bag full of tools, radically different from Gateway.

"This is a different kind of fun.

"We don't know how well the program will work.

"Any real results will be one month . . . Six months from now. . . ."

An Austrialian-born, practicing anaesthesiologist quietly commented. "I'm here because you've got more to give me than the AMA has."

The introductory session was over. We were ready for H+. It was a bumpy ride.

The program had been designed by Barbara Collier and Cathy Kachur, the experienced professional trainers and Monroe addicts, who did the paper work in San Diego. When Barbara, the head trainer for the course, got to Virginia, she met her co-trainers for the first time.

We found the first tapes repetitive and boring: We were absorbing a new technique by rote. There was no intellectual challenge. We simply laid down, listened—and, often, slept. By the end of the second day, I was beginning to question searchingly the wisdom of having joined the maiden voyage; I toyed with the idea of packing my bags. I had anticipated hiccups in the training, but not boredom, nor kindergarten games.

Barbara Collier completed the long days of training, and hastened up Robert's Mountain for lengthy consultations with Bob, who sat up, waiting for the reports.

* * * *

The course turned up for the better. We began to see the forest instead of individual trees. Bob later expressed his deep gratitude that we had been able to make a valuable contribution to the program. We, for our parts, welcomed his flexibility and his readiness to accept our comments.

We continued to absorb lessons. What was lacking in that first H+ course was the metaphysical or spiritual contacts we had all experienced in Gateway and other courses. But that, too, came.

One evening, we sat around a cluster of lighted globes whose opaque surfaces project an unending whirl of variegated, kaleidoscopic patterns. They were, it turned out, Lori Lights, remnants of that fantasy project created years earlier by Monroe and Charley Tart. That night, in the darkened David Francis Hall auditorium, they served as beacons for contemplation.

We talked of critical points at which our lives had changed. A former musician spoke of a moment of revelation when he knew he no longer needed alcohol and drugs. An older man told the moving story of an accident in which his foot was nearly severed from his body, when he was far from any help; the power of an unknown force raised the load under which he was pinned, and allowed him to get to a hospital for surgery. He added the doctors had told him he would never have feeling in the foot again. He does.

One of our number groped for an experience, and spoke of driving down a road in Germany when he was in the armed forces, a full colonel rumbling in the back seat. He discovered the switch for the lights on the unfamiliar car just seconds before his vehicle would have been demolished by an oncoming truck. Another spoke of a miraculous rescue from probable death while sailing a catamaran in a risky confluence of ocean currents in the Caribbean.

A woman recounted a singular incident on a Yucatan beach when she knew a parent died, later confirmed, even to the minute, by a phone call. Someone else had a similar experience, knowing the instant his mother died. Confirmation came from his father half an hour later, by phone.

A young mother wanting to cross a street with her child, saved by a voice from stepping into the path of an unseen truck; when she looked around to thank the speaker, no one was there.

The stories were not all breath-taking, but by sharing experiences we normally did not voice, we finally changed from an inchoate gaggle into a cohesive group.

It became a week of laughter, huge exhilaration, and of hard work. We ate enormously of the vegetarian fare at the Center, we walked and played and meditated on our own, and we knew something important was happening in our lives, although we also recognized the results would take a while to tally.

On the final evening, Bob Monroe sat in his chair, stroking the back of his head. Then he slipped into gear... "So, what're you going to do now?

"Let's assume you didn't pick up anything infect-u-ous, but got some things you can take home with you, like souvenirs. You're going to display a bit of it to the family and friends. Put it on the coffee table, then try it in the bedroom, maybe, and then it'll end up on the closet shelf.

"Is that what you're going to do with it?

"These are some principal goods. The key is to use them next week.

"It's critically important you tell us. We learned from your early ability to meld the tapes.

"You've got to let us know what's happening."

"You see, we've been trying to get spatial up till now, when it really isn't spatial at all.

"You can swallow and digest these things. You're one of the few....

"You don't have to labor in rice paddies or pull sentry duty on the Tibetan border.

"How lucky you are to be able to make that quantum jump."

Bob began to wind down the first H+ training course.

"This is the Quiet Wave. Not something what will be publicized on your local talk show. Something that will not look for publicity.

"You are the progenitors. That implies and imagines that something else takes place beyond this stage. Until, eventually, you become a full-fledged member of the H+ Fellowship.

"What's that? Only the H+ Fellowship itself can decide.

"As Progenitors, you will come across someone who needs an H+ function badly. You've got the figurative tool kit to help; you can't help but share it.

"You'll say, 'Yes, I have the means to help that person.' "

* * * *

Bugs remained to be ironed out in the H+ program. When I first heard Monroe brainstorming the concept in April, 1987, he was talking of a commitment to anonymous service, and an outright obligation to bring in new members. At the training session, he turned aside direct questions on the implementation of H+, adding he would put his thoughts into a letter, so as not to be misinterpreted.

Within weeks, we got a letter which said, in part, "You do have an obligation—not to me or the Institute—but to others and yourself. It is to be of service where and when the opportunity arises. It is very important that you understand the nature of this...You will encounter others who need the help that H+ provides...It is a gift you can give, a service you can perform better than anyone else."

Bob went on that he had no idea what the H+ Fellowship he had often mentioned in his talks was. "It is not yet in existence. The activities and structure of such a Fellowship will be in the hands of (the) membership, not I (sic) or the Institute."

And he included a purely voluntary commitment—"a tickler"—which reminded us of the need to practice, and to expand the group of people who use the functions. Nothing more.

* * * *

But then, in David Francis Hall, Monroe's thoughts continued to spin out. "How we're going to disseminate the program, we're not sure yet. We'll set some type of goal, and then introduce it into people's lives.

The question of publicity arose. "It's your discretion. We ask you not to create displays: Don't make a spectacular out of it for the media. Stay out of the tabloids."

And then, farewell: "You're all Gateway graduates. You all have a cleanness about you. You have a clarity of purpose."

Someone murmured, "I feel we have been touched by God."

And the week came to its end. There were tears as we crunched in a tight circle around a U.S. Postal Service worker who is a Cherokee Indian and was one of the outstanding members of our intake. Slowly we swayed to an imperceptible rhythm. Without pattern, individuals haltingly brought forth statements of love and of purpose.

It happened that I stayed at the Center for a night after all others had left. I rattled like a pea in a pod, trying to break the feeling of unaccustomed aloneness in that building which held so many memories. I sat alone on the deck, staring out into the dark, reliving moments of booming laughter and of ecstasy, recalling quiet moments of revelation and the deep, shattering recognition of Self.

I went back into the building and prowled the corridors, glanced into empty Chec Units, and wondered what countless, vibrant memories the living energy of their cedar-paneled walls secreted. It was as if the boards echoed, once again alive to the far-reaching experiences of those who had donned headsets and contemplated There.

Wherever I went on that solitary night, I felt alone, yet accompanied. There was a comforting wisp of animate but unseen presence in the Center.

My memory subsided, and I considered the H+ week I had just lived. No one knew, or dared guess, in October, 1987, where the new program would go. Would it fizzle, as we returned to our accustomed work-and-home routines?

Would we find the moments to summon our recall and make a quick plea for help in any given situation? Would those of us mired in pressurized jobs be too exhausted by the end of the day to devote time to practice the necessary functions, to keep up and expand the effectiveness of what we had learned?

We knew H+ had been guided to Monroe over a period of years, as have all of his programs. It was something of value that Bob, at least, felt the Helpers wanted humankind to know and utilize. I had the strong feeling that night in the Center that that Guidance had now been passed on to us, to do with as we chose.

After my departure, there came a disappointing lull. Bob and the Institute promised that the tapes to reinforce what we had absorbed at the Center and to teach us new functions, would be available "within a month."

As the delay stretched on, I practiced what I had learned in Virginia with a fair degree of consistency, and I proved to my own satisfaction that those functions I used repeatedly worked; the experiences gave me considerable hope that the rest of the exercises would do what they were intended to. Others I talked to in those early days after the maiden voyage seemed equally optimistic.

The courses in the winter of 1988, went better. By spring, and H+IV, Dave Mulvoy and others had ironed out the bugs, the course had been tightened up and was intense. The Russells came over from England to participate, and found the experience valuable; they started planning to give a version of the course in Britain, with the Institute's blessing. For the first time, non-Gateway graduates were trained, and they encountered no problems; to the contrary, several said they wanted thereafter to do a Gateway course. A psychiatrist, and a lawyer who work with AIDS patients attended, and hoped to devise ways H+ could be useful to those afflicted.

Scoffers who knew little about the program and had not worked with the tapes could say all Bob Monroe had done in H+ was to reinforce work or sleep or physical habits already buried deep in our psyches. Indeed, some of the exercises seemed to be merely extensions of common sense. But regardless of how H+ functions, evidence began accumulating that the program did work for individuals, and Bob commented that he was amazed at the ingenuity of some H+ graduates, who devised new applications for H+ exercises.

Book III

Who Is Bob Monroe?

Views of Associates

A number of people have observed and worked with Bob Monroe over a period of years, some of them closely, some sporadically. Practically everyone who has ever met and listened to Bob is sure he is, at the very least, an extraordinary individual. "Genius" is the descriptive most often applied to him. But that touches only the Here-and-Now Monroe, and there are other elusive qualities of his that send friends into reflective silences, or bursts of lyrical homage. The simple truth is that Bob Monroe is both opaque and transparent: His being generates more questions than it answers.

Some of those who have known Bob Monroe in various stages of his development have tried to answer a difficult question: Just who is Bob Monroe?

* * * *

At the beginning of *Beyond Biofeedback*, Elmer and Alyce Green wrote: "In a way, this book is a preview of what we think will be scientifically studied in the coming A significant factor in that science will be 'self-awareness.'"[1] Elmer Green is perhaps in the best position of all to put Bob Monroe into perspective: He has know Bob for twenty years and kept abreast of Monroe from afar, and he is on top of developments in all the related, clinical psi fields.

There is more of a connection between the two: The earliest lab equipment used by Monroe in Virginia was derived from Biofeedback technology. Elmer Green has been, in some ways, a Dutch uncle, yet a seeker and a teacher parallel to Bob Monroe.

"They all fit in," Elmer says of the better and lesser known Supra-Conscious explorers of our time. "All of them have their place in the Planetary Mind. It has more aspects than any one can fulfill.

"Jack Schwarz, Swami Rama, Ram Dass. . .all of them. And Bob Monroe. Their surging ideas. The memories they raise. . .They all have roles as teachers in the unfoldment of The Plan."

When Elmer first met Monroe at the 1969 Council Grove, "I wondered why he was so depressed. I asked him if his concept of God might be wrong.

"I said, 'You're thinking in human terms, but you're dealing in the cosmos. You've been told that other civilizations are far ahead of us. You believe it.'

"Bob replied, 'They told me I'd be the keeper of the pumping plant.' It was no wonder he was depressed.

"Don't forget, Bob is an engineer. He wanted to go somewhere, but he hadn't developed his spiritual side. He was passive in that respect.

"Bob didn't meet the good entities at first; that was the source of his depression.

He'd run into the self-satisfied entities who are not filled with love. At that time, he was working at a lower level of consciousness.

"Every time you get in a jam, there are entities who snatch you out. Bob was an agent and was to be protected, but he hadn't yet reached the level of awareness where there's much compassion.

"There's a lot of medium stuff—like some channeling—that's no good. It depends on where the source is. What level. Cayce's sources are high level. (Shay St. John's) Miranon was, too.

"Above a certain level, the nature of the entities begins to change. One encounters Jesus, Buddha, and they help one to achieve enlightenment.

"But you have to meet the enemy first."

Dr. Green reflected on Bob Monroe's "Beyond God" theories. "They're not new with him. *The Tibetan*, quoted by Alice Ann Bailey, said the same thing. Madame Blavatsky talked of 'a pivotal God.' Zeus was a cultural god.

"Apparently all these sources were aiming toward the same progression: The thoughtform of Being.

"The question with Bob is whether he has gone through the Initiation. If so, he doesn't have to go into thousand-year cycles any more.

"Behind every thoughtform, there's something else. Everything is Mind and modification. The Infinite is Mind, not a God.

"Edgar Cayce talked also of cellular rejuvenation. Aurobindo said, 'You do not die till you want to.' We can transform our cellular material using our minds.

"Every cell of your body is a cell of your mind. Once you gain control of your mind at all levels—not just the conscious level...if every cell is under control, and you can take your mind out of your body and return, you are reaching the breakthrough point.

"It's the kind of thing the yogi does who can stop his heart, underwater, and return to his body later....

"I hope that Bob has not been too materialistic to hinder his breakthrough."

Elmer Green sees Monroe's H+ program as a new version of this process, which ordinary people can apply to themselves. But he is wary that metaphysical powers may be disseminated to people who are not ready to handle them.

Green last saw Monroe in 1978. "I asked Bob to remove my name from his board of advisers then, when he started marketing Gateway, because I didn't feel businessmen should go through the program. It should be reserved for people who are not involved with their egos."

When a student anchors himself and allows his mind to work compassionately, he can become eternal, not merely immortal. If you don't become a-karmic, you're stuck with your future: "If you don't take the power and move towards a higher level of transpersonal development, you get stuck in the sewage pumping station.

"What Bob Monroe is doing is unique. There's nothing like him in India, Europe or America. He has developed a mode people can understand. It's old wine in new skins, but that's fine."

* * * *

Dr. Art Gladman, the Oakland Biofeedback specialist and psychiatrist, is a member of the Institute's board and a longtime friend of Bob. Gladman says, "He's a rare bird."

Is Monroe a "Walk-In," as others have hazarded? The scientifically-trained, but unorthodox M.D. says, "I don't want to speculate.

"Bob's a very special human being. His ways of perceiving and his ways of functioning are very different from the norm.

"You get the feeling Bob knows a lot more than he gives out.

"I'm surprised he was successful at Mutual Broadcasting. How he could have been successful in business at all is beyond me. His view of reality just doesn't fit in with the corporate style of New York City at all.

"This boy's a prophet. There's no question about it.

"There will come a time when he's heard.

"But look at what happened to others: They were only recognized fifty years after their deaths."

* * * *

Dr. Stuart Twemlow, the martial arts expert and psychiatrist who examined Monroe exhaustively at Topeka, assisted Monroe at the early Gateways and periodically has been a Monroe trainer, gives these insights:

"Bob believes thinking can influence facts: that his thoughts create reality. That's why he won't say anything negative about people.

"You have to be very careful in what you think, or your thoughts may become self-fulfilling prophecy. It's at a level beyond pure logic.

"That may be why Bob defends his father. He says to himself, 'I'd better not think Father was tyrannical.' "

Who is Bob Monroe? "He's an enigmatic character...there's something very peculiar about him...not quite human.

"He's a warm, pleasant-natured guy, unprepossessing. He likes a good laugh...he has the traditional white southern gentleman's view of loyalty. He's genuinely kind-hearted on the etheric level.

"But when you look at him from time to time, you become aware of a depth in his eyes which is not of this world...His voice is disembodied. He's a shell through which something is being channeled.

"He's a true 'As If' character.

"He's many things to many people.

"I suppose I know more about his psyche than anyone else. He's a very healthy person in that area. His responses are not 'normal.' They're different. But overall, he's quite integrated.

"One time when he was in a lot worse health than he is now, he told me he wanted to die. He described himself to me as 'already dead,' waiting to move on.

"But he said he had been told he was the Gatekeeper, or the gas station attendant who was Here to fill the tanks of people who were moving on.

"There's a mystical quality to him, even though he's typically American in his pioneering way."

Twemlow thinks Monroe's role is to calm people in coming times of crisis.

"There is a group of people who *know* that certain things are happening. A sense of transformation is starting. When it arrives, we will all act in certain ways."

* * * *

Professor Charles Tart—the parapsychologist at the University of California, Davis, and author of countless publications—the first man to put Monroe into a lab for examination—comments: "In ancient Greece, the philosophers were members of mystical religions. They were given the technologies to go Out-Of-Body. They were a small number of people, but they were very influential.

"Think that today some eight million people have had Near Death Experiences. They have been initiated into the highest mysteries.

"Now, they can read Bob Monroe, and say, 'Hey, this guy's been there, too.' If all of them ever get together and organize, they'll be a powerful spiritual movement.

"Bob's a genuine American mystic. He arose spontaneously out of the mainstream of American culture. He's archetypical, as American as apple-pie.

"We in the United States have been living on spiritual junk food.

"Bob Monroe offers something different. He represents homegrown American spirituality." Even though Monroe sternly refuses to put a spiritual label on what he does or experiences.

"I have a very wide view of the spiritual spectrum, from Buddhists to mystical Catholics. I think we as a culture need people like Bob.

"Why him? Why is he the one who has done all of it? Why him instead of his neighbor?

"He and I have discussed it. But we have never come to a satisfactory answer.

"He's such a good example of the man who is successful yet decent.

"Americans can appreciate his worldly success; he's the kind of guy who doesn't lust for power, and doesn't climb over other people's bodies to get to the top. That's important.

"His target audience is people who are reasonably educated, who are trying to get a genuine spiritual basis for their lives...for whom the old-time traditions just don't work any more.

"Of course, it's interesting he comes from a background in the world of communications. Another coincidence. With a capital C?

"I'm not comfortable speculating. I'd like to believe the world operates according to a design, but I can't prove it."

* * * *

Bill Schul, Ph.D., is a writer, and has been a Monroe trainer. He has done considerable experimentation with the power of pyramids, and with the psychic powers of animals.

"Bob's an interesting individual. It all depends on how we look at the manifestation. If we look at life as moving in and out of form, then we don't get caught in the schematic. I don't think of Bob as moving from Planet A to Planet B, Vulcan, Mars.

"We're dealing with a variety of energy systems. We're from the Universe. We're the thought in the mind of God. The dream of Brahma.

"Bob has identified the levels and retained his identity within them. He is able to flow in and out better than most of us.

"He's not entirely an inhabitant of Planet Earth. But none of us are. He has a wide experiential background which takes him out of the usual, and places him in the citizenship of Advanced Being.

"You have to think of an enlightened person as being on a continuum. He doesn't suddenly go from A to Z. There are many scales which criss-cross and interweave. But we perceive another in our illusions, and we are disappointed if he does not seem to be as high on the scale as we had expected.

"Bob has kept the Institute open by keeping it within the disciplines of engineering and science, in terms of fields rather than religion.

"Bob would be the first to say he's not a teacher, but he certainly helps us grow. He is a sharer. A journeyer. A traveler on some paths that have helped others travel their paths.

"He has given access to several levels of consciousness. People go to the Institute, learn, share, and move on.

"Bob sometimes makes it difficult to follow, difficult to work with him.

"He's an ingenious person. He's not the same today he was yesterday. Bob's learning. You can't expect any more from anyone."

Schul and Monroe met in the late 1960s, and their lives crossed. "Bob has helped me. A lot has happened since then. He's grown, I've grown.

"Then it was time for me to move on. We had shared."

* * * *

Whitley Strieber is the best-selling author who attended Gateway in January, 1987. Since then he has gone on, exploring the Supra-Conscious in his own way, with the often-terrifying help of the Visitors. Strieber's life changed dramatically well before he went to Virginia; what has happened since is a progression, combining his own adventures and the benefit of Monroe training.

Whitley regards the time he devoted to absorbing Bob Monroe's techniques as vital to that progression, and he has done as Bob urges: Taken the gift of the Monroe tools and used them for his own purposes. He has boldly unleashed his curiosity, and to the extent possible, integrates what he learns in his daily life.

It is tempting to speculate that Strieber's experiences are an "advance" on Monroe's, in humanity's experience of other realms. In fact, of course, it is fatuous to talk of superiority or inferiority in Altered-State experiences. At best, one can think in terms of parallels.

Strieber is the first to say his episodes are simply "at different vibratory levels" and perhaps in a different realm from Monroe's. There are many avenues, and many stages to physical man's accommodation with the Supra-Conscious.

Part of Strieber's learning program, conceived and orchestrated by the Visitors, has been to shatter his belief in the reality of physical experience. "We're actors on a stage, but we don't know we're acting.

"Life is an addiction which we have to learn to break.

"We're locked into our bodies, hooked by our senses and our needs. Energy was directed at Bob to enable him to unhook and move to other levels."

Monroe helped Strieber to "break out of the duality" Society imposes: the limitations of believing in Good versus Evil; Right versus Wrong.

"Bob says, 'You don't need the anchor. Free yourself from the fear. Escape from cliches: There is no good or evil, only positive and negative energy.

"Managing energy is what life is all about. After death, we go on and manage energy at other levels.

"Bob's work is to help people realize the body is purely a jumping-off point, a wellspring, or a safehouse.

"This is, as Bob says, the Learning School. We're all students; there are no gurus: The ones we call gurus in this physical life are babies. Buddha, for instance, found he was a little baby when he got to the next level."

Another purpose of his progression has been to take Strieber through his fears. He refers to it as "a planned program over eighteen months."

Gateway helped Strieber come to an understanding of death. Yet Strieber retains some of his fears, for good reason.

"Fear has to be my brother. I wouldn't want to lose it; if I did, I would lose the zest of battle. The enemy is your best friend; no air is as sweet as that which you breathe when you have vanquished your enemy."

His life has taken on a depth of perception and of purpose that Strieber attributes in part to his time at the Institute.

He describes his work now as, "taking people to other levels, to the possibility of new relationships in the physical and non-physical, using skills I learned from Bob." It is a subject he deals with in *Transformation.*

Bob Monroe's success? "Bob is about the noticing. He brought it all about. He started something resonating. In the physical realm, he has been enormously successful."

Monroe's resonating opened a heretofore secluded, shrouded world to countless people, far beyond the realization of the general public.

* * * *

Chris Lenz is the student of Eastern disciplines who had opportunities to observe Bob closely over a number of years in the late 1970s and early '80s. He reflects "the viewpoint of the traditional yoga."

Lenz observes, "Bob has never had what the Indians call *satsang*—companionship. It has been a lonely, uphill fight all the way, to get to this place called Home. If you don't come across your sense of purpose while you are There, the physical world looks dry and dusty.

"Creative men and mystics of the past have been legion in their complaints about those states in which fear, sadness, anxiety, depression, and the glaring brilliance of all their lacks roam hotly through them, uncontrolled, unwilled, and unstoppable.

"I called Bob a while ago and mentioned I was going through this state. I said, 'But you know all about this.' He replied, 'Only too well.'

"He has apparently chosen a more difficult way.

"Bob Monroe is a man who has tried to go the spiritual journey alone, living on the edge, and help others along the way. But he's a fiercely independent man.

"Think of his communication with all kinds of teachers, with others on the globe who have different identities at night. Even to make an analogy of them is impossible.

"Just imagine bringing your consciousness down to the size of a molecule and then enlarging it to the size of the galaxy, and then bringing it back down again; back up; back down, all night long. It's no wonder he looks tired in the morning!

"Stu Twemlow and someone else once made up a test for spiritual maturity. Of all the people they gave the test to, Bob scored highest.

"He does sense the higher powers, and I think part of him does want to surrender to them.

"But he's not prepared to put it on the line, and surrender enough.

"I wonder if it is some sort of pride or some sort of miscommunication that prevents Bob from finding others of like being.

"He repeatedly credits his associates with the ability to receive communication at his level of being; he doesn't bow to their limitations and lack of maturity.

"People regard Bob as a sort of 'divine father' who is privy to levels of power far beyond the normal. People give their power—in today's jargon—to Bob Monroe.

"He leads people to believe in a beautiful future; that they will be powerful in this world and the next; that the world is right at last.

"Then they realize they have to take their power back, if they are going to survive." Bob does, in fact, give that power back to the individual.

"It's a type of manipulation." Lenz pauses and checks his wording. "No. . .Bob feels it's his contribution for the greater good of us all.

"It's as if you see the grand design, know where every piece of the jigsaw fits, envision the light and the splendor. And still have the cold chills of financial fears in the middle of the night.

"I used to tag along behind him, clearing up the promises. The trials of Bob's life at the time: The continual money problems, the continual management problems; the continual traveling and working, with little time off, and no real promise of more money or security.

"I used to do a lot of agonizing in Charlottesville.

Bob's life, Chris Lenz concludes, "is in some ways tragic, but it's perfect for him.

"Being the Sorcerer's Apprentice was good training."

* * * *

Two of the three San Diego "girls," Barbara Collier and Mary White, spend an evening trying to determine who Bob Monroe really is.

Mary is forthright: "I think the only aspects of Bob Monroe which take place Here are his bodily functions, like eating, shaving, the like.

"He has graduated to a plane we can only guess at. He's an Entity. He's not a straight human being. Even the first time we saw him, back there in Montana in '77, we thought, 'This guy's not of this Earth. He's never all Here.'

"If a stranger walked in and heard him talking, of course, he'd run out yelling, 'The man belongs in the booby factory.' By today's standards in society, maybe that's true.

"But are those standards valid?"

Barbara Collier interjects, "Don't underestimate his wife, Nancy." Mary White nods, "'Nancy helps keep him earthbound when he has to be. But she recognizes his commitment, and she doesn't try to inhibit it."

Mary returns to Bob. "Talk about enlightenment! Over the years, you see changes in him. By 1982, he seemed almost transparent to me, in the physical. I thought, 'He's not going to last.'

Mary White is a calm woman who makes her way very successfully in the business world, but is also at home in the metaphysical.

She pauses, draws a breath and says: "Bob Monroe's the Gatekeeper. He lives from the Energy of the Light. He's Merlin, the magician of the universe."

Mary continues quietly, "He's one of the Avatars, one of many.[2]

"Some people get their power through music, others have it in a different way. Bob gets it through electronics *and* music, and other sources as well.

"Most of the people who go to the Institute have no belief in Jesus or God. They're beyond the fear of death. They have gone through, gone beyond that theology, and they're trying to understand the Here and Now.

"People want to keep the glow of Monroe with them when they leave the Institute, but they can't do it. Or at least they think they can't. In fact, it's always with them.

"You never lose it once you have it. It only takes very little to bring it back to its full radiance."

Mary continues, "We have a fine golden thread which connects us with Robert. . .It's almost as if it were a thread of destiny."

Barbara adds, "I don't care what people think of him. What he has given me is priceless."

Mary: "He's not selling anything any more.

"It's as if he has been told not to worry; things will take care of themselves. Everything is going according to some design.

"But he doesn't have a design, does he? At least not one we're able to perceive."

Barbara asks, "What's going to happen when he's gone?

"For instance, I think people at H+ have made the breakthrough because they believe Bob.

"Because they believe him, they believe H+ will work.

"When he's no longer Here in the physical, talking of his belief. . .his Knowing. . .will it work for others. . .? Can the Institute, in fact, exist without him?"

* * * *

Karen Malik, the longtime Monroe trainer, pauses. "He's an artist," she hazards, "but a visionary, well before his time.

"An artist usually sees beyond what is present. . .sees the larger picture.

"I don't see him as a businessman. He's an entertainer. He knows the quality of the show must go on.

"I don't think he has ever understood or admitted the magnitude of his experience or his creativity.

"Oh, he'll say, 'I've got a tiger by the tail,' but he says it self-deprecatingly.

"Basically, he's a very lonely guy, who's way ahead of his time.

"He was given a very powerful tool to bring into the world. The tool was beyond his level of understanding at the beginning. He has succeeded in keeping it very straight by not considering himself a guru.

"He's a good, good man."

* * * *

One of the most interesting characters around Roberts Mountain Farm is Joe McMoneagle, the barrel of a man who holds no official position with the Monroe Institute, but is married to Bob's step-daughter, Nancy Lea, and who now represents the Monroe interests in the New Land community.

McMoneagle is very much his own person. He is the fifth generation man in his family to have designed and, literally, built his house with his own hands. He served as a U.S. Army Warrant Officer with distinction for twenty years, in a series of at-times hair-raising overseas, classified activities. He has written a novel, and has a professional remote-viewing consultancy firm, under contract to the Stanford Research Institute in California.

The intriguing question of predestination in Bob's life arises: Is Monroe a creation of his own entity? Did he choose, before his entry into physical life, to fill the role he has now nearly played out?

Joe McMoneagle circumvents a direct answer. "The things Bob does that work are those he meant to do. Maybe he did well with Cable TV and not in modular home construction, and he judges segments of those episodes as failures.

"In fact, while he was doing them, he was also developing Hemi-Sync and working towards the Institute as it is today. These are by far the major accomplishments of his life.

"Bob tends to apply the culture's Left Brain standards to himself, while his true greatness is his Right Brain creativity.

"Sometimes, you can't see the goodness in yourself; you can't realize you have progressed, but other people can, and they benefit from you.

"You may not reach the goal you have established for yourself, but you accomplish much along the way.

"In *JOOB,* Bob dared to speak from the heart, from his core. He came across with integrity, laid his bones bare. Here was a guy who had done it, in agony. It was a valuable contribution to Mankind.

"But now, he still finds himself in the disconcerting position of wanting to discover more, ever more."

In his son-in-law's eyes, Bob Monroe sometimes needs to pause to assimilate and integrate what he has already learned.

"He's got a curious, eighteen-year-old mind and seven decades of life-knowledge crammed into a body which won't keep functioning forever. He knows that and he's fighting what he perceives to be that limitation, tooth and nail."

There arises, as in any discussion of Bob Monroe, the ticklish question of his relationships with people who have at one time or another been close to him.

"It's a question of communication," says Joe. "For instance, he's constantly saying how non-emotional he is, when, in fact, he's one of the most sensitive and emotional men I've ever met.

"He gives too many mixed messages. They cause people to misread him, constantly." The unanswered question that hovers is whether Monroe deliberately mixes his messages, to keep followers off-balance.

"People who choose to enter a relationship with Bob do so ninety-nine percent of the time for other than humanistic, altruistic motives. They base their approach on their view that he's better than human.

"In fact, Bob's just like you and me in some ways, only more so.

"Look at his Gateway Voyage appearances. He uses emotion there for his purposes. He's in his own element.

"He really cares when he is teaching people, but that doesn't mean they should latch onto him.

"He's not totally aware of the public persona he has built up over the years. Bob carries the Father persona with him. The New Age Light and Love people come, expecting to take. They hear him saying, 'Daddy knows best.'

"Then he is perceived to be withdrawing his support of the children. The relationship changes, and the children get angry. Who's to say whether he or the children are responsible?

"For years, people have sucked him dry.

"They say, 'He owes it to us.' Only a few have stuck with him, and given him anything in return."

Then, Joe McMoneagle says with a slight but compassionate grin, "There's nothing more sensitive than a trained remote-viewer. Sometimes, I can feel Bob's pain through his eyes and his skin.

"I think it makes him angry when I do it. He doesn't want anyone to know his pain."

And there's the loneliness. "If he lets someone get close to him, it shows he's a conventional human being after all."

Did Bob Monroe have to suffer through the agonies of Altered State exploration in order to become a teacher? Joe McMoneagle thinks it's a possible explanation.

"But a lot of what he endured was training for him; to allow him to grow out of the kind of enculturation and attachment we all have to deal with.

"Bob lives, therefore he gives.

"He creates knowledge. Bob imparts a degree of that knowledge to show us where he is going, and where, perhaps, we are going, too. The existence of knowledge is sufficient. It's not necessary to be taught.

"The greatest thing that can be said about Bob Monroe is that he has lived...The fact that he has lived and shared human knowledge is important...very important!

"His gift is to Mankind. It's an idealistic view.

"Our job is to go out into the world and learn, surviving in a sea of realities."

* * * *

Mrs. Joseph McMoneagle is Nancy Lea Honeycutt or, more often, just Scooter. Except for the time out, when she was away working for publishers, she has been closely associated with Bob Monroe since the mid-late 1960s.

Nancy Lea leans back in her directorial chair at the Institute.

"Bob's in his contemplative period." Scooter suspects he has been asking himself if there is purpose to what he has experienced, or if the whole has been an exercise in futility. His philosophy, as it appears to have developed, she likens to Nietzsche, and to Sartre's existentialism: totally devoid of positive or negative.

Why has Bob not encountered anyone in this life who knows precisely what he is talking about? Is Bob Monroe truly unique? Nancy Lea theorizes there may be a few other people who have done the deep, mystical exploring Bob is involved in now, but they are well hidden. "Perhaps they'll come out of the woodwork when *Ultimate Journey* appears."

Scooter examines Bob, the teacher-showman: "His style of communication sometimes leads to misunderstanding. He ought to find some way to telegraph to people, 'This is a joke.' "

Who knows how many of the multitude of ideas Bob spins off are meant in jest, and how many he hopes will take root?

"He advocates, 'Everything is possible,' and people take him at his word. It's part of his mysticism.

"He's a true Renaissance Man. He has an incredible level of creativity.

"He has been able to break through many of the restrictions imposed on us by the culture: His philosophy, his way of behavior, his way of thinking.

"He defies a lot of stereotyped roles, and he gets away with it.

"He enhances other people's lives simply by sharing his thoughts.

"He's the most human non-human I've ever met.

"By non-human, I mean someone who knows how to play by human rules, but somehow places himself outside those rules.

"He can punch your buttons, and have his buttons punched, too. That's his human side.

"He's the Great White Father to many people. And the Great Exasperator to many, as well.

"It's like watching a boy flying a kite outside. While he's there, he talks about being an astronaut.

"Then he goes into his room, lies down, has an OOB, and he *is* an astronaut.

"It's the most fun game he's ever been in.

"Now, Bob's the philosopher. The old, wise man."

Scooter is well aware many of the people who come to the Institute come because of Bob's presence, and want the personal contact with him.

"But after he has made his exit, the Institute will go on. The idea is not Bob-dependent.

"It remains...How to get in touch with your consciousness: You are more than your physical body. That, too, may expand.

"If, for instance, someone dies and communicates with the Institute. That would then become knowledge and could help make it part of humanity's belief system.

"We have wonderful minds here. The Institute will expand and improve; the technology will grow."

* * * *

Ronald and Jill Russell are the British couple who have attended Gateway, Guidelines, the Professional Seminar, and H+, and who have now established the "Monroe Outpost" in Cambridge.

When they first met Bob Monroe, "We both had the feeling he had known us before. Maybe forever. The first time we ever spoke to him, one-on-one, at the end of our Gateway, in summer 1986, he said, 'I've always known where you were.'

"To Jill, he said, 'You're as radiant as I have known you would be.'

"The most precious time we had was when he took us on a tour of the New Land in his car—with the gas gauge showing red all the way.

"It was a conducted tour. But there was something else going on beneath this. It's difficult to say what it was."

Then Russ changes pace. "Of course, there are certain circumstances under which I wouldn't trust him an inch. I wouldn't play cards with him, for instance.

"No way would I, thank you very much.

"But, in other ways...if he phoned us in England or communicated non-verbally...and said, 'Would you come over, there's work for you here in Virginia,' there's no doubt we would come. Even if, when we got there, he looked up in surprise and said, 'Hey, what are you doing here?'

"Everyone has his own views and responses to Bob. But they change as you get to know him better; and they change as you find out what's going on. . . ."

Russ continues, "I don't think one can ever say what *is* going on, though. Maybe only at that precise moment.

"One's whole view of Bob does shift. I'm only talking at this moment. It's quite possible this is a whole lot of rubbish, as of now in this everyday reality."

What is Bob Monroe? "If he'd lived a few centuries ago, he would be counted today among the mystics.

"He stands there still, but with the added element that he's one of the very few who can link the mystical world with the world of contemporary physics: These two worlds which are increasingly close together. Bob has knowledge of both. He brings his knowledge of one to the other.

"He's a past master at moving from everyday life to the altered state, and dwelling there as long as he wishes."

Bob rejected the commercialization and the power-trip lure of his OOB ability. Instead, "He asked, 'Where is this really going?'

"Lawrence LeShan talks of the 'Transpsychic Reality' where 'Time is the Eternal Now,' and one is conscious of the total harmony of all creation, at one with nature and with everything.

"Bob can move into this reality—perhaps spend all of his time there.

"In this state of consciousness, he can make statements such as those on the H+ tapes: 'You can change your view of reality.'

"From anyone else, you would think the man was crazy. But when Bob says it, your reaction is, 'It's acceptable. Why shouldn't I believe him?'

"When you have gained some awareness of Bob, you *know* he knows what he's talking about.

"It seems clear that his own experiences, his awareness of the infinite range of human potential have altered his spiritual views. Occasionally, you get some glimpses of this, although he's pretty canny at holding it all within.

"If he released these views, they would color the feelings of the people to whom he is talking.

"Bob is an Enabler. At the Institute, they call him a Facilitator. There's a great difference between him and the more conventional type of teacher.

"He says, 'Here are the doors. You can open them and find out what's behind them."

Russ says, clearly and calmly, "I can't think of anyone I've come across with whom I could compare him.

"He's amongst the three or four who've had the greatest influence on me. . .for whom I've had the greatest respect and, I suppose one can say, the greatest love.

"But these impressions are fragmentary.

"Is it possible at one moment to get a comprehensive view of the Old Chap? He's elusive."

Russ, a writer, says of Bob's books: "I don't like them. They're difficult to read.

"He's gone so far beyond them.

"He's moved into a further reality. . .a rarer state of consciousness.

"He's like an old trout. . .you think you've got him, but he slips out of your fingers, just as you try to pull him out of the stream.

"He seems to switch off from time to time. Maybe he gets bored. You can't bridge that gap.

"'I love him this side of idolatry.' Shakespeare? Maybe. Anyway, it's a good comment. I'll let it stand.

"Bob is saying, whatever develops in sensory reality over the next decades, we can cope.

"What manner of man can envision this and know it can be done?

"It's out of the realm of mysticism. It has nothing to do with the paranormal. It's visionary.

"And yet, Bob has the practical ability, for instance, to get H+ going. To sort it all out. His Left and Right Brain hemispheres are operating at full stretch.

"This is where Bob is singled out. He has developed his own brain to a degree given to few people.

"Bob is a living example of Hemi-Synchronization. He's Hemi-Sync incarnate.

"Apart from that, there's the spiritual dimension, which one feels rather than perceives. But it's there for the person who can tune in.

"He's There. He knows Other People.

"He is All. He is One...

"You can see it in him...the totality of awareness...in this overweight bear of a man who is so full of love."

* * * *

Kaye Andres went to a Gateway in January, 1987 and thereafter commented, "Bob's one hell of a showman. He stages things like mad. He suckers people in, playfully, but there's a steeliness to him that he keeps hidden. I wouldn't want to go to the mat with Bob.

"He spends considerable time in Focus 12—buzzes in and buzzes out. Listens for a little bit, then takes off.

"But he's extremely lovable.

"He's standard brand, less personality bound. He has seen it through his Out-of-Body travels. Sex is an aspect of humanity not necessarily linked with another human being: That's his perception."

Kaye thinks of Bob Monroe as a terribly lonely man. "If there were a way for him to open lines to other people...."

She was talking in early 1988; her last exposure to Bob Monroe was in June, 1987. "He has gone through his second-level guidance, gone through Inspec;[3] now he's dealing with his own death issues. He's looking at some blank walls.

"There's a bind there. His ego is involved. It's part of his alone-ness and his skepticism, which impedes his total going for broke.

"There's a great deal of self-knowledge and self-reflection which he carries with his own self.

"He might be freer when he's dead. It will lift the responsibility he feels he has towards others.

"I want to hear his fears, his early fears. His sacrifices.

"He's not going naked. If he could do so, it would serve me so heart-breakingly well...nakedness I can recognize. That's the place for acceptance.

"What I see in him is what I see in me. There are parts of him which are me. I feel a great compassion for him...a great cuddling. No negativity."

On a deeper level, Kaye Andres sees Bob as "one of a vaster number of people present on this planet than I have any idea of....

"People who are offered to the rest of us in a variety of ways. They have a variety of backgrounds and training, and they also have a variety of infusions...you might call them 'Divine Hits.'

"Bob is riding the wave, singing the siren song of the New Heaven and the New Earth for those of us who are attracted by his tones.

"I'm learning to recognize those who sing the song, whether I hear it or not.

"Bob doesn't have a perfectly-polished halo.

"Each of us needs to recognize we can only be led by those who have human flaws."

Nancy

The person who knows Bob Monroe best is Nancy Penn Monroe. Her experience of the metaphysical world is not as vast as Bob's, but is still a useful and joyful basis for their deep understanding and their love for each other.

Nancy says, almost in a whisper, "Also, we're good friends. We share.

"He doesn't tell me everything. I can't be his mentor."

In turn, Nancy's greatest gift to him is her gentle acceptance of Bob as he is. Nancy chides Bob, humors him—and lets him be.

"The best thing about our marriage is that we're best friends."

The marriage has endured longer than any of Bob's previous matrimonial liaisons, and undoubtedly for good reason. "Bob's ability to communicate is his greatest gift. He's so gentle."

Bob's not moody. "Oh, sometimes, he's very quiet."

Nancy recalls an article she once read about an Oriental tree, encrusted in a thick, forbidding layer of porous bark. "If you strip away that crust, you find the trunk of the tree is Light, pure Light.

"That's Bob. He has stripped off all the outer bark of teaching, training, dogma—the encrustation of society—and he shows the Light.

"It's not always easy, living in the shadow of the oak."

Nancy once found Bob watching the sun rise at Whistlefield. He turned to her with tears in his eyes. "I've just been to church.

"A lot of people call him an oddball. Maybe. But really he's a loner. Because he doesn't conform to the expected patterns of behavior or belief, he is forced into the chill of isolation. It gets really cold out There.

"There's a part of me that admires so much a person who can be different. Who can be an individual.

"He's not afraid of criticism. He stands up to be counted, and lets the chips fall where they may.

She turns quietly passionate: "What is it out There that makes him feel so alone? He's on the leading edge of something!"

* * * *

Bob Monroe is regarded by many, often including his own staff, as the Source; they feel they must deal exclusively with him, in private." I have difficulty with some of his friends. They come to the house to talk with Bob, and they exclude me, deliberately."

Nancy has at times complained to Bob. He is sympathetic, but his response is always the same: Encouragement to Nancy to do her own thing.

It is bleak comfort for Nancy. "Sometimes I feel so small and picky!"

Nancy speculates on the factor of jealousy—or envy—of Bob. She uses a description, "Spiritual Ph.D.'s," to categorize many who don't measure up to Bob in her eyes. "Years ago, he was very receptive to the adulation given him. But he's been bamboozled so many times: People offered him big financial deals, but really they wanted to take over the Institute. When Bob became aware of their intentions, and cooled toward them, they became disgruntled and stabbed him in the back.

"People don't understand he's not in competition with them. He only competes with himself.

"He's happy when someone takes one of his ideas and runs with it. Who was it—Emerson?—who said, 'You recognize your genius in someone else's work.'"

Nancy cited examples of a well-known institute and a famous, channeled entity both of which, in 1988, were exploiting schemes parallel to, if not copied from, Monroe pioneering.

"His creative generosity is unbelievable. The man's grown up. He's a Giver. It was hard to convince him that people sap at him. Sap his energy.

"He's trusting and tender-hearted to a fault.

"I used to get all hot and bothered, but Bob would say, 'Honey, let it go. Don't worry. The trick is to stay ahead of them. Forget it.

"Come on and fly with me. Get on the Interstate.'

"He's always pressing ahead to new horizons.

"I'm the tortoise, he's the hare, way up the line. I keep thinking, 'Where are my Seven League Boots?

"Bob's attitude towards money today is simply that he doesn't want to have to be worried about it.

"He's saddened by people who misjudge or discover he does not match their expectations, and then turn on him," says Nancy. "Now, he's in full retreat."

* * * *

Inevitably, there's the subject of women. Bob is, after all, a Scorpio. There are those, indeed, who think most of the males around the Monroe Institute are Scorpios, but the theory has not been checked.

One recurrent question among Gateway Voyagers is whether Bob attracts ladies when he's Out of Body. Nancy says, "There have been times when I felt tremendous female Energy during the night.

"Nowadays, I don't try to protect myself when he's Out-of-Body.

"But he has never reported to me that he's playing footsie with women out There.

"Of course women like to think he's coming to see them at night. He's a very human and very dynamic man."

Almost everyone who visits the Monroes at home, notes that the subject of sex rears its wondrous head often in conversation, and quite naturally, because they consider it an interesting, normal, and vital part of life. Both leave little doubt in the listener's mind that theirs has been a rapturous union, on all levels of consciousness.

"There aren't many people who understand that there's an aspect of spiritual love—for lack of a better word—which isn't commonly experienced," says Nancy.

A "best friends" relationship opens both man and woman to the concept of total giving, of body as well as emotion. Nancy recalls Cyrano de Bergerac's line to Roxanne about "the blinding, soaring music" of love.

Some couples who do metaphysical exercises together have reported stupendous experiences, far beyond the usual orgasm, while they were consciously aware, in the Altered State. They say they do not become their partner's entity, but that the merging is complete. Other pairs even think they have gone OOB as one ethereal body. One woman described the experience: "It's as if I have to stop and put on a garment—my body—when I return."

Nancy comments, "What we're talking about is a blending of energies most people think they can attain only through sex.

"But that's light years away from the truth. It's the light of the candle, compared to the sun.

"There's no real description for it.

"Sometimes, I think of a seemingly empty bottle. You blow smoke into it, and watch it eddy. The essence has supplanted the original contents.

"You are that essence, down to your toes, until you equalize and return to your physical self."

* * * *

Nancy Monroe frankly does not know why Bob has so consistently avoided reference to "spirituality," but she will not speculate. She does say, "He's deeply moral. His attitude is *laissez-faire*. . .allowing others to do their thing.

"His beliefs are expressed best in his concept of Loosh.[1] It's the Unseen Language: The ability we all have—if only we can develop it—to tap those wavelengths which permit us to communicate with everything—plants, animals, other energies. It's a huge, all-enveloping concept."

In *Far Journeys*, Monroe refers often to Inspec, which is as close as he came, prior to *Ultimate Journey*, to talking of the Deity. "He doesn't like labels. They're limiting."

When *FJ* was in preparation, Bob brought the early morning's production into breakfast and read it aloud. When he got to the sections dealing with the Inspecs, he often broke down, voice choked, tears filling his eyes.

There is one passage which contains a description of an Inspec protecting him from the Light. Bob simply could not bring himself to read it aloud, even to his wife. Nancy says, "There are some things beyond Inspec he just can't talk about at all."[2]

Nancy won't cry in front of Bob. Why? "Maybe I don't want to embarrass him. Men get squeamish when women cry. But I get choked up. Not that I'm a pillar of strength for him. I just try to be.

"And then he turns to me and says something like, 'You don't need to defend me. I'm indefensible.'"

* * * *

One evening in a local restaurant, Nancy examines her martini carefully before she answers another question.

"He's flying by the seat of his britches. He's in the vanguard, on the edge of the

Wave. The hardest part is *interpretation*. . .to explain the raw data of the unexplainable.

"He says he's in his contemplative years, but he's far from being a monk.

"Time's his most valuable commodity."

It's a fact Bob himself is acutely aware of, as he works on his various projects.

Nancy Monroe says. "I'm sure he gets his direction in his sleep, then he gets up to mull it over, during his morning Quiet Time," in the simple, comfortable sitting alcove off the kitchen. "It's up to him to figure it all out, as it always has been.

"Then, when he has made his discovery, he's smiling, as if They told him, 'Well, you made the connection again, after all!'

"The H+ program, for instance.

"When you look at it, it's really the practical enunciation of the Gateway Affirmation, isn't it?. . .'I *am* more than my physical body. . . . '

"It's a big breakthrough, which he had to figure out on his own, after Guidance gave him the clues."

Suddenly, Nancy softly but firmly lashes out at the surrounding society: "The true conspiracy is pampering our physical bodies. Look at cosmetic advertising—the stuff they throw at us to make us think our physical body is the be all and end all!

"It actively promotes neglect of the real Us. The Inner Self. The spiritual side. It's outrageous!" The cry of a full woman who knows Here as well as There, and has made her choice, in concert with her physical husband.

The penultimate word is Bob Monroe's. "I don't know how I can explain Nancy's value to me. She's a female with extraordinary depth. She's been in conflict with her cultural upbringing. She has experienced the agonies and ecstasies of motherhood." The Progenitor gropes for words.

"Maybe if I tell you that the words in the Explorer 19 tape ("Love, Fear and Christ Consciousness") are hers, although voiced by someone else. . .that's her stuff." Bob Monroe could have paid his wife no higher compliment.

What is the most difficult part of living with Bob Monroe? Nancy's reply comes quickly. "It's my wanting to be more for him. I simply don't have enough facets.

"But it's important I not call him a saint."

Conclusion: So, Who Is The *Real* Bob Monroe?

It's time to brush in the final daubs of pigment in the portrait of Bob Monroe.

Holding Bob steadily in focus long enough to capture a true likeness is an exercise in frustration. Then, too, ordinary human senses give only a superficial impression. They cannot delve into those unseen and unheard crannies which must also be at least hinted in the portrait, nor can they feel with him. The finished canvas should be as rich and as evocative as that of a master's parable in oils, yet it is necessarily two-dimensional, telling of more. Much of the model can only be surmised because he is a man of many-layered paradoxes, and—even if not in the clinical sense—of several personalities. That Bob cannot completely portray himself is evident. For another human being, the task of rendering Bob Monroe is complexity to the nth degree.

Given his paradoxes and his shielded sides, it's still an absorbing game to try, with the help of everyone who contributed to this book, to answer, finally: Who is Bob Monroe?

Most of those who believe in and think they know Monroe will speculate that his contacts in Altered Consciousness have been no accident, but rather are a mystical partnership.

Not all, but some will carry the speculation farther: that, indeed, Bob's whole life falls into a distinguishable pattern which has led to his situation today. There is nothing new to mysticism; even skeptics will grudgingly acknowledge there are events in the lives of people through recorded history which defy rational explanation. The "spiritual experience" is probably the most generally-accepted existential evidence of Supra-Conscious activity in human life, but there are many others.

In our own day, inquiries into the paranormal have become a serious matter, even if only among a few. Edgar Cayce is, for instance, far more than a cult figure beloved of graduate hippies and smalltown discussion groups. Bill Wilson and Dr. Bob Smith relied on Guidance in the birth and adolescence of Alcoholics Anonymous. The New Age has a hard, very serious core behind the camouflage of crystals, healers, and pitchmen.

* * * *

Has Bob Monroe succeeded by any index we can apply in our achievement-happy, result-oriented, success-driven world? And if he has succeeded, in what?

Monroe has come close to several identifiable successes in a lifetime of effort. The first has been to find his identity. It has taken his entire lifespan, true, and has been incredibly expensive, exhausting, frightening, lonely, selfish—and beneficial. If you protest that a lifetime is an inordinate amount of time to spend examining oneself,

Charley Tart, for one, retorts: "Well, don't we all spend most of our lives figuring out who we are?"

The difference is that Bob Monroe went on the search with an engineer's single-minded, methodical, unflinching approach, and with considerable financial resources.

Bob's second success was initially a by-product of the first, but then far superseded it in importance. It is that Monroe's engineering approach has helped to de-mystify what others refer to as the occult, the supernatural or supernormal, even the metaphysical, for many other people. Monroe has pragmatically put experience of the Supra-Conscious within the grasp of the average, earthbound human who is willing to exercise curiosity, dares to innovate, adds a bit of courage and effort to the search, and then integrates what he finds into his daily life.

On the way to that achievement, he brought the OOB experience out of the closet, and assured a large number of people their fears for their sanity were groundless. He also told people it was OK to be a bit flaky, to zoom covertly around non-physical planes, having a ball, and incidentally collecting knowledge vital to themselves.

He has succeeded, too, although as yet only modestly, in introducing a potent new technology in some branches of medicine, in education—both fields where a new approach is sorely needed—and, conceivably in business. With recent developments in science, it is conceivable, also, that his tools-of-the-mind may be far more useful than has heretofore been suspected. He has founded a technology that begs for exploitation in modernistic-but-pragmatic realms.

Serious or lighthearted, any one of these is a major achievement in a man's physical lifetime.

There is also a good chance that Monroe will be far more significant in the years to come than he has been able to prove thus far, as the ripple effect of his work spreads, and the world of Supra-Consciousness becomes a field for more serious study and broader experience. If, that is, we humans have the time and the wisdom to explore the possibilities.

* * * *

Monroe's first demystification was *Journeys Out of the Body*, which was not the first work on the subject, but did help publicize OOB's—theretofore scarifying experiences known to but not admitted by an appreciable percentage of the population. *JOOB* came at a time when drugs were seeping into the culture; drugs, whatever else they did, opened people's minds. Monroe provided an access to the same kind of consciousness without artificial or chemical substances.

Then came the courses: Few who have passed through the Monroe Institute can claim their lives have not been changed by the experience—even if it has taken some time for differences to make themselves apparent. The changes are intensely personal: they touch ego, pride, material acquisition, and, especially, fear, hence one's basic outlook on life itself. The student may look at the bridgehead to There and lose his Fear of the Unknown. He often emerges with a confident new sense of self-purpose; frequently, he comes to know his Inner Self. If only one person in one course has so benefited, Monroe would have been a success; in fact, thousands have grown and expanded as a direct result of Monroe's techniques. Apart from personal progress for many, application of his methods in professional life is where the real future action lies.

There is the debate, at times passionate, on Bob's exclusion, from the Monroe

Institute, of the spiritual ingredient which so many participants experience. It is dictated by Engineer Bob's physical-life background and makeup. Monroe adamantly regards himself as a "facilitator." He leans over backwards to avoid the guru label, and, in the way of his own upbringing, to insure he does not foist his own views on others.

But omission of the spiritual issue is the result, as well, of his own and others' non-physical explorations.

Until *Far Journeys* and later, *Ultimate Journey*, Monroe ducked the key question of whether there is a spiritual presence or component in his life. Apart from the indications in his writings, any answer to the question can only come in the observer's resonating with the man—both the Left Brain'ed and the Right Brain'ed Bob Monroe.

Is Bob's approach to The All purely that of the inquiring technologist? Does it make any difference? The Institute does not deal in Good versus Evil, but in constructive, beneficial, positive energies. The ultimate is a state of being Beyond God in which energies become "the operators of the lasers that make the hologram."

Monroe stands on his written and spoken record, which has helped many to find spiritual comfort and sustenance. Whether he does or does not have the same comfort is a matter between Bob and his Guides.

Arguments about this void in Institute training come from both sides. Some contend the majority of students have some form of spiritual experience while going through a Gateway, regardless of their initial intent, so why ignore that powerful presence in the curriculum? It is often the sharpening of contact with a power greater than ourselves, and it can be as powerful as the Near Death Experience, elaborated by Kenneth Ring in *Heading Toward Omega.*[1] Some feel the lack of guidance, or even tutorial discussion, keenly.

Others agree with Bob that spiritual learning, if it takes place at all, is a very private, individual matter. Some feel that any spiritual ingredient would necessarily limit the programs' appeal, and would in itself be a limiting factor on students.

There is a school of thought that the Institute provides a transportation system, akin, for instance, to those illuminated signs in department store elevators: "Alight here for advanced consciousness in all sizes and styles." Or another analogy might be to the maps one sees in subway systems: You know there are restaurants, theaters, hotels, apartments, playgrounds up above, but the map doesn't tell you where they are. The traveler gets out at a station, climbs the steps, and explores the cityscape on his own. You make your own reality; or it is tailored to your requirements.

Almost all Institute students are products of Western civilization; Monroe pours gentle skepticism on the "appurtenances" and institutions of that society. He allows no reference, either, to Eastern philosophical thought, which arrives at basically the same conclusions, if by different routes.

All major theological schools are wholly compatible with the results achieved by Bob's methods, but the Institute suggests previous belief systems are inadequate to deal with the Truth. It encourages no specific replacements. The vacuum that can then occur may cause some bewilderment.

For instance, Bob Monroe rejects the blatant aspects of the New Age, but in failing to outline—not impose—serious guidelines for consideration, he may inadvertently encourage some students in the exploration of the New Age's flakier side shows and totems.

Bob Monroe cannot be all things to all men—non-spiritual technologist, and spiritual pathfinder. Though as much as he may reject even the concept of spirituality, he comes close to enunciating role for many people—by his actions, his giving, his humility, and his words.

Perhaps the best evidence of the true spirituality of Bob Monroe—whatever else he may choose to call it—is contained in two guided-meditation tapes which often bring listeners to tears. One is called "The Visit," the other, "Moment of Revelation." In each, Bob leads the participant along a gentle, soft path to a point of rhapsodic truth, of oneness, cleansing, healing—and knowing. "Moment of Revelation" nears its close with these words: "Use this knowledge without greed, and always in the service of the Creator."

* * * *

When Bob Monroe goes out from Roberts Mountain into the physical, material world, he often doesn't quite fit. His movements are slow, but there's a wide-eyed air of naivete to him. He sits in a restaurant and offers humble, near-childish delight to a waitress who brings him a plain hamburger. Bob shows turn-of-the-century courtesy and genuine concern for others—up to a point. In another age, he might have been a cavalier, though it's hard to picture him as a man of the sword; more likely, a bardic courtier, who pleased yet humbled others with his words.

Though he's an engineer, he watches a mechanic perform a minor repair on his car with genuine innocence—exuding an air of helplessness. But, when roused, he's equally capable of a technologist's trenchant disgust with slipshod workmanship, or the businessman's abrasive impatience with bureaucratic indifference.

It's hard to believe this is a man who has made millions of dollars in his life, whose daredevil adventures in both the physical and non-physical worlds defy description. But that's all part of the Monroe Paradox.

After a long day of work, Bob leans back in a much-worn executive chair in the Lab, behind him a fifteen-inch reel of tape spinning on a studio deck. It plays the original master of Titus Moody's New England-dry comments on politics and the world, a Monroe Productions spin-off from the old Fred Allen radio show. Not much in the world or the nation has changed, says, Bob. But he's sad that few, in the 1980s, cotton to the humor of three decades ago.

Then he switches reels, and puts on the master of some late night Manhattan-style piano music, also recorded in the early 1950s. The notes glide evocatively through the speakers. He whispers softly, "We're still romantics, aren't we?"

But, despite the open encouragement that seems to issue from his Real World openness, a sign in muted neon seems often to flash from an impenetrable fence around him: "Beware. No Trespassing beyond this point."

* * * *

Bob sounds good. He uses all the techniques of the master showman. He is often thought of as a brilliant practitioner of the art of communication.

But there are any number of instances when members of an audience have found themselves wrapt in his words, thinking they understand his drift, only thereafter to stare blankly at one another with some embarrassment, and ask, "What did he really say?" Bob's words loop smoothly into the ear, but when they get to the brain for integration, they may prove to have been more dumbfounding than helpful.

Likewise, Bob's writing style is not always clear. He is justifiably proud of his dialogue-scripting. He studied journalism.

When Bob wants to make himself absolutely clear, he does so, and he leaves no doubt in the listener's mind.

When he chooses to be obscure, he can be as vague as a practiced diplomat. In any conversation that touches on one of his many private preserves, Monroe controls the flow, answers those questions he wants to, though often obliquely.

Even in relaxed chat, Bob frequently cloaks his meaning in metaphor or, more often, lapses, not entirely consciously, into that elliptical style which is a form of obfuscation. Sometimes he just plain rambles, enjoying the moment, and maybe even the confusion it creates.

One of the problems in understanding Monroe is that much of the Knowing he deals with is so far from the ken of 'normal' human beings, he cannot find words to express his meaning. How do you describe the indescribable?

* * * *

The physical Bob Monroe is puzzled by all that has gone into the makeup of his Here-and-Now being. As a matter of generational outlook, he has never considered counseling or group therapy for himself; either would have been a ludicrous exercise anyway. Bob, the action man, never spent much time reflecting on his past until he started to think about this book. What came out in his recollections often surprised him. While ruminating just before one of our final conversations, he suddenly said: "If you are able to figure out an emotional pattern for me in all this, you'll be doing me a great service."

Monroe's introspection is of a different type, more detached-reportorial-intellectual, far less self-obsessed-emotional than the style to which we have become so accustomed in the 1980s: His self-examination has to do with his experiences There. The results are the meat of his books and his training courses. Psychologists and counselors might argue that Monroe cannot teach adequately without full self-knowledge, even some form of psychoanalysis; that he's "coming too much from intellect, not enough from the heart." Bob would say courteously that they are welcome to their points of view.

Monroe examines the enigma that is himself with considerable understatement: "I can't reject the conclusions that have become obvious to me, no matter how unorthodox they are.

"I'm not conventional in my approach to human consciousness. I take the engineering approach. Elmer Green and Stu Twemlow take the medical. I hit some good flatted sixths, and came out right." He does not feed into the equation the facts that he has always been a courageous, perhaps even foolhardy, risk-taking researcher, to benefit himself and others.

Bob draws a parallel to the paradoxes that existed in Duke Ellington. One night at the Gift House, before watching "Star Trek IV" ("a nice fairy tale") yet again, Bob put on some Ellington music. "Mood Indigo," "Tenderly," and "Solitude" laced the warm air from the carefully-placed speakers.

Bob's face was in reverent repose as he followed the intricate bass sax work of Johnny Hodges, and Cootie Williams' trumpet. He reveled in the meticulous piano phrasing and the unusual styling that was the Ellington trademark: "He was a pacesetter, five years ahead of the other big bands. Unorthdox, but he did it."

Bob, the white border-state gentleman, feels a true sense of companionship with the black musician who inspired him, not just in music. Ellington came from a middle-class family which was uncomfortable when the bandleader billed himself as "Duke Ellington and his Jungle Boys." Bob embarrassed his with a whole skein of antics. Both came from comfortable backgrounds. More to the point, Ellington was years ahead of his time. "He knew how to make the unorthodox work with the broad public; that was his trick. No one else ever used flatted sixths to end a piece before.

"Ellington's aim was to affect people's emotions with his music, when other bands didn't go that deep. His instrument was the whole damn orchestra. He conducted it from the keyboard, using chords to cue the band. We do have parallels."

It is not too difficult to catalogue the influences that shaped the human Monroe. In achieving the crest of Roberts Mountain, Bob Monroe has had to discard much of what he absorbed from 1915 to the 1950s, but some of the externals remain, indelibly engraved in his personality.

He is outwardly still a post-Victorian gentleman, shaped by the mentality of a far more sedate time.

But, "What seemed to be conventional in my background actually wasn't." Bob Monroe never attributes direct influence to either parent, but he quickly repeats a key refrain:

"There wasn't a Bible on display in our living room, and Lexington was a Southern town. I assume everyone around us went to church regularly, but my parents went maybe once a month, as a social requirement. There was that sort of difference.

"It wasn't conventional that my mother was an M.D., when few women were. Nor was it conventional that my father was a professor of romance languages at a Midwestern university during the Depression," when French and Spanish were not exactly bread-and-butter priorities. "My parents were far more intellectually and philosophically tolerant than most."

The strongest overt influence in Monroe's upbringing was The Professor: remote, strong-willed, non-emotional, pragmatic, attractive to both women and men; a man who always considered himself a gardener or farmer as much as an academic.

It is significant that, in the memories of Dorothy Monroe Kahler and her brothers, Bob and Emmett, the role their mother played is far less to the fore. She is a nearly-ethereal figure who was present in their childhoods, often tried to temper the forthright edicts of their Father (with discreet handouts of money, for instance) but whose part in their upbringing is hardly mentioned.

There is never, in the conversation of any of the three siblings, reference to Mrs. Monroe's medical practice; she was an accomplished musician, but her cello-playing is not a joyously-recalled ingredient in their lives—even though two of the three children became decidedly musical in their adult years. There can be no doubt the children loved their mother, but she is always cast in shadow by the strong presence of Father.

Monroe made no effort to check the data after an Explorer reported the name and the Italian town of residence of his mother in her new physical life. She was a physical memory, nothing more. He was happy she would now have an opportunity to enjoy the music she had missed last time around. His reaction speaks of a sense of detachment, even of a lack of curiosity, that is remarkable.

* * * *

Bob Monroe turns to examine a few of the crossroads of his life. The formative influences, or, as Bob likes to call them, "the patterns," began to emerge at an early age. One was the early need for music, and wiggling his way into the church choir. Another was, of course, flying. "I was only five or six when I saw that Gates Brothers Air Show in Lexington and Ed Lund's fatal crash. It didn't frighten me."

The first time he realized he could drown, in the pond in Kentucky while little more than a baby, gave him his first intimation of mortality. The flash of intuition sticks with him to this day. How many of us remember so precisely the first time we knew we were mortal?

There was always the knowledge and exercise of his precocious mechanical ability: scavenging parts and rebuilding a racing car in the yard in his early teens.

Next came the self-confidence that grew when he took the furlough from Ohio State and went on the road. "I spent nearly a year looking for work in the middle of the Depression." Life was raw. Bob slept in boxcars, and in downtown-rescue-mission dormitories. "But when I came back and had a goal, I had no trouble finding that job grinding saw blades."

* * * *

From boyhood till his 40's, Bob Monroe led a life which was above-average in excitement and achievement, but otherwise not out of the ordinary. He was the all-American go-getter, hometown-boy-made-good. After his life changed radically in 1958, his personality inevitably altered in a devolution that extends into his contemplative years.

Now, the physical Bob Monroe likes people in the same way many philosophers do: They espouse and work idealistically for the good of mankind, but want little or nothing to do with the seething mass, or with any but a small, comfortable band of close associates. Even most of this inner group, in the case of Bob Monroe, is necessarily excluded from the deepest of his visions.

Humankind is, in Monroe's view, billions of scenario-scripters acting out their complex roles of learning. The actors cast themselves in their own scripts before they came on stage. If they digress too far from the plot they chose, they come back in other lives to rehearse their roles again and again until they have perfected them. Only then can they move on from, say, kindergarten to elementary school plays. The dramas of grade school, junior high, and beyond are still a considerable ways down the pike. The craft the novice actors learn Here is, in Bob's view, useful only insofar as it applies to the Broadway out There.

It just happens Monroe has been given certain stage directions he can pass on. He also helps provide cues, prompts, costumes, and backdrops for a few, chosen players in the Learning School theatre.

In Monroe's universal acting studio, the physical world is a warm-up exercise; its demands contribute to the skill of the players. Bob's is a cosmic academy of stage, and television. Perhaps most accurate of all, it is a school run by a man who knows Here's three rings are sheer illusion.

* * * *

Bob Monroe radiates a warm appeal of conviction, especially when he is performing for a Gateway group: He woos men and women alike with voice, eyes and gestures. He's the seductive barker, the carnival pitchman, on the rim of the baby spot, inviting you in to learn the secrets of the illusion. "You've tried the competition. C'mon now, I'll just hold up the tent-flap, you sneak in under it and join me in the greatest adventure physical life has to offer."

Is his warm enticement merely the adroit ringmaster offering Huck and Becky a chance to play flamboyant roles under the Big Top? Or is it an invitation born of love for humans—even if only for some—to demystify the circus, and reveal All.

Emotional entanglement, even of the platonic kind, is a risk Monroe seeks to avoid. It has not always been so, but Bob's close friendships have been notably few. Time after time, Bob Monroe has shown those around him how vulnerable he is to the play of emotion—and how much he wishes he weren't.

Most males today take their adventure vicariously, in manufactured escapism. Monroe makes his own escape, and it's not to a mindless narcosis.

But has Bob Monroe consistently done something many males in our society do, namely used adventure to stifle feeling which, if let run rampant, would prove intolerable?

One indication, apart from his absorption in exploration, might be that Monroe continues to smoke; nicotine helps to stifle emotion, as well as energy.

* * * *

From earliest boyhood, Bob Monroe has lived audaciously. He has thrived on pushing himself to the limit, on creating situations which limned the risk of death. What was Monroe trying to prove with his physical-life derring-do? The pop-psych answers might be that Bob felt "insecure or rejected," or "lacked a sense of identity," or suffered from "low self-worth," and therefore had to prove himself, or over-achieve.

But, in accustoming himself from early life to danger, was Bob, perhaps, sketching a mental and psychological landscape for a far more important canvas? Was he unwittingly accommodating himself to fear?

One of Bob's worlds was that of the masculine daredevil; he might have found happiness as a Hollywood stunt man, or an old-fashioned, barnstorming air-circus pilot.

He felt himself attracted to types similar to himself who had flying, music and mechanics as common denominators. His three closest friends, two of them from pre-OOB days, were also adventurers; each died in an air crash.

Harry Bullock, the childhood friend, early on was a whiz at fixing cars and later studied mechanical engineering. He was hooked on jazz, and was Monroe's source for a lot of the old shellac records that got Bob started on the musical path.

Edgar Wynn, the partner in the air-charter business, had the same characteristics. "He was a real cafe society figure. We'd be at a nightclub, and he'd pick up a trumpet and play the lead in the band." Edgar was a flyer who also dabbled in ham radio.

Agnew Bahnson, the pal in Winston-Salem, was an engineer; he loved to fly, and he especially loved his music after a few drinks, when everyone else had gone to bed. "He was a true Atlantean." Monroe hastens to amend the statement. "Well, not really. But what I call an Atlantean."

Bob gave his active love to these three, as he has to a few others since. It's a precious gift, as it is for anyone, to give and to receive.

In his relationships with women, Monroe acknowledges the obvious-that he's a romantic, although he professes to be unaware of the appeal he has—even at seventy-three—for women.

Although he's so very private, Bob lavishes a feeling of ethereal love on his students.

Yet it's part of the Monroe paradox, and part of the Monroe image, that Bob gets uncomfortable when the talk turns to heart; the engineer takes over. Bob pours out love, but hopes you won't notice it, because "real men" don't.

* * * *

There was a memorable British film some years ago, starring Tom Courtenay, called *The Loneliness of The Long Distance Runner.* It's a title that could almost precisely be applied to the Ultimate Adventurer, except that "Loneliness" implies a certain degree of self-pity, and that's not part of Bob Monroe's luggage.

Monroe does admit he has been driven, but he reflects no worry about competition or successors; to the contrary, there's plenty of room on the track for all, the more the merrier. There just aren't many runners who can stay the distance.

That he is lonesome is a factor quietly and sadly mentioned by all those who have spent fruitful time in his orbit. His sense of apartness started in childhood, and continues: Bob has felt "different" all his life.

The enormity and the implication of the unedited material he has brought forth, set him apart from most, but not quite all, of his fellowmen. His is a solitary burden that must be comparable to that felt by other visionaries, magicians, mystics, and the like, down through time. Some have gone out into the populace, others have chosen to emphasize their sense of apartness by leading a cloistered existence.

One might think that the serious seers of our time might get together and share their knowledge. It would be a rare clambake indeed, should it ever come to pass. The chances that it will are minimal, for a variety of identifiable and many other less obvious reasons. When and if necessary, people such as Swami Rama, Rolling Thunder, Jack Schwarz, advanced Buddhists and Hindus, mystic Christians, Africans, and Aborigines can probably communicate to the extent necessary on their inner planes, anyway. Meantime, each follows his fairly isolated path.

There is, too, a characteristic of Monroe which separates him from most seers: He has explored out of his own pure, individual curiosity, and it has required enormous courage to do so. Others have arrived at their stages of enlightenment in the course of an esoteric tradition or schooling; the trail has been at least partly blazed for them. Bob Monroe did it on his own.

Monroe could have gone to India soon after the OOB's started, and learned how to handle them. In the 1960s, the ashrams of India at times seemed to resemble Magic Mountain East.

But, Bob says, phlegmatically, "My terror wasn't big enough. As the terror declined, I became less inclined to go elsewhere. I didn't want to drop all the Western culture that surrounded me, which I would have had to, to absorb Eastern disciplines."

His emphasis was and remained on the American-ness of his experience, and there may have been higher reason for that, too: There are many from the square world who are attracted to Monroe precisely because he doesn't have any sub-Continent hocus-pocus in his resume.

Monroe, the Left-Brained operator, was comfortable in New York, and opted to see the adventures through on his own. "The loneliness was assuaged by my rationale that what I was experiencing was not part of the Here and Now reality."

It would not have been difficult for Bob to beat a far more public drum than he has. In the early days, before J.Z. Knight and Ramtha, and Penny Torres and Mafu, Bob gave lectures and seminars before he gave courses. He could have used *JOOB* as a public relations springboard. He could have forced himself into public attention by writing articles. He could have scrambled for television time as a talking head on various esoteric subjects. He could, in short, have marketed himself far more successfully, as he had earlier marketed his radio productions. He could have inserted himself, much later, into the inner circle of the Institute of Noetic Sciences, the leading American metaphysical clearinghouse/think tank.

He chose not to do any of these things. He withdrew. The miles of taped exploration—both his own and those compiled by others—lie unused at the Institute. Except in the books and in his appearances in front of Institute groups, Bob rarely discusses the content of his voyages.

Bob's attitude is that he is available if anyone cares to drop by for a chat. Rarely does Bob Monroe pick up the telephone. And for this, too, there must be reason.

* * * *

Is the true significance of Bob Monroe's thirty years of Out-of-Body Experience that he should have flown in the Supra-Consciousness so he could act as a channel to pass the Knowledge on? Is Bob Monroe a teacher of the few?

Elmer Green says: "Bob's more a disciple, than a teacher. He's doing what Roberto Assagioli called "psychosynthesis." Real teachers no longer have to incarnate.

"Bob Monroe can instruct because his mediumistic body allows his mental, physical, and emotional energies to be separated."

Dr. Green's standards are exacting, and his vocabulary precise. If Elmer won't accept Bob Monroe as a teacher because he's too tangibly physical, less evolved humans might be allowed leeway to believe Monroe's mission has been to teach.

Has Monroe chosen or been forced into physical suffering on behalf of those who are guided to him to learn? Monroe shifts uncomfortably when the subject comes up. "It's all a matter of perspective. What I have... endured..." he stumbles over the word. "...is one form of learning, but no greater than, for instance, the man who has gone through military combat, been severely wounded, had his guts hang out, and been patched up. It's just a different experience."

Why did Bob choose this particular role? He has a typically-obscure explanation: "This little finger that I am is really only doing what I am supposed to be doing. I'm still the pumping station attendant.

"The real question is, what am I pumping?" The question, if there is, indeed, a question, would be whether Bob is imparting Knowledge or Technique. Bob thinks his role is to disseminate his technology. Others may feel that what he has discovered in his forays is just as important.

Monroe has taught much, and this is where his immediate significance lies. His example has reached thousands. He doesn't have prime-time ratings, and doesn't seek them. His is the late-night audience, or those who prefer reading or listening to goggling.

There is reason—although, of course, it cannot be proven—to think that the influence of Monroe's teaching is spreading. It's the ripple effect, but there is a more esoteric explanation for it, as well, propounded by Dr. Rupert Sheldrake, who attended a Monroe Gateway in 1983.

"If something like (morphic) resonance actually happens, then when patterns of activity are done in a similar way—as similarly as possible to the way they have been done before—then those who are doing the participating will indeed be put into a real type of connection with those who have done them before, right back to the very first time they were done." [2]

In simple contrast, Bob Monroe puts it this way: "If it can be done once, it can be repeated. If it can be done twice, it can be learned."

* * * *

Public awareness of Altered States of Consciousness is growing, perhaps more under-than overground, because it's still not a subject one can casually mention at a lunch counter in Nebraska. A quizzical Bill Moyers listens to the eminent Joseph Campbell discourse on myths and consciousness on Public Broadcastings System (PBS), and reflects polite Texan absorption with what Campbell has to say. But he deftly reflects that degree of incredulity which springs from a society of self-protective institutions, anchored in assumptions one is not encouraged to challenge.

There is some, limited scientific work being done to legitimatize the paranormal. Robert Monroe has welcomed and subjected himself to examination. Elmer and Alyce Green examine Rolling Thunder, Swami Rama, and Jack Schwarz.[3] Individuals who are well known in the field, Dr. John Lilly, Hal Puthoff, Russell Targ, "Blue" Harary, Joe McMoneagle, and many others, have subjected themselves to tests. Such scientists know there is something out There with which we can be (or are) in touch. They seek to devise ways to make their knowledge more palatable in the scientific pantheon of our society.

The Stanford Research Institute (now SRI International) is trying to push the frontiers of parapsychological acceptability ever farther by devising laboratory experiments which will intrigue and convince "straight" scientists, and through them, society at large. The Institute of Noetic Sciences uses its high profile to somewhat the same end. Isolated research units elsewhere strive to expand the borders of scientific recognition, usually with minimal funds at their disposal. Almost all of the big names in the field have at one time or another called on Bob Monroe to learn about and from him. Yet despite the warm regard with which he is held as a person, Monroe remains outside even the limited parapsychology establishment. He monitors its progress, but Bob is not part of the action.

Monroe has reluctantly come to realize the experiences of his pupils are the greatest validation he can expect, although he undoubtedly secretly would like to prove the unprovable before he departs.

Stuart Twemlow is blunt. Even today, "Bob's real role is pure research—playing around, like Elmer Green and Charley Tart in the good old days. Stuff like the Explorer tapes."

Sympathetic academics like Twemlow grumble that Bob's attention has wandered from the main goal, investigating. He is inconsistent, although no one contends that Bob is a dilettante. Monroe has a precious gift, they say, which could be of enormous benefit to mankind, if it were open to more outside scrutiny. Even admiring critics think Bob is overly-protective of self, yet they see the commercialization of his operations as a major shortcoming.

Raymond Waldkoetter, the U.S. Army psychologist who has known Bob since 1970, takes a worried look at the present and the immediate future. "If Bob hasn't already, he must soon articulate his objectives and insights for the long-range picture. His special knowledge must be shared in some fashion. It cannot be applied only when he is prepared to develop some new facet. His extrasensory gifts will need to be installed before his possible transformation beyond death."

* * * *

The subject of Bob Monroe's ego (in the colloquial sense) often comes up in discussion. Some say Bob has no ego, and they point to his willingness to share his techniques with any and all who find their way to the Institute. Others are well aware Bob has a very definite sense of his human as well as his non-physical self.

One of the Monroe paradoxes is that, when he is in the Left Brain function, he realizes that recognition is a "carrier wave for information. If that's ego, OK. We're entitled to it." When Monroe is operating from the Right Brain, he is notably selfless, humble, warm, totally giving.

It is remarkable that Monroe still genuinely underestimates his mystique and his magnetism. Yet it is a sign of the gentle Right Brain man that he is oblivious to the rapture he evokes in some of his audience. Even as he accepts heartfelt gratitude and affection, he seems silently to pass them on to those who have guided him.

Since about 1976, his life has been notable for the absence of people who have been able to stick with him over a period of time. Down deep, Bob recognizes he could have avoided the rebuffs and disappointments if he had compromised, but he didn't.

Lack of compromise is not necessarily a perjorative, even in this age. A few tested and proven friends can join him, because they appreciate, usually from their own experience, something of what he is about. He operates a system in which the fittest will rally around him, through no doing of his own, except his books.

What is now the Gateway Voyage program started out as Mentronics 5000: Bob wanted to train only that number of people in his techniques as a data base. It became apparent that demand was far more than that relative handful; it is on the increase and will probably gain more momentum.

If one accepts that Bob Monroe does truly live and experience a life beyond the ken of most of us, there is something more in his posture of exclusivity. Monroe's lack of worldly pride lies in his rejection of the role of leader, teacher, guru, or cultist—roles he could easily have claimed. But Bob is truly humble; how can anyone who has had Out-of-Body Experiences in such far reaches not be?

Until he reaches that invisible border at which he splits from society's ethic, Monroe gives of himself, as teacher. He makes as many of the soothing noises expected by society as he can. At the border, he turns to his pupils and says, "You've got the tools, you're on your own. Find out for yourself."

At that point, Bob's attitude swings to the exclusive and the private, self-centered. Society could charge him with disloyalty, exploitation, ignoring the code-of-conduct, refusing to fess up, etc. But Monroe shrugs indifferently. He has far more important fish to fry than to listen to the din of social expectation. He confides what he chooses in his books and his courses; the rest remains proprietary information.

Elmer Green regards Bob with friendly objectivity: "Bob Monroe's work is healthy as long as he doesn't leave out the compassion. He has the kind of power that can be grasped by the ego, and not used to benefit the group. If you work for humanity, you're OK."

Monroe counters, at another time and another place, that the concept of service does not necessarily apply only to humanity in physical life; it may be service elsewhere.

Stuart Twemlow has observed Monroe professionally and as a friend over a number of years: "Bob's knocking his head against the wall. He should concentrate on giving workshops, expanding the knowledge of his techniques, challenging the existing philosophy of science.

"He should ask himself if he isn't already successful enough," in terms of the extent to which his techniques have penetrated the culture. Twemlow continues, "Bob knows his tapes work. That should be enough."

Bob will always be a soloist. If he's part of a team, it's his team. Almost all of his remarkable catalogue of physical adventures were independent trials of courage. With the exception of a few early ventures in sports and music, Monroe has either been the leader of the band or gone off on his own in search of some other scores.

The Explorers were working for him when they formed that happy, selfless team at Whistlefield: "They brought me unqualified, joyous fun. It was eager participation, full-fledged sharing; satisfying pure curiosity, truly a team effort. No self-aggrandizement. We had no second-class citizens. For the first time, I had people I could talk with.

"I was dumping money into it, sure, but I didn't think of myself as a leader or boss type. I was the sparkplug." Yet the Explorers did nothing he had not pioneered. He took responsibility for the wellbeing of those who worked with him. He was the unquestioned commander of the squadron.

When dealing with the enormity of his personal voyage, Monroe often simply cannot bring others all the way along. It can be hinted at to some, but it cannot be adequately discussed in full. It can only be experienced, and there are few who have had even remotely parallel journeys. Some of them are in direct, physical contact with Monroe.

Monroe's real Being is the one that voyages to far reaches at still-unpredictable times. The pulls between his two main roles—even his two (or more) personalities—inevitably appear to be ego-exercises in the only arena visible to other humans. Monroe has to march to his own drummer, one heard from afar, not to the thump of society's tympany.

There is a reverse side to this coin, too, and it is an unfortunate—or, perhaps, purposeful—one. If purposeful, that intent is, however, obscure. It is that Bob, in the eyes of many of his admirers, as well as those who are not so enraptured of him and his work, must control everything around him, exclusively. His response is straightforward: "If someone else will take the responsibility, including paying the bills, he can have the authority."

Bob always makes a point of asking his students to report back. Many who have been at the Center do so; they usually get no acknowledgement or thanks. The information is perhaps read by Bob or Scooter, then put aside. It does not circulate to others who might find it useful or encouraging. The one-way information flow discourages many people from maintaining contact, or contributing their results more than once. Monroe responds, succinctly, "To get the information out as it should be done would take two more full-time people. It's a growing problem—how to pay for it. We just do the best we can."

* * * *

A major Monroe characteristic has been the exaggerated pull between Right and Left Brain functions, throughout his life. On the one hand, he is the gadget-minded hi-tech enthusiast, mechanical engineer, plane-and-glider pilot, financially-versed show biz producer-entrepreneur-businessman. On the other, the script-writer, musician, radio and TV director.

We are born with only Right Brain innocence, then spend much of our lives absorbing Left Brain rules and attitudes because they are what society demands. Now, restless Consciousness-neophytes devote much time trying to achieve enlightenment or awareness by shucking off the Left Brain rigidity they acquired along the way.

The peculiar aspect of this societal minuet, according to Bob Monroe, is that the Left Brain abilities anyone learns and practices Here are valuable There, and are even a primary reason the entity has come to Earth. It is not the material trappings which are valuable, but even the acquisitive techniques humans learn. In other words, one has to be able to survive in the physical, Left Brain society to be of value There.

Monroe calls Earth the Predator System, which formed even as the first living beings emerged. That system now threatens the continued existence of the human species. Will Mankind end its own existence through Left Brain excess? It can be hypothesized that too many entities have logged too many lifetimes in sharpening their addiction to wealth-power cycles; not enough are gathering the necessary Right Brain'ed escape velocity to save the Earth, and to graduate; the system has ruptured. It's morphic resonance proven to a fare-thee-well, in a rather nasty way.

The idea of surviving the Apocalypse is not new. Any number of religious sects have inner groups which are specially trained in survival. Concern about physical prevalence had its most widespread recent outbreak in the 1970s, and then, not only among Monroe's West Coast adherents. Most survivalist and self-sufficiency groups fall apart because of Right Brain-Left Brain disputes among their adherents.

Right Brain-Left Brain divergence in an individual can be a source of great discomfort, illness, even what society calls insanity. Overcoming the Right Brain-Left Brain dichotomy is one of the things the Monroe Institute's Gateway and Guidelines programs are all about; "Integrate!" is one of the keywords of Monroe-ism.

* * * *

Bob Monroe does not see himself as a part of the Consciousness Movement. He provides more conservative keys to reality than others, offered through glitzy mail order brochures, or sales extravaganzas. Monroe is also quick to repeat that he holds no exclusive access to Supra-Conscious Reality: "There are thousands of other ways to achieve the same thing."

But Bob has been out in front, leading quietly, from the beginning. He has stuck steadfast to his course, not jumped on bandwagons as they have started to roll. Monroe has never been trendy. He has always been intensely pragmatic, in a very pragmatic society.

Bob only began to encounter difficulty with the "leeches" of the New Age when he went public with his experiences. Before that, in the closed circle of the original Explorers and a few trusted outsiders, he had no need to erect defenses against criticism, attempts at takeover, and unwanted expectations.

Where Monroe differentiates himself from the mainstream of publicized New Age practitioners is that he has consistently tried to apply scientific method to himself and his techniques, while others simply don't bother. They sell, sell, sell; Monroe and his supporters softly underline the thousands upon thousands of pioneering, wearying lab hours that have gone into development of Hemi-Sync technology.

It is possible to make a distinction between soft and hard New Age. Another description might be frivolous and serious, although the frivolous branch is harmless, well-intentioned and admirable. It just lacks substance.

Monroe is one branch of serious, hard New Age or Consciousness. The person to whom Bob today most often appeals is the individual who has made a success of his workaday life, but feels an inner void. He or she is often hard-nosed: A seeker who wants to find the Inner Self, is prepared to pay the market price, and—often—intends to apply his new abilities in Left Brain situations.

Only, more often than not, something unexpected happens to the student as he goes through the Monroe course, and his life changes in ways he could not have predicted. Other people are retreads who come to Virginia after having sampled quick-fix New Age seminars, and found they do not provide lasting or deep assistance.

When he is in his tough, Left Brain "modality," Bob can come close to rejecting the soft New Age. He is dismayed by the contradiction that some say they have glimpsed the pristine vision he has seen, but seek to use it only for major material profit to themselves.

Bob Monroe has told people where he comes from, in *JOOB* and *FJ* and, for that matter, where he is going, in *UJ*. But still, most of Bob Monroe's problems with people have been the encumbering thoughts others have laid on him, and their beseeching of him to assume responsibility for themselves.

Monroe has consistently, coolly, unemotionally repeated, over and over, "Take what you get here. Practice it. Use it. Apply it in your daily lives." He doesn't have to add, "Take responsibility for yourselves."

* * * *

In *JOOB*, Bob Monroe wrote, "Three times I have 'gone' to a place I cannot find words to describe accurately. . . . To me, it was a place or a condition of pure peace, yet exquisite emotion. It was as if you were floating in warm soft clouds where there is no up or down, where nothing exists as a separate piece of matter. . . The cloud in which you float is swept by rays of light in shapes and hues that are constantly changing. . . All are familiar to you. This is where you belong. This is Home."[4]

During the early months of 1988, Bob Monroe was particularly occupied with the nature of enslavement: Human bondage to the institutions of our time—government, media, financial institutions—whatever form they might take. One chilly morning in February, he came to rest over sausage and eggs in a spick-and-span new coffeeshop across from the colonial courthouse of Amherst, Virginia.

"At the Institute, we're sometimes accused of brain-washing, but what's more an example of brain-washing than advertising? The techniques these days are so refined, they can get you when you think you're paying attention to something else. That's legal.

Try to stop it, and you'd have a fight on your hands.

"We are the latest victims of the Predator Society. And there doesn't seem to be any way out." If economies collapse and populations are winnowed, Bob thinks another form of Predator Society will inevitably eventually emerge: That the Aquarian Age, about which so much has been written, is an illusion; a construct of beseeching human minds.

The Aquarian Age is, in short, a "fallacy of the New Age. Unless the New Age can make the breakthrough which frees the human from being predators.

"The need is to circumvent those who prey on Mankind."

The way to circumvent or repulse the predators, both in the physical and non-physical realms, is positive, constructive, and beneficial Conscious Awareness. It's an unprovable certainty that others beside Bob Monroe have arrived at, both in times past and in the physical present.

* * * *

Bob and Nancy Monroe had a glorious time, playing with Dr. John Lilly in his sensory-deprivation flotation tank in the hills behind Malibu in the 1970's. Lilly, the serious scientist with an impressive track record, became a cult figure during the Hippie period, largely because of his work with dolphins. He and Monroe talked the same language, but Bob did not strike a responsive chord among the flower-and-drug culture of the early 1970's. Perhaps Bob's Guidance was different.

One question that always arises when people discuss Bob Monroe is the extent to which he is guided in his activities. Some people believe everything Monroe does in his Right Brain activity is at the behest of his Supra-Conscious self, or his Non-Physical Friends.

Bob says he has not always been in touch with the same "Helper," as such." His Helpers are usually not single entities, but clusters. "The whole Inspec series (in *Far Journeys*) is not operational any longer. That work is completed, from their point of view and mine. Any continued association would distort and be injurious to my life here.

"Now, I'm learning in other modalities, not a physical one.

"Once you're into them, they seem very real; you don't know they are a synthesis." The trips are not the same kind of local traffic OOB's as Monroe described in *Journeys Out of Body*.

It's this change in style, or level of understanding—or profundity—that makes the late 1980's Bob Monroe so hard to understand, and separates him from many of the more well-known oracles of our time. Bob's path of discovery has been a singular one, perhaps not meant for general dissemination. Whether this is Bob's own Supra-Conscious decision, or the action of Guidance at work is a question that perhaps even Bob cannot answer.

"I started this experience around 1983, when I began to write *Far Journeys*, and described as much of it as I could in the book.

"It's an exquisite freedom, which is equally difficult to write about. It's continuing."

Bob Monroe has been given a framework, or has had the courage to accept challenges proffered by his Non-Physical Friends: Challenges which would daunt many, if not most, of us.

Usually, a question has been made apparent to him, and then Bob's inner voice says, "Go on, dummy. Figure it out!" The solutions to the challenges have come to him, over long periods of suffering, trial and error, financial loss.

Although Bob Monroe today has difficulty describing his sources of learning There, they are probably not entirely dissimilar to those mentioned by Elmer Green and John Lilly, although, of course, Monroe uses no third-party, but is himself at one time, explorer, channel, and consumer of the information; and he receives his input in private. The ultimate source, for Monroe, Cayce, Lilly, J.Z. Knight, Penny Torres, and many others, appears to be similar, or much the same: There is a unanimity, in general outline, of the information humans obtain from Supra-Conscious sources.

* * * *

It's the getting to the ultimate source that is different, and perhaps here is where Helpers—or Angels, Protectors, Friends, Supervisors, Guides, Gods (the designation varies)—play a distinguishing role. It is possible the guides encountered by one individual may belong to a cluster which is considerably different from those which are tuned to the waveforms of other Supra-Conscious groups. Interpretations also may be different, and meanings may be shaded by the fact of transmission through the physical persona of the human channel.

This difference, too, may be theorized: As there may be levels of attainment in Consciousness, so there may be levels of knowing. The more important and belief-shaking the knowledge, the more centered, focussed, accomplished must be the person handling and disseminating it in full awareness. He must have been tested, again and again. He must be fearless. It takes proven courage, not only to go to the far reaches, but to confront awesome Truth. The physical-life transmitter cannot have been in mind-numb trance. He must witness and experience the information in a fully aware state, so he is convinced of the knowing himself, and so that he will be able to report effectively. Here, too, protective Helpers can assist, but the job of the transmitter is a gravely lonely one.

Monroe touched on it when he talked with the first H+ class. Someone brashly asked him if he were going to stay alive till the turn of the century.

Bob listened to the query, and his face instantly masked. He stared over the heads of the class, at a far wall, and then reluctantly but courteously, started to muse out loud. As he talked, he almost visibly gained balance. He cuddled his coffee cup, sighted along his plastic stirrer at the goal he, at first—as ever alone—had seen.

"Hang on till 2000, then go home for thousand years? That's pretty good. But I'd still have one last loop around. I don't want to spend another thousand years in the loop—even if it's only a hiccup. I'd have that one final run to make....

Someone interjected: "Is there anything about this we would understand?"

"No, nothing you would understand with this consciousness.

"I currently tell Gateway participants my goal was to be in the service of humankind. Then, because of some contact with some Non-Physical Friends, I understood there could be another goal.

"H+ is the (my) major effort to introduce a coordinated system."

If Bob Monroe's primary role since 1958 has been to provide one conduit for the current increase in consciousness by perfecting Gateway and, latterly, Guidelines, the above passage may indicate that, starting about the mid-1970s, he also began slowly to develop a secondary approach to something broader than what is usually meant by the word "consciousness."

The parallel path has resulted in the H+ program which is distinguished from the others by the fact that it is designed for all, and does not require any previous conscious attainment, in the usual sense of the word. If Gateway provides access to consciousness, H+ is an avenue to mastery.

The Russells of Cambridge advance a theory that the opening of H+ marks Bob's transition from the role of pure engineer-technologist to the spiritually-evolved seer. Bob admits that by about 1985, he had all the information he needed. Presumably by then, he had ended the long quest for his own identity. The broad-based H+ program is the result.

* * * *

In his seventies, Bob Monroe is ending three decades of mind-numbing discernment. *Ultimate Journey* is an attempt to "convert a Belief System into a Know System: It's a hard-nosed look at the fear of death. But, do I tell it like it is, or like most people want to hear?"

As he discussed the thrust of the book with relatives and friends, Bob found himself under increasing pressure to tell it like it is, not to gloss over the discomfiting aspects of his experiences There, which had been his initial inclination, and which fly in the face of Society's belief system. One of his confidants challenged him: "Who are you to decide what people are able to take and what they shouldn't see? Put it all in, and let them decide."

Bob yielded, but the decision cost him time. "In a book like this, you've got to watch every word, because they quote you out of context." It was slow going, well into 1989, but Monroe was determined to write the truth as he experienced it, gruelling and unsettling though it might prove to others.

Bob described *UJ* thus: "People won't be able to say it's fantasy, because there's too much reality to it. The basic premise is that the Truth does set you free. That illusions bind you.

"Their Right Brains will say, 'I've been living under these conditions all this time?' And then maybe they'll begin to understand the nature of this reality, at least."

Bob Monroe remarks, "One of my Non-Physical Friends asked, 'Why are you people so concerned about death? It's nothing compared to the agony, noise, shock of being born.'

"We are more than our physical bodies.

"The OOB is a birth process," Bob continues.

"Once you get past the early fear barrier, you'd be surprised at the difference it makes."

* * * *

Peter Russell wrote *The Global Brain* before he was aware that Bob Monroe had done precisely what he had in mind: Taken the basics of Biofeedback, and constructed a technique on them, using good sound waves as a medium, to enable novices to leap into The All.

Bob simplifies and reiterates his refrain to the novices who come to the Center, "You might set out wanting to climb the mountain. But on the way, you find a nice looping path, and it leads you down into a valley. The valley's pretty attractive, so you decide to stay there a while. Or maybe you just like the path, so you stay on it, but don't quite get to the ridge." It's the searching that counts. And the lingering to make unexpected discoveries along the way. "That's part of the learning system. You can live Here better, and take more with you when you go."

Sometimes his voice nudges students to a threshold from which their altered-consciousness takes them to a close approximation of the clinical Near Death Experience. They emerge with the confidence of first-stage Knowledge. Once the student gets past fear, he can go as far as he chooses.

In contrast to Monroe's at-times threatening, disagreeable experiences while exploring, the majority of Monroe Institute students have pleasant, even euphoric voyages. There are some who automatically become Explorers: "The rare ones who come along and take to Focus 21, and then start to look around. They have the greatest promise, because they have curiosity."

If they have overcome their fears, Gateway graduates face an unsettling problem, especially when they leave the comforting cocoon of the Center. "Did what I saw really happen? Can I continue to believe it out here in the "real world?" What is real?"

Unless they are prepared to work on their Supra-Conscious with steadfast devotion, many find their experiences at home often fall off. Expanded exploration takes time and intense concentration; Real World concerns dominate daily life and thought; society demands conformity. There's no one to talk to. They are on their own with their guides, but without Bob.

* * * *

What is Bob Monroe really doing in his Out-of-Body exploration now, in his seventy-fourth year? As Bob replies, his eyes glaze over in that now-familiar sign of detachment.

"It's a testing. If I don't learn something, it is repeated. In some ways, it's far more difficult than any physical matter tests.

"I'm not doing it against my will. I have foreknowledge of the learning system. But I don't know the pain of learning in advance."

Why does Monroe, still at it after thirty years of OOB's, continue to encounter downright unpleasantness There at times? "I take my Left Brain with me. I don't necessarily accept what I perceive. I'm still in an exploring mode." He switches to an illustration that harks back to his youthful theatre days.

"I have a tendency to go backstage to see how they built the sets. If I were emotionally involved with the illusion, I would be anguished by the sight of the flats and the cyclorama." The stage manager wants to keep some of his tricks secret, and rebuffs the inquisitive Monroe.

"In encountering a difficult illusion, sometimes I'll meet an intelligent non-physical Being. He approaches me, not necessarily in a hostile mode. Really, he doesn't care." The stranger is, in other words, as curious or as indifferent as is Monroe himself.

"To a great extent, what I have encountered is not within our human belief system structures." The engineer adds, "I've been as pragmatic or objective as possible in my observations of these adventures.

Monroe glances down at his stubby fingers, made to grip a steering wheel. "It's like I know there's a truck around that curve. I can't see it, but I know it's there.

"I'm pulled into the curve, but I'm not going to slow down. I could willfully say no, I don't want to continue around that bend."

But Monroe doesn't say no. His sense of adventure and curiosity are still high. And, perhaps most important, he has overcome fear.

"There are no landmarks, now, on these trips. They have no relationship to time/space activities.

"It's direct-experience type stuff. I'll give you an illustration, but it's only a poor comparison." Another analogy from his past as a competitive driver follows.

"It's as if you were driving a sports car around a racing track: The trick is to go around at a certain high speed and stay on the circuit, not spin-out.

"Any number of things can happen to make it difficult. You learn as you go round, and you increase your speed.

"You keep trying to do it until you're able to complete the course in a specified time.

"The race course is impersonal, just as the Universe is. It's not there to kill you. There's competition out There, but the competitors don't care about me. They're just trying to compete, not to kill me, although that's part of the game, too. They are just as impersonal."

Elmer Green says of Bob, "If he doesn't have to go through the thousand-year cycle, it's because he has taken the First Initiation. When you get to the Fifth Initiation, you have taken control of all the cells of your body. That's when you can really move through walls."

Monroe has never identified another human being in his current travels. The entities he has observed There are from other civilizations.

"It's as if we're talking about two entirely different things.

"Everything I have encountered is a total stranger. Some of them are teams, or clusters.

"The whole thing has nothing to do with Earth activities. I don't see how I could possibly integrate the experiences I have There with life Here."

* * * *

Once, Monroe seemed to toy with Mike D'Orso, a reporter for a Norfolk paper, who was doing a piece for the Sunday magazine. Where did we come from? Who or what established and guides this system, this planet, this Universe?

'Just somebody having some fun,' he says.

Somebody?

'Some intelligent energy field.'

Energy field?

'An energy being. Something the average human would call God.

'There are graduates from this school of compressed learning we call Earth who are doing this in other places,' he says. 'It's a lot of fun, creating species, weaving just the right delicate balances for life on a planet.'

Monroe knows how much fun it can be, he says, because he has seen it.

'Just a small demonstration,' he says of the energy-being who escorted him during one of his OOB's. The being, says Monroe, created a solar system for Monroe's viewing pleasure.

'It was as if someone was making it snow, and creating snowballs, and tossing them out like fiery suns, as it were. Just having fun.

It was, in fact, just fun and games, says Monroe, that got the whole ball rolling here on Earth. The consciousness that created Earth, says Monroe, began tinkering with its toy, decided to try out its creation firsthand, in human form, and things got out of hand.

'To really feel how it is, it had to get down into it. Only it didn't figure out the addiction of life as a human. It thought it was in for a quick shot and out. But things don't happen that way.'

So all this is a result of an accident, or a great cosmic mistake?

'Not a mistake,' says Monroe, 'an experiment.' [6]

Bob Monroe actually was not playing with the incredulous, quizzical reporter; he was speaking from experience, as a keeper of the knowledge, a Merlin who exudes Love but simultaneously remains remote, as if there were that elastic fence surrounding him: It gives a little bit, invisibly, then snaps back into its protective place. The inscrutable mask goes up behind the fence, and the bystander asks, "Did I see and hear right?"

* * * *

Back at the Gift House, Bob heaves into a comfortable position on the sofa in front of the fireplace. The TV zapper lies untouched on the table. Dan Rather has done his gloomy best, "Wheel of Fortune" and "Jeopardy" have played their games, and there isn't a football match-up in sight.

Bob talks quietly of the consensus of reputable seers, channelers, people of insight, that grave times are ahead as the millennium wanes.

"My Non-Physical Friends tell me practically every day: 'Don't you see it? It's coming. The Wave of Change is building. It's visible now, and it's going to get a lot bigger.' "

Is Bob, at root, talking about Earth Changes, such as those channeled by Edgar Cayce, in the sense of massive geological upheaval?

"It doesn't look like it, as it's presented to me. I see empty cities. Economic collapse. My Friends tell me, 'If you believe anything less, you're kidding yourself.'

"Our economy is based on the fact that if we don't buy more in 1990 than we did in 1989, the country's in trouble. We're conned into unnecessary buying.

"Our "democracy" allows the predators to work, because 'that's the way it always has been.'

"All men are not created equal. One Man, One Vote is a concept we have been sold emotionally.

"How much pressure can our civilization take?

"When too many pots boil over....

"I think we have ten years, maximum...We're a domino system.

"The message is, 'Enjoy what you have now. Now's the time. Soon enough there won't be any.' "

Is the Supra-Conscious issuing a license to be escapist, hedonistic, thus encouraging the Decline and Fall? That, of course, was not the intent. It was a purely personal message for Bob Monroe.

Why did Monroe not go public with warnings? Others have been saying the same.

Bob Monroe's answer is that only an increase in appreciation of Higher Consciousness can help, "But I don't know of any single event that would cause even an appreciable segment of the population to achieve Conscious awareness.

"The second coming of Jesus? The media would tear him apart.

"The scientists would say, "We need to test him before we can accept him."

Those are words of someone who might be called the rankest cynic. Yet Bob Monroe's statement merits examination. Serious people are convinced he does voyage to There and come back with information which is arguably not solely of his own imagining.

"The only way you can superimpose another reality on humans is to hit them repeatedly with that two-by-four between the eyes."

When *Ultimate Journey* is in full circulation, the ritualistic God-Fearing of this world will probably turn on Monroe. Who, they will ask, is this singular individual who dares to set himself up as a heretic propagandist?

Their pained outcries won't be as unsettling as some of the more basic issues raised by Monroe's outright questioning of the God concept.

Bob would never engage in a doctrinal argument with a believer in God. As always, he says, "Don't take it from me; go out there and see for yourself," which is a very humble suggestion. He even gives Gateway students the key to the Library, the repository of all knowledge. It's not the act of an ego-driven dogmatist who has much to protect.

Monroe probably truly wishes others could join him out There to overcome the loneliness of his position, and report back to Mankind what they learn.

Monroe's quiet contention is that he has gone beyond belief to the Knowing. The inevitable question then arises, in our society: 'How can you know? Prove it!' To which there can be no more definitive answer than to someone else's "knowledge" of God: Is my knowledge superior to yours?

Where Monroe's Beyond-God construct is more easily open to debate is in his concept that the Universe is impersonal. It implies that there is no benificence and that there are no miracles. Yet there is a body of data, ranging from the certified miracles of the Roman Catholic Church to mystical healing to the inexplicable, "ordinary" events at work in the lives of many, that seem to indicate one or more watchful, beneficial presences.

Bob does not dispute that great and small miracles do happen in the existence of many people. He is likewise a firm believer in what may be called faith-self-healing, although he attributes such "miracles" to the work of the Supra-Conscious, not to any external "spiritual" power.

If the Universe is impersonal, as Monroe describes it, can there be loving, protective "Spirits", "Guides", "Angels", or "Gods" who care for and guide the physical human? Monroe has flatly told Gateway audiences the main task of the non-physical Friends is to protect and help the Explorers.

If people were able to overcome their inculcated defenses and try to accept what they could understand of Bob's own Know System, there would still be the problem of language. All of what he observes and all communication when Bob is exploring is non-verbal. Translation into human language and therefore into our understanding is difficult at best.

"Too often, we don't look beyond the experience; we get wrapped up in local traffic vocabulary and rules.

"Anything less than catastrophe probably won't change our awareness. I secretly think that's why it's going to happen."

* * * *

Many of the early pioneers of Consciousness used LSD which, in laboratory quality and quantity, proved useful as a mind-liberating hallucinogenic, as well as helpful in the treatment of some mental illness. Its subsequent banning was a hysterical, if understandable, over-reaction to the quality of underground LSD and the bad or fatal trips it caused in casual experimenters.

What do the drugs of today's culture do? Crack and crystal, cocaine, heroin, even marijuana and hash, all liberate the user from the perceived "reality" of his situation, although they do not induce the same Altered State as LSD. The most common mind-altering chemical is, of course, alcohol.

* * * *

There is much in Bob Monroe's personality which hints at the addictive. He is compulsive and a perfectionist. He is deeply emotional. He has had great difficulty in getting rid of his sense of responsibility for others. He's a workaholic.

He continues to smoke when he well knows he should not. The list can stretch on at some length. Bob refuses alcohol, having experienced it and known its mind-dimming effects; he feels genuinely upset when he sees booze working in others.

Many practicing alcoholics and drug-addicts are fully aware, while they are practicing, that they are effectively on the road to suicidal death. They have looked over the brink, perhaps even been in the chasm, and survived—for reasons which often baffle them. For some, the bottoming-out process just prior to entering Alcoholics Anonymous, Narcotics Anonymous, or one of the other addiction programs is equivalent to a Near Death Experience (NDE).

Dr. Kenneth Ring, in *Heading Toward Omega* underlines the spiritual component in the post-NDE lives of his subjects. The description of the ways in which the lives of some have changed as a result of their NDE's are remarkably similar to the change that takes place among some members of AA and other Twelve-Step programs.

What can probably be said is that prolonged exposure or addiction to chemical substances is one avenue of preparation for a re-evaluation of the individual's spiritual beliefs and, perhaps, a considerable change in the pattern of his life.

The theory that addiction is actually a form of spiritual quest in itself seems quietly to be growing in acceptance. No one knows how many AA members have experienced, before or during recovery, peak-moment "spiritual awakenings," or what others might call "transcendent experiences."

AA could be viewed as one access road to the Supra-Conscious. Among those who truly recover are many who form a quiet, resilient, calm, balanced, often-fearless element in our society, serenely in touch with and guided by their Higher Power.

The turnabouts that recovery from addiction and NDE's seem to provoke, in turn, are also similar to those some Monroe students experience.

Bob Monroe chose not to propagate his methods broadly, after the early days. He deals in a field which is far less easily identifiable than alcoholism, drugs, overeating, or any of the other addictions, except one: the addiction to life itself.

If pursued, Monroe's techniques offer the same kind of accommodation with physical life that AA provides, even if Monroe adamantly refuses to call his a "spiritual program."

Bob Monroe's technology is another access channel to a way of physical life that is balanced, where so many of our lives lack that element. Further, Monroe's techniques offer what might be called an alternative to the addiction to physical-life, in helping the student rid himself of fear of the unknown, accumulate escape velocity, and eventually get to There.

* * * *

A number of people who listened to Bob talking in various settings during the latter part of 1987 and early 1988 felt sure he had recently experienced some kind of a spiritual awakening, or that his view of the "spiritual" had changed. Bob's answer is elliptical.

"I'll talk about 'spiritual' with anyone, if he can define what he means by the word. Is it a synonym for growth? The kind of growth I recognize doesn't seem to fit.

"I do know that the concept of the Ultimate God watching over you is not my department. There is something very much wrong with that picture, to me.

"It's like five hundred years from now, the remnants of the human race may revere the automobile. They won't know what it was used for, but they'll know it did something, and they'll worship it.

"So it is with prayer today."

Bob Monroe's voice drops to the barely audible, as he leans forward over a formica table strewn with left-over crinkle french fries.

"I have an open option. I can stay in the physical, or I can leave. I can say, 'I've had enough of this.' I think I can make my exit at any time.

"I'm not sure what keeps me here. It's as if I'm waiting for something. . . waiting for some event.

"I have no idea what the event will be. . . all I know is that it is one major event that I have yet to experience.

"Strain? Yes and no. But I'm acclimated to it. . . ." And Bob Monroe's voice trails off.

If Monroe is reluctant to talk about spirituality, or even abrasive in his allusions to it, many of his graduates are not. In fact, as previously noted, many—perhaps even an overwhelming majority—wish there were some active spiritual component or guidance in the Monroe courses, to help them integrate what happens to them in the Chec Units.

Again, there is a correlation between the results—for some—of working with Monroe's tapes and the "core experience" of Dr. Kenneth Ring's NDE'ers. Monroe issues a challenge for a definition of spirituality, but Ring has come up with a modest one—a synthesis from the experiences of his subjects—which seems highly adequate and applicable. Ring calls the experience a "Universalistically Spiritual Orientation," and defines its seven elements thus:

1. A tendency to characterize oneself as spiritual rather than religious per se.

2. A feeling of being inwardly close to God.

3. A de-emphasis of the formal aspects of religious life and worship.

4. A conviction that there is life after death, regardless of religious belief.

5. An openness to the doctrine of reincarnation (and a general sympathy toward Eastern religion).

6. A belief in the essential underlying unity of all religions.

7. A desire for a religion embracing all humanity. [7]

There would probably not be many Monroe graduates who would find major objections to the above compendium, although Bob might.

The intriguing, unanswerable question is why Monroe bends so far over backwards to avoid even acknowledgement of the spiritual element his courses seem almost involuntarily to bring into, or reinforce in, people's lives.

Upbringing? Live-and-let-live philosophy? Don't-tread-on-me individuality? Or is it that, in his Ultimate Journey beyond God, Monroe has found no hint of loving comfort in the impersonal Universe, and therefore rejects what he may see as the deistic coddling of the lower, close-in planes of exploration? Few have gone as far as he in their Altered-State contemplation. Most of us stay fairly close to this planet, where the guideposts are, perhaps purposefully, still pretty familiar.

Here is one of Dr. Ring's salient comments on NDE's:

(They), in my view, represent a brief but powerful thrust into higher state of consciousness. . . . However, the NDE is not a breakthrough that occurs as a result of a long period of voluntary spiritual training. Rather it is an involuntary and sudden propulsion, usually without warning or preparation, into a realm of profound spiritual illumination. . . . A journey into higher consciousness, I am saying, has effects that are independent of the way it is attained. [8]

Kenneth Ring extrapolates from his deep study of Near Death Experiencers. Bob Monroe's students often have similar experiences; those experiences—that knowledge of differing scenarios and choices—can be tapped, using Monroe's techniques.

If there is no Time and no Space, other dimensions exist, parallel to ours; each is a tiny milli-iota of the energy-knowledge—and the dimensions—available in The All.

* * * *

The other side of Bob Monroe's loneliness is the exhilaration of exploring the unknown: "It's an exquisite freedom, which is equally difficult to write about. When you take the fear-induced concepts out, things have a different texture."

The man who can't talk spiritual says, "I turned it over to my Higher Self, and I felt more free."

A major limitation on the joy of exploration is the ego of the physical self. "We don't like to admit it," says Bob Monroe, "but it's there and has to be overcome.

"You have to use your antenna. When you meet a luminous being, you wake up a little bit.

"When you resonate with that Light Figure, you can't even talk about it." It's the most isolating of all factors.

"We keep looking for Big Brother; but if we find him, we resent Him." Searching the Supra-Consciousness for what most would consider spiritual truth isn't, per se, an answer. "The relationship with the greater consciousness pattern isn't the way we have the illusion it is.

"Where does that leave us? I'd suggest you note how great your investment in the established belief system is.

"The biggest temptation is to attribute a great mystical pattern to the entire physical/non-physical Universe." Engineers don't like to admit they can believe in something that defies neat explanation.

"The Left Brain can chew, devour, divine the meaning of what you experience, then calculate it."

* * * *

Even if Bob Monroe would like to be known simply as a disinterested bystander who reports his findings, he is also a self-designated "revolutionist" who records events and theories the establishment has great difficulty in swallowing.

He has chosen or been selected to be an up-front, resident iconoclast, or has set himself up as a target. By whom? The answer to that question depends on your perception of the Universe.

"The basic illusion is: Love will conquer all. It's ongoing propaganda."

There's only sadness as Bob says that. It's part of the Monroe paradox, too: when operating out of his Right Brain, Bob gives forth that almost overpowering sense of unreserved love for all those within his range.

Bob's adamant statement would horrify New Agers, who feel there is too much "talking from the head," not enough "from the heart." The New Age, whatever its other shortcomings, pins much faith and a lot of practice time on the spreading of Love and Light—heart over mind. Some believe that Rupert Sheldrake's morphogenic resonance theory is actually now operating in this energy field, and that it has caused a delay in the apocalyptic changes we on this planet have scripted for our habitat and ourselves.

Bob Monroe muses, "If you put ten scientists in a room, only two might be able to accept Sheldrake. The culture cuts too deeply." It's a flat comment from a man who has felt rejection deeply.

"No single individual can change what's coming. Nor even any group."

Bob Monroe is at the very least a human being to whom remarkable things have happened which make him a link between levels of consciousness not generally experienced, and our own mundane life.

Very, very few if any have chosen to venture far out on Monroe's Interstate alone, to risk the fears, rebuffs, bruising, rejection, pain, agony, and loneliness the exploration has cost Monroe.

If nothing else, Bob's courage makes him worthy of recognition and respect.

* * * *

It's obviously impossible to fit Bob Monroe into any tidy, grounded category. Too many people, over the years, have in effect said, simply, "Oh, Bob Monroe? Sure. Nice guy. Great theories, but they don't really fit in with what anyone else is doing." In fact, by using our imaginations, it is possible to develop a hypothesis which makes Monroe and his work potentially of great significance in our physical world. The wonder is that he has been so ignored by so many for so long.

There are those who will always claim that Bob has a wild imagination or has intriguing hallucinations and capitalizes on them in his books and training courses. Their comforting rationale is that Monroe ranks with Jules Verne or H.G. Wells, or perhaps Isaac Azimov and Tom Robbins, and should be treated as an author of fiction; or, better still, ignored. Others may claim that he is a charlatan who foists dubious "knowledge" on willing supplicants. If either or both charges are true, where's the proof?

Against them, however, are several arguments. The most persuasive is that thousands of people have gone through Monroe's Gateway, have had experiences which defy Left-Brain "logic," and have thereafter registered remarkable change in their lives. Other thousands—perhaps, over the years, tens of thousands, from all over the world—have written Bob words of profuse thanks that his books have assured them they are not alone in their OOB experiences; that they truly are more than their physical bodies.

These two groups are best exemplified in the simple statement of one student: "I don't care if he's a fraud or not, he has helped me." It underlines the truism that any judgment on Bob Monroe has to be subjective.

On the surface, Bob's Hemi-Sync courses and tapes provide members of the public who wish to use them with a method of learning Self, of coming to terms with fear, perhaps of doing some entertaining voyaging and gaining some spiritual guidance. Who gets to a Monroe course is a matter of accident, just as it was an accident that Monroe—and Whitley Strieber—had the experiences they have written about. Or that people have Near Death Experiences.

Cynics whose fears bind them tightly to religious, academic, scientific, political, and/or financial institutions, will always find it upsetting to try to accept the manner of thought exemplified by Monroe and others in the transpersonal world. "Professional" guilds and associations—from the American Medical Association to the National Rifle Association—provide cozy, self-buttressing fortresses for their initiates and impose their belief systems on society; people are told they must abide within the boundary limits dictated by arbitrary priests of the various righteous temples. If you sortie outside those limits, you may find truths which could undermine the establishments' comforting, protective, all-inclusive walls. It was a lesson the founders of the science of Chaos had to learn the hard way as they innovated, scrounged for computer-time and money, and began to scream for recognition.

One of Bob Monroe's basic precepts is: "Man has no limitations." Time and again, people who have been through a Gateway course or had a similar experience say, "I found I had no boundaries."

Those professional observers who are open-minded are convinced that Monroe has at least had experiences which are genuine to him, and that they are a step in the search to establish an acceptable science of psi. They also accept that Monroe's techniques allow others to have subjective experiences which transcend the readily understandable.

* * * *

Is Bob Monroe a Walk-In? The concept is generally credited to the writer Ruth Montgomery, but has been discussed elsewhere by people interested in inexplicable phenomena.[9] It is one of the lesser myths of our time.

Monroe himself rejects the suggestion that he is a spirit who has taken over someone's physical body. His memory of his own childhood is too clear, he says, to support such an argument. "I have too many of the characteristics I started with.

"If the Walk-In exists, I have never encountered one. It's only a speculative concept."

But then, he continues, "What's the difference between a Ramtha and a Walk-In? Ramtha could easily say, 'I'm going to stay. JZ can't have her body back.'

"Or the difference between Walk-Ins and the centuries-old idea of possession?

"Or, to be more concrete, what's the difference between Walk-Ins and people who have multiple personalities? Who are those people?

"I could easily see that 'Walk-In' is another way of explaining how just one of the many personalities in all of us takes over.

"There is ten times as much supporting data for the multiple personality explanation as there is for the Walk-In concept."

In the next breath, Monroe makes a typically paradoxical statement. One of the tests some people apply to see whether an individual is a Walk-In, is the degree of emotional attachment the person has to events in his past. If he feels little emotion about major happenings which "normally" would arouse strong feelings, well then, perhaps he is a Walk-In.

Bob says: "Look at my peak experiences: I don't have the emotional input when I recall them. I remember the emotions of the time, but the emotions themselves don't arise again."

But is the 'Walk-In' perhaps a way of describing another phenomenon?

* * * *

There is one aspect of psi investigation which is widely known and which forms part of this mosaic.

An appreciable proportion of the population believes there might be visitors from other planets among us. Some think certain humans might have been abducted by space visitors, or inoculated and otherwise influenced by what are often called Extra-Terrestrials. There is a still-growing literature on the subject.

Whitley Strieber is pursuing a line of investigation which may well shed more light on some aspects of the phenomenon he has encountered.

Dr. Kenneth Ring takes the general subject seriously enough to be conducting a study on Unidentified Flying Object (Ufo) abductees: "Both Near-Death Experiences and Ufo close encounters," he argues, "are transcendental experiences that bring about a profound spiritual reorientation in those who undergo them." In both, he says, a similar sequence of events is reported in case after case. He plans to do "a careful comparative study" of Ufo contactees, but in the meantime, he is willing to bet that they, like NDE survivors, are "the leading edge, lifting the planet to a higher evolution." [10]

Bob Monroe is not an Extra-Terrestrial nor the physical incarnation of a delegate from an Unidentified Flying Object, nor is there any evidence at all he has been abducted, inoculated, had implants and then been returned to physical life by a Ufo.

Monroe says of Ufo's, "I have a hard time handling the government secrecy. It's a great mystery to me. It's impossible to have that much smoke over thirty years without some fire, some place." He cites examples from his own circle of acquaintances: reliable, experienced pilots who so routinely sight Ufo's, they don't bother to fill out the immediately-classified government forms any longer.

"The idea that they're a visual manifestation of another part of the Universe is very acceptable to me.

"Why they're here is another story.

"I don't subscribe to the 'space brothers' theory. The Universe is far too impersonal for that. It's not necessarily benevolent, except in the same way we treat our dogs and cats.

"We're no more than an interesting planet. A curiosity.

"I have no desire to go to the other end of the Universe. The other planets don't interest me. I've made no recent attempt to go to Mars or Arcturus 25. They're as bad off, or as well off, as we are.

"I haven't played around in Time/Space for a long time. It's like, how you gonna keep me down on the farm, now that I've seen Paree? The physical Universe is the farm for me."

But part of Bob Monroe's legacy are keys which may help us understand and put to positive use some remarkable phenomena which are happening all around us.

Carry the example into the realm of super-computers and the people who operate them. What would their perceptions, their theories, their concepts be if they had the freedom of simultaneous access to Supra-Consciousness while working at their keyboards, or dreaming up new programs?

No one would wish the scientists of Chaos to volunteer for true Near Death Experiences. Nor do they have to bottom-out as the result of a chemical addiction.

The quickest way they can get in touch with the liberating Supra-Conscious is by using Bob Monroe's techniques—a technology which is as close to the scientific method as there is available, and therefore appealing to their own bent of mind. The possibilities are fascinating to contemplate.

* * * *

If the blocks to progress along the Interstate to Supra-Consciousness can be identified as, generally, twofold, we have made some progress. The first obstacle is our attachment to that which we know in physical life, indeed, our addiction to life as we know it: The comfort of belonging to various groups, of having the tangible evidence of material well-being, of "fitting-in" or conforming to what society expects of us. Monroe, the revolutionist, quietly urges his students to be more than their physical selves—to break out of society's mold. It takes one kind of courage.

The second obstacle to progress is fear, and it comes in many more than the old fifty-seven varieties. We are literally riddled with fears. The advertising to which we voluntarily submit plays on our anxieties about health, hygiene, financial security, conformism, acceptability—on-and-on, in a litany of "life-or-death," socially-acceptable musts.

It might be argued that there are two levels of fear. The first, fairly readily identifiable, is the level of social fear, above, with which we are drearily familiar, and by which we are hamstrung.

The second level of fear is Fear of Death . . . Fear of the Unknown. Remember the childhood warning, "If you don't do such-and-such, the bogeyman will get you?"

Bob Monroe talks of the impersonal Universe and, drily, unemotionally, recounts experiences he has had in which non-physical entities have jolted him, perhaps without meaning to. They were just going about their business, as he was.

Bob says, 'Go away, you don't bother me,' and continues his Supra-Conscious journey. Recall the race-track analogy: No driver is out to maim another, but accidents happen. Bob says, in effect, 'They're all part of the game. The other drivers have their job, I have mine.'

Budd Hopkins ends *Missing Time,* his investigation of Ufo abductions, with this statement: "I have no solutions to the open-ended problems (his book raises), and least of all to the profound issue of their human toll. I do not believe the Ufo phenomenon is malign or evilly-intentioned. I fear, instead, that it is merely indifferent, though I fervently hope to be proven wrong." [11]

There are many humans who are not as courageous as Monroe—people who carry their fears with them constantly in physical life, and, when they make their first moves into the Altered State of Consciousness.

Their fears are so deep-rooted, they think they open themselves to the negative, exploitative curiosity of grasping entities. Whereas it is entirely possible they are, in effect, dreaming-up these entities as part of their cultural construct—a carryover from the fright in which they live their physical lives. They have not protected themselves by confronting fear. The self-sustaining chink in their armor is the black hole of fear.

The formula is simple and effective, and has been used countless times by people far less experienced than Bob Monroe. It is merely a refusal to give in to fear.

Few people who open themselves wholly to the Monroe experience harbor fear thereafter, including fear of the unknown. Likewise, few who have been through the Monroe Institute have had bad trips. Bob has pioneered, worked through the levels of fear, and signposted the way, so the rest of us could follow along his Interstate without being subjected to the abject terror and the rough rides he took.

Abandoning of fear, concommitantly, clears the way for the human to attain pure Higher Conscious Awareness, where he is protected and meets truly beneficial, loving entities from dimensions which elude our easy definition. Monroe provides a dual key: Loss of fear and the positive Gateway Affirmation which, seen in this light, is incredibly important.

Once again, it must be reiterated Monroe's is not the only way. Yoga will eventually get its conscientious follower to Higher Consciousness. Various forms of Buddhism will achieve it, with time. A Near Death Experience, or a severe bout with chemical dependency may do so. Teachers of various schools, including some Western religious thought, can achieve the same aim. That there are many ways is a testament to the diversity of life and culture on this planet.

But Robert Monroe offers a path which seems almost designed to suit Twentieth Century America. Many could usefully follow it, to search without dogma, to demystify the seemingly-ominous, and to explore constructively the other dimensions hypothesized by Carl Jung, Jacques Vallee and others.

If we follow this readily-available path, we as a species might learn from the universal mind, of which we are a part, much to our advantage. We might be then in a position to head for the what Peter Russell and others call the Fifth Evolution.

* * * *

A proportion of Dr. Kenneth Ring's sample of core-experience NDE subjects had what he termed "Prophetic Visions (PVs)." In *Heading Toward Omega,* Ring synthesizes these visions. His subjects sometimes saw the entirety of Earth's history, but their future-view was short, and generally contained images of massive geological shifts and climatic change, followed by economic-political-military upheaval, leading to what many think of as the Aquarian Age.

Decades earlier, Edgar Cayce channeled the approach of massive "earth changes." There was a consistent drumroll of apocalyptic warnings during the 1970s. Monroe Institute Explorer Tape No. 9, reports much the same information from two sources: Tom Campbell and his Helper, Thor, recorded in September 1976; and Shay St. John with Miranon, around the same time. It was in that psychological atmosphere that the Feathered Pipe Gateway group decided to try to buy Rainbow Ranch as a refuge and West Coast center. Ramtha, Mafu, and other channels today often give similar, dire warnings. Skeptics will immediately pounce to note that dates have come and gone, and the Earth still exists, its poles where they were yesterday, the continents still in their accustomed places.

Dr. Ring's subjects who had PV's almost unanimously predicted catastrophe in 1988. That same time-frame has cropped up in many other prognostications.

Bob Monroe and others who deal with non-physical Friends underline that they are not very good at time, since they don't deal in it themselves. And, they will add, the time factor is not the important one. Human behavior is.

The Altered-State warnings are unanimously directed to Mankind. They appeal for calmer, more balanced, selfless and loving behavior, and emphasize that the attainment of a state of collective Supra-Consciousness is the way to achieve planetary and individual survival. It is the path to the Global Brain sketched by Peter Russell.

One school of thought points out that, towards the end of each century or millennium, people get anxious; prognosticators promise Doomsday. According to this theory, it is a matter of scale, but there is nothing particularly unique to the anxiety about the mess humankind finds itself in now. Ronald Russell, the Cambridge historian and British self-styled "Monrology" buff, puts it succinctly, "Don't worry the grandchildren. Eat up the ice cream on your plate."

But is it, this time, merely a matter of going about one's daily affairs, and disregarding the warnings?

Can the relatively few positive, constructive, beneficial energies amongst us absorb or convert the negative, destructive energy of the Predators in time to save the Learning School for Mankind, and for the Universe?

The gloomy say there's only a faint chance Earth can survive as a human habitat. Dis-equilibrium, the familiar, interwoven cause-and-effect chain of negativity—population growth, capital expenditure, land use, water resources, fossil fuels, pollution, climate, and human nature—is beyond correction. If a Third World nuclear war doesn't get us, the combination of the Greenhouse Effect and the depleted ozone layer, or something else, will.

Set against this despondency are those who feel optimistic, and who are working in their own, individual and joint ways to make Earth a better place to inhabit. There are grass-roots movements trying to avert the planet's headlong decline by many methods, including world-wide prayer and meditation. People of Consciousness work quietly in small ways, in small towns and communities, to reverse the trend. Some would even say the good-thinkers have already been successful, at least in postponing calamity from dates now past.

In Bob Monroe's Institute, you learn the reason for Earth is so that entities can pick up knowledge Here that is useful There. Our habitat performs a valuable and perhaps unique function. Although some dimensions and lifeforms may be indifferent to the occupants of this planet, others need us and it.

It would be in their interest to help at least some humans survive a cataclysm. There are indicators or precedents, if you buy the Lemuria and Atlantis legends, the Hopi legends, even Noah and the flood. Or you might be willing to accept another theory.

Let's bring the inquiry into sharper relief. If there is any realistic hope at all of finding solutions to what the Club of Rome[12] called Mankind's *problematique*, the lead must probably come from America's can-do society—from a culture that has also, because of its greed, caused more than its share of the debacle. For that matter, could the new-look open, responsible Soviet Union help in a joint effort?

* * * *

Think back to the glorious-tragic days of "Imagine" and the flower children who wanted to love the planet to health, until they were overtaken by the negative energies of rampant drug abuse. Behind the love-ins there was an intellectual movement afoot, some of its politically-motivated, much of it idealistic, to transform the world, or at least the United States. Students for a Democratic Society spawned a lot of psychologists and social engineers, many, if not all, of whom had seen other realms of consciousness with the help of LSD.

Recall the days of the Stockholm Conference on the Environment, and the near-panicky reaction of many in the 1970s. The world was going to hell in a handbasket. People scrambled to find salvation, solutions, and survival—among them Monroe's cadre on the West Coast. Bob himself conceived of the New Land community at the time, and withdrew into his isolation.

After Vietnam and Watergate the protestors had their chance at responsibility, under President Carter. It was the premature, incandescent zenith of Michael Murphy's Esalen and the innovative core of the Aquarian Conspiracy. The mid-to-late 1970s was a time of intense, dervish-dance excitement in those circles; a seed was planted, perhaps symbolized best by Baba Ram Dass, ex-Richard Alpert, one of the acknowledged LSD experimenters. Books poured forth. The decade's spokesmen became national figures. Many of them came to see Bob Monroe, who, however, remained aloof from the excesses of the period.

* * * *

The book that summarized it all and codified the dream was Marilyn Ferguson's *The Aquarian Conspiracy*, a passionate catalogue already obsolescent by the time it was published in 1980. American society found the reformers under Carter wanting: All that talk, so many drug-inspired dreams, and so little action! The flame of the Aquarian Conspiracy spluttered; in came Reaganomics.

In the public mind, the threat of global ecological catastrophe receded into complacency. People bought big cars again. The long-hairs of the 1960s shifted to Yuppie hair-stylists. They kicked drugs, settled into marriage—at least temporarily—bred kids, bought or sold insurance and mortgages. Everyone loaded his MasterCard.

Under Reagan, no funds were available to support the flaky research and the networking necessary to engineer the dream of social transformation. With the power cut off from their hothouses, those who lived to implement the Aquarian Conspiracy could no longer succeed.

The Movement didn't die; it hung out somewhat obscurely. The fastidiously respectable Institute for Noetic Sciences (IONS), took over where the slightly suspect Aquarian Conspiracy left off. IONS is new establishment, inspired by ex-astronaut Ed Mitchell, and volubly presided over by Willis Harman, formerly of Stanford Research International; Charley Tart is a Fellow. IONS sponsors conferences on altruism and exceptional abilities, and gives grants; it also is involved in a venture to promote fruitful contact between heavy and mediumweights from the United States and the Union of Soviet Socialist Republic, in recognition that it's time for something more than missile rattling.

The other facet of the Consciousness Movement which emerged in the 1980s was its popular face, epitomized by the various name-authors and artists who contribute to the popular stereotype of New Age. Even *Time-Life* Inc., which keeps its horn-rimmed bifocals riveted on trends and the bottom line, jumped in with a hype letter to subscribers:

> *Atlantis. Stonehenge. Nazca. The Great Pyramid. ESP. Telepathy. Channeling. Clairvoyance. Mystic Powers. Ufos. Reincarnation. Psychic healing. Miracles.*
>
> *Now you can learn more about unexplained phenomena than you ever thought possible!*
>
> *Dear Reader,*
>
> *. . . If you are one of those people who can't just settle for leaving the unknown unexplored (as I suspect you are), I invite you to gain a bold new understanding of all kinds of paranormal phenomena in. . . the penetrating new series from Time-Life Books that dares you to satisfy your curiosity about the unexplained for yourself. . . .*

The late John D. MacDonald sugar-coated his serious messages in the "Travis McGee" and other novels. Years of Asimov and Bradbury sci-fi, even Star Trek, have conditioned us to fictional mind-bending, or a new form of mythology. What are Lucas and Spielberg really saying?

The popularists of our time, perhaps operating on guidance, have established the new space-age myths, and even the heroes, of our culture.

In considering the field of Consciousness, it is useful to think of Dr. Jacques Vallee's theory of absurdity, or what he calls "metalogic" in his book, *Dimension*: That the people of the Secret Commonwealth purposely obscure themselves and their artifacts, but have consistently dropped hints for the perceptive to pick up.

Is it too far-fetched to think that some pop culture entertainment and the softer New Age manifestations may serve a dual purpose: To acquaint the broad public with Consciousness, but to divert its attention from the serious yet obscure purpose of the Secret Commonwealth?

If an actor can be president, an actress can quite realistically be Advance Woman for

Consciousness. Shirley MacLaine's hear-and-tell experiences groove onto the bookstands and TV network. JZ Knight is a 1980s version of the all-American success story. It has all been an effervescent, wonderful, giddy fad—past-life regressions, self-discovery workshops, crystals, and pyramids. The entertainment fantasists of our society have done much, and deserve credit, for promoting acceptance of matters beyond conventional comprehension. Time-Life bestows its seal of approval!

The Hippies are now pushing into their forties. The world of scams and bottom lines really isn't everything. Some remember, over the years of child-rearing and car payments, the dreams and visions of the Sixties. Wasn't there more to it than just a neat psychedelic memory? Is there a chance to recapture and act on the dream, without drugs? What could the expanded-but-sober and straight mind accomplish? Some of them, indeed, are active in the hard sciences.

Those who are supposed to may become curious: A fleeting memory may be triggered, they may feel a nudge, and they might begin to wonder whether there isn't something of value behind the flashing lights on the marquee. They don't have to look far. The world of Consciousness has become easily accessible; it's no longer underground.

Joseph Campbell discourses with Bill Moyers, once of the White House and CBS, on Public Television about the role of the myth and Altered Consciousness in history and in our society. The Greeks, says Charley Tart, were well aware of the Supra-Conscious.

It's a big leap, but could those who are now assuming responsibility, at least for this nation, perhaps still do something in a society where brains seemed too often to be atrophying, whose institutions were visibly going bankrupt?

The quiet, new, surface Movement got a lot of tongue-in-cheek publicity at the time of the Harmonic Convergence celebration in August, 1987. Yet a number of previously-straight people said privately they could never have imagined themselves participating in such a festival, a year earlier, "but then, around January, something I don't understand happened, and I started to think differently."

The soft New Age serves a very serious purpose.

If someone wanted to get a very serious message out to people in the United States, how better to do it than to use the blatant hype we so enjoy.

* * * *

Bob Monroe does not fit into the IONS or the Shirley MacLaine mode. He refused to join the Pied Pipers of Consciousness.

Bob's IQ has never been doubted. He is pragmatic. He has known what he is doing, if no one else has.

Elmer Green and Stuart Twemlow say he should have stayed in pure research. Had it been of paramount importance to him, Monroe could have joined the serious Consciousness troops in their laboratories. He could have cooperated and courted further scientific "validation." He could have done many things to join the mainstream of the hard, earnest New Age.

No one except Bob will ever know where his Guidance leaves off and the human Bob Monroe takes over. Monroe answers the question loosely. To him, cause-and-effect are still important.

For whatever reason, Bob purposefully chose to stay fiercely independent at an Institute and in a lab he paid for, built, equipped and ran, to concentrate on exploring and on perfecting and training his techniques.

Perhaps intuitively, he positioned himself to be available to those who need him. He went commercial, but in an ultra-conservative way.

Bob deliberately chose to turn his Institute into a non-profit organization (idealism), backed by product—books, tapes and courses (acceptable commercialism), all in keeping with the American ethic. He insists "you pays for what you gets."

Throughout the years of turmoil and financial stringency, Monroe has remained firmly—some say obdurately—in charge of himself and the scope of his activities.

* * * *

Contact with the Supra-Consciousness can be beneficial to your health, can improve your (Universal) mind and can, let us suppose, be constructive to the healing of this planet.

Apart from the help you can give, any solutions to Earth's *problematique* would probably have to be technological. The United States is still, albeit barely, the world's scientific innovator and leader.

We, as a nation, remain to be convinced of the reality of the threat to Earth, to the point of mobilizing, selectively or across the board, our vast technological resources. Bob Monroe is not sure we ever will wake up, as a society.

Yet despite the egregious materialism of our era, something is going on. A rapidly-growing, but untold number of people—not just a handful of academics, yogis, novelists, and moviemakers—feel the time has come to accept things that cannot be rationally explained. We've tried everything else.

An underlying theme in James Gleick's book on Chaos is the frequency with which he writes that leading men in the new field worked on "intuition." [13] Their discoveries have challenged the rules in economics, ecology, biology, medicine, physics, climatology, and mathematics. Some of the images pictured in Gleick's book, look not-unfamiliar to the Altered-State voyager.

At a Pasadena New Age exposition in the spring of 1988, the number of short-haired, short-sleeved males who attended serious workshops was surprising; Pasadena itself is techno city. Southern California is aerospace, computers and hi-tech—and earthquakes. The gurus of the Seventies have faded into the hills, to be replaced by channelers. Could they, in turn, be succeeded by engineers?

It is significant that, increasingly, those who feel pulled to the Monroe Institute come from the technological leagues: scientists, engineers, doctors, and educators. Not a lot of professionals are willing to investigate the Altered State, yet; but the mix in course attendance has tilted. Some of them, at least, come because their disciplines no longer provide satisfactory answers; their underlying assumptions look more and more shaky. Significantly, too, there has often been a majority of males at most Monroe courses. In New Age workshops, women have previously always outnumbered men.

Behind the glitzy face of the New Age, serious researchers work to establish what they unfailingly refer to as "new paradigms." Their work would normally take a long time to trickle down to the public, yet that public has been prepared for revolutionary shifts in knowledge by show biz. In fact, it could be argued that the public, and especially the younger element in our population, is way ahead of establishment institutions, precisely because of the "escapist" entertainment business.

All the projections and warnings about our future sound ominous; maybe it's time to get serious, like now.

But until now, humanity has shrugged in dismay: The interlocking problems are too vast. We despair; no one individual can help or make a difference. The problem has been to find the hard core of the New Age which holds out a chance of some positive results. The earnest ones may decide to slice through the glitterdust to find the firmament.

People of Consciousness are optimistic in the face of dismay. They argue there is something we can do. We can make a Conscious contribution.

Some of the new seekers may land at a place untainted by European or Asian cross-enculturation—pure American, therefore easy to get a handle on.

And the protagonist in this arena is a Horatio Alger figure. A Rip van Winkle-Charles Lindbergh-Duke Ellington-Neil Armstrong who actually hasn't been asleep, just ignored...adventurer, millionaire, show biz veteran, technologist. He even represents the old, bygone United States where you tipped your hat to women, who were always ladies. He's a father figure who has a track record, some of it even in the fast lane. He's tough, no-nonsense, not airy-fairy or pie-in-the-sky. Anyone can identify with Bob Monroe, even if some people call him a mystic. Hell, he's our mystic.

He's going to tell even the roughest part like it is, but he doesn't gild the easier aspects, either. Just maybe he has the right tools for a very difficult job.

Monroe and Charley Tart significantly chose to call Monroe's trips Out-of-Body Experiences, not "astral projections." Mysticism is a word the Left Brain'ed establishment has degraded, for its own reasons, but it covers an element of our lives which has been missing and is much needed.

In other societies, older than ours, there has usually been a mystic-mythic ingredient. The Christians survived the decline and fall of the Roman Empire. Britain has its Merlin and its Druids; Germany has the Nibelungen; France has the Merovingians. The American Indians have their traditions and their mystical beliefs; South and Central America have the Aztecs, Mayans and Incas. What do we have that we can call our own?

Except for Henry David Thoreau and the Transcendentalists, and William James, we don't have much of a metaphysical tradition. The Theosophists and Urantia have never really caught on. Spiritualism still exists, but has never become a major movement. We've been too busy getting some of the good stuff for ourselves to worry about anything that was esoteric or "occult." Even the words sounded foreign.

Bob Monroe is a core American, operating inside the United States at a time when nation and planet need all the serious help they can get from within, from native sources they can accept and credit.

We are today a Superpower which has spread its material addiction and outlook on life throughout the world even, increasingly, into the Communist sphere, like margarine. But we have had nothing but materialism to spread.

It could be argued that we have needed and lacked the restraint and the idealism provided by a mystical tradition, as a balancing factor in our society.

Bob Monroe would never claim to be unique; many others say he is. He is quick to point out there are many ways to reach the awareness he knows and deals in.

Other cultures, especially Eastern ones, have recognized the vacuum in us and tried to help. The Sufis are at work in the West; Gurdjiev's followers, likewise; Yogis such as

Swami Rama have come to live among us; Buddhist monks are a relatively common sight; the American Indian is finally being recognized as a source of wisdom. They have surfaced because we do not have our own tradition of Conscious awareness, and organized religions have not provided the true spirituality the independent-minded increasingly seek.

Consciousness is a component which is coming at us from a bewildering variety of sources, and it's even being boosted by all the hyperbole of American marketing. It could, finally, begin to emerge as a factor in our lives. Charley Tart, on the lecture circuit, calls it "Mindfulness, not Mindlessness" and urges his listeners to sample the cuisine.

Because we are pragmatic Americans, it has to come in recognizable, acceptable form. One of the major, if little-credited, forces that has, indirectly as well as directly, made Consciousness a new factor in our material society is Bob Monroe, a unique creation of our own, acquisitive America.

Whether the coming of Awareness is too late is yet a moot question. But there is a growing, surface feeling in the United States, as well as elsewhere, that it may be time to examine myths and tap the mystical. Bob Monroe offers the tools to do so.

Perhaps a force newly-discerned is finally succeeding in nudging the human species. It is not yet broadly acknowledged nor fully compelling. Its recognition is hindered by many conflicting cross-currents, perhaps purposefully strewn as red herrings along its path. Perhaps, too, it is a collaborative force available only to those designated to heed, or the gifted, to implement on behalf of all of us, or even some of us.

That notable series of incidences, generally grouped under the heading of advancing Conscious Awareness which we have catalogued, seemed to intertwine in the late 1980s.

True survival is an Inner Self, Whole Brain, Consciousness activity and is the antithesis of the "survival" preached in the Left-Brain material jungle. It's nirvana or utopia; can one attain it and still live in the everyday world?

There is no reason to believe one cannot do both. The Right Brain does have a necessary role in the progression; however, gaining full use of it is a stumbling block for many of us who are beset by Left Brain preoccupations.

There is ample evidence down through the ages of people who have made creative breakthroughs based on dreams, intuition or, some said, magical, or mystical guidance. Creativity, in this sense, encompasses everything from physics to painting, mathematics to music.

In many cases, historically, breakthroughs—or masterpieces—seem to have come as the result of a random, even "accidental" process, sometimes called divine inspiration; in other cases, revelation is the result of years of devoted study, exercise, and meditation. How some innovations actually occurred to the person who introduced them is a matter we have tended to ignore, because it was highly private or frowned upon in public discussion. The discovery or the revelation came to the individual, no doubt, in a rush—a surge of knowing the rightness of what he was about; with that surge came the sure knowledge, too, that he had transcended his limitations.

Today, not only have disciplines become constricted, but sub-disciplines won't talk to each other. The early difficulties of the Chaotists are cases in point: it took years for some of the innovators to find that others were working along parallel lines, not quite, but almost just down the office corridor.

One of the remedies to this era of burrowing specialization is to lift the practitioners out of their confining tunnels. Cross-disciplinary conferences can do it, true.

But there is a more effective way: If the Chaotists can tap in on their Supra-Consciousnesses, they can perhaps draw on a super information bank, have some pretty nifty non-verbal communication with colleagues or others, visualize where they are headed, even, conceivably, see where and how their work fits into the universal scheme of things.

What are the methods which access the Consciousness easily, allow one to draw upon its knowledge, be guided by it, and apply that knowledge in ordinary physical existence? The deep-eyed mystic atop Roberts Mountain in Virginia, again, readily admits his is not the only way.

But the Hemi-Sync process allows quick contact with Self and Consciousness; perhaps it offers, as well, some form of spiritual guidance, and the chance to explore a fund of un-human wisdom to anyone who has the courage and the initiative to set out on the voyage.

This modern highway to Consciousness, totally in keeping with our times, permits the human being not only to "survive" and better himself in the surroundings of the material world, but, might help him pull through the worst a maligned environment may throw at him and his fellows, when the chips are down.

Hemi-Sync is one stepping stone to the practical utilization of Consciousness. It's radically different from the techniques of other, more historic disciplines. It is easily available, and it can be expanded upon by the practitioner, on his own or in a group.

Recall Bob's key statement: "If it can be done once, it can be done twice. If it can be done twice, it can be taught." His is almost a practical slogan for Rupert Sheldrake's morphogenic resonance.

Think back to the persistent question of our man from Dallas: "Bob, what is the biggest illusion?" Until Monroe, with his huge, fetching grin, on the last day of that Gateway said: "The biggest illusion is that man has limitations."

Monroe's techniques have thus far been learned by relatively few people. There is perhaps just a chance an expanded circle can develop ways of using Hemi-Sync to open their minds, and find help to solve riddles and develop technologies which might, just in time, contribute to maintaining the planet for human life.

Perhaps not as broadly dramatic but nonetheless important, Hemi-Sync provides curative relief for people who suffer in various ways; it could help in primary and higher education, when our school and university systems are in dire trouble; the applications may be endless, if some members of some establishments can be gently convinced their disciplines sorely need help from what they now regard as unorthodox sources.

It is here the lesson of Chaos is particularly apt. The Chaos scientists broke out of the protective barricades of entrenched academic schools into the wasteland, to discover that those nagging, unanswered questions the sciences had theretofore ignored actually had trails and patterns and significance. The Chaotists gradually convinced others, and founded their own camp of knowledge, outside the circle of firelight.

* * * *

Monroe's significance is that he has utilized the incidence of his OOB's to accumulate knowledge which he has then made available to others: Bob is the first known Westerner to offer a technological channel to practically anyone who cares to try it, linking earthly life with the Supra-Conscious world.

Others have adapted his laborious experiments and the thousands of hours of lab work, and issued their own methods of Supra-Conscious attainment. Although Monroe may not respect his competitors and imitators, he acknowledges them humbly and freely; they have simply done what he has always urged—used his tools. Bob reserves his admiration for those who use his work to clear their own paths.

His search has been novel, bold, and unique. He has accumulated a body of experience which gives him a detached view of physical life, while still being very much an earthy part of it. His impressions of the value and meaning of our world and its institutions are similar to those of other mystical visionaries, except that the physical Monroe is a trade-marked product of Main Street culture.

He offers an active, vividly American exploratory conduit to knowledge. He has even, half-playfully, toyed with the idea of opening store-front Hemi-Sync self discovery centers in shopping malls.

Edgar Cayce, the all-American psychic, was a passive provider of information, basically for passive, healing consumption. Monroe offers enormous possibilities for further, active exploration, productive research and implementation to those who previously thought they were merely human minds and bodies.

* * * *

Kenneth Ring, for one, seems convinced that the New Age of Consciousness has begun. One of its manifestations is the seemingly random selection of people who have Near Death Experiences, and the lesser number of those who are then transformed in spiritual terms. His theory, drawing on work by John White, Professor John T. Robinson, a zoologist at the University of Wisconsin, Rupert Sheldrake, and Peter Russell, among others, is dramatically and cogently posed in the concluding chapter of *Heading Toward Omega.*

Another transformation, remarkably similar to that analyzed by Dr. Ring, is the change that takes place in some, not all, of the people who attend the Monroe Institute.

We are now aware of the role myth plays in our lives. Dr. Jacques Vallee speculates in *Dimensions* that our civilization's myths may have been provided down the millennia by life from other realities—the "Secret Commonwealth."

Chaotists use new tools to write manuals and assemble workbenches which will allow a new branch of scientific-technological exploration. If given the space in which to work, they might be able to provide Techno-Man an accommodation and a cooperation with those far-glimpsed realities. They do not have to have Near Death Experiences to gain access to those realities.

Look at it another way. Bob Monroe initially set out to train five thousand people. It was, he figured, a good number to get the ball rolling or, as Sheldrake might have said, to set up a morphic resonance field. Five thousand people could certainly do what one hundred allegorical monkeys could. Now, there have been considerably more than that number who have passed through the Gateway. All have been affected by it, although some have not chosen to use their access to higher consciousness.

So perhaps the guided purpose of the Monroe Institute is to continue training, to help push the paradigm shift, or set the next evolution on its way. And specifically, it may be hypothesized, the role of the Institute is to be available to train the Left Brain'ed scientist-technologists of our society.

Whether humanity gets to the Fifth Evolution or not is, after all, our choice. Monroe has done his best to get a vibratory resonance started in that population to which he particularly appeals.

If we use the tools Monroe provides and the access of the NDE'rs and all the other routes available to Mankind, perhaps we will learn to live in a reality other than the previously-scripted scenario—a reality which at the moment barely exists in the physical realm.

H+ is a new departure, and may slowly establish its own resonance, presumably in a broader audience than that to which Gateway appeals.

The point is that Monroe has done precisely what Peter Russell said needs to be done to set humanity on course, and has established a technique which lends itself to the resonance of habit postulated by Sheldrake. This is in itself a major contribution.

Is it stretching the possible to its limits...does the possible have limits, for that matter?...to speculate that the technology developed by Bob Monroe may provide the space needed by others to solve the *problematique*? Monroe himself is far too humble to make such a claim. But the signs may indicate otherwise.

The Chaotists need the ability to step into the room they have not yet found—to be able to work in Supra-Consciousness, to explore the world of the Secret Commonwealth. Perhaps it is here, in offering Vallee's "Invisible College" of extra-mural scientific investigators—and the Chaotists—one or more added dimensions to work in, that Bob Monroe's true role and importance lie.

What could the Chaotists do if they were able to work in a state of No Time, No Space?

Recall, if you will, a remark Monroe made at that Gateway course in April, 1987: "Service to humankind is a fine goal, but there are other forms, far more important. For instance, there might be other intelligent life Here. We might know, if we knew how to communicate better non-verbally."

The Chaotists' shop, to be specific, could be a combination of the Supra-Conscious/Inner Self access a Gateway student attains, coupled with some special H+ functions. If nothing else, that shop would probably operate on the principles of love, not fear and anger.

* * * *

One Virginia evening in late 1987, Bob Monroe sat in the Burger Stand in the crossroads village near the Institute. The local traffic was home, watching TV. It was some months before *Chaos* and *Dimensions* and the Joe Campbell Show came into public view.

He wasn't grouchy—Bob rarely is—but he was despairing of the future. He was saying things like:

"No single individual can change what's coming. Nor even any group.

"The only way you can superimpose another reality on humans is to hit them repeatedly with that two-by-four between the eyes."

Monroe was in his pensive years, ripened and a bit chastened by his experiences with mortal man. He was, on the one hand, even more isolated than he had ever been in his life. On the other, he still confidently rode the wave of his unique talent. A wave that, if perceived even only by a few, could have a profound effect on many people in the future. Would that possibility be grasped by those who could use it?

Bob didn't reflect loneliness. There was no self-pity in his comments. But he yearned for the peace of There.

"I'm a lover of what we are culturally. I'm addicted. I enjoy the toys of our culture. I'm a technocrat."

"I truly love this civilization. The real base of it...I guess...is that from my perspective, I can't do anything to prevent its decline. It wouldn't matter if I did go public." He mentioned some precautions he has taken in the construction of his own house, but then immediately grins. "When there's no more fuel oil, they won't do much good anyway. We get our electricity from West Virginia. When that's cut off....

The latest contribution of Bob Monroe and his Friends is the H+ Program. "The hard core of it is that some of us humans will be able to cope. Over the next five to ten years...I don't know how many it will affect. But I do know the implications.

"When it comes....

"We'll take Joe The Cat. He'll go into the woods and hunt, and his coat will get furry in winter. He'll survive. Will we? Can we?"

Bob mentions a couple of neighbors, brothers who live near Roberts Mountain Farm, who work occasionally for money, but grow their own food and are largely self-sufficient. They have a refrigerator and a freezer, both of which they use, but, "They've survived before without them. They can do it again.

"Everyone is scared by the projections. But what do they do? They run away from them and keep right on in their same old ways."

Is Bob's post-Apocalypse scenario provided by the Friends? "It's hard to handle. It's incomprehensible in this culture.

"I'm narrow-banded now. I'm down to some facets which concern places, events, people in another perspective....

"I'm having difficulty accepting...it's a reality I'm having trouble with...." The words drift off once again into a hanging silence.

"It's so much of a pattern. Antithetical. If you have trouble with it, they're saying, stick your foot in the water. It's already tickling your toes.

"The Hippies of the 1960s saw it, and they went into drugs, because they couldn't handle it. They resigned from the world.

"People just can't conceive of a lifestyle of deprivation. It doesn't compute with the industrial culture."

A new beginning? "Sure. It has happened before. I understand there have been many other cultures. In one, the energies just got disgusted and took off. All of them, I guess.

"We'll start over again, and build another civilization." The universal mind will have stored our knowledge in The Library, available for the next go-round.

"The things we consider worth saving aren't. Our science is local traffic.

"We aren't getting the message.

"So they slice the brain and make pictures. So what?

"When I think of the brain, I think of the energy that flows through the system. But I haven't heard any scientist say he knows what Thought is.

"It would be nice if we could put a big H+ in the sky, so everyone could see it, and realize there was a chance. We can't do it without hi-tech, but maybe it can be done."

Bob Monroe shifts planes, to the far reaches.

"It's that part of me I can't talk about. It's not part of our human belief system. It doesn't fit any human category." The Know System.

"I treat it with some amusement. That part of me has a sort of observer status, because there's nothing I can do about it.

"That part rarely exercises full attention to what I do and what I think."

"Some people might say, 'It's the God in me.' Only God doesn't fit."

The impersonal Universe perceived by Bob Monroe is a chilly place. Bob's explorations are suited to Bob's needs. What he has derived from them, and made freely available to those who, in turn, need his technology, could help this planet and its residents to survive and even to link up with the Consciousness of other realms heretofore out of our ken.

It may be that the Monroe Paradox has tossed out some vital keys to a more balanced planetary life, to be fashioned by people he has never heard of. And if happiness is balance, these keys could lead to considerably more happiness than we at the moment could imagine.

Is it possible that the time of the bulky man who shuffles out the door in tattered canvas shoes and checked lumberjack shirt has finally come? Have his life and his discoveries been an intricate design, jig-sawed by energies only some discern—images to be elaborated by those who now begin to have visions?

Is Bob Monroe an unlikely hero in a world starved of heroes—a mythical figure in a planet bankrupt of truly spiritual leaders? It may take some patience yet to tell.

There is so much about Robert A. Monroe that defies physical understanding....

Appendix I

The Monroe Technology

The Monroe Institute's Hemi-Sync Process

[Below are excerpts from a monograph published by, and available from the Monroe Institute. It is by F. Holmes (Skip) Atwater, who is, according to the accompanying biographical note, "A college instructor, scientific investigator and behavioral engineer. He specializes in the design and application of methods for developing advanced human potentials. He has been a technical consultant to the Monroe Institute since 1977."]

Hemi-Sync is an auditory guidance system which is said to employ the use of sound pulses to induce a Frequency Following Response in the human brain. It is reported that the Hemi-Sync process can heighten selected awareness and performance while creating a relaxed state. Hemi-Sync is more than this, however, and an extensive evaluation is warranted. Hemi-Sync involves the physics of resonant entrainment, brain-waves and their relationship to the behavioral psychology of consciousness, and the physiology of the brain.

....The physics of entrainment: What is of concern here are the electromagnetic properties called brain waves. The electrochemical activity of the brain results in the production of electromagnetic wave forms (brain waves) which can be objectively measured with sensitive equipment. Brain waves change frequencies based on neural activity within the brain. Because neural activity is electrochemical, brain function can be externally modified through an introduction of specific chemicals (mind-altering drugs) or by altering the brain's magnetic environment (entrainment). Caffeine, nicotine, and alcohol are mind-altering drugs, whereas sunspots and heterodyning radio and microwave frequencies are entrainment environments.

Beyond these obvious things, the senses of sight, touch and hearing provide for easy access to the neural functions of the brain. Each of these senses responds to wave-form activity within the surrounding environment and transmits information to the brain by means of electron pulse stimulation....

The senses of sight, touch, and hearing by their very nature provide a fertile medium for entertainment of brain waves and, therefore, neural brain function...(In addition to strobe light displays), other practices such as humming (mantras, resonant tuning), autogenic training, and/or biofeedback can also be used to break down the homeostasis of resonant objects (Tart, 1975).

The strobe entrainment effect involves only one of the sensory channels mentioned previously as being neural avenues capable of transporting entrainment signals. The kinesthetic sense of touch is another...in the case of Hemi-Sync, the sense of hearing provides the neural avenues by which entrainment signals can be introduced into the electromagnetic cranial environment. The Frequency Following Response of

Hemi-Sync is in fact the well-established principle of entrainment. Sound pulses are used to entrain brain waves.

Brain Waves and the Behavioral Psychology of Consciousness:

One of the biggest criticisms of brain wave research is characterized by the popular notion that one can't tell what a person is thinking by measuring their brain wave patterns. By way of analogy, this is like saying that one can't tell what information is in a computer by simply measuring voltages present at various points. There is probably some human resistance here to others being able to "get inside one's head" and to know who one really is, or what one is really thinking....

Measuring brain waves is somewhat similar to measuring telephone line voltage. When, through the measurement of line voltage, one determines the telephone is in use, this does not reveal what is being said over the telephone. The same is true of brain waves. When, through the measurement of brain wave frequencies and associative patterns, it is detected that an individual is in REM sleep (dreaming), this does not reveal the dream content. This can only be discovered if the experimenter awakens the subject and asks him to describe his dream.

But brain waves are more than just discrete (single) states of consciousness. They represent the electrochemical environment through which perceived reality is manifest. Perceived reality changes, depending on the state of consciousness of the perceiver (Tart, 1975). Some states of consciousness provide limited views of reality while others provide an expanded awareness of reality. For the most part, states of consciousness change in response to immediate socio-environmental surroundings. (The psychologist would call these, changes in ego states or subpersonalities)....

Hemi-Sync and the Physiology of the Brain:

Hemi-Sync's Frequency Following Response (FFR) is applied through the use of unique phenomena called binaural beats. Unlike the gross effect of strobe entrainment...the FFR of Hemi-Sync provides the user with access to and control of highly specific discrete states of consciousness....

Binaural beats are not the result of electronically mixed signals, are not recordable by device and, to be detected, require the combined action of both ears. Binaural beats exist as a consequence of the interaction of perception with the brain (Oster, 1973).

Binaural beats were discovered in 1839 by a German experimenter named H.W. Dove. The human ability to "hear" binaural beats appears to be the result of evolutionary adaptation. Many evolved species can detect binaural beats because of their brain structure. The frequencies at which binaural beats can be detected change depending on the size of the species' cranium. In the human, binaural beats can be detected when carrier waves are below about 1000 Hz. Below 1000 Hz, the length of the signal is longer then the diameter of the human skull....

Because sound frequencies below 1000 Hz curve around the skull, incoming signals below 1000 Hz are heard by both ears. But due to the distance between the ears, the brain "hears" the inputs from the ears as out of phase with each other. As the sound waves passes around the skull, each ear gets a different portion of the wave. It is this wave-form phase difference which allows for accurate location of sounds below 1000

Hz....

The relevant issue here is that it is this innate ability of the brain to detect wave form phase differences which gives rise to binaural beats. When signals of two different frequencies are presented through headphones...the brain detects phase differences between these signals....

With headphones on...pulse stimulation provides relevant information to the higher centers of the brain.... This anomaly (the difference in electron pulse stimulation) comes and goes as the two different frequency wave forms mesh in and out of phase. As a result...an amplitude modulated standing wave (the binaural beat) is generated within the sound-processing centers of the brain itself. This standing wave acts to entrain brain waves—the FFR of Hemi-Sync. It is important to grasp the fact that no one ever *hears* binaural beats. One only thinks something is heard.

Beyond the Basics:

The term Hemi-Sync was chosen because many of the states of consciousness available through this technology are the result of wave forms of equal amplitude and frequency in both hemispheres of the brain. The reason for this is physiological. Each ear is 'hard-wired' (so to speak) to both hemispheres of the brain....

The complexities of an effective Hemi-Sync signal are amazing. Each state of consciousness is not represented by one simple brain wave. Each...involves a milieu of inner-mixing of wave forms.... For each discrete state of consciousness, each area of the brain resonates at a specific brain wave frequency because it performs a localized function (Luria, 1970). To entrain a particular state of consciousness, then, one must identify these complex wave forms and mimic them through the use of binaural beats, multiplexed carrier signals and heterodyned binaural beats. This is the Hemi-Sync process.

The Monroe Institute has been identifying these states of consciousness and developing Hemi-Sync signals for almost two decades. The process of developing effective Hemi-Sync signals has been as complex as the function of the brain itself. Under laboratory conditions, many subjects were tested for their responsees to binaural beats. Records were kept as to the effect each binaural beat frequency had on these subjects. Then binaural beats were mixed and records were again kept on the subjects' responses. After many months (in some cases, years), test results began to show population-wide similar responses to specific mixes of binaural beats, which laid the foundation for what is now called Hemi-Sync (Monroe, 1982). The individual binaural beats within these unique mixes entrained separate areas of the brain to different frequencies, effectively discrete states of consciousness.

In the case of the state of consciousness coined Focus 10 (mind awake, body asleep), for example, the cerebellum, which works below the level of consciousness and deals with muscles and body functions, must be entrained to a Delta frequency. Under these conditions (a Delta brain wave within the cerebellum), the body is asleep. The "mind awake" half of Focus 10 is achieved by entraining the cerebral cortex to a low Beta frequency. The subject's exposure to these individual binaural beats is timed, introducing the Delta cerebellum signal first and later mixing in the low Beta cerebral cortex signal. The mixing of these two binaural beats produces a complex Hemi-Sync signal. This Focus 10 Hemi-Sync signal also seems to have a soothing entrainment effect on the limbic system (the brain's emotional center) as evidenced by the many subjects who report that Focus 10 is a very pleasant experience....

As stated before, states of consciousness are subject to change in response to immediate socio-environmental surroundings as well as drugs. . . . Individuals can, however, learn to control hemispheric dominance through the disciplines of Biofeedback, yogic breathing and others (Budzynski, 1986).

But Hemi-Sync is the only method of learning to control both hempispheric specialization and/or interaction, and brain wave frequencies. The result of such control is the minimizing of the effectiveness of the human brain, or, put another way, the effective employment of appropriate states of consciousness to state-specific environments or situations.

Hemi-Sync beats can be generated to either facilitate inter-hemispheric integration or facilitate left/right hemispheric dominance. If a state of consciousness is desired which requires inter-hemispheric processing, then conventional Hemi-Sync binaural beats are used. . . . With conventional Hemi-Sync binaural beats, the standing waves are in phase and synchronous in both hemispheres. . . and information passes freely between them. . . .

If a state of consciousness is desired which requires hemispheric specialization or dominance, or hemispheric entrainment to different brain waves, then unconventional Hemi-Sync binaural beats are used. An unconventional Hemi-Sync binaural beat is one in which the amplitude modulated standing wave in one (selected) hemisphere is attenuated. . . . Specific states of consciousness which are attainable with unconventional Hemi-Sync binaural beats include those states which require hemispheric specialization or dominance.

Note: *The above is the 1987 version of the Atwater paper. A second working draft was issued in August, 1988.*

* * * *

Excerpt from Monroe Institute Professional Division newsletter, "Breakthrough," March, 1985.

. . . If Theta is the best learning state, how do we achieve it? It happens that Theta is the 'slipperiest' of the four EEG ranges. The only time most of us are in Theta is during the hypnagogic state—on the way into sleep—and during the hypnopompic state—on the way out of sleep. Both of these states are normally of short duration—a few minutes or less. Only highly-experienced meditators can achieve and hold the Theta state for an extended period of time. Unless we are willing to discipline ourselves through years of meditation practice, extended periods of Theta state might seem unattainable.

Listening to only a Theta signal often results in sliding right down into Delta—sleep. To prevent this, a Beta signal is superimposed on the Theta, which brings about relaxed alertness. But this relaxed alertness is of a special kind, for Hemi-Sync synchronizes the brain's hemispheres. There has been so much discussion about hemispheric symmetry in the past decade that we are sure you are aware of the importance of having both hemispheres of the brain function as a unit. There is near universal agreement that a balanced personality is desirable—one in which the rational and intuitive aspects work in harmony. Hemi-Sync helps accomplish this and the effect it has upon students is dramatic.

* * * *

Appendix II

Research Developments Reported in Monroe Institute Publications

Monroe, Robert A.: The Hemi-Sync Process. Monroe Institute Bulletin 1982.

______: The Hemi-Sync Synthesizer. Monroe Institute Breakthrough, 1985.

Analysis of Hemi-Sync Effect on Brain:

Edrington, Devon: "Your Fabulous Brain/Mind," Work done at Tacoma Community College. No date (1982/83?)

Schul, Bill D. Ph.D.: "Effects of Audio Signals on Brainwaves." Covers experiments in 1980/81. No date.

Projects

Education:

Brown, Jo Dee: "Hemi-Sync in The Classroom." Reports results in first and second grades, rising to sixth grade, using Synthesizer in Tacoma schools. Breakthrough March 1986.

Carroll, Gregory D.: "Brain Hemisphere Synchronization and Musical Learning," at University of North Carolina, Greensboro. No date. Available from Monroe Institute. Covers experiments 1984.

______: "Hemi-Sync and Music Interval Identification," paper for Monroe Professional Seminar October 1985.

______: "Brain Hemisphere Synchronization and Musical Learning" by Greg Carroll. Tests with freshmen. Breakthrough June 1987.

Edrington, Devon: "A Palliative for Wandering Attention." At Tacoma Community College. No Date. Probably circa 1985. Use in classroom for concentrated learning; led to use in Tacoma Schools by Jo Dee Brown. (See also Breakthrough December 1983)

______: "Hyperamnesia Experiment." Spring 1981. Higher grades of control group hearing tapes during course. Breakthrough 1982/83?

Kramer, Terry D., L.C.S.W., M.F.C.C. "Report of Classroom Demonstration of Hemi-Sync." One-time test of "Concentration" tape in evening college class. Breakthrough 1982/83?

Martin, Ann 'Morning Dove,' M.A., Gateway/Guidelines Trainer. "High Tech Vision Quest: Similarities of Gateway Programs of Native Americans and MI Gateway Programs" Similarities to Metis-Cherokee ritual. Paper for Professional Seminar August 1986.

General:

Baker, Deborah, Ph.D.: "Effects of Rest and Hemi-Sync Compared to Effects of Rest and Guided Imagery on the Enhancement of Creativity in Problem-Solving" at New Orleans/Metairie. Uses Flotation. Counseling psychologist and Hypnotherapist. Breakthrough December 1985.

Carstens, Richard: "Integration of Yoga and Hemi-Sync." Uses Hemi-Sync in psychiatric as well as general Yoga instruction. Breakthrough December 1984.

Hastings, Arthur Ph.D. "Tests of the Sleep-Induction Technique" (Mentions also lab interest by Dr. Joe Kamiya, Director of the Psychophysiology of Consciousness Lab, University of California Medical School, San Francisco.) 1975.

Medical:

Bowen, Barbara: "Hemi-Sync and the Art of Moving Teeth." Movement of Teeth in Jaw astonishing to orthodontist. Breakthrough September 1985.

Brill, Ron Ph.D.: "Introducing Hemi-Sync to Health Care Practitioners". Paper for Professional Seminar August 1986.

Carter, Gari: "A Personal Testimonial on the Emergency Treatment Tapes," at Orange, Virginia. Personal account of 1982 reconstructive facial surgery success using MI tapes. Breakthrough August 1983.

Dahlberg, Albert Ph.D., M.D. and Theresa 'Winter' Pope, M.A.: "Channeling Medical Information: Interface Between Two Dimensions." Prof. of Medical Science at Brown University and Psychologist, Psychic, Guidelines Trainer report on the medical clairvoyance work all over the world. Traditional and unorthodox therapies. Paper for Professional Seminar August 1986.

Edgar, David Ed.D.: "Experience with Surgical Tapes." Skin cancer surgery; reports quick recovery using MI surgical tapes. Breakthrough March 1983.

Gilbert, Nicola: "Results of Emergency Treatment Tapes Used in Splenectomy." Personal account of help from Hemi-Sync in splenectomy surgery at University of Virginia Hospital. Breakthrough June 1986.

Gold, Jean: "Hemi-Sync and Vision Improvement" describing results of her experiences as patient: Vision improvement, actual movement of eyes. Breakthrough March 1983.

Gray, John Harvey: "Professional Report." Master Instructor in Reiki Healing—channeling Energy to body cells. Uses Focus 10-15 to enhance own healing of patients. June 1985.

Jones, Fowler C., Ed.D.: Associate Professor of Psychiatry (Psychology), University of Kansas College of Health Sciences. "Anecdotal Report"—relief of pain in cancer patient. Breakthrough September 1985.

Lasko, Edward: "Integration of Hemi-Sync into a Diversified Health Clinic." Biofeedback Therapist and Hypnotherapist at clinic in Latrobe, Pennsylvania. Pain control. Breakthrough September 1986.

Roalfe, Robert, M.D.: Oakland Anesthesiologist. "Results of Emergency Treatment Tapes Used in Back Surgery" Comparative results from back surgery on Dr. Art Gladman. Anecdotal. Breakthrough June 1986.

Wessbecher, Harrald: Gateway and GO Trainer, Germany. "The Effects of Hemi-Sync with Hypnosis and Magnetic Healing." Several case histories. Breakthrough March 1985.

Psychiatric/Psychological:

Bright, Kathryn A. M.A.: Dance-movement Therapist. "Autism Helped by Hemi-Sync." Breakthrough March 1983.

Brill, Ron Ph.D.: "Applications of Monroe Hemi-Sync Tapes to Treatment of Behaviorally-disordered Retarded Clients" use in ninety-day program, residential care facility for severely retarded. Two case histories.

Clausing, Dan: "Practical Application of Hemi-Sync in Regressive Therapy—or—Repress It or Regress It." Hypnotherapist's paper for Professional Seminar August 1986.

Domin, Ruth, M.H.R.: "Use of Monroe Institute Tapes by Hospice of Chattanooga Patients." Case histories and details. Breakthrough March 1986.

Levy, Edwin Z., M.D.: "Constructive Work in Psychiatric Treatment Seems Aided by Use of Monroe Tapes," Psychiatrist, Topeka, Kansas. Professional Seminar October 1985

———: "Patients' reactions to Hemi-Sync Tapes." Anecdotal. Breakthrough December 1986.

Malik, Karen: "Biofeedback: What and Why." Director of Biofeedback program, Oakland, California and Gateway Trainer. Paper for Professional Seminar, August 1986.

Morris, Suzanne Evans Ph.D. "Effects of Music and Hemi-Sync on a Child with a Seizure Disorder," Case history with single brain-damaged child. Breakthrough August 1983.

———: Facilitation of Learning: The Use of Music and Hemi-Sync with Children with Developmental Disabilities." Speech-Language Pathologist working with children five months to eight years old. Breakthrough December 1985. Full paper printed separately.

———: "Music and Hemi-Sync: Impact on Learning." Special Edition of Breakthrough, March 1987.

Reed, John C., M.D.: "A First-Hand Account of HP-10"; medical acupuncture, healing, stress relief, etc. . Work with a compulsive overeater, member of OA. Breakthrough September 1985.

Russell, Jill: "Hemi-Sync and Remedial Therapy." Therapist in Cambridge, England and voluntary worker with Chaplaincy at Addenbrooke's Hospital. Anecdotal experiences with tapes. Breakthrough June 1987.

Salley, Ron, Ph.D.: "Multiple Personality: The Question of Split Possession and Mediumship," Clinical Psychologist, Richmond, Virginia. Hypnotherapy of multi-personality patient using information from an Explorer. Paper for Professional Seminar October 1985.

Tollaksen, Robert, M.A.: "Discovering The Shadow: A Discussion of the Views of the Discovery tapes for Release of The Dark Side." Biofeedback psychologist in pain clinic at Memorial Hospital, Saint Joseph, Missouri. Case studies. Breakthrough June 1986.

Travis, Dr. Paul and Marion: "Hemi-Sync with Alcohol Abuse Patients." Psychiatrist and psychologist in Washington, D.C. Using Hemi-Sync tapes to dehabituate two patients. Breakthrough December 1983.

Wulfhorst, Laura: Anecdotal account of Hemi-Sync use with one elderly patient at home-care center. Cupertino, California. Breakthrough August 1983.

Business/Corporate:

Jones, James; "Making The Connection." Consultant and Trainer. Hemi-Sync in Management. Breakthrough September 1986.

Keen, Michael: "Hemi-Sync and Auto-Racing." Director, Mentronics Systems (UK), distributor of Hemi-Sync in United Kingdom. Several drivers using tapes in racing and rallying. Record-breaking laps. Breakthrough December 1986.

Appendix III

Explorer Logs

A glance at the log sheets of a few Explorer sessions is tantalizing in the extreme. The actual material channeled by the Explorers remains on tape, locked away, awaiting the availability of money to transcribe, edit, and publish the wealth of information that has come into the Monroe Institute from the Non-Physical Friends.

Below is a very modest sampling of subject matter and a few of the responses Explorers have brought in. Some of the headings represent forty-five minutes of tape; others sessions are as short as four or five minutes. The excerpted logs below cover, in part only, the channelings of a number of Explorers in the 1980s.

Monitor-Explorer Relationship:

Advice to Explorers
Monitor's Role
Explorer-Monitor
Explorer Experiences
Motivating Explorers
Matching Explorers and Monitors

Sources of Information:

Several energy systems

Sleep/Dreams:

OOB's, sleep and dreams (multiple); Contact with dreamer
Lucid dreaming and OOB's (multiple)
"First Dream State" and dream guides
Dream interpretation
Energy infusion during sleep

OOB's

OOB and Spirituality
Techniques

Illness, Health and Healing:

Health and Diet
Healing and Cancer
AIDS (Cancer and AIDS; multiple discussions)
Alzheimer's Disease
Information from "The Library" on drugs
Avoiding emotional attachment in healing

Death and Transition:

Near Death Experiences; Practicing a dying process (multiple sessions)
Nature of death (multiple)
Transition process (ditto)
Relationship of Purpose to death choice
Experiences/Alternatives/Options/Personality after death (many sessions)
Five alternatives to physical life, after death
Death: Contact and discussion with guardian
Consciousness beyond space and time
Consciousness before, during and after life
Communications after death

Nature of Non-Physical:

Levels, organization and working with non-physical existence
Energies' relationship to time and space
Contact with 'Grey Energy'; 'X Energy'; 'Big Energy'

Guides/Teachers/Masters:

Guides and teachers
Nature of Guidance
Masters

Reincarnation/Past Lives:

Reincarnation (multiple)
Child's memory of past lives

Soul:

Unfolding of Soul; metamorphosis

Origin of Earth:

'Big Bang' Theory
Origin

Time:

Concept of Time

Gravity:

Formula for Gravity/Prana
Scientists who understand Gravity
Overcoming Gravity

Human Origin:

Origin of Humans
Dawn of Man
Primitive Man

Jesus:

Jesus and Christ Consciousness (multiple)
Crucifixion and Resurrection

Entering the Physical:

Ways of Soul entering
Purposes

Male and Female Energy:

Balancing the two Energies
Male and Female

Chakras:

Physical and Mental Meaning

Purposes of Human Existence:

Purpose

Nature of Reality

Earth Observers:

Observe Transition
Transition

Pyramids:

Purpose, building

Crystals:

Information

Other Universes:

Parallel and Alternate Universes; Systems of Universes; Gateways between them
Exploration of non-physical Crystal Group. Questions about; characteristics of; life and times of; group discussion.
On another planet; planet in another system; another planet—relationship to fear
Visit to 'lower' life forms
Intelligent beings in another universe
Place of no duality
Orion system
Fluid group; dense liquid environment
Pleiades Group
Extra-Terrestrial Life
Another galaxy tries to communicate
Aliens on Earth, 10,000 BC
CD-120

Appendix IV

The Formulae

When called upon to autograph copies of his books, Bob Monroe looks intently at the individual and does either of two things: a) He writes a dedicatory phrase, "See you in . . . .", and fills in the level of Supra-Conscious attainment appropriate to the designee; or, b) Bob at times scrawls cryptic formulae in the books. No one, to my knowledge, has succeeded in deciphering them. Here is a selection, culled from various sources:

"From 21:

1. $$\frac{F^2 + 3C\ (6K + 8) = CRL}{T + 4p}$$

2. $$\frac{8C + R^2\ (5N + 12) = VMO!}{T - 3p}$$

3. $$\frac{4L + N^2\ (S + 3) = MVC}{T + 6p}$$

4. $$\frac{6N + L\ (R^2 + 5) = STC}{T + 2p}$$

5. $$\frac{3K + N^2\ (5C + B) = EAS}{T + 4p}$$

6. $$\frac{K + N^2\ (3L + G) = BTH}{2T + P}$$

7. $$\frac{5R + N^2\ (5 + 3) = AVT!}{T - 2p}$$

Appendix V

Acknowledgments:

In addition to those named in the text, I owe a special debt of gratitude to the late Ruth Domin and to Rosalind McKnight, who took the trouble to dig deep into their personal files for material not otherwise available. To Llana Baldwin and especially to Brian O'Reilly, both of whom were involved from the start. To the San Diegans, particularly to Barbara Collier. To Jill and Ronald Russell, of the Monroe Outpost, UK, for consistent transatlantic suggestion, encouragement and counsel. To the New York support base, Vivian Love, Elizabeth Hepburn and Ben Bryant. To Ed Cooney for trenchant advice. To BethAnn Christopher and Vivian Berg who provided vital material serendipitously - well, more or less. To Prof. Charley Tart, advocate and dragon-slayer. To Stuart and Linda Robinson. To Peter and Caroline Alevra. To Alex Pearson, under whose roof some of it happened. To Tara, Philip and Vanessa, who doubted. To Norb. To Nancy Monroe for coffee, pancakes and shopping advice. And to Bob, for so much.

Bibliography and Reading

Out-of-Body:

Black, David, "Ekstasy: Out-of-the-Body Experiences." New York: Bobbs-Merrill, 1975.

Gabbard, Glen O. and Twemlow, Stuart W. "With The Eyes Of The Mind." New York: Praeger/Greenwood, 1984.

Lilly, John C., M.D. "The Center of the Cyclone." New York: Julian Press, 1972; reprinted Bantam, 1973.

Monroe, Robert A. "Journeys Out Of The Body." Doubleday, 1971. Second, updated edition, 1977.

___, "Far Journeys." Doubleday, 1985.

___, "Ultimate Journey," (Work-in-Progress, 1989)

Puharich, Andrija: "Beyond Telepathy," Doubleday, Garden City, 1962.

Rogo, D. Scott: "Leaving The Body: A Complete Guide to Astral Projection," Prentice Hall Press/Simon & Schuster, New York, 1983.

_____: "Mind Beyond the Body," Penguin Books, 1978.

Aquarian and New Age:

Ferguson, Marilyn: "The Aquarian Conspiracy: Personal and Social Transformation in the 1980s." Jeremy P. Tarcher, Los Angeles, 1980.

Dass, Ram: "The Only Dance There Is," Anchor/Doubleday 1974.

Fitzhugh, Elisabeth Y.: "The Orion Material—Perspectives of Awareness," Synchronicity Press, Takoma Park, MD, 1988.
Lake, Catherine: "Linking Up," Donning Publishers, Norfolk, VA, 1988.
Montgomery, Ruth: "Strangers Among Us," Coward, McCann, Geoghegan, NY 1979.
Roberts, Jane: "The Nature of Personal Reality: A Seth Book," Prentice-Hall, 1974.
Smith, Adam: "Powers of Mind," Random House, NY 1975.
Young, Meredith Lady: "Agartha," Stillpoint Publishing, Walpole, NH 1984.

Ufos, &c.

Berlitz, Charles: "Atlantis—The Eighth Continent," Fawcett Crest, 1984.
Fawcett, Lawrence and Greenwood, Barry J.: "Clear Intent," Prentice-Hall, Englewood Cliffs, NJ, 1984.
Fowler, Raymond E.: "Ufos: Interplanetary Visitors." Bantam NY, 1979.
_____: The Andreasson Affair, Prentice-Hall, 1979.
Friedman, Stanton T.: "MJ-12: The Evidence So Far" October 1987 and updates. Privately available from Friedman, UFORI, P.O. Box 3584, Fredericton, NB, E3A 5JB, Canada.
Fuller, John G.: "The Interrupted Journey," Dial Press, 1966.
_____: "Incident at Exeter," G.P. Putnam's-Berkley Medallion, NY 1966.
_____: "The Ghost of Flight 401," Berkley Medallion Books 1978.
Hopkins, Budd: "Missing Time," Ballantine/Random House NY, 1981.
Hynek, J. Allen.: "The Ufo Experience," Henry Regnery Co., 1972.
Jung, Carl: "Flying Saucers," Harcourt, Brace & World, 1959. Signet, 1969. (Originally published as "Ein Moderner Mythus von Dingen, die am Himmel gesehen werden," Rascher et Cie., Zurich, 1958.)
Omega Foundation: Richard Grossinger, Michael Grosso and others at Symposium on "Angels, Aliens and Archetypes," San Francisco, November 1987. Cassette tapes available from Sound Photosynthesis, P.O. Box 2111, Mill Valley, CA 94942.
Strieber, Whitley: "Communion," Avon Books NY 1987.
_____: "Transformation," William Morrow, 1988.
Vallee, Jacques: "Dimensions - A Casebook of Alien Contact," Contemporary Books, Chicago 1988.
_____: "Anatomy of a Phenomenon," Henry Regnery, Chicago, 1965.

Edgar Cayce:

Stearn, Jess: "Edgar Cayce—The Sleeping Prophet," Doubleday, Garden City 1967.
Sugrue, Thomas: "There Is A River, The Story of Edgar Cayce," Henry Holt 1942; reprinted Dell, NY 1966.
Cayce, Edgar Evans and Hugh Lynn: "Edgar Cayce on Atlantis," Warner Books 1968.

Scientific, Technical, Theoretical, Philosophical.

Assagioli, Roberto: "Psychosynthesis," Hobbs, Dorman & Co., 1965; Viking 1971; Penguin, 1976.
Baigent, Michael; Leigh, Richard; and Lincoln, Henry: "Holy Blood, Holy Grail," Dell, New York, 1983.

Bentov, Itzhak: "Stalking The Wild Pendulum," Wildwood House Ltd., London, 1978: Fontana/Collins, London 1979.
Boyd, Doug: "Rolling Thunder," Delta/Dell NY, 1974.
Campbell, Joseph: "Myths to Live By," Bantam, 1972.
_____: "The Masks of God" (Three volumes: Primitive, Oriental, Occidental). Viking ca. 1972.
_____ and Moyers, Bill: "The Power of Myth," Doubleday, 1988.
Capra, Fritjof: "The Tao of Physics," Shambhala, Berkeley, 1975.
Evans-Wentz, W.Y.: "The Tibetan Book of the Dead," OUP/Galaxy, NY 1960.
Gleick, James: "Chaos—Making A New Science," Viking Penguin, NY 1987.
Goldberg, Philip: "The Intuitive Edge," Tarcher, Los Angeles, 1983.
Green, Elmer E. and Alyce M.: "Beyond Biofeedback," Delta/Dell, NY 1977.
Gribbin, John: "Time Warps," Delacorte Press/Eleanor Friede, NY; J.M. Dent, London, 1979.
Gris, Henry and Dick, William: "The New Soviet Psychic Discoveries," Prentice-Hall 1978.
Grosso, Michael: "The Final Choice," Stillpoint, Walpole NH, 1986.
Grosso, Michael, Grossinger, Richard Tapes: See Omega Foundation.
Gustaitis, Rasa, "Turning On," Signet/New American Library 1970.
Haraldsson, Erlendur: "Modern Miracles—An Investigative Report on Psychic Phenomenon Associated with Sathya Sai Baba," Fawcett-Columbine Ballantine, 1988.
Hutchison, Michael: "MegaBrain," Beech Tree Books/William Morrow, NY, 1986.
Leonard, George B.: "The Transformation," Delacorte Press, NY, 1972.
Maslow, A.H.: "The Farther Reaches of Human Nature," Viking Press, 1971; Penguin, 1976.
Murphet, Howard: "Sai Baba, Man of Miracles," Samuel Weiser, NY, 1973.
Pearce, Joseph Chilton: "The Crack in the Cosmic Egg," Pocket Books, 1972.
_____: "Exploring the Crack in the Cosmic Egg," Julian Press, NY, 1974.
Ring, Kenneth: "Life At Death," Quill, NY, 1982.
_____: "Heading Toward Omega," Quill/William Morrow, 1984.
Russell, Peter: "The Global Brain," Tarcher, Los Angeles, 1983. Published as "The Awakening Earth—The Global Brain," Routledge, London, 1982; Arkana, London, 1988.
Schul, Bill D., Ph.D. and Pettit, Ed: "Pyramid Power—A New Reality," revised edition, Stillpoint Publishing, Walpole NH, 1986.
Schultz, Johannes and Luthe, Wolfgang: "Autogenic Training: A Psychophysiological Approach in Psychotherapy," Grune & Stratton, New York, 1959.
Schwarz, Jack: "Human Energy Systems," E.P. Dutton, NY, 1980.
Sheldrake, Rupert: "A New Science of Life," Tarcher, Los Angeles; Blond and Briggs, London, 1981.
_____: "The Presence of the Past," Times Books/Random House, 1988.
Solomon, David, Ed.D.: "LSD: The Consciousness-Expanding Drug," G.P. Putnam's, NY, 1964.
Targ, Russell and Harary, Keith: "The Mind Race," Villard/Random House, NY, 1984.
Tart, Charles T.: "Altered States of Consciousness." Joseph Wiley & Sons, NY, 1969.
_____: "States of Consciousness." E.P. Dutton, NY, 1975.
_____: "Psi: Scientific Studies of The Psychic Realm," E.P. Dutton, NY, 1977.
_____: "Waking Up," New Science Library/Shambhala, Boston, 1986.
Tolstoy, Nikolai: "The Quest for Merlin," Little, Brown, Boston, 1985.

Toth, Max and Nielsen, Greg: "Pyramid Power." Warner/Destiny, NY, 1974.
Waters, Frank: "The Book of the Hopi," Viking Press, NY, 1963.
White, John: "Pole Shift," Doubleday, 1980.
Whiteman, J.H.M.: "The Mystical Life," Faber & Faber, London, 1961.
_____: "Old and New Evidence on the Meaning of Life, Vol. I: An Introduction to Scientific Mysticism," Colin Smythe, Gerrards Cross, England, 1986.
Wolman, B. and Ullman, M. (Eds): "Handbook of States of Consciousness," van Nostrand Reinhold, NY, 1986.

Magazine Articles

Albrecht, Mark and Alexander, Brooks: "Thanatology: Death and Dying" in Spiritual Counterfeits Project Journal, April 1977.
Arpita: "Science and Service: The Yoga of Swami Rama" in Yoga Journal, May/June 1983.
Bassior, Jean-Noel: "Astral Travel," New Age Journal, November/December 1988.
Black, David in Penthouse, 1976. Further details unknown.
Bygraves, William: "Barbarian Warrior who died 35,000 years ago. Or so she would have us believe." Sunday Times Magazine, London, February 1988.
Kubler-Ross, Elisabeth—Interview with: "Cosmopolitan Magazine," February 1980, reprinted from "Human Behavior," date and writer unknown; quoted in undated Monroe Institute Bulletin.
Dickinson, Terence: "The Zeta Reticuli Incident" in Astronomy, December 1974.
Kron, Joan: "The Out-of-Body Trip: What a Way to Go!", New York, December 27, 1976-January 3, 1977, p. 66.
National Enquirer, February 15, 1976.
Reston, James Jr.: "Mission to a Mind," "Omni," undated photocopy, 1984

Learned Journal Articles

Atwater, F. Holmes: "The Monroe Institute's Hemi-Sync Process: Theoretical Perspective," privately published 1987; updated in working draft August 1988.
Green, Elmer E. and Alyce M.: "Biofeedback and States of Consciousness" chapter in "Handbook of States of Consciousness," Wolman and Ullman.
_____ and others: "Biobehavioral Treatment of Essential Hypertension: A Group Outcome Study" in Biofeedback and Self-Regulation, Vol. II, No. 4, 1986.
_____: "Human Potential: The Interface Between 'Psychophysiologic Self-Regulation' and 'Intervention'," Chapter for Golden Thread Continuum, Menninger Foundation, January 1988.
Tart, Charles T.: "A Second Psychophysiological Study of Out-of-the-Body Experiences in a Gifted Subject," in Parapsychology, December 1967.
_____: "Science and the Sources of Value" in Phoenix: New Directions in the Study of Man, Palo Alto, Summer 1979.
_____: "The Controversy About Psi: Two Psychological Theories," in Journal of Parapsychology, December 1982.
_____: "Acknowledging and Dealing with the Fear of Psi" in The Journal of the American Society for Psychical Research, April 1984.
_____ and Labore, Catherine M.: "Attitudes toward Strongly Functioning Psi: A

Preliminary Survey" in Journal for Psychical Research, April 1986.
_____: "Consciousness, Altered States and Worlds of Experience," in Journal of Transpersonal Psychology, 1986, Vol. 18, No. 2.
_____: "Psychics' Fears of Psychic Powers," in Journal of the American Society for Psychical Research, July 1986.

Fiction

Asimov, Isaac: "The Foundation Series" (four novels) and "The Galactic Empire Novels" (three books) reprinted by Del Rey/Ballantine, NY, 1960s-1980s.
Robbins, Tom: "Still Life with Woodpecker," Bantam, 1980.
Stapledon, Olaf: "Star Maker," reprinted with "Last and First Men," Dover Publications, NY, 1986.

Alcoholism/Addiction

Alcoholics Anonymous: "Alcoholics Anonymous Comes of Age," AA World Services, NY, 1957.
_____, "Dr. Bob and the Good Oldtimers," AA, 1980.
_____, "Pass it On. The Biography of Bill Wilson," AA, 1984.
Bob P.: "Unforgettable Bill W." in *Readers Digest*, April, 1986.
Burton, Shirley and Kiley, Leo: "Beyond Addictions, Beyond Boundaries," Proceedings of the First National Conference on Addictions and Consciousness, Brookridge Institute, San Mateo, CA, 1986.
Kurtz, Ernest: "AA, The Story." (Formerly: "Not-God"), Revised edition, Harper & Row, New York, 1988.
ReVision, The Journal of Consciousness and Change, Fall 1987 (Vol. 10, No. 2). Special issue: Spirituality, Alcoholism and Drug Abuse: Transpersonal Aspects of Addiction.
Whitfield, Charles L., M.D.: Alcoholism & Spirituality, A Transpersonal Approach," Thomas W. Perrin Inc., Rutherford, NJ. 1985.

Footnotes

Prologue:

1. "Omni," 1984, "Mission to A Mind" by James Reston, Jr.

Book One

1940s:

1. See *Far Journeys.*
2. Taken from "Preview Excerpts from *Far Journeys,*" undated paper by Bob Monroe, probably about 1982.

1950s:

1. The "sleep-learning deal" eventually, and over a period of many years, evolved into Monroe's patented Hemi-Sync process. See Bob Monroe and the Professionals, Book II.
2. Andrija Puharich, *Beyond Telepathy,* Doubleday, New York, 1962, p. 67.
3. The Explorers were and are a loose grouping of people clustered around Bob Monroe who go Out-Of-Body to develop useful information, primarily for Bob but, in later years, for the Institute.

1960s:

1. Charles Tart, "States of Consciousness and State Specific Sciences," in "Science," 1972, 176:1203-10.
2. Glen O. Gabbard and Stuart W. Twemlow, "With The Eyes Of The Mind, An Empirical Analysis of Out-of-Body States," Praeger/Greenwood Press 1984, p. 5.
3. Charles Tart, "Altered States of Consciousness, A Book of Readings," John Wiley & Sons, New York 1969. Second Edition, Doubleday 1972.
4. Charles Tart, "A Second Psychophysiological Study of Out-of-the-Body Experiences in a Gifted Subject." Parapsychology, December 1967. The first study dealt with the OOB's of a Miss Z. Bob was, of course, Mr. X.
5. See *Chaos* by James Gleick.
6. See "Not With A Wand, Nor Lightly," Chapter One, *JOOB.*

1970s:

1. The Focus levels used by the Monroe Institute refer to various levels of Conscious Awareness. Focus 10 is "Mind Awake, Body Asleep." Focus 12, the "State of Advanced Conscious Awareness." Focus 15 is "No Time, No Space." Focus 21 is the border between Here and There.
2. In later years, for instance, Monroe provided Joe McMoneagle with a special tape which improved his remote-viewing skill.
3. For fuller discussion of the Hemi-Sync technology, please see "The Professionals" chapter in Book II and Appendix II.
4. Jane Roberts, *The Nature of Personal Reality: A Seth Book*, Prentice-Hall 1974, p. 311ff. The "I" in the text refers to Jane's husband and chronicler, Robert Butts.
5. *Cosmopolitan*, February 1980. Reprinted from *Human Behavior.*
6. Elmer and Alyce Green, *Beyond Biofeedback*, p. 218.
7. The similarities between Council Grove and the parapsychological community, and the rise of the science of Chaos are unmistakable. See Gleick, *Chaos.*
8. "National Enquirer," February 15, 1976. About fifteen hundred people wrote in after the article appeared. Seven hundred of them "reported experiences in which they felt their consciousness was separated from the physical body." Some of these, in turn, were used in the Gabbard-Twemlow survey which forms the statistical base for their book, *With The Eyes of the Mind.*
9. Gabbard and Twemlow, p. 208.
10. David Black in *Penthouse*, 1976.
11. Lilly, "The Center of The Cyclone, An Autobiography of Inner Space," Bantam Books, 1972 and "The Deep Self, Profound Relaxation and the Tank Isolation Technique," Warner Books, 1977.
12. D. Scott Rogo, "Leaving The Body, A Complete Guide to Astral Projection. A Step-by-Step Presentation of Eight Different Systems of Out-of-Body Travel," Prentice-Hall Press, New York, 1983, Pp. 88ff.
13. The indiscriminate opposition of conservative and fundamentalist Christians to the New Age gained strength in the late 1980s. Over Easter weekend 1988, the Christian Broadcasting Network transmitted one of five segments of a John Ankerberg expose′ of the New Age. On the panel questioned by Ankerberg were Brooks Alexander, Tal Brooke (identified simply as a former assistant to Sai Baba), and Dave Hunt, ("Author and Researcher"). Elmer and Alyce Green wer singled out for criticism in the Easter segment; Monroe, Kubler-Ross, Moody and others were not. A request to an 800 telephone number for a "free" brochure, "The Facts On The New Age Movement" brought a reply which said, in part, "Program materials are available on request as 'premium' items to contributors. To facilitate your request, you may simply indicate your request and the amount of your gift on this letter, and return them to this office in the enclosed envelope."
14. Tart, "Science and the Source of Value," Phoenix: New Directions in the Study of Man, Vol. III, No. 1, Summer 1979.

1980s:

1. Miranon, in fact, announced that he was graduating from earthbound-levels, or in

Monroe terms, going beyond Level 49.
2. For a popular description of a rescue mission, see "The Ghost of Flight 401" by John G. Fuller, Berkley-Medallion 1978, Pp. 197ff. Two Eastern Airlines pilots apparently successfully freed the soul of a flight engineer killed in a Miami crash from the physical realm, and thereby stopped the haunting of certain Eastern planes.
3. Meredith Lady Young, "Agartha: A Journey to the Stars," Stillpoint Publishing, Walpole, NH 1984. p. 36.
4. "The Armies of 1990" by Peter McCormick, "Omni" 1983. Photocopy, further undated.
5. See Book II, Professional Division section. Devon Edrington's work on the use of Hemi-Sync in education virtually stopped with his death in 1986.
6. Tart, "Open Mind," Vol. III, No. 3, Winter 1986.
7. Michael Hutchison, "MegaBrain," Beach Tree Books, William Morrow, 1986. p. 224.
8. Bob neglected his visit to Jane Roberts and his conversation with Seth in April, 1973. During the late 1960s and early 1970s he and Nancy did a lot of traveling, looking up early Consciousness people. He may well have met other channels during that time. The first Explorers probably started reporting in the late 1960s; whether they qualify as channels as opposed to OOB travelers is a moot point. The 1975 date in Bob's treatise is a flexible time notation. I was given a figure of a total of three thousand hours of taped Explorer sessions, up to the end of 1987, by one of the lab monitors, far more than the eight hundred Bob cites. All of which is merely numbers play.
9. Tart, article based on a paper for an American Psychological Association symposium at Los Angeles, August, 1981.
10. Tart, "Consciousness, Altered States and World of Experience", The Journal of Transpersonal Psychology, 1986, Vol. 18, No. 2.
11. Doug Boyd, "Rolling Thunder," p. 269.
12. Boyd, p. 123.
13. For fuller discussion of the program, see Book II, Chapter on H+.
14. Inevitably, others had the same idea. At an inventors' show in Los Angeles, an entrepreneur demonstrated what appeared to be heavy-framed, wired, dark glasses, which he claimed did the job by a combination of sensory-deprivation, sound signal, and light display. ABC-News' peripatetic Charlie Murphy chanced upon an establishment in the Paradise Shopping Center in Corta Madera, Marin County, California, in late 1988, which called itself "New Age Tune-Up." In the first "Universe of You" storefront, customers lounged in hammock-like swings, wearing bulky spectacle-frames similar to those used by optometrists when checking patients' eyes. The lenses flashed psychedelically. Through headphones, customers heard music and, presumably, subliminal signals. For twelve dollars they got a forty-five-minute session and apparently found the treatment efficacious. Randy Adamadama, who started life as Randall Stevens, developed the system which, he said, synchronized the hemispheres of the brain. (ABC News, November 16, 1988.)

Book Two

Gateway:

1. Kenneth Ring, *Heading Toward Omega*, p. 90.
2. Copyright 1987, Robert Rosenthal. Reprinted by permission.

Guidelines:

1. Stephen Bladd later became one of the three Monroe Institute "core trainers," with Dave Mulvey and Darlene Miller.
2. I have subsequently tried to check the existence of such a group, but with no success. However, since the Guidelines episode, considerable further altered-state information has become available to me which reinforces and adds significance to the experience. There is also apparently a connection between the Brotherhood, the monastery, the guild town, and the symbol I was shown during my Gateway.
3. See also Book II, Explorers chapter.
4. Reprinted by permission of copyright owner, Ronald Russell.

Bob Monroe And The Professionals:

1. New York *Times*, May 25, 1975.
2. See Appendix II for Atwater's detailed description and analysis of the Hemi-Sync technique and for details of the Hemi-Sync Synthesizer. Appendix III lists papers and articles published by the Monroe Institute which have bearing on the use of Hemi-Sync.
3. A good thirteen years after Bob took out his patent on Hemi-Sync, other techniques to elevate consciousness mechanically—apart from those which were imitations or copies—received publicity. The August, 1988 edition of *Omni's* "Wholemind Newsletter" carried a piece on the work of neuroscientist Michael Persinger at Laurentian University in Sudbury, Ontario, who has developed "an experimental headpiece resembling a motorcycle helmet. Fitted with magnets, the device beam(s) a low-level magnetic field at (the) temporal lobes—brain areas associated wth dreamy states, time distortions, spinning sensations, and assorted odd psychic phenomena.... Like most of Persinger's fifty test subjects, (a student) spent a half hour immersed in ecstatic, mystical, visionary experiences....Persinger aims to probe the neuro-mechanisms behind religious revelations. He also thinks that his helmet could eventually be used to produce transcendental experiences in nonreligious people suffering from death anxiety." *Omni* followed up with a full-length piece on Persinger's research into the facilitation of the Mystical Experience in its December, 1988 issue.

Applications of Monroe Technology:

1. Expanded discussion of this subject is in Book III, "Who is Bob Monroe."
2. Appendix II contains technical discussions from the same report.

Consciousness and Science:

1. John G. Fuller, *The Ghost of Flight 401*, Berkley Medallion Books, 1978.

Explorers:

1. See Appendix IV.

Book Three

Views of Associates:

1. Greens, P. 2.
2. Avatar: "An entity regarded as an extreme or notably complete manifestation of a kind; exemplar; archetype. 2. Hindu Mythology: The descent to Earth of a deity in human or animal form." *American Heritage Dictionary.*
3. See *Far Journeys.*

Nancy:

1. See *Far Journeys.*
2. See *Ultimate Journey.*

Conclusion:

1. Kenneth Ring, *Heading Toward Omega*, Quill/William Morrow, 1984.
2. Dr. Rupert Sheldrake in the Alister Hardy Memorial Lecture at the Hardy Research Centre for the Study of Religious and Transcendent Experience at Manchester College, Oxford, December, 1987.
3. After his experiences with the Greens at the Menninger Foundation in the early 1970s, Swami Rama established the Himalayan Institute, which since 1978 has been located at Honesdale, Pennsylvania. Jack Schwarz continues his work on healing and *Human Energy Fields* (E.P. Dutton, 1980) at the Altheia Psycho-Physical Foundation in Grants Pass, Oregon. "Rolling Thunder" was the subject of the 1974 book by Doug Boyd.
4. *JOOB*, Pp. 123-124.
5. "*Pas de Lieu Rhone que Nous:* A language professor father, now in another reality, used this to wake up students in his class in French, claiming it was an old and famous French proverb. Some worked earnestly for hours trying to solve the enigma. It may be very appropriate here, too. To find the solution, say it in your mind or vocalize it, using a French accent. Listen to what you are saying. . . . See you in Home - or along the way." *Far Journeys.*
6. Mike D'Orso in *The Virginian-Pilot/Ledger-Star* "Tidewater Living" Section, Sunday, May 18, 1986.
7. Ring, *Heading Toward Omega*, p. 146.
8. Ring, *Omega*, Pp. 170-171.
9. *Strangers Among Us*, Coward, McCann, Geoghegan 1979.
10. Tracy Cochran in the *Omni* "Wholemind Newsletter," September, 1988.
11. Hopkins, *Missing Time*, p. 231.
12. The Club of Rome was the international organization of thoughtful businessmen, scientists, and academics which commissioned the landmark studies, "Limits to Growth" and "Mankind at the Turning Point" which did much to elevate environmental consciousness throughout the western world.
13. See also *The Intuitive Edge* by Philip Goldberg, Tarcher, Los Angeles, 1983.

* * * *

Copyright Permissions:

Excerpt from *The Nature of Personal Reality* by Jane Roberts, Copyright 1974. Reprinted by permission of the publisher, Prentice-Hall, Inc., Englewood Cliffs, NJ.

Excerpt from *Agartha: A Journey to the Stars* by Meredith Lady Young, Copyright 1984. Reprinted by permission of Stillpoint Publishing, Walpole, NH.

Excerpts from *Rolling Thunder* by Doug Boyd, Copyright 1974. Reprinted by permission of Random House Inc., New York, NY.

Excerpts from *Powers of Mind* by Adam Smith, Copyright 1975. Reprinted by permission of Random House, Inc.

Monroe Institute paper on "The Hemi Sync Process" by F. Holmes Atwater, Copyright 1987. Reprinted by permission of the author, F. Holmes Atwater.

Article, "Thanatology: Death and Dying" by Mark Albrecht and Brooks Alexander, Copyright 1977. Reprinted by permission of the Spiritual Counterfeits Project. P. O. Box 4308, Berkeley, CA.

Excerpt from *Missing Time* by Budd Hopkins, Copyright 1981. Reprinted by permission of Ballantine Books/Random House, New York.

Robert with his mother, Georgia Monroe, 1915

Robert with his sisters, Margaret and Dorothy, 1917

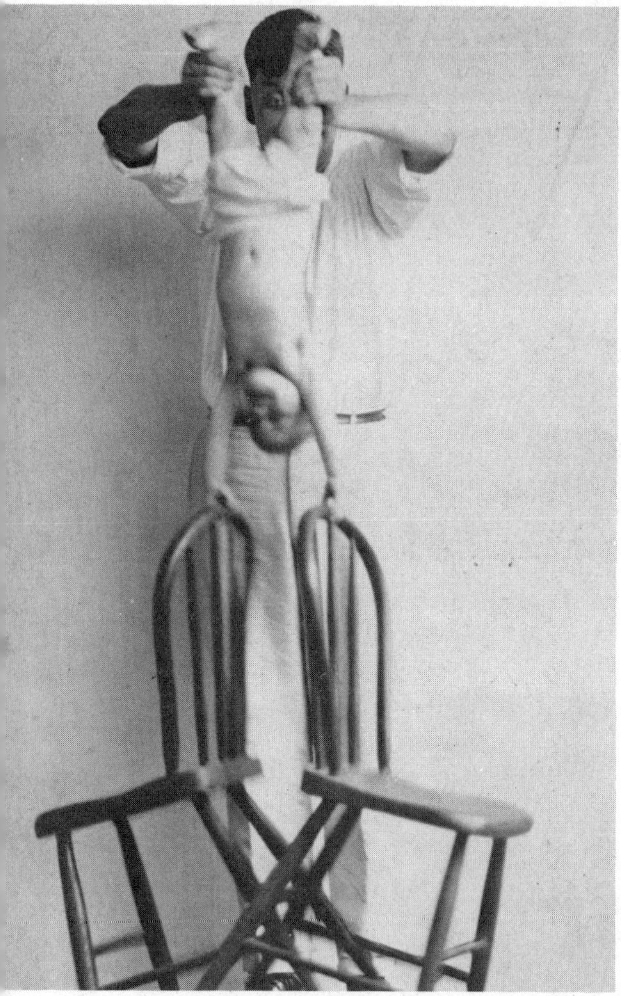

Robert testing his strength with his father, Robert Emmett, 1916

Robert Monroe, 1919

The Monroe children, Robert, Dorothy, Margaret, and Emmett, in Lexington, Kentucky, 1925

Robert Emmett Monroe (father), 1948

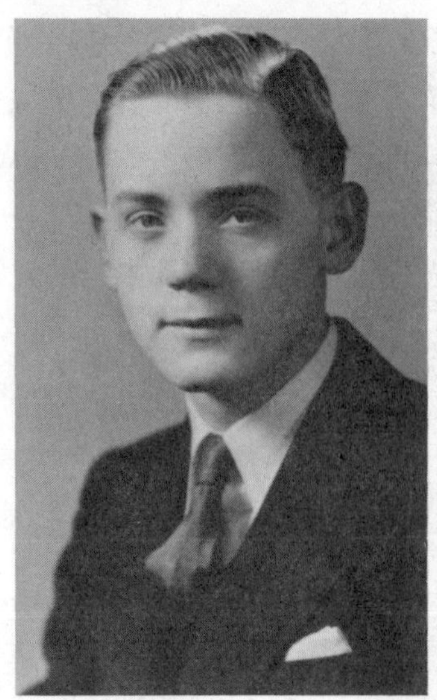

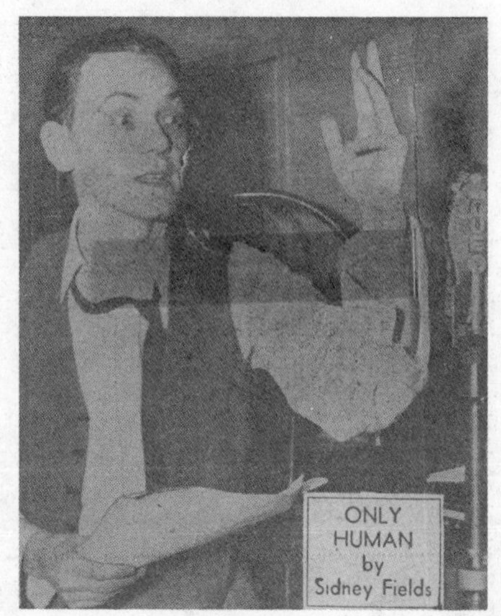

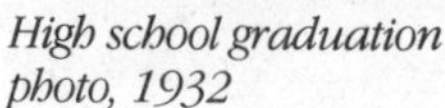

High school graduation photo, 1932

ONLY
HUMAN
by
Sidney Fields

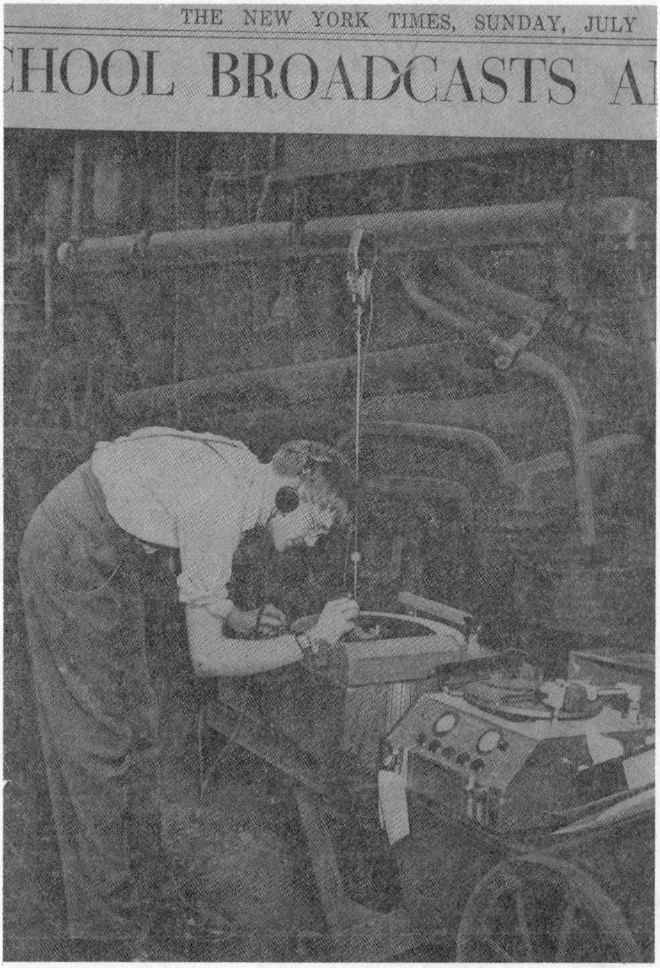

THE NEW YORK TIMES, SUNDAY, JULY
CHOOL BROADCASTS A

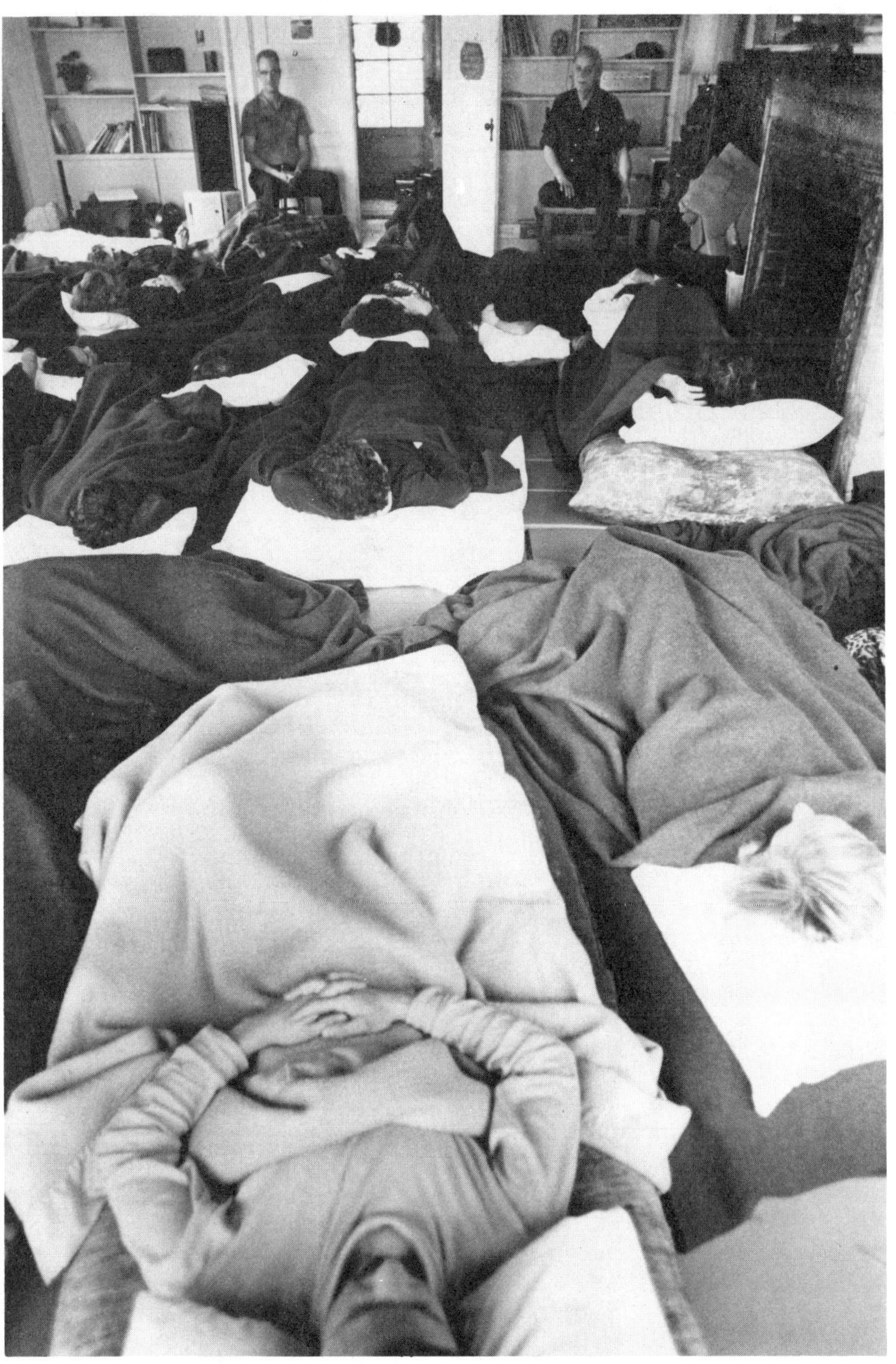

The first Gateway Program, Esalen, 1973. Photograph by Hella Hammid

Publicity photo, 1940's.

Robert's twenty-seven acre estate in Westchester County, New York, where he had his first OBEs. Notice pyramid-shaped, copper covered roof.

Publicity photo, 1960's.

Contemplative moment at Feathered Pipe Ranch, Montana, 1976

Addressing his program participants at a Gateway Program in Virginia, 1987. Photograph by Nancy Conroy

Robert as producer and director of programs in Spanish and Portuguese for the Coordination of InterAmerican Affairs, 1940's.

Robert's family from left to right: Robert; wife, Mary; brother, Emmett, and his wife, Alice; brother-in-law, John Kahler; sister, Dorothy. Seated from left to right: Donna Kahler; Georgia and Robert Emmett Monroe; Jacqueline Kahler.

INDEX

ABOUT THE AUTHOR

Bayard Stockton is the former Bonn bureau chief for *Newsweek,* a past contributor to ABC radio and TV and the BBC World Service "Outlook" program. He has held various public affairs positions for corporations and received California Associated Press awards for documentary and commentary. He is presently working on a second book about the programs of Robert Monroe called *Lift Off! - Bob Monroe's Gateway. . . And Beyond.*